Tamaki Nozomu Presents Dive In The Vampire Bund 2

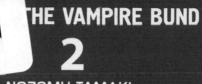

THE VAMPIRE BUND

2

NOZOMU TAMAKI

ちくしょう！詮索好きのパンドラめ、小悪魔め
これがお前の見たかったものか？

呪いあれ！嘘吐きのデリラめ、毒蛇め！
今やお前に自由などない！

お前の夢に描いた思惑の外にあるものよ
私を見つめることができるのか
私を思うことに耐えられるのか
地獄の劫火に身を曝す
この忌まわしいガーゴイルとて
しかしひそかに天国に焦がれているのだ
ひそやかに……
ひそやかに……

Damn you! You little prying Pandora!
You little demon is this what you wanted to see?

Curse you! You little lying Delilah!
You little viper! now you cannot ever be free! Damn you... Curse you...

Stranger than you dreamt it can you even dare to look
or bear to think of me.
this loathsome gargoyle, who burns in hell,
*but secretly yearns for heaven, secretly...*secretly...*

Dive in the Vampire Bund
VOLUME 2

story & art by Nozomu Tamaki

STAFF CREDITS

translation   **Adrienne Beck**
adaptation   **Janet Houck**
lettering   **Roland Amago**
layout   **Bambi Eloriaga-Amago**
cover design   **Nicky Lim**
proofreader   **Shanti Whitesides**
editor   **Adam Arnold**

publisher   **Jason DeAngelis**
   Seven Seas Entertainment

DIVE IN THE VAMPIRE BUND VOLUME 2
Copyright © 2013 Nozomu Tamaki
First published in Japan in 2013 by MEDIA FACTORY, Inc.
English translation rights reserved by Seven Seas Entertainment, LLC.
under the license from MEDIA FACTORY, Inc., Tokyo, Japan.

ISBN: 978-1-626920-18-7
Printed in Canada
First Printing: October 2013
10 9 8 7 6 5 4 3 2 1

FOLLOW US ONLINE: www.gomanga.com

READING DIRECTIONS

This book reads from *right to left*, Japanese style.
If this is your first time reading manga, you start
reading from the top right panel on each page and
take it from there. If you get lost, just follow the
numbered diagram here. It may seem backwards
at first, but you'll get the hang of it! Have fun!!

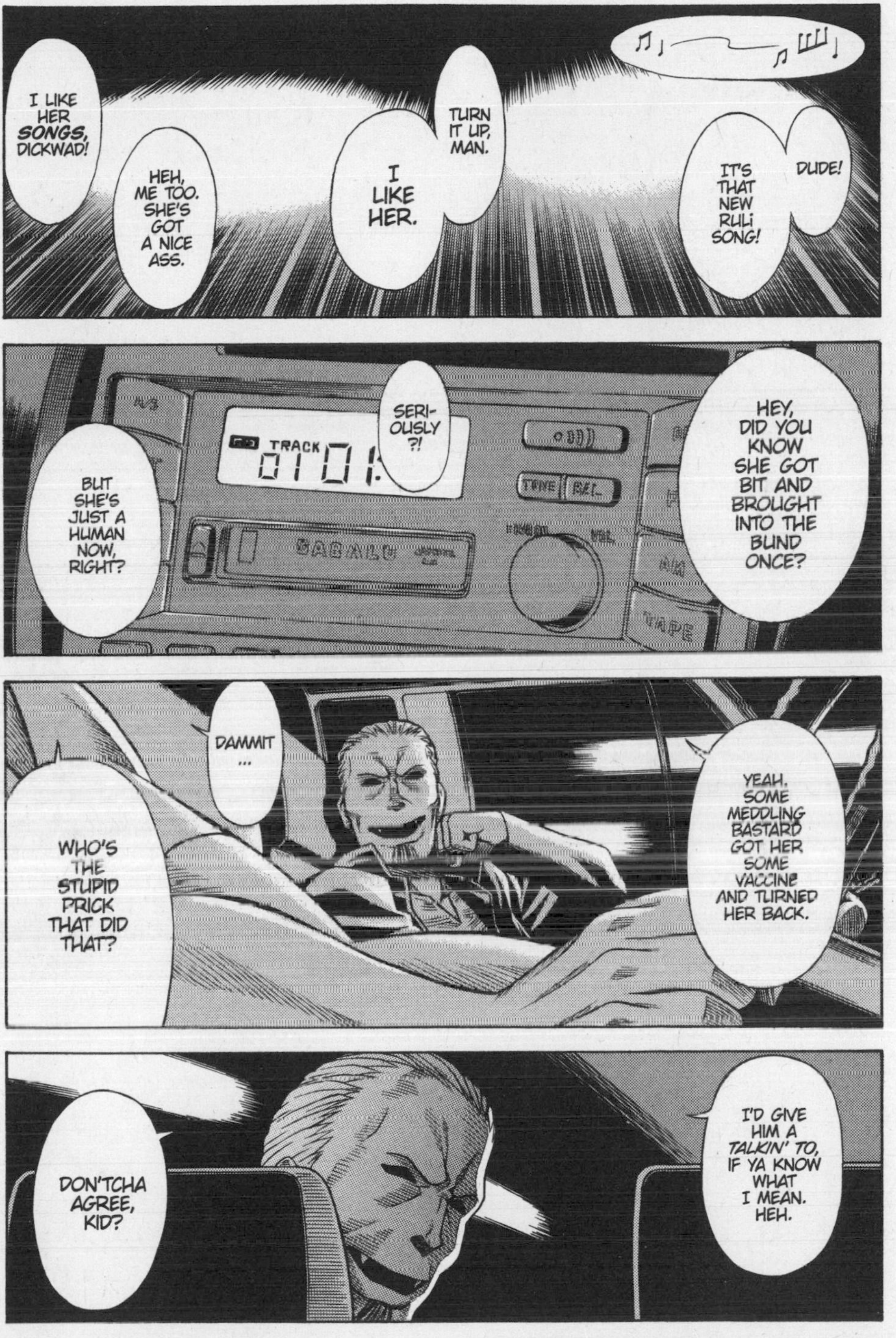
DUDE!
IT'S THAT NEW RULi SONG!
TURN IT UP, MAN.
I LIKE HER.
HEH, ME TOO. SHE'S GOT A NICE ASS.
I LIKE HER *SONGS*, DICKWAD!
HEY, DID YOU KNOW SHE GOT BIT AND BROUGHT INTO THE BUND ONCE?
SERIOUSLY?!
TRACK
BUT SHE'S JUST A HUMAN NOW, RIGHT?
TAPE
YEAH. SOME MEDDLING BASTARD GOT HER SOME VACCINE AND TURNED HER BACK.
DAMMIT ...
WHO'S THE STUPID PRICK THAT DID THAT?
I'D GIVE HIM A *TALKIN' TO*, IF YA KNOW WHAT I MEAN. HEH.
DON'TCHA AGREE, KID?

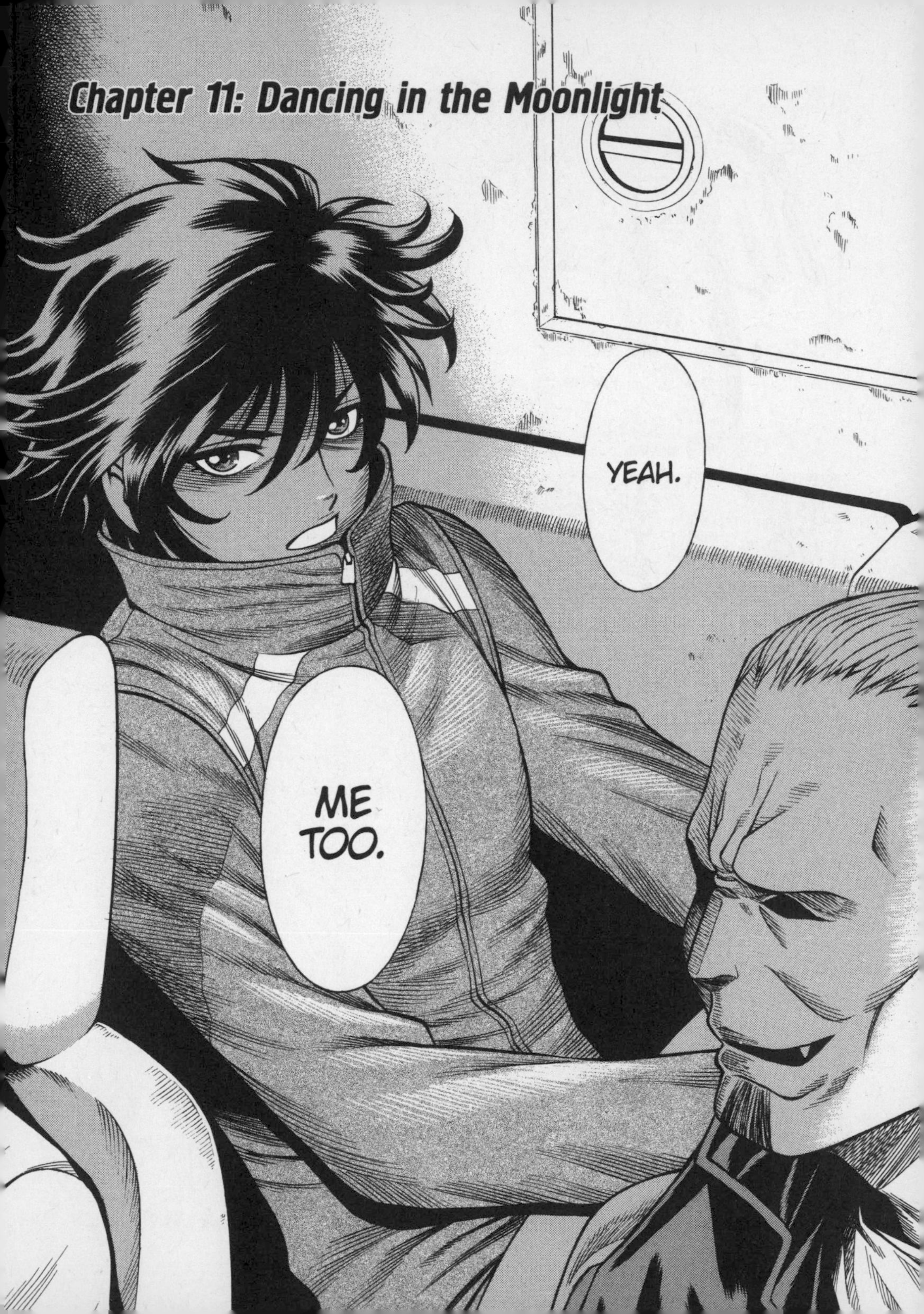
Chapter 11: Dancing in the Moonlight
YEAH.
ME TOO.

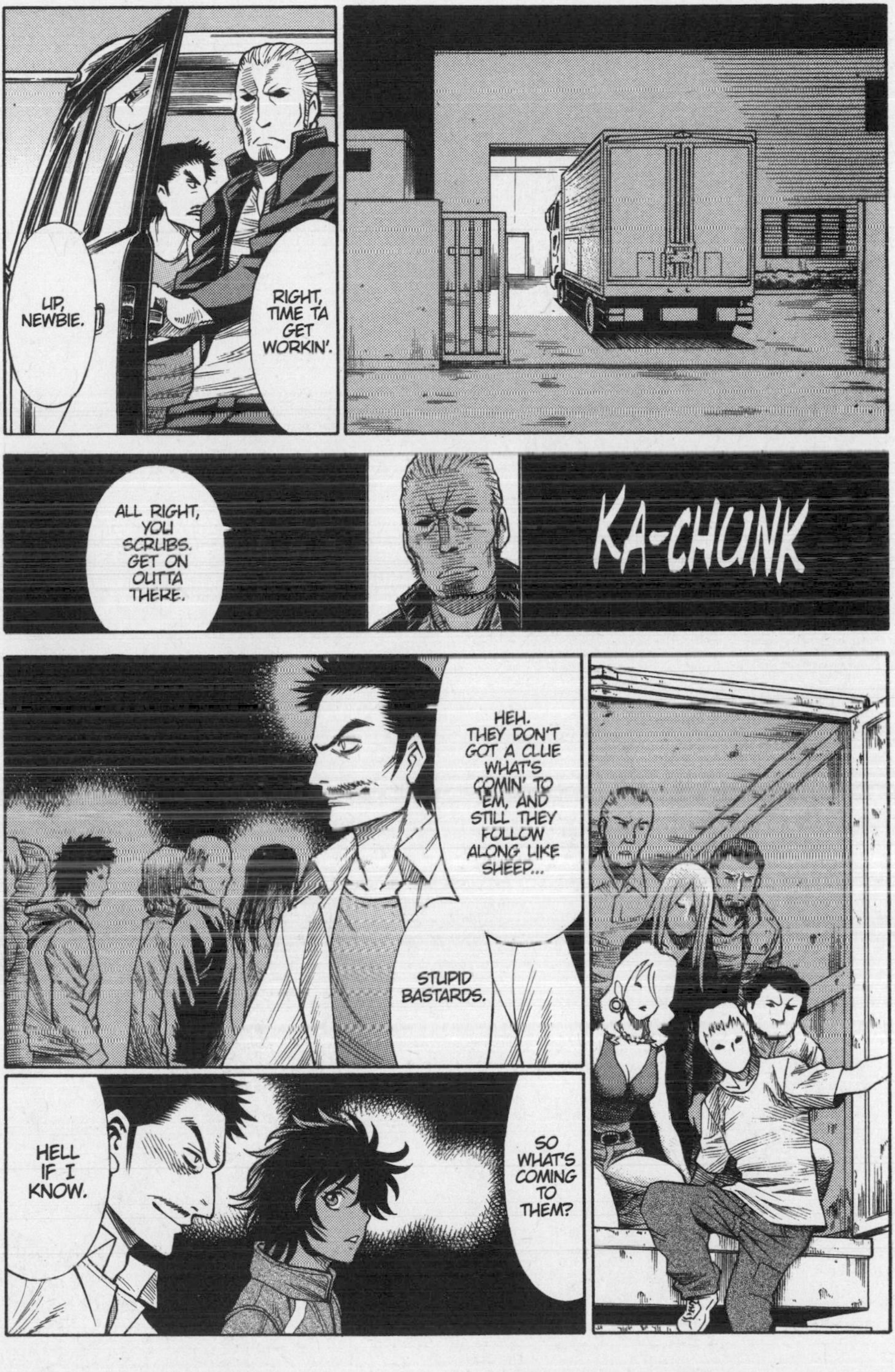
RIGHT, TIME TA GET WORKIN'.
UP, NEWBIE.
KA-CHUNK
ALL RIGHT, YOU SCRUBS. GET ON OUTTA THERE.
HEH. THEY DON'T GOT A CLUE WHAT'S COMIN' TO 'EM, AND STILL THEY FOLLOW ALONG LIKE SHEEP...
STUPID BASTARDS.
SO WHAT'S COMING TO THEM?
HELL IF I KNOW.

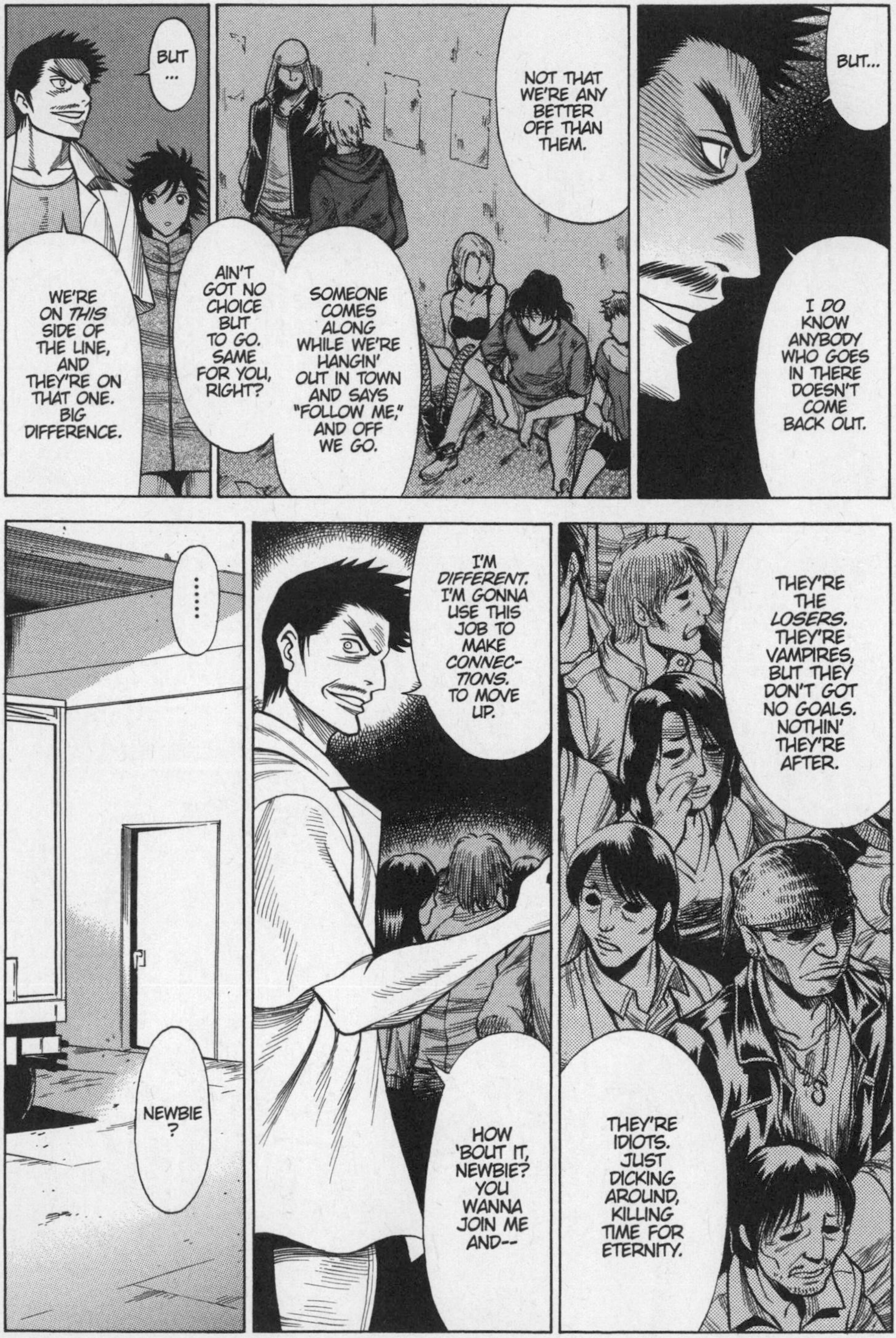
BUT...
I *DO* KNOW ANYBODY WHO GOES IN THERE DOESN'T COME BACK OUT.
NOT THAT WE'RE ANY BETTER OFF THAN THEM.
SOMEONE COMES ALONG WHILE WE'RE HANGIN' OUT IN TOWN AND SAYS "FOLLOW ME," AND OFF WE GO.
AIN'T GOT NO CHOICE BUT TO GO. SAME FOR YOU, RIGHT?
BUT ...
WE'RE ON *THIS* SIDE OF THE LINE, AND THEY'RE ON THAT ONE. BIG DIFFERENCE.
THEY'RE THE *LOSERS.* THEY'RE VAMPIRES, BUT THEY DON'T GOT NO GOALS. NOTHIN' THEY'RE AFTER.
THEY'RE IDIOTS. JUST DICKING AROUND, KILLING TIME FOR ETERNITY.
I'M *DIFFERENT.* I'M GONNA USE THIS JOB TO MAKE *CONNECTIONS.* TO MOVE UP.
HOW 'BOUT IT, NEWBIE? YOU WANNA JOIN ME AND--
......
NEWBIE ?

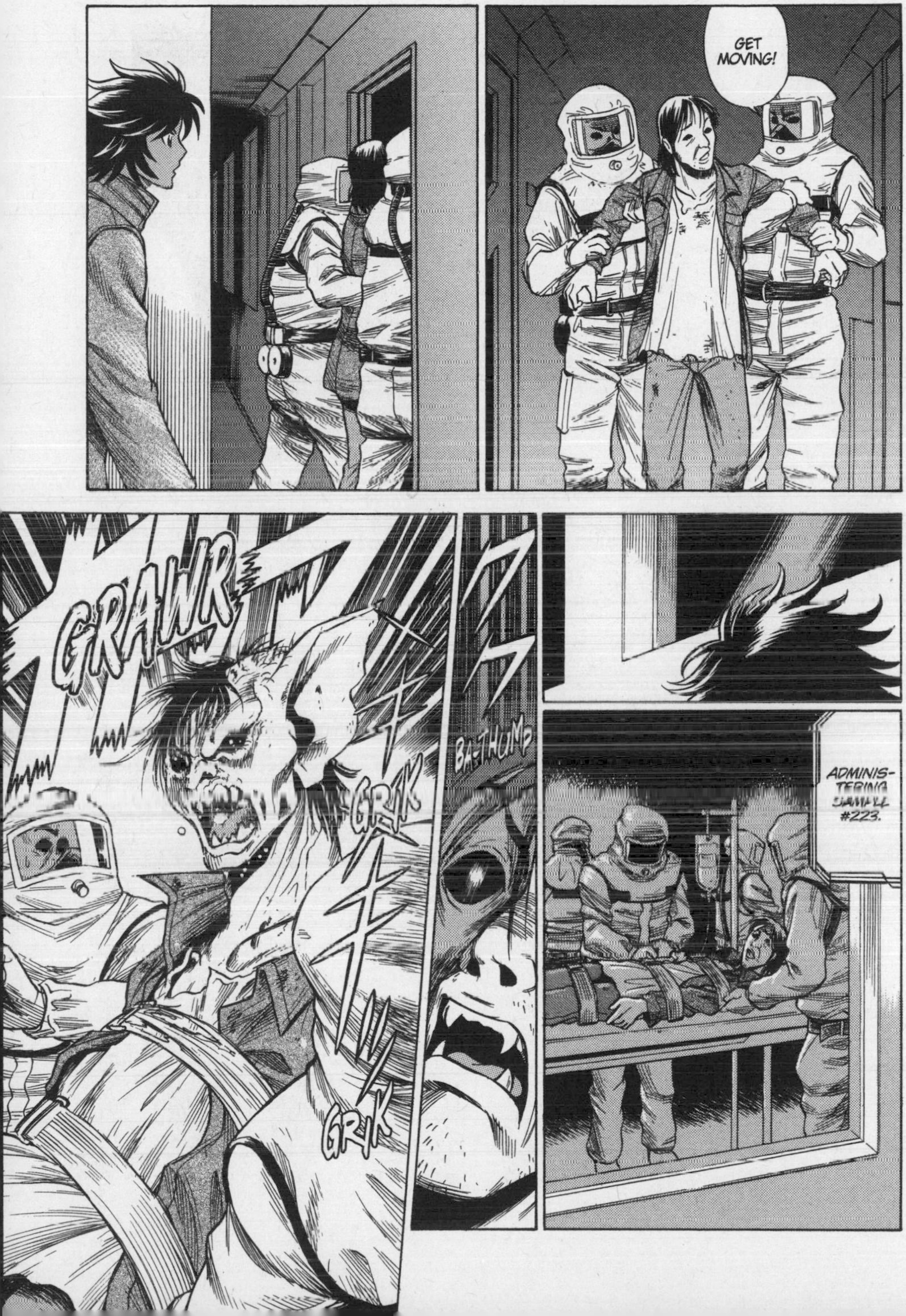
GET MOVING!
ADMINIS-
TERING
SAMPLE
#223.
BATHUMP
GRAWR
GRIK
GRIK

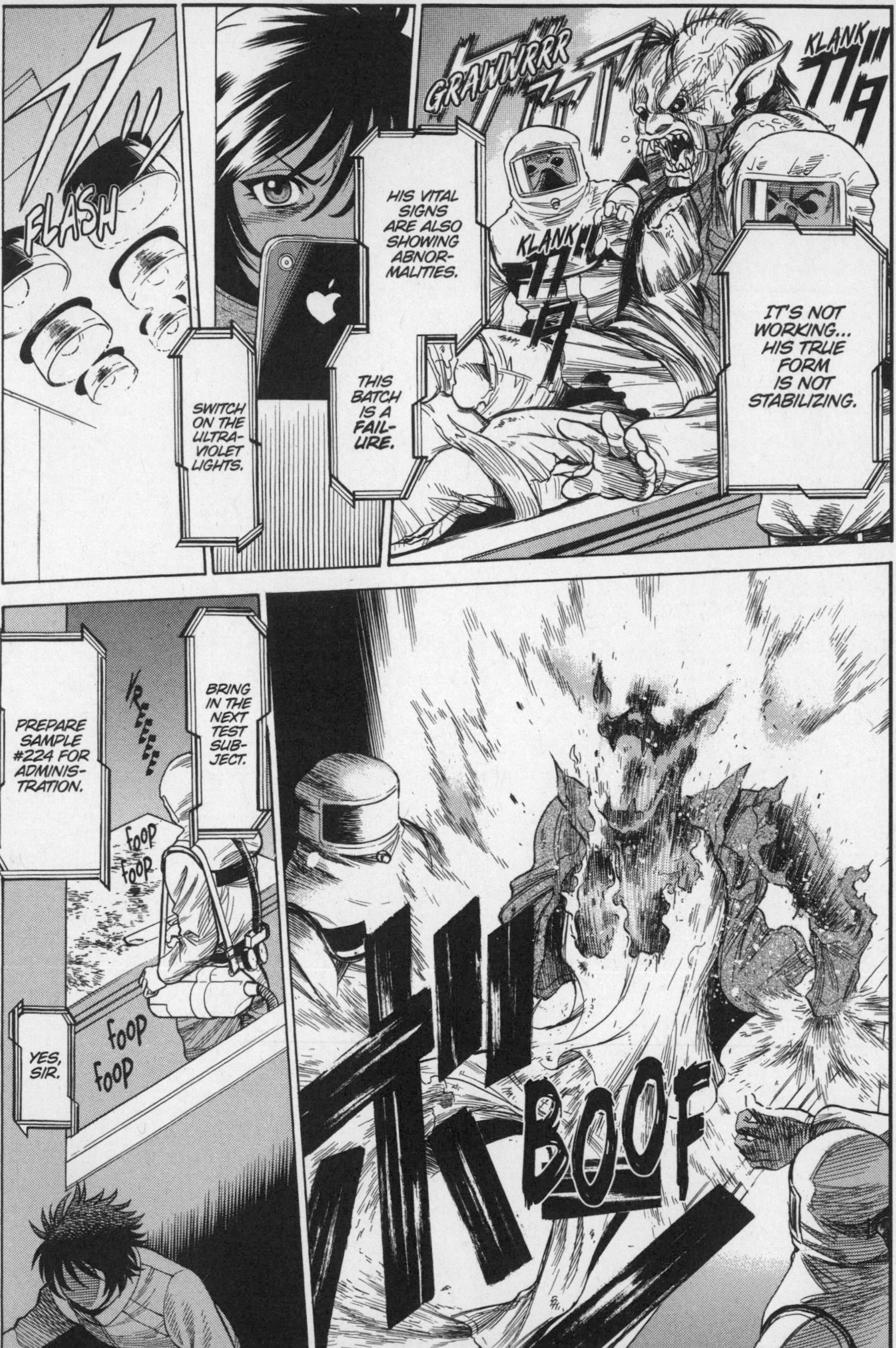
GRAWWRRR
KLANK
IT'S NOT WORKING... HIS TRUE FORM IS NOT STABILIZING.
KLANK
HIS VITAL SIGNS ARE ALSO SHOWING ABNOR-MALITIES.
THIS BATCH IS A FAIL-URE.
SWITCH ON THE ULTRA-VIOLET LIGHTS.
FLASH
BOOF
BRING IN THE NEXT TEST SUB-JECT.
PREPARE SAMPLE #224 FOR ADMINIS-TRATION.
VREEEEE
foop foop
YES, SIR.
foop foop

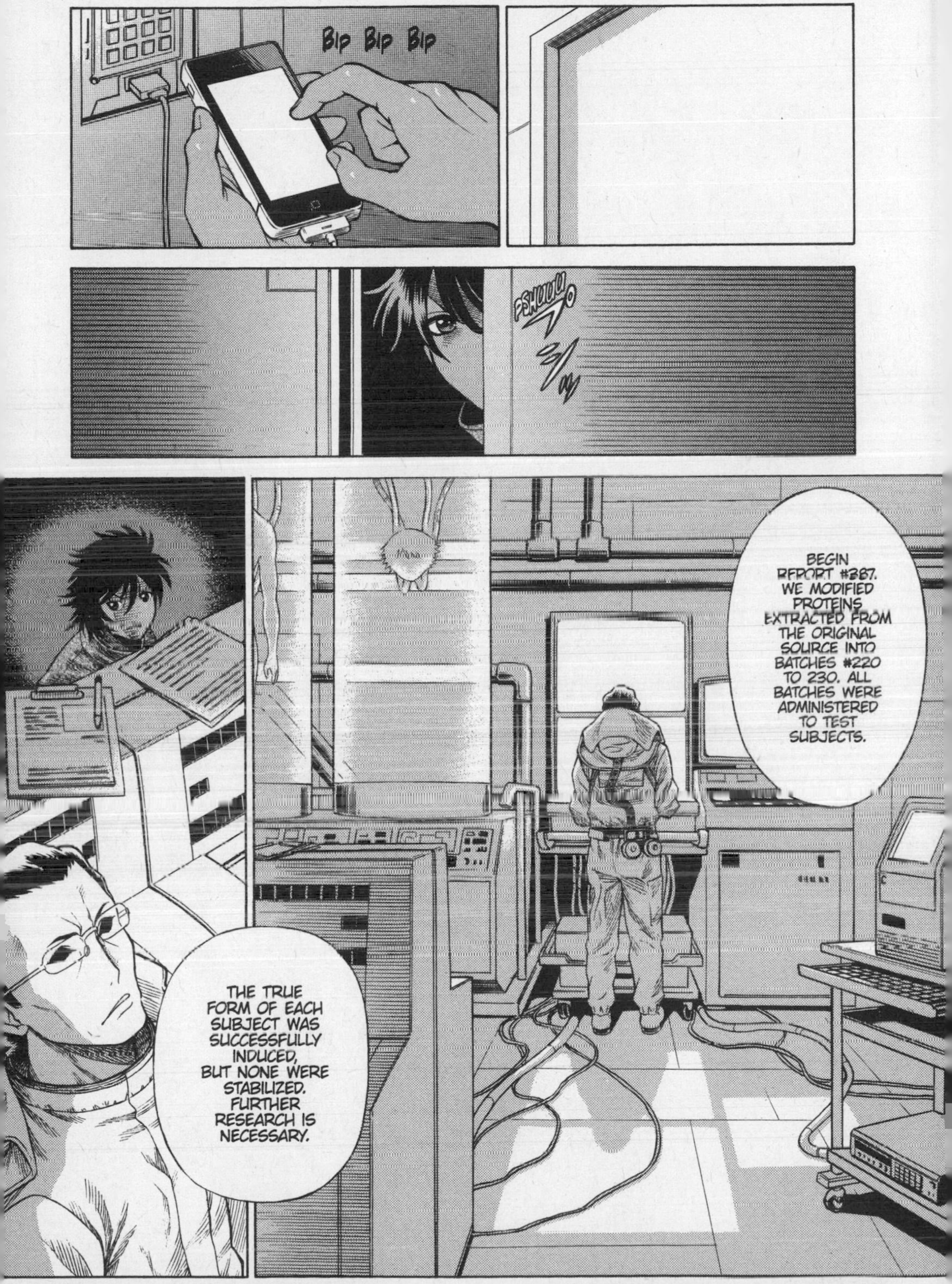
Bip Bip Bip
PSHUUU
BEGIN REPORT #387. WE MODIFIED PROTEINS EXTRACTED FROM THE ORIGINAL SOURCE INTO BATCHES #220 TO 230. ALL BATCHES WERE ADMINISTERED TO TEST SUBJECTS.
THE TRUE FORM OF EACH SUBJECT WAS SUCCESSFULLY INDUCED, BUT NONE WERE STABILIZED. FURTHER RESEARCH IS NECESSARY.

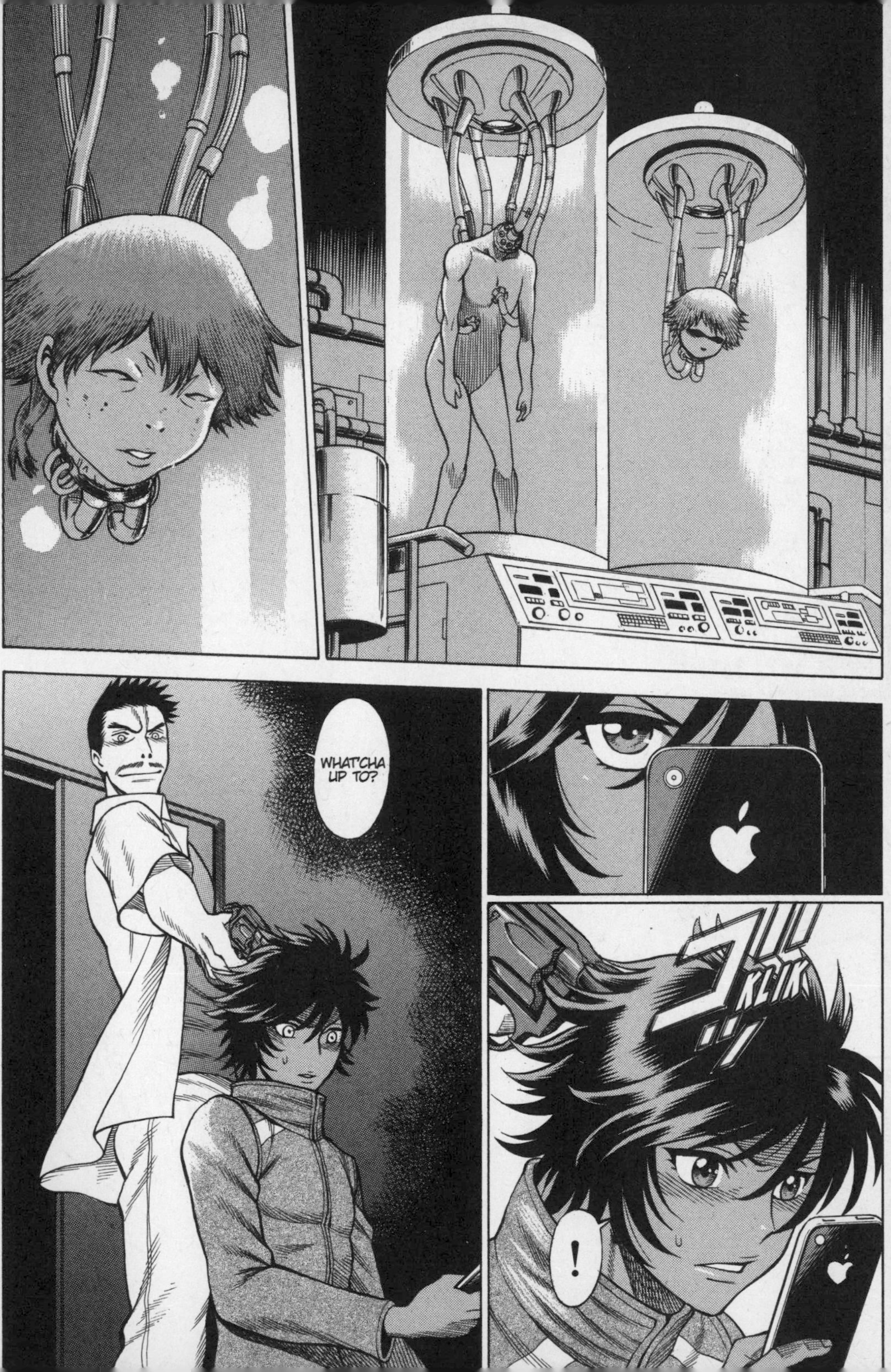
KLIK
!
WHAT'CHA UP TO?

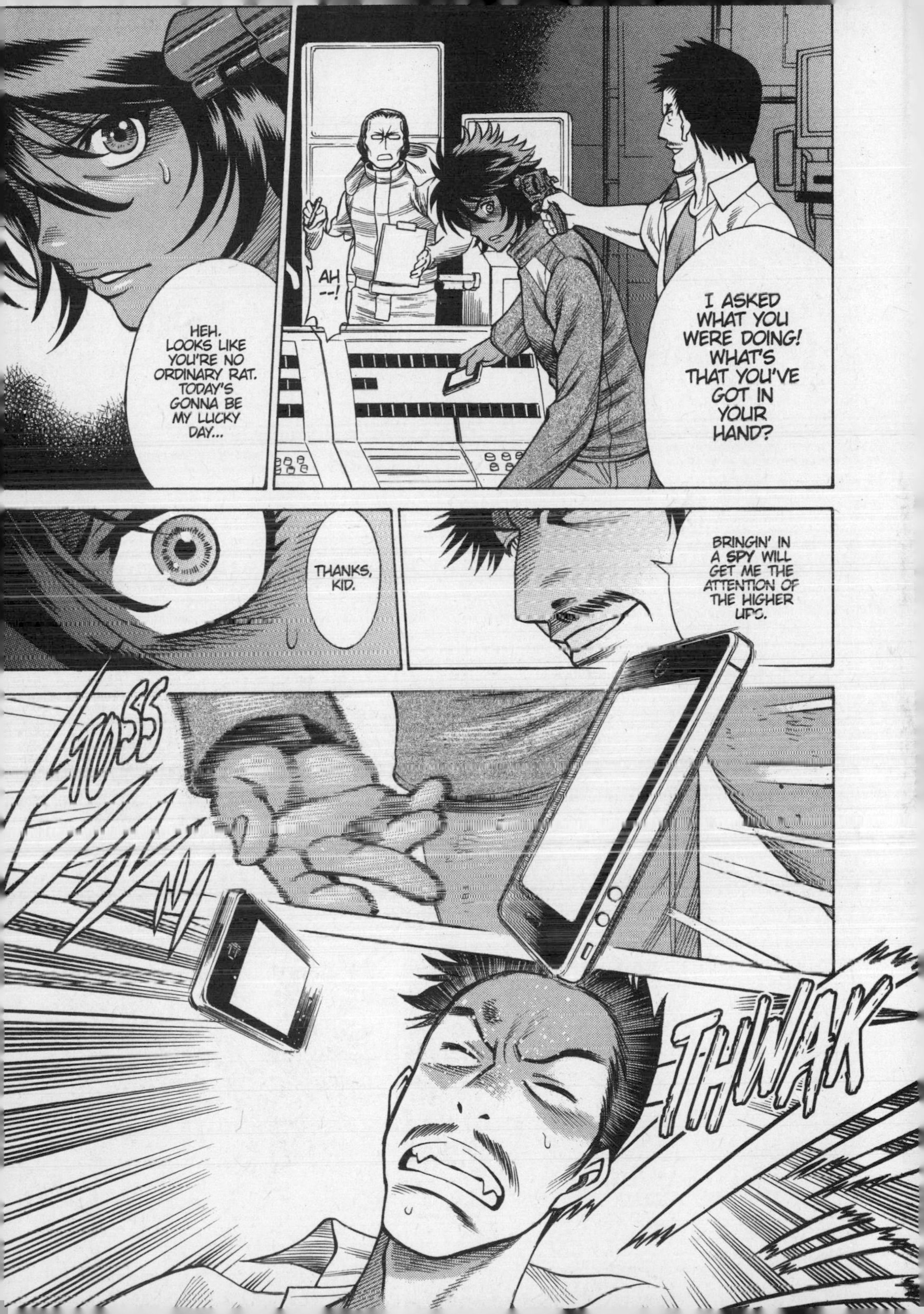
I ASKED WHAT YOU WERE DOING! WHAT'S THAT YOU'VE GOT IN YOUR HAND?
AH --!
HEH. LOOKS LIKE YOU'RE NO ORDINARY RAT. TODAY'S GONNA BE MY LUCKY DAY...
BRINGIN' IN A SPY WILL GET ME THE ATTENTION OF THE HIGHER UPS.
THANKS, KID.
TOSS
THWAK

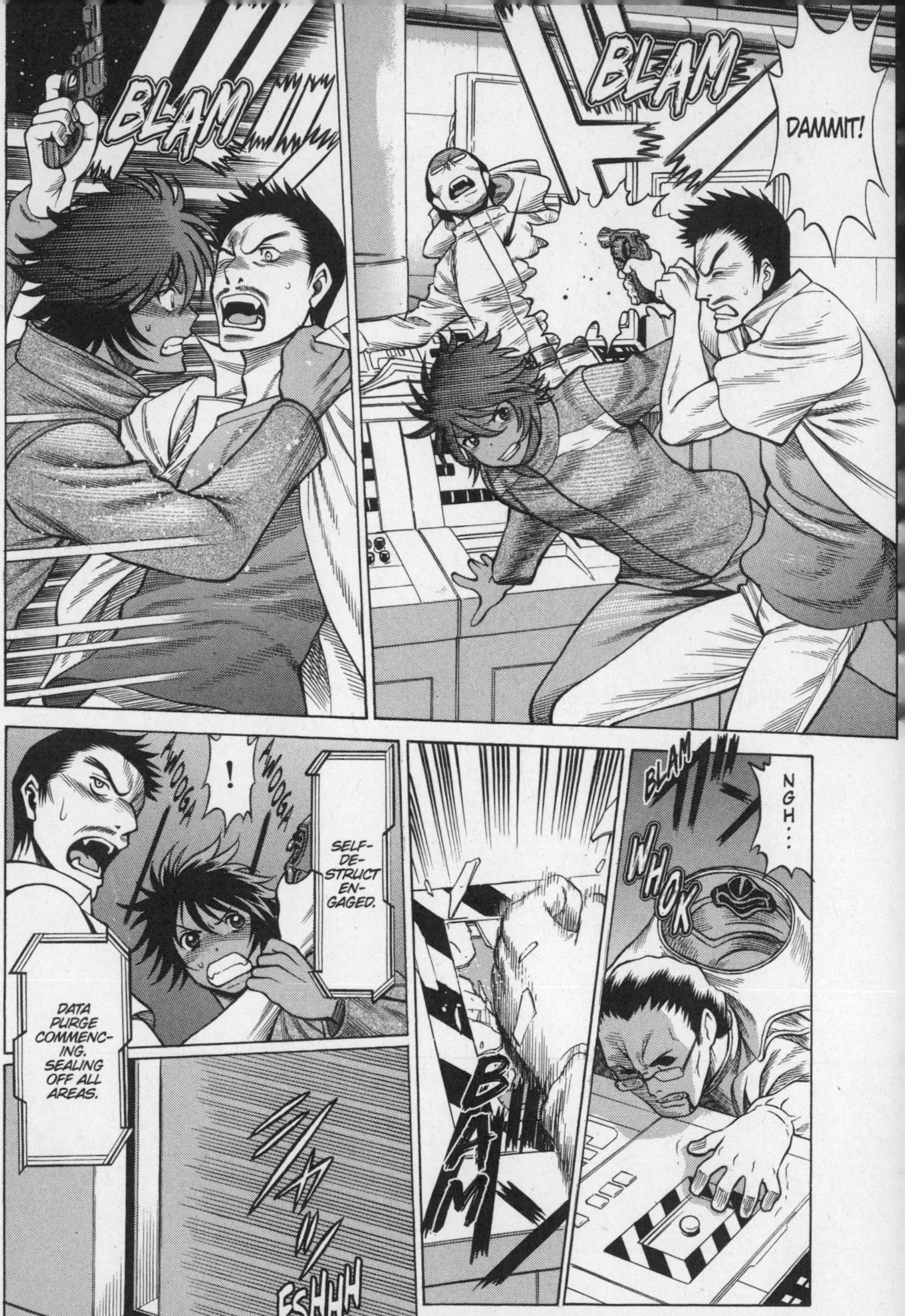
BLAM
DAMMIT!
BLAM
BLAM
NGH...
WHOK
BAM
AWOOGA
!
AWOOGA
SELF-DESTRUCT ENGAGED.
DATA PURGE COMMENCING. SEALING OFF ALL AREAS.
FSHHH

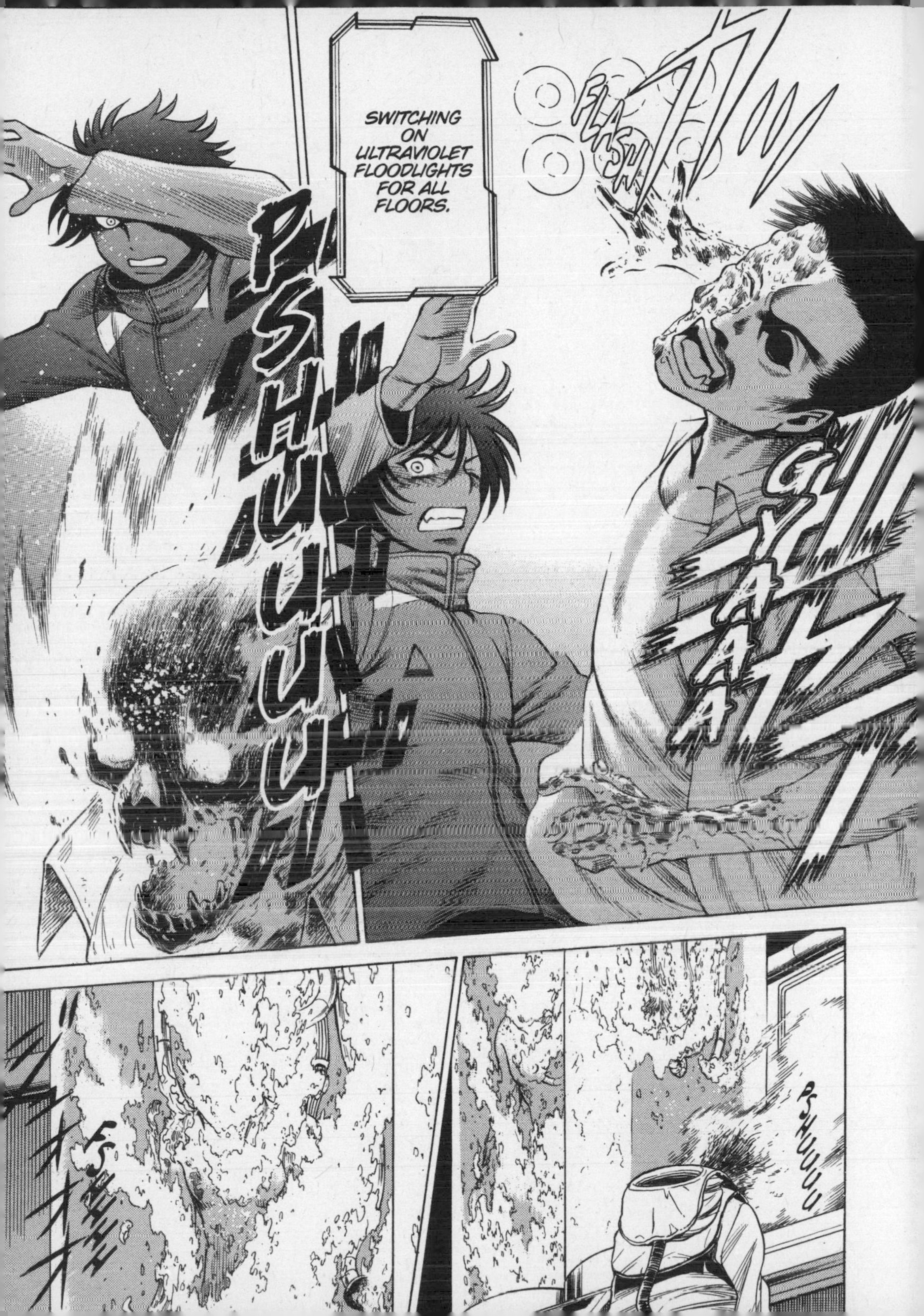
FLASH
SWITCHING ON ULTRAVIOLET FLOODLIGHTS FOR ALL FLOORS.
GYAAAA
PSHUUUU
PSHUUUU
FSSHHH

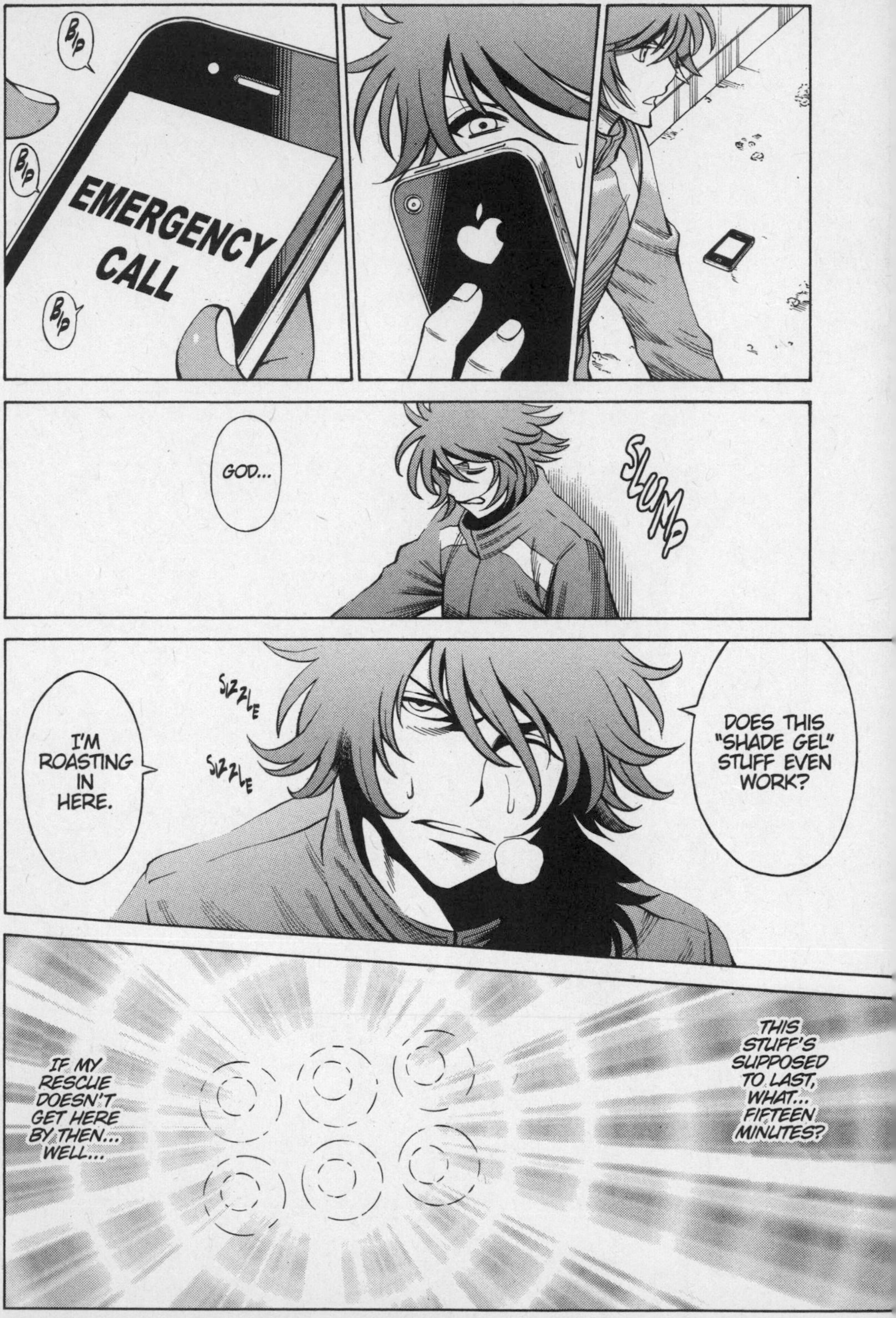
BIP
BIP
EMERGENCY CALL
BIP
SLUMP
GOD...
DOES THIS "SHADE GEL" STUFF EVEN WORK?
SIZZLE
SIZZLE
I'M ROASTING IN HERE.
THIS STUFF'S SUPPOSED TO LAST, WHAT... FIFTEEN MINUTES?
IF MY RESCUE DOESN'T GET HERE BY THEN... WELL...

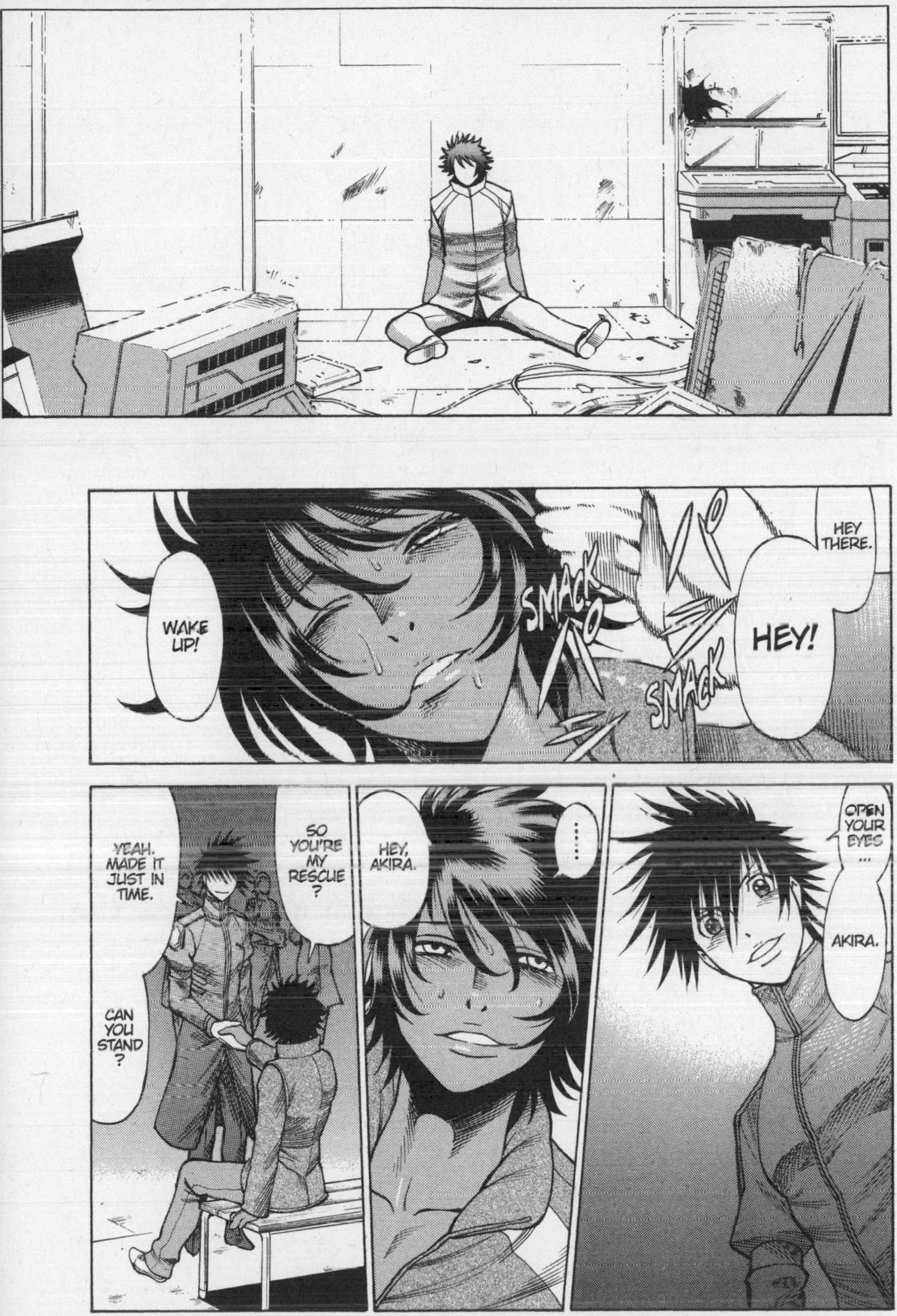
HEY THERE.
SMACK
HEY!
SMACK
WAKE UP!
OPEN YOUR EYES...
AKIRA.
......
HEY, AKIRA.
SO YOU'RE MY RESCUE?
YEAH. MADE IT JUST IN TIME.
CAN YOU STAND?

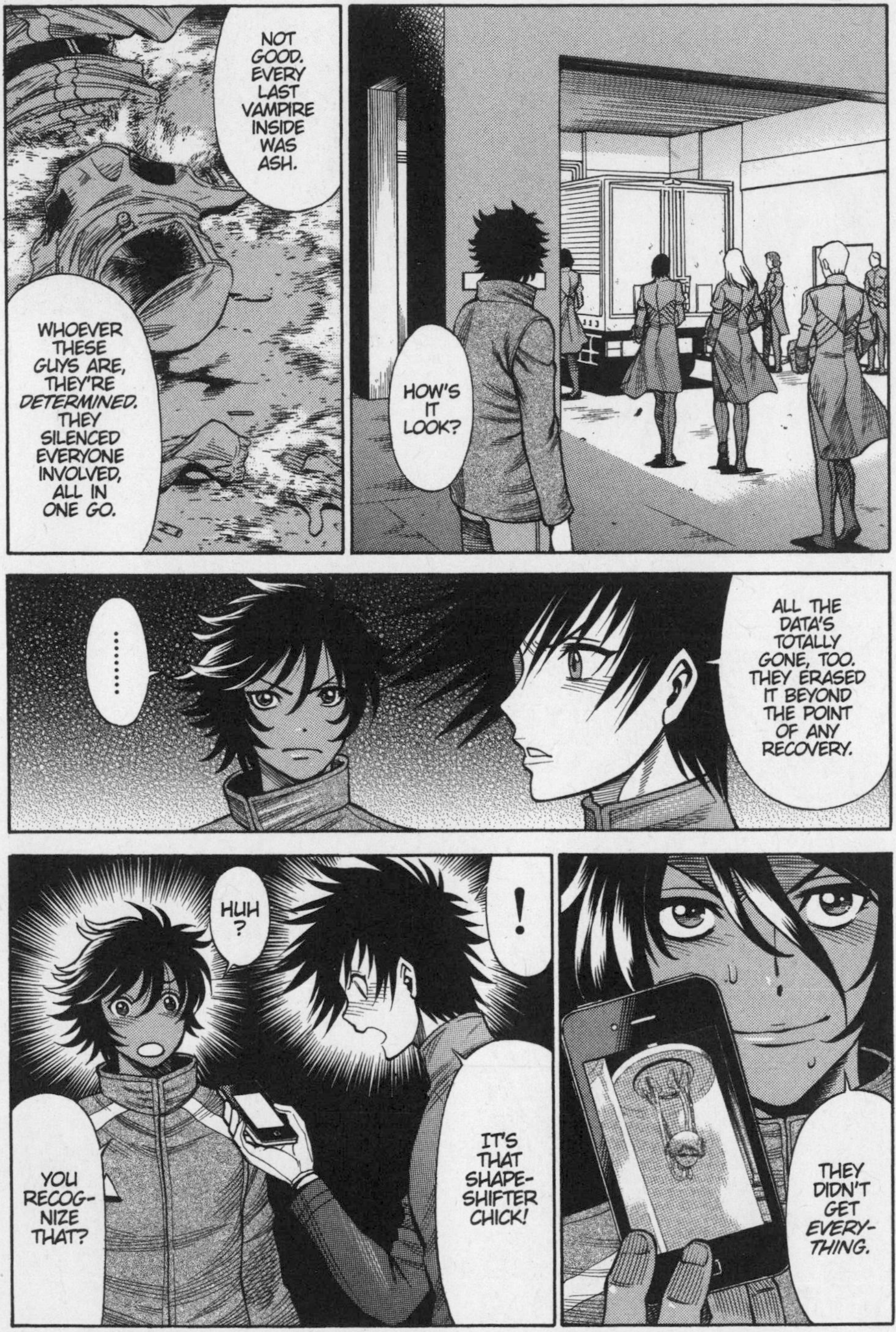
HOW'S IT LOOK?
NOT GOOD. EVERY LAST VAMPIRE INSIDE WAS ASH.
WHOEVER THESE GUYS ARE, THEY'RE *DETERMINED.* THEY SILENCED EVERYONE INVOLVED, ALL IN ONE GO.
ALL THE DATA'S TOTALLY GONE, TOO. THEY ERASED IT BEYOND THE POINT OF ANY RECOVERY.
....
THEY DIDN'T GET *EVERYTHING.*
!
HUH?
IT'S THAT SHAPE-SHIFTER CHICK!
YOU RECOGNIZE THAT?

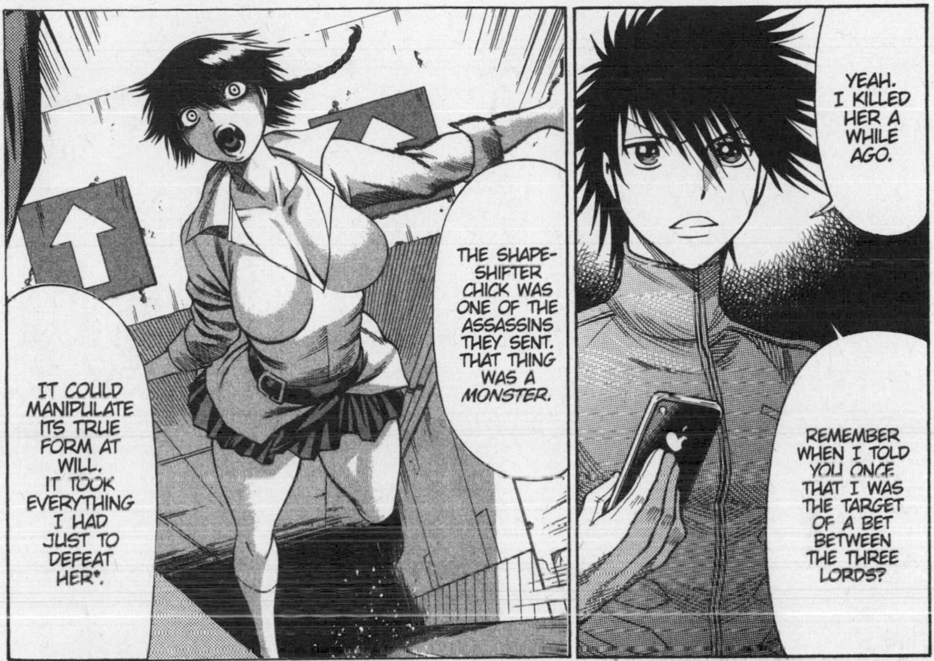
YEAH. I KILLED HER A WHILE AGO.
REMEMBER WHEN I TOLD YOU ONCE THAT I WAS THE TARGET OF A BET BETWEEN THE THREE LORDS?
THE SHAPE-SHIFTER CHICK WAS ONE OF THE ASSASSINS THEY SENT. THAT THING WAS A *MONSTER*.
IT COULD MANIPULATE ITS TRUE FORM AT WILL. IT TOOK EVERYTHING I HAD JUST TO DEFEAT HER*.

*Back in Dance in the Vampire Bund Vol. 4.

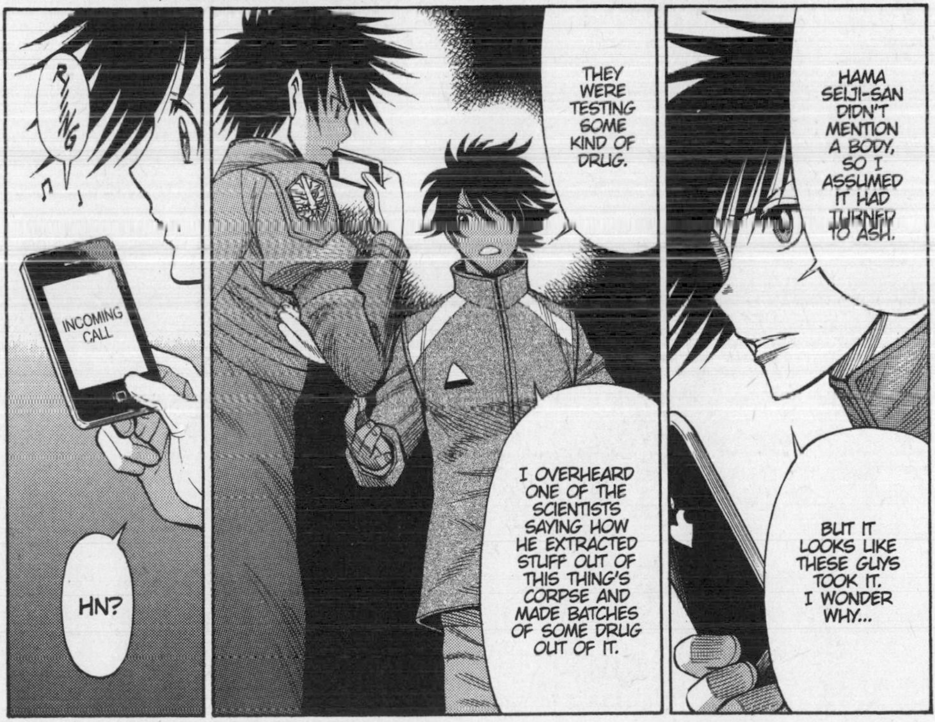
HAMA SEIJI-SAN DIDN'T MENTION A BODY, SO I ASSUMED IT HAD TURNED TO ASH.
BUT IT LOOKS LIKE THESE GUYS TOOK IT. I WONDER WHY...
THEY WERE TESTING SOME KIND OF DRUG.
I OVERHEARD ONE OF THE SCIENTISTS SAYING HOW HE EXTRACTED STUFF OUT OF THIS THING'S CORPSE AND MADE BATCHES OF SOME DRUG OUT OF IT.
RIING
INCOMING CALL
HN?

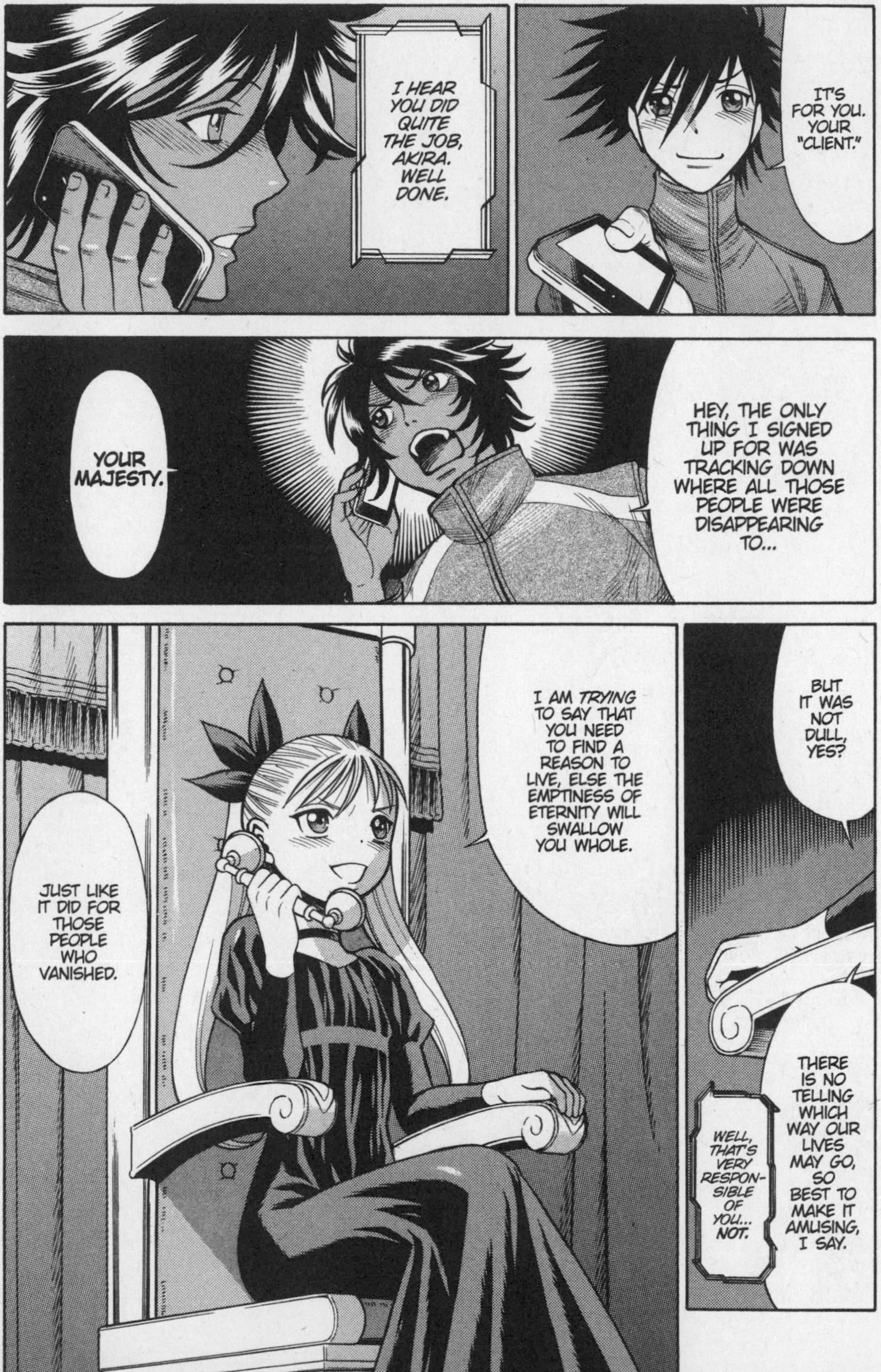
IT'S FOR YOU. YOUR "CLIENT."
I HEAR YOU DID QUITE THE JOB, AKIRA. WELL DONE.
HEY, THE ONLY THING I SIGNED UP FOR WAS TRACKING DOWN WHERE ALL THOSE PEOPLE WERE DISAPPEARING TO...
YOUR MAJESTY.
BUT IT WAS NOT DULL, YES?
THERE IS NO TELLING WHICH WAY OUR LIVES MAY GO, SO BEST TO MAKE IT AMUSING, I SAY.
WELL, THAT'S VERY RESPONSIBLE OF YOU... NOT.
I AM *TRYING* TO SAY THAT YOU NEED TO FIND A REASON TO LIVE, ELSE THE EMPTINESS OF ETERNITY WILL SWALLOW YOU WHOLE.
JUST LIKE IT DID FOR THOSE PEOPLE WHO VANISHED.

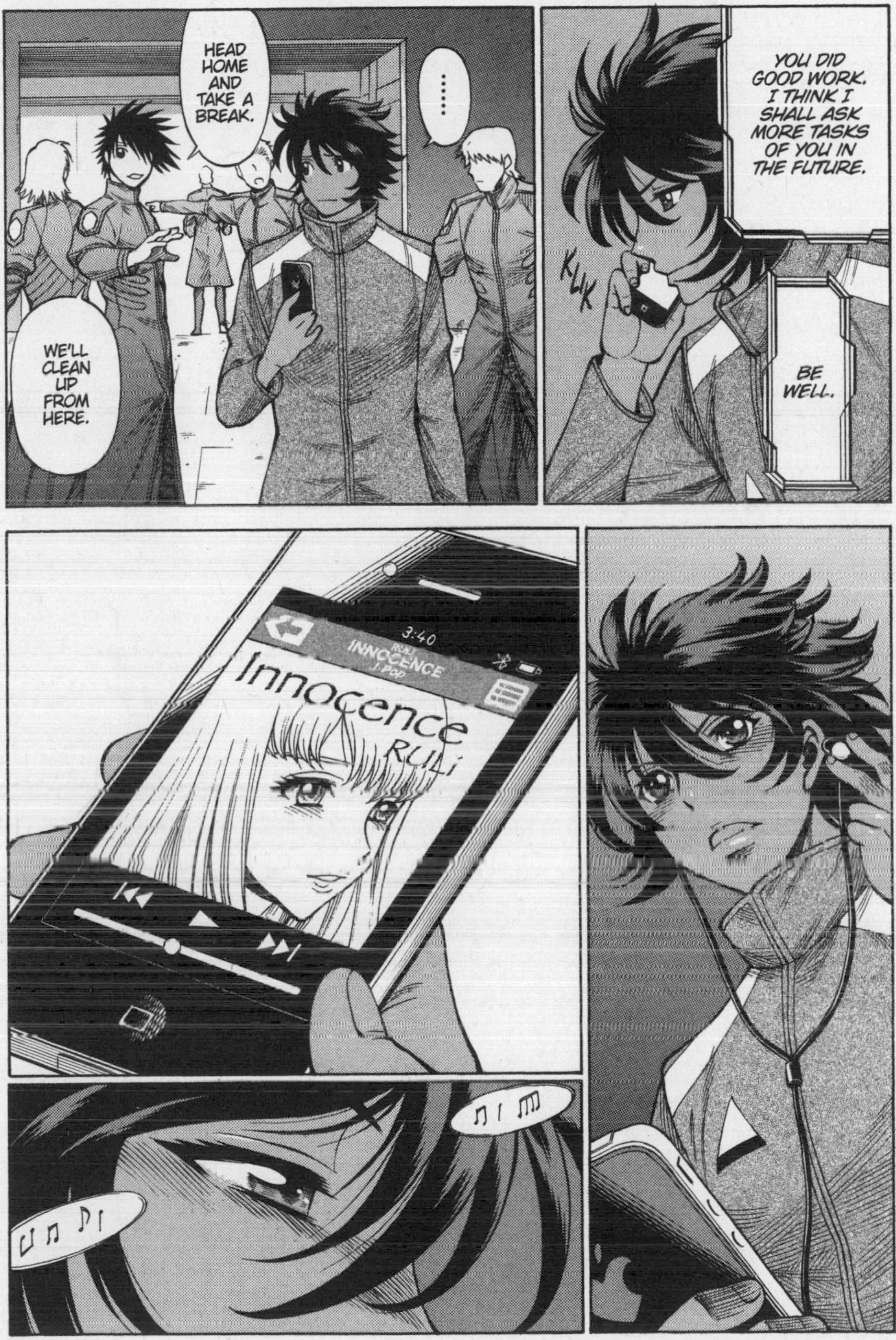
YOU DID GOOD WORK. I THINK I SHALL ASK MORE TASKS OF YOU IN THE FUTURE.
KLIK
BE WELL.
HEAD HOME AND TAKE A BREAK.
......
WE'LL CLEAN UP FROM HERE.
3:40
INNOCENCE
Innocence
RULi

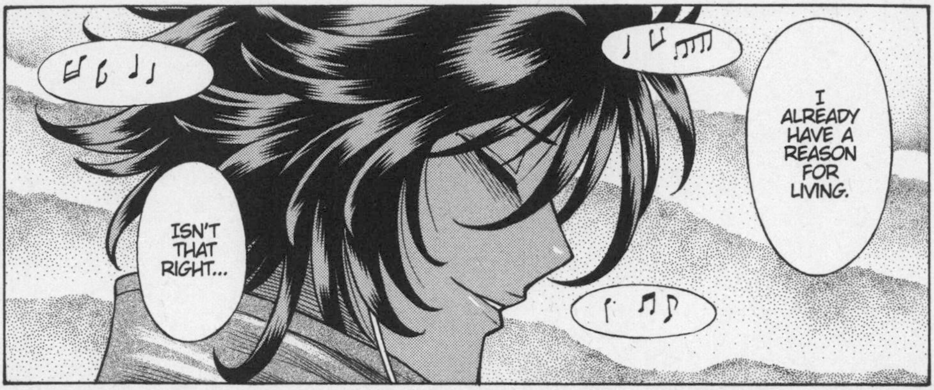
I ALREADY HAVE A REASON FOR LIVING.
ISN'T THAT RIGHT...
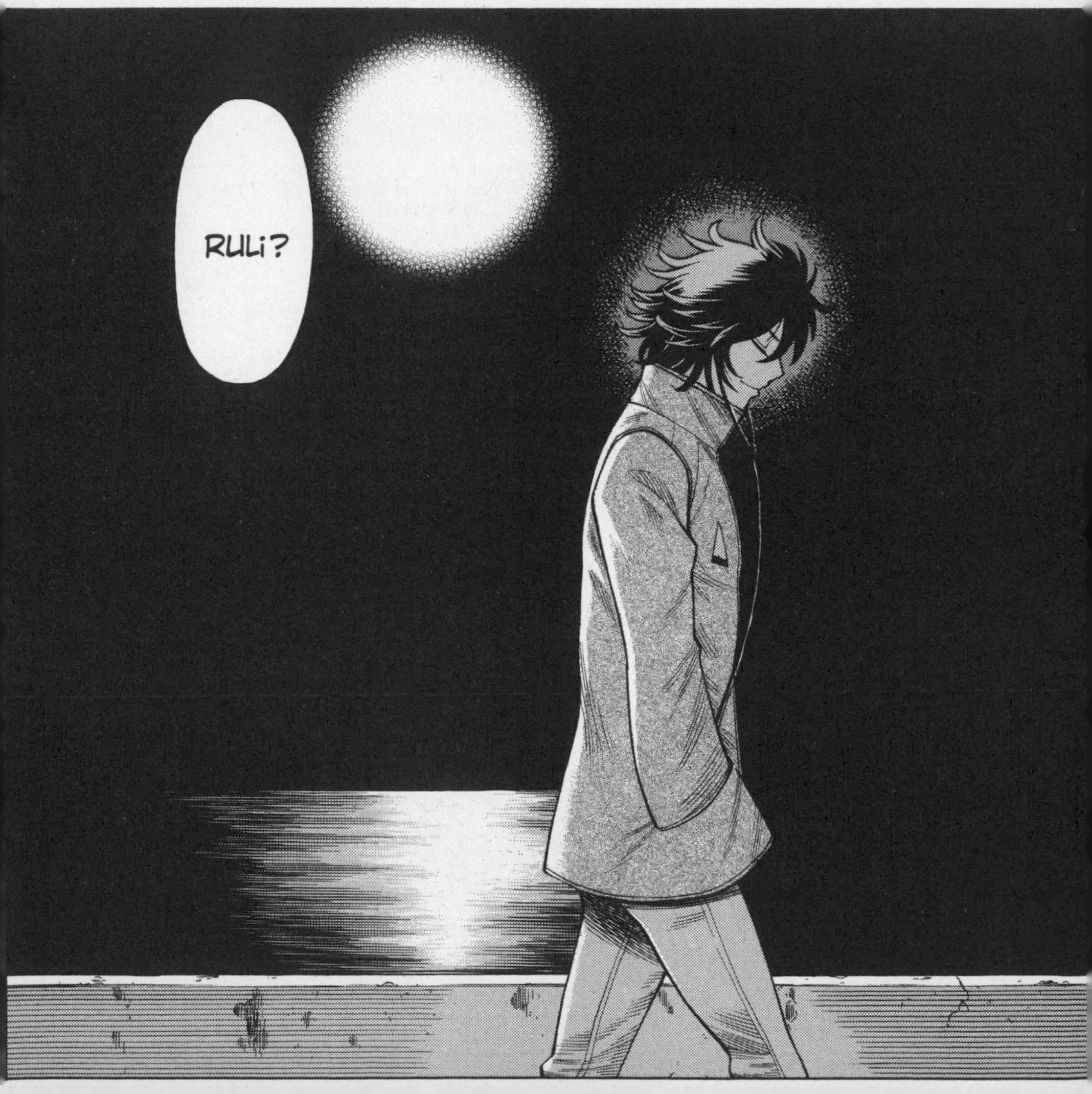
RULI?

ABOUT THIS STORY...

This volume begins a few weeks after the events in *Dive in the Vampire Bund Vol. 1*. Placed in the overall story arc, it fits somewhere in the middle of Volume 6 of *Dance in the Vampire Bund*, while the Bund was still enjoying a short period of peace. The facility Akira infiltrated here was the one responsible for experimenting on the drug which Rozenmann intended to use on Mina in Volume 12 of the main story. The decapitated body Akira found floating in the tubes was that of Ivanovic's shapeshifter assassin, sent after Mina's Akira in Volume 4.

DIVE IN THE VAMPIRE BUND

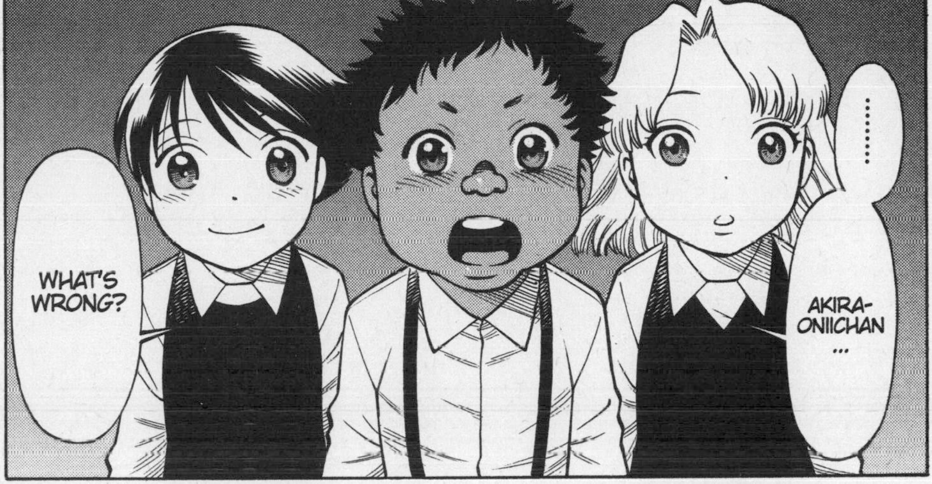
......
AKIRA-ONIICHAN ...
WHAT'S WRONG?

Chapter 12: Cross the Sea

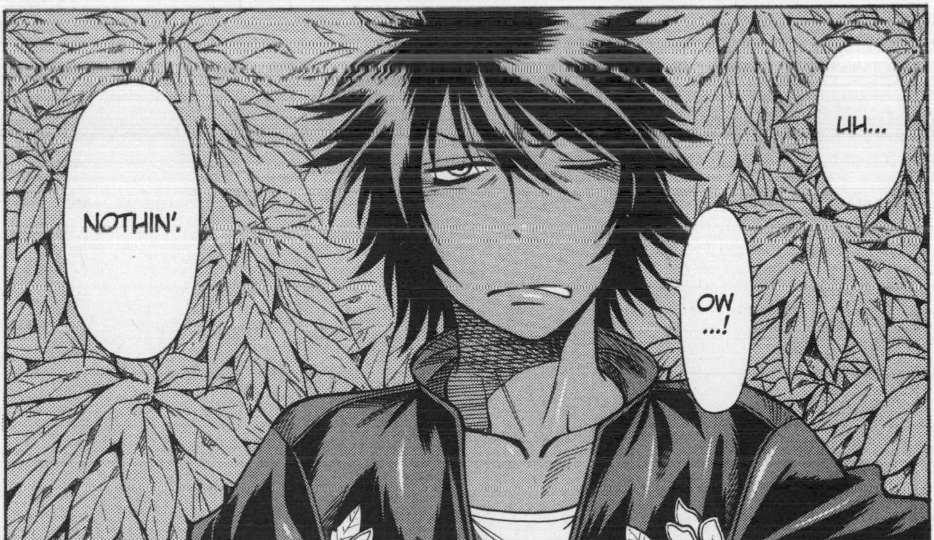
UH...
OW ...!
NOTHIN'.

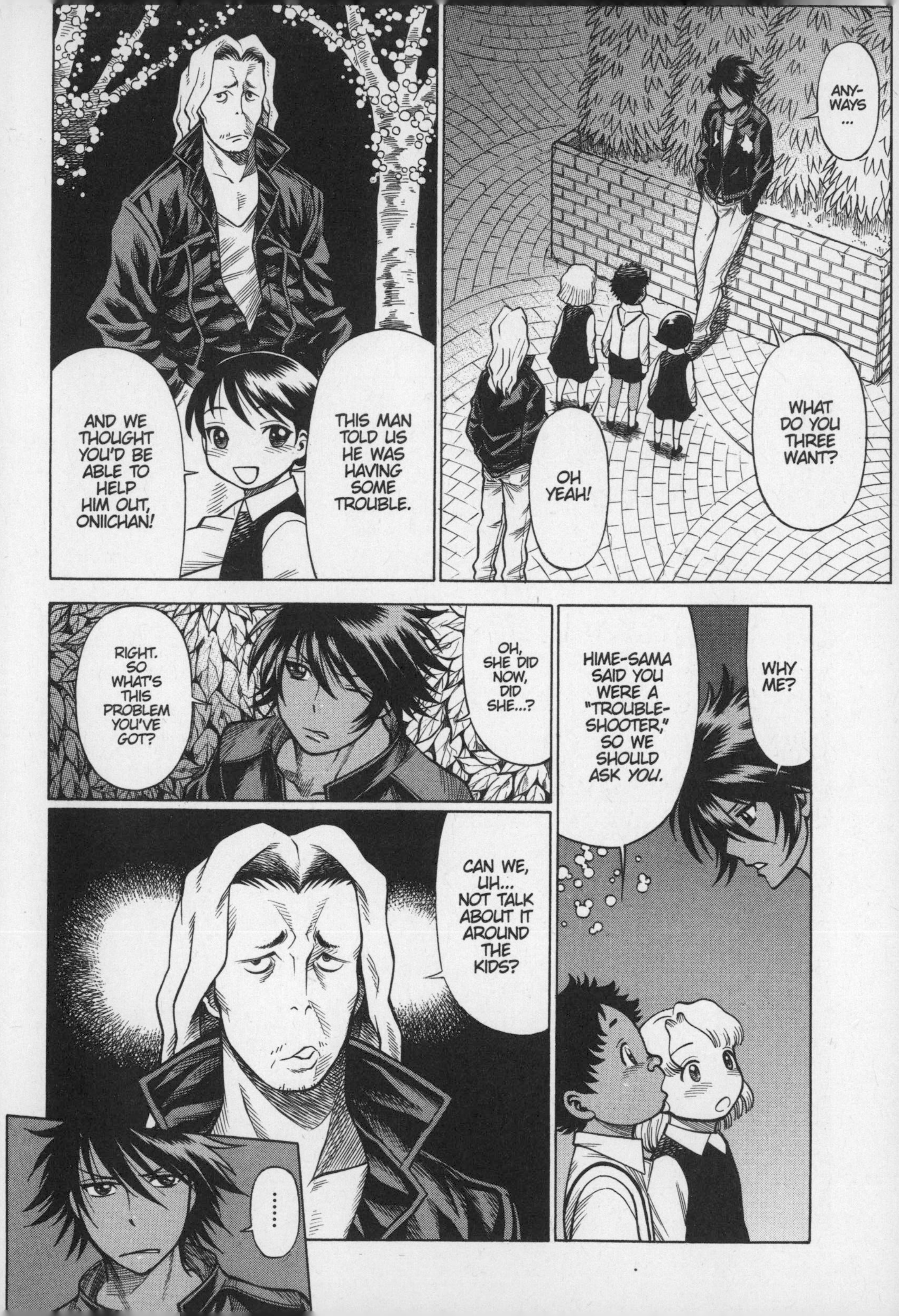
ANY-WAYS ...
WHAT DO YOU THREE WANT?
OH YEAH!
THIS MAN TOLD US HE WAS HAVING SOME TROUBLE.
AND WE THOUGHT YOU'D BE ABLE TO HELP HIM OUT, ONIICHAN!
WHY ME?
HIME-SAMA SAID YOU WERE A "TROUBLE-SHOOTER," SO WE SHOULD ASK YOU.
OH, SHE DID NOW, DID SHE...?
RIGHT. SO WHAT'S THIS PROBLEM YOU'VE GOT?
CAN WE, UH... NOT TALK ABOUT IT AROUND THE KIDS?
......

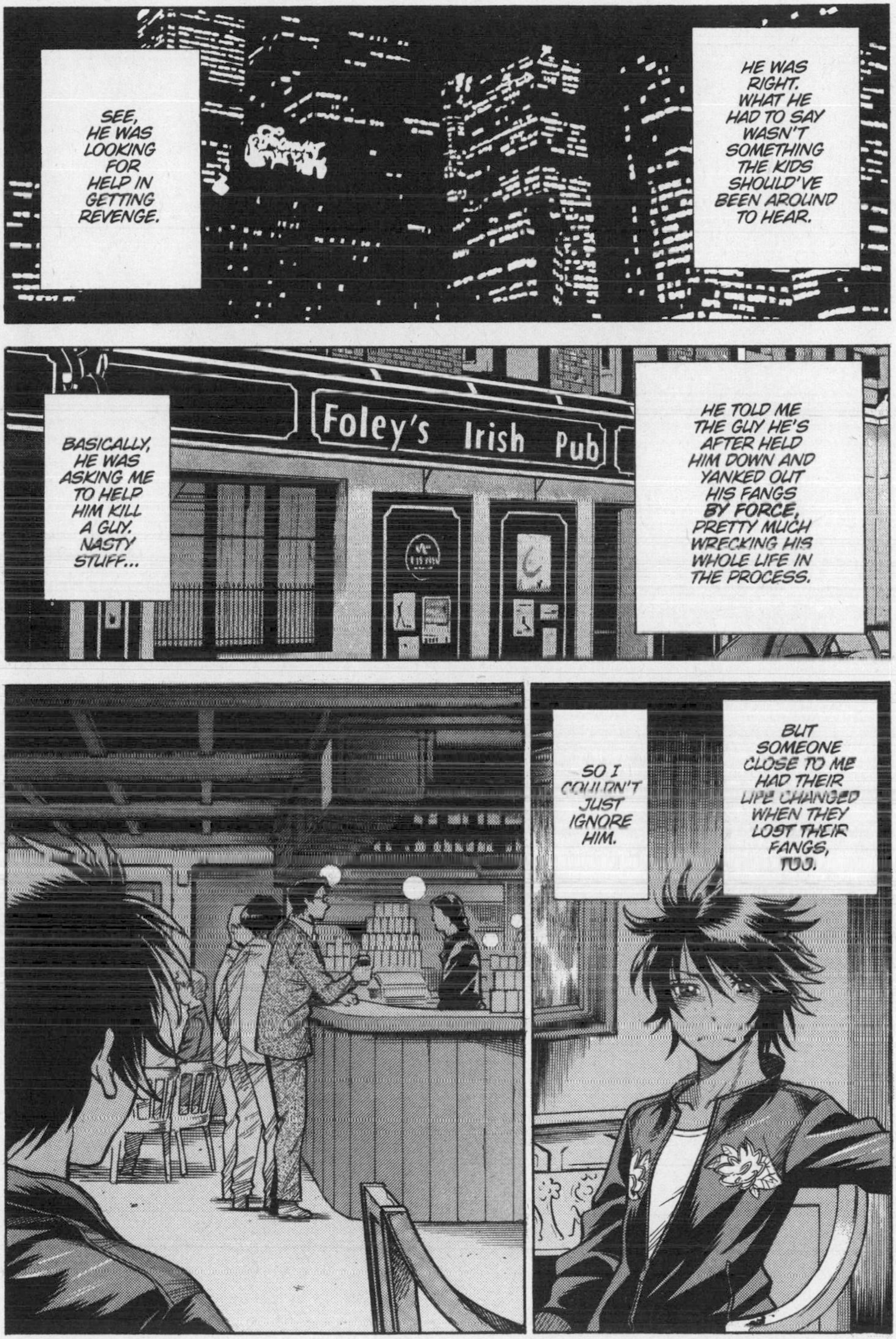
HE WAS RIGHT. WHAT HE HAD TO SAY WASN'T SOMETHING THE KIDS SHOULD'VE BEEN AROUND TO HEAR.
SEE, HE WAS LOOKING FOR HELP IN GETTING REVENGE.
HE TOLD ME THE GUY HE'S AFTER HELD HIM DOWN AND YANKED OUT HIS FANGS BY FORCE, PRETTY MUCH WRECKING HIS WHOLE LIFE IN THE PROCESS.
Foley's Irish Pub
BASICALLY, HE WAS ASKING ME TO HELP HIM KILL A GUY. NASTY STUFF...
BUT SOMEONE CLOSE TO ME HAD THEIR LIFE CHANGED WHEN THEY LOST THEIR FANGS, TOO.
SO I COULDN'T JUST IGNORE HIM.

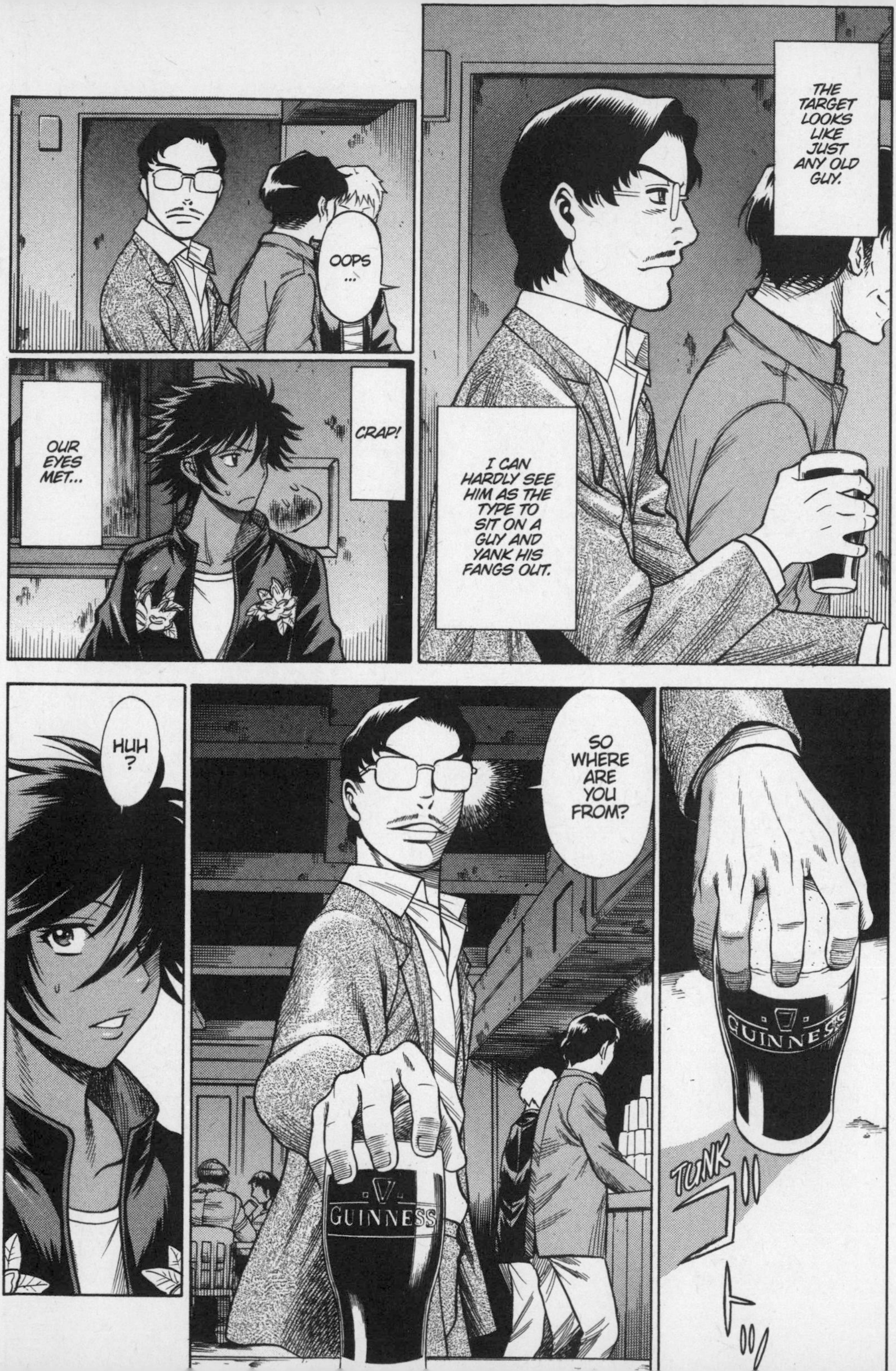

THE TARGET LOOKS LIKE JUST ANY OLD GUY.
I CAN HARDLY SEE HIM AS THE TYPE TO SIT ON A GUY AND YANK HIS FANGS OUT.
OOPS ...
CRAP!
OUR EYES MET...
TUNK
SO WHERE ARE YOU FROM?
HUH ?

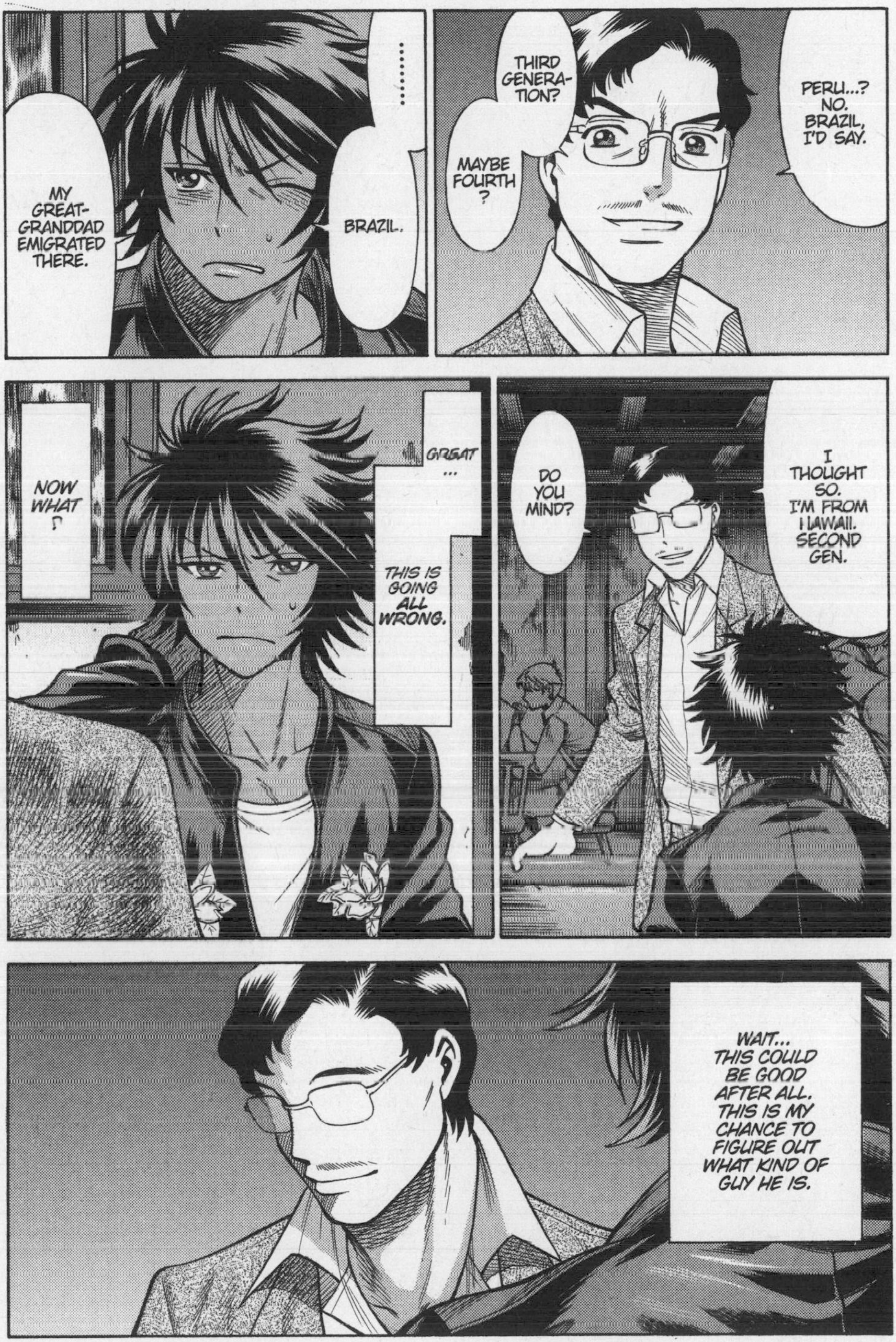
PERU...? NO. BRAZIL, I'D SAY.
THIRD GENERATION?
MAYBE FOURTH?
......
BRAZIL.
MY GREAT-GRANDDAD EMIGRATED THERE.
I THOUGHT SO. I'M FROM HAWAII. SECOND GEN.
DO YOU MIND?
GREAT...
THIS IS GOING ALL WRONG.
NOW WHAT?
WAIT... THIS COULD BE GOOD AFTER ALL. THIS IS MY CHANCE TO FIGURE OUT WHAT KIND OF GUY HE IS.

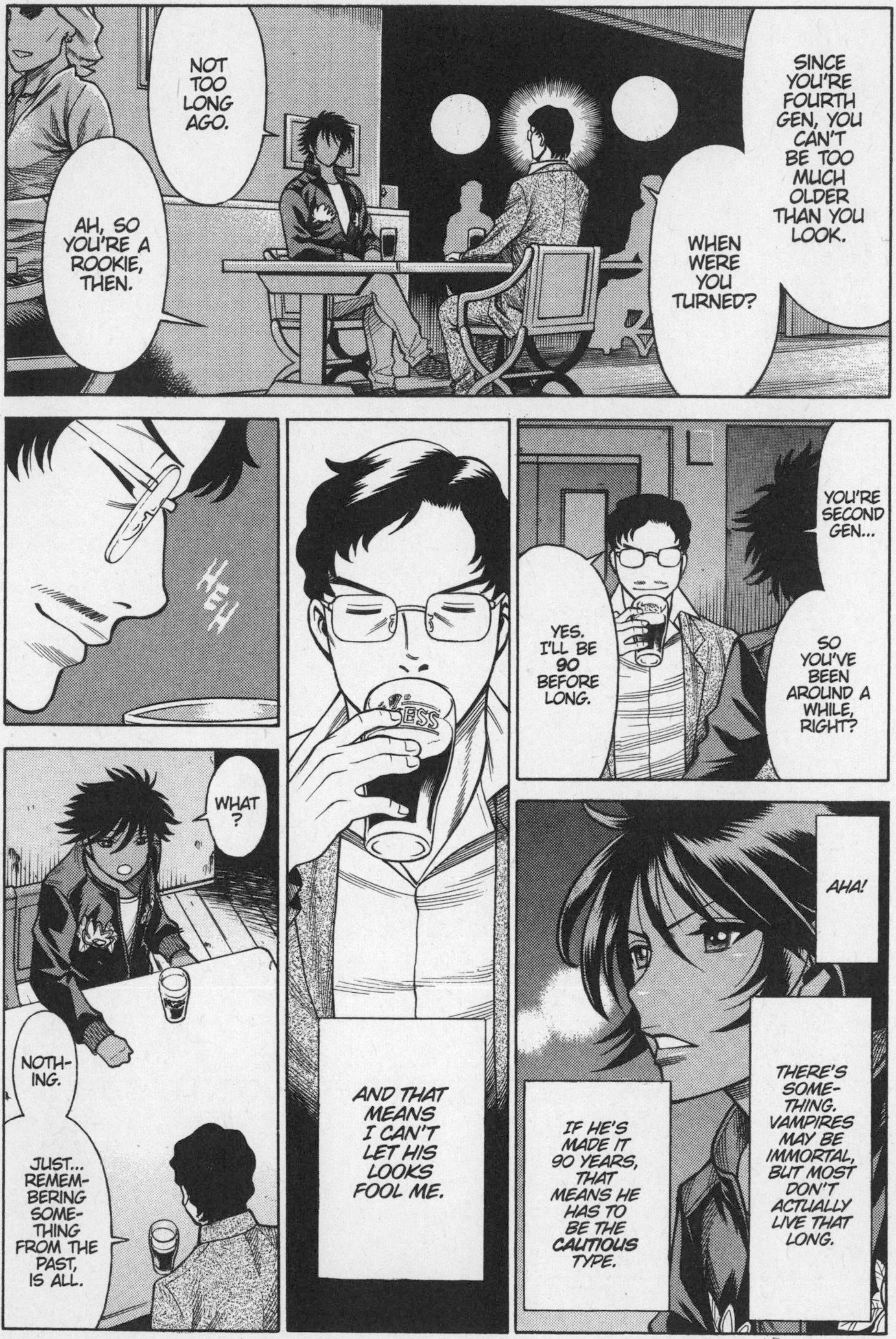
SINCE YOU'RE FOURTH GEN, YOU CAN'T BE TOO MUCH OLDER THAN YOU LOOK.
WHEN WERE YOU TURNED?
NOT TOO LONG AGO.
AH, SO YOU'RE A ROOKIE, THEN.
YOU'RE SECOND GEN...
SO YOU'VE BEEN AROUND A WHILE, RIGHT?
YES. I'LL BE 90 BEFORE LONG.
AHA!
THERE'S SOME-THING. VAMPIRES MAY BE IMMORTAL, BUT MOST DON'T ACTUALLY LIVE THAT LONG.
IF HE'S MADE IT 90 YEARS, THAT MEANS HE HAS TO BE THE CAUTIOUS TYPE.
AND THAT MEANS I CAN'T LET HIS LOOKS FOOL ME.
HEH
WHAT?
NOTH-ING.
JUST... REMEM-BERING SOME-THING FROM THE PAST, IS ALL.

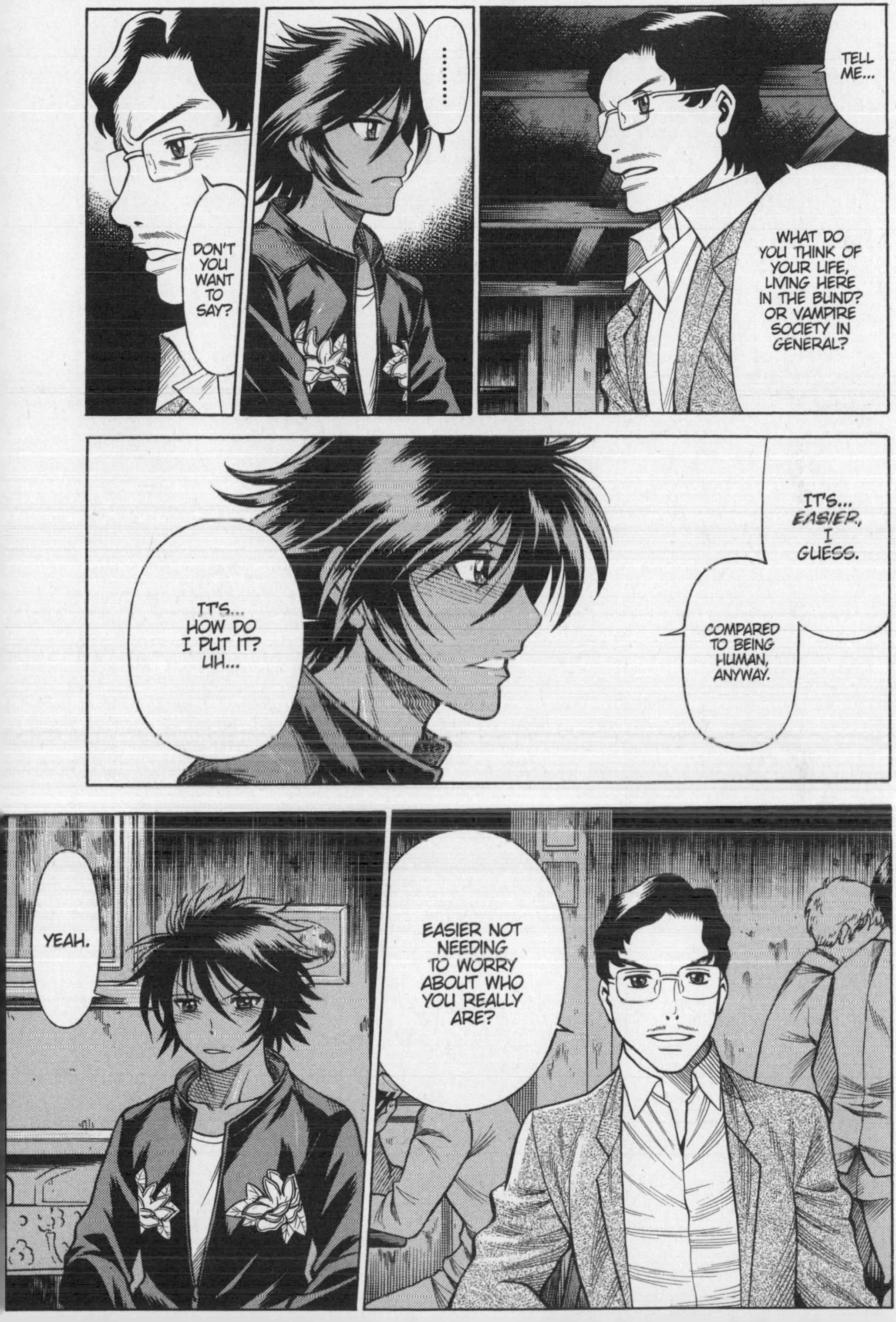
TELL ME...
WHAT DO YOU THINK OF YOUR LIFE, LIVING HERE IN THE BUND? OR VAMPIRE SOCIETY IN GENERAL?
......
DON'T YOU WANT TO SAY?
IT'S... *EASIER*, I GUESS.
COMPARED TO BEING HUMAN, ANYWAY.
IT'S... HOW DO I PUT IT? UH...
EASIER NOT NEEDING TO WORRY ABOUT WHO YOU REALLY ARE?
YEAH.

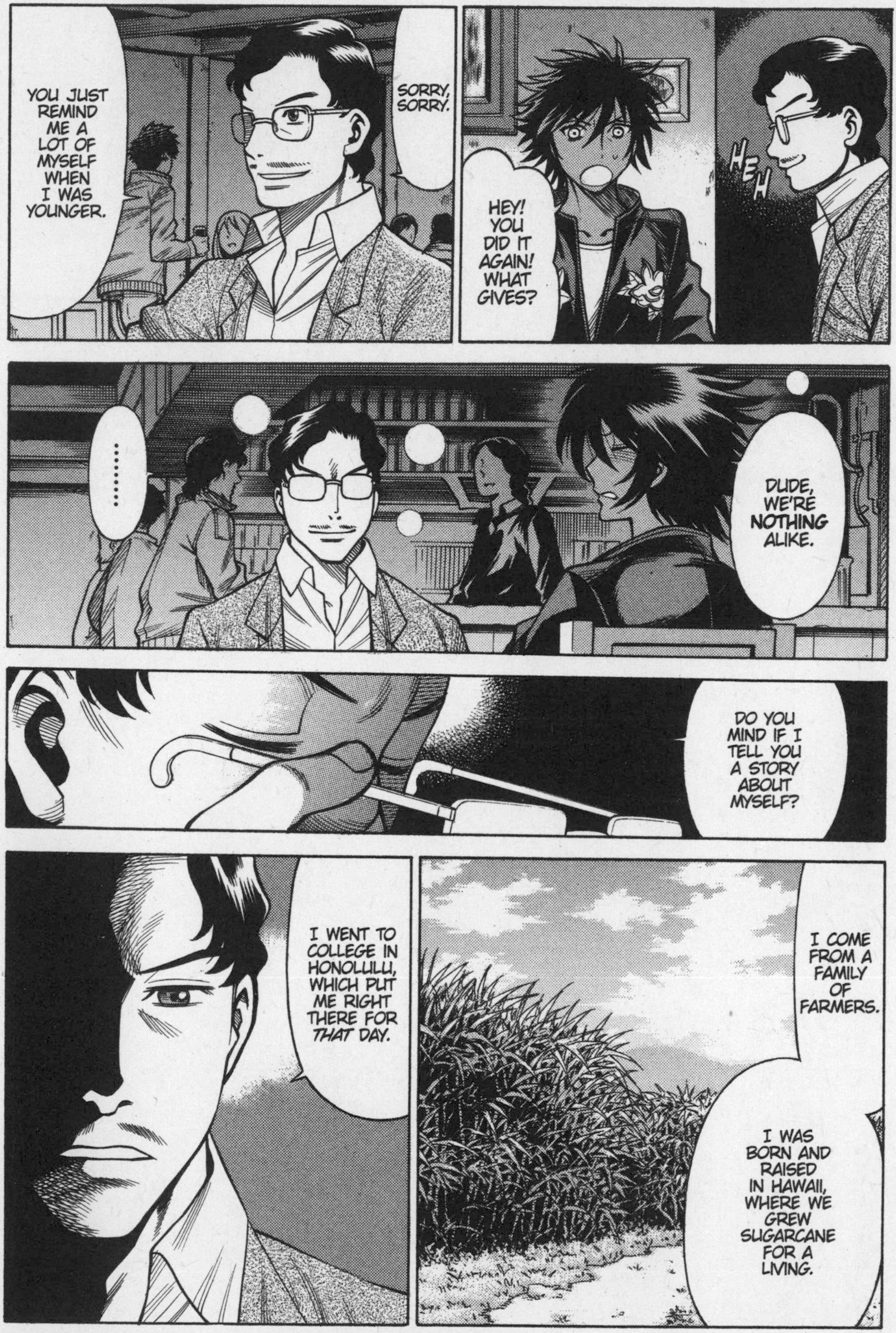
HEH
HEY! YOU DID IT AGAIN! WHAT GIVES?
SORRY, SORRY.
YOU JUST REMIND ME A LOT OF MYSELF WHEN I WAS YOUNGER.
DUDE, WE'RE **NOTHING** ALIKE.
……
DO YOU MIND IF I TELL YOU A STORY ABOUT MYSELF?
I COME FROM A FAMILY OF FARMERS.
I WAS BORN AND RAISED IN HAWAII, WHERE WE GREW SUGARCANE FOR A LIVING.
I WENT TO COLLEGE IN HONOLULU, WHICH PUT ME RIGHT THERE FOR *THAT* DAY.

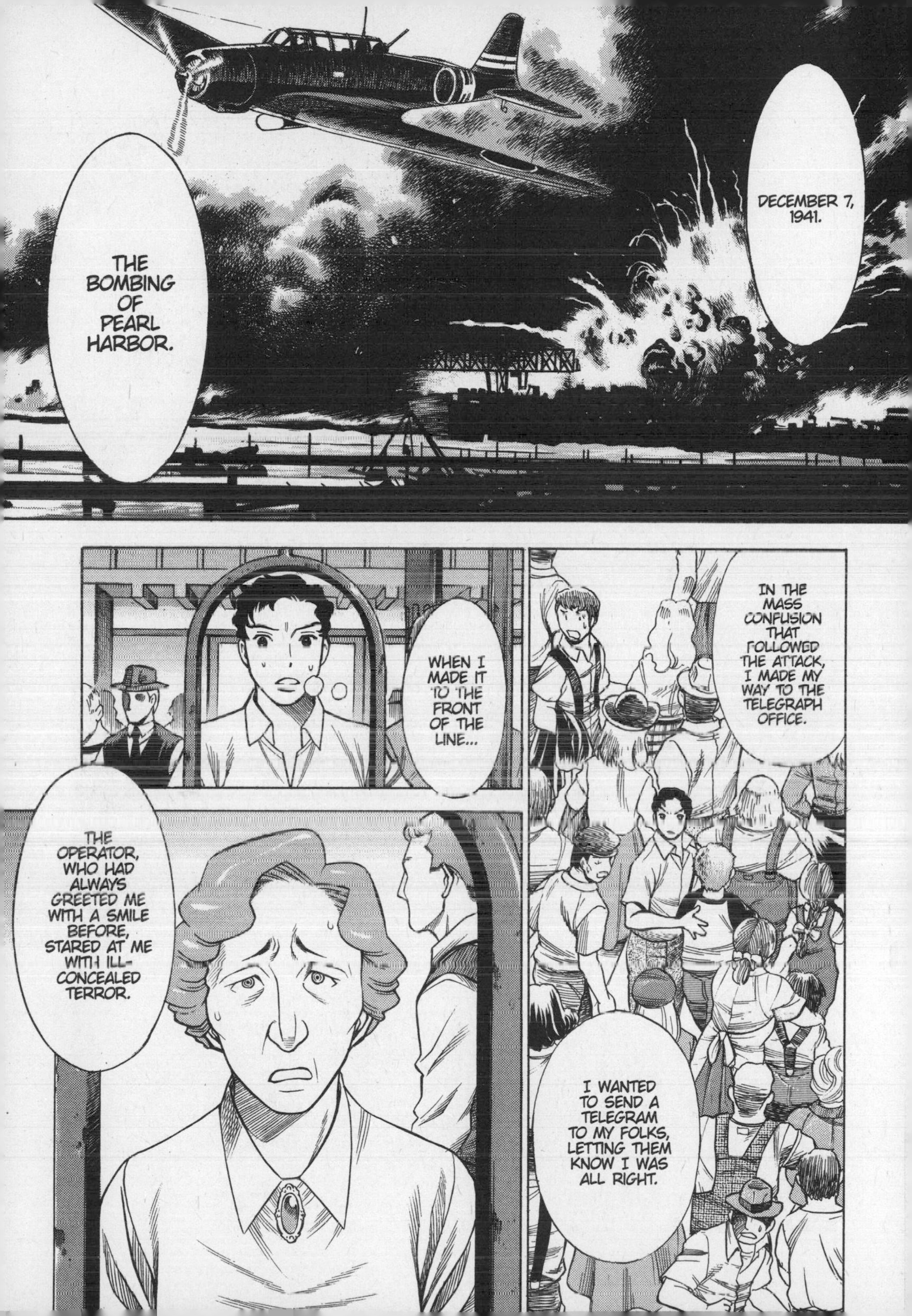
DECEMBER 7, 1941.
THE BOMBING OF PEARL HARBOR.
IN THE MASS CONFUSION THAT FOLLOWED THE ATTACK, I MADE MY WAY TO THE TELEGRAPH OFFICE.
I WANTED TO SEND A TELEGRAM TO MY FOLKS, LETTING THEM KNOW I WAS ALL RIGHT.
WHEN I MADE IT TO THE FRONT OF THE LINE...
THE OPERATOR, WHO HAD ALWAYS GREETED ME WITH A SMILE BEFORE, STARED AT ME WITH ILL-CONCEALED TERROR.

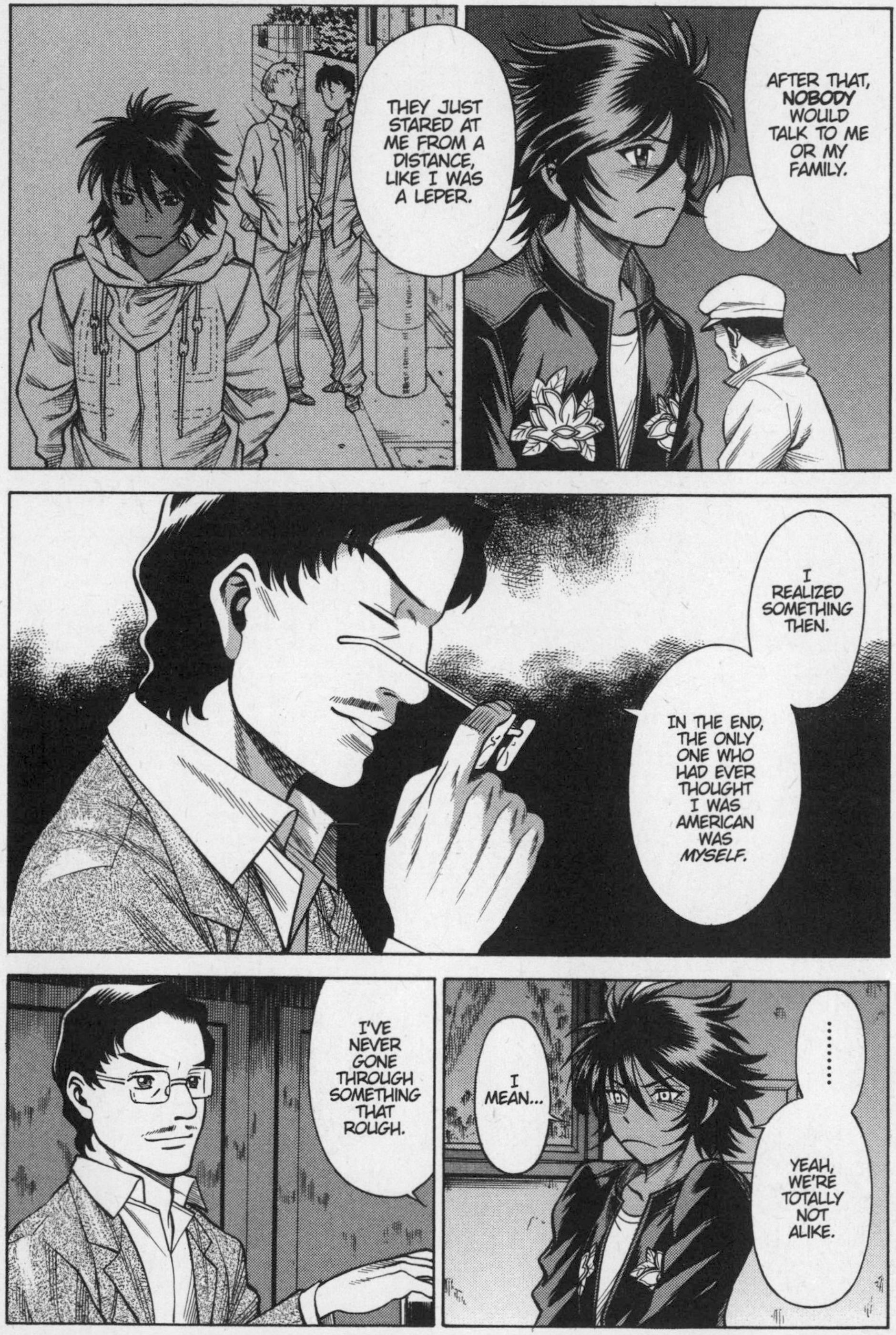
AFTER THAT, **NOBODY** WOULD TALK TO ME OR MY FAMILY.
THEY JUST STARED AT ME FROM A DISTANCE, LIKE I WAS A LEPER.
I REALIZED SOMETHING THEN.
IN THE END, THE ONLY ONE WHO HAD EVER THOUGHT I WAS AMERICAN WAS *MYSELF.*
......
YEAH, WE'RE TOTALLY NOT ALIKE.
I MEAN...
I'VE NEVER GONE THROUGH SOMETHING THAT ROUGH.

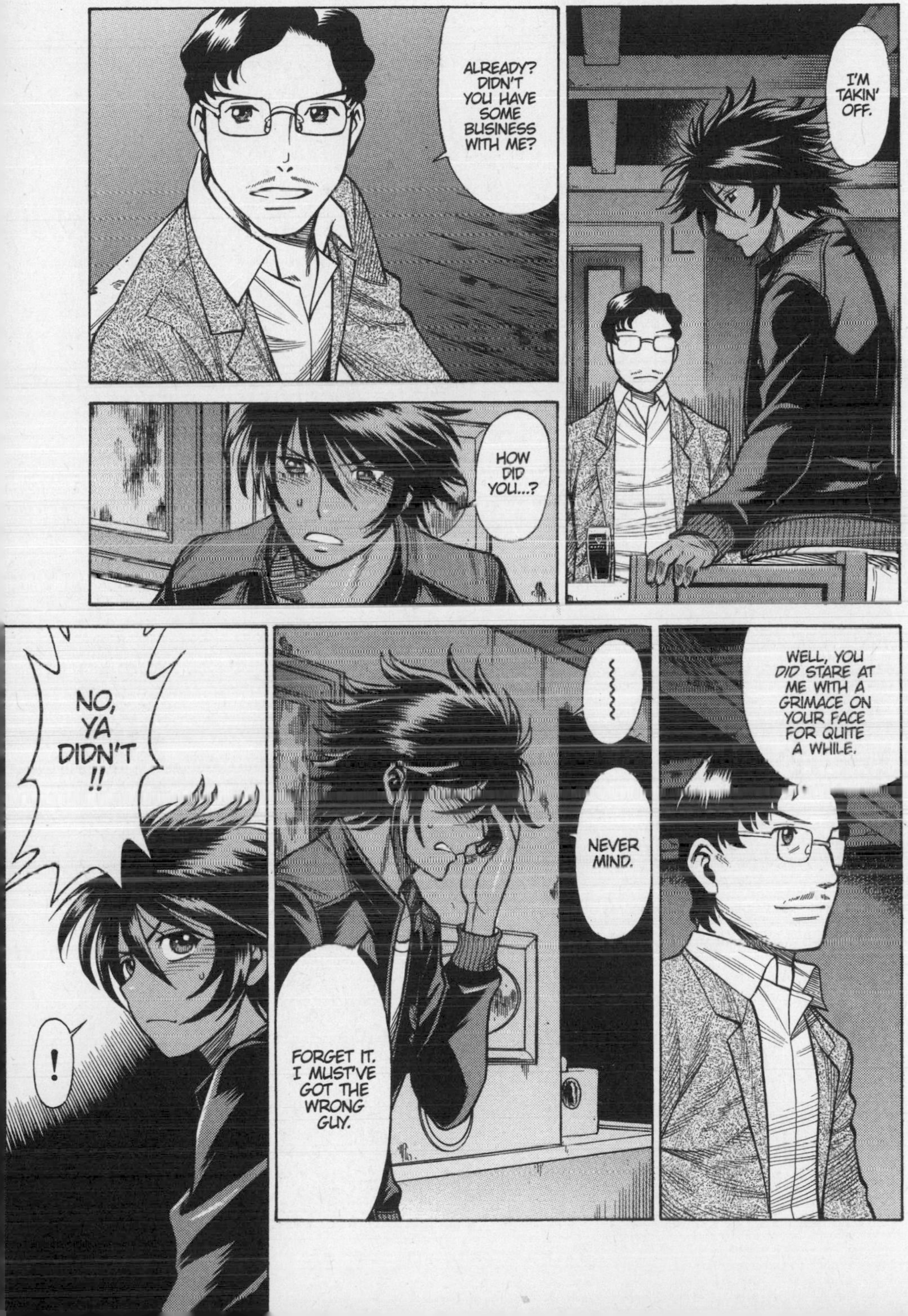
I'M TAKIN' OFF.
ALREADY? DIDN'T YOU HAVE SOME BUSINESS WITH ME?
HOW DID YOU...?
WELL, YOU *DID* STARE AT ME WITH A GRIMACE ON YOUR FACE FOR QUITE A WHILE.
NEVER MIND.
FORGET IT. I MUST'VE GOT THE WRONG GUY.
NO, YA DIDN'T !!
!

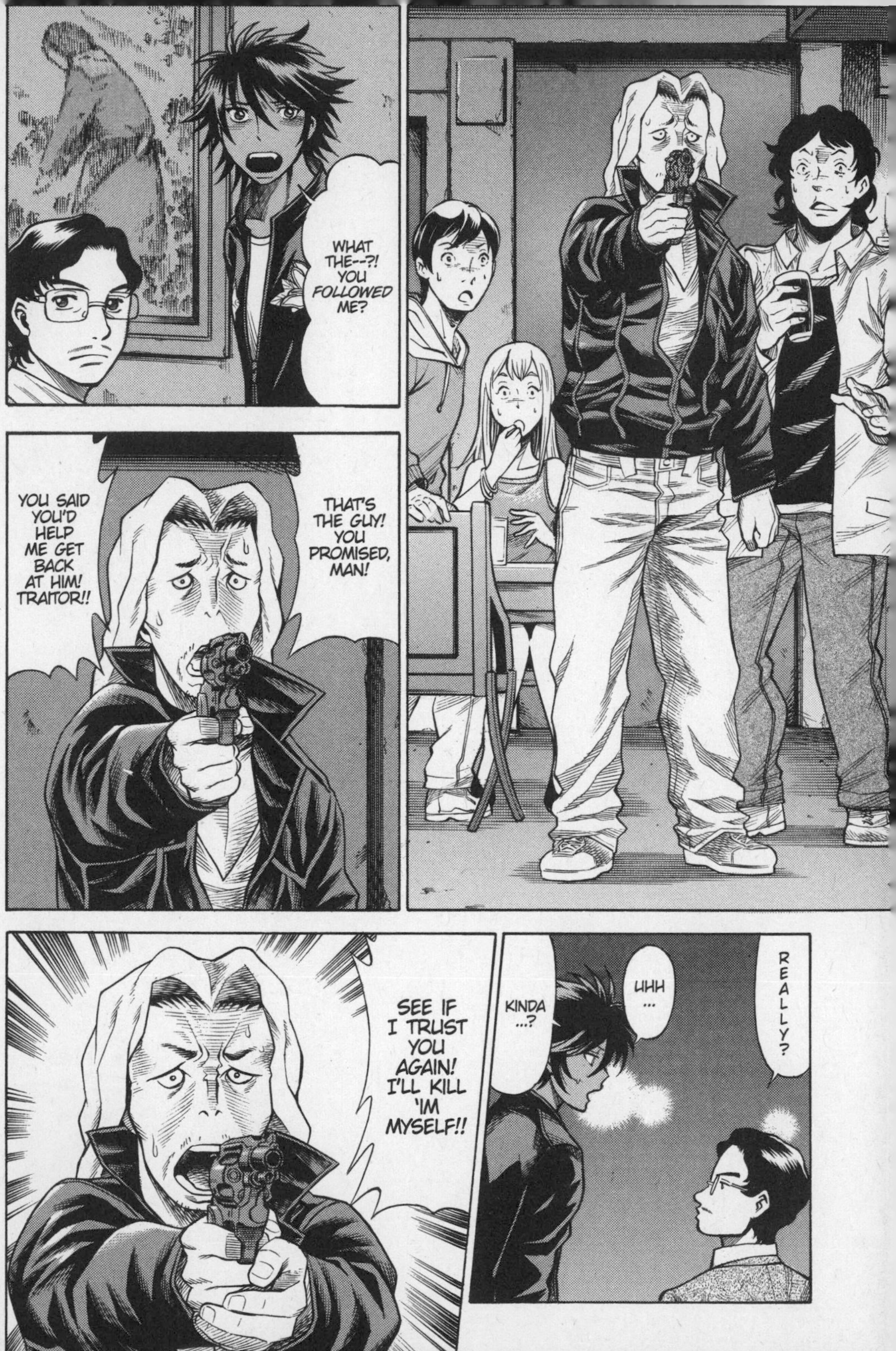
WHAT THE--?! YOU FOLLOWED ME?
THAT'S THE GUY! YOU PROMISED, MAN!
YOU SAID YOU'D HELP ME GET BACK AT HIM! TRAITOR!!
REALLY?
UHH ...
KINDA ...?
SEE IF I TRUST YOU AGAIN! I'LL KILL 'IM MYSELF!!

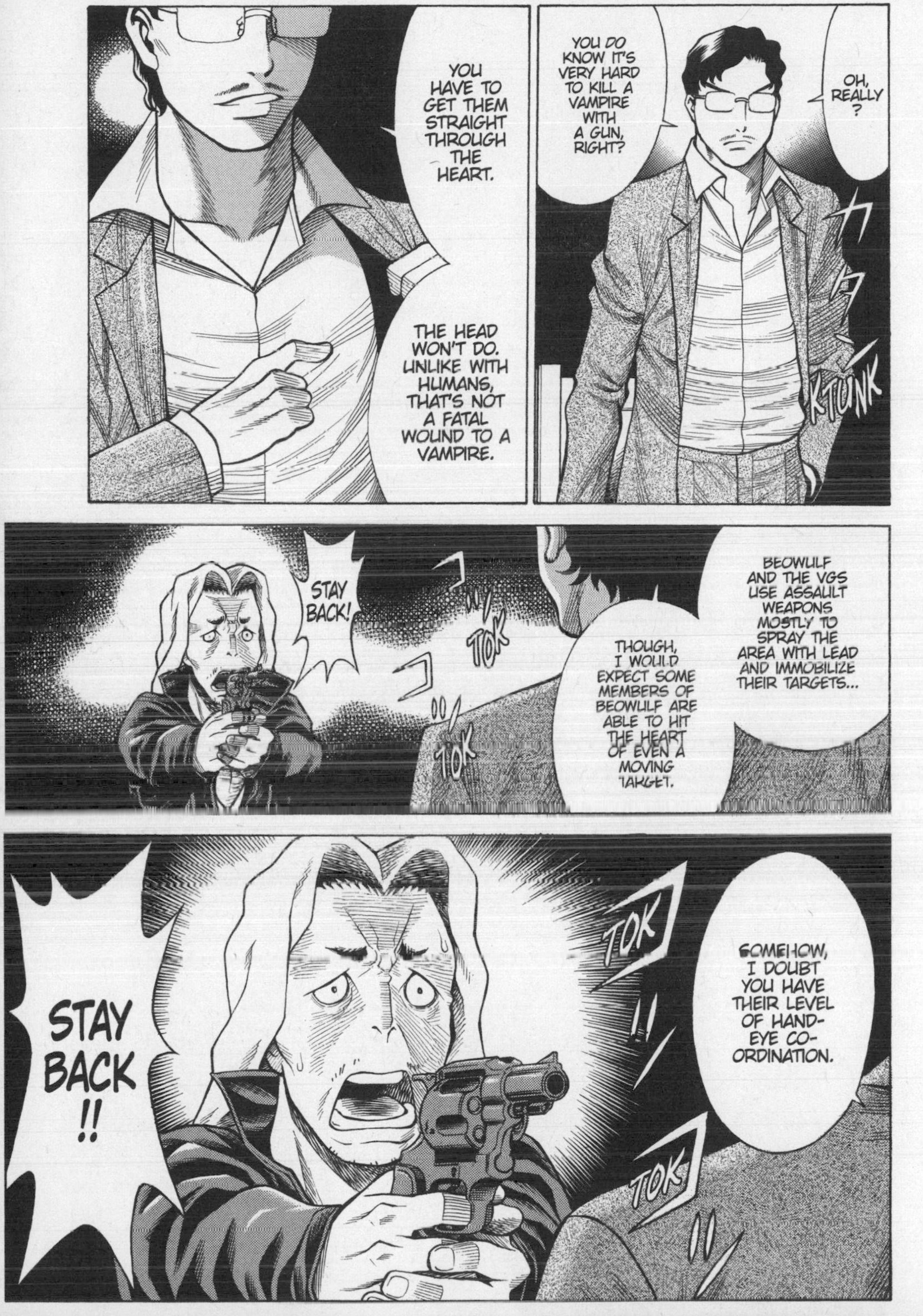
OH, REALLY?
YOU DO KNOW IT'S VERY HARD TO KILL A VAMPIRE WITH A GUN, RIGHT?
KTUNK
YOU HAVE TO GET THEM STRAIGHT THROUGH THE HEART.
THE HEAD WON'T DO. UNLIKE WITH HUMANS, THAT'S NOT A FATAL WOUND TO A VAMPIRE.
BEOWULF AND THE VGS USE ASSAULT WEAPONS MOSTLY TO SPRAY THE AREA WITH LEAD AND IMMOBILIZE THEIR TARGETS...
THOUGH, I WOULD EXPECT SOME MEMBERS OF BEOWULF ARE ABLE TO HIT THE HEART OF EVEN A MOVING TARGET.
TOK
TOK
STAY BACK!
SOMEHOW, I DOUBT YOU HAVE THEIR LEVEL OF HAND-EYE CO-ORDINATION.
TOK
TOK
STAY BACK !!

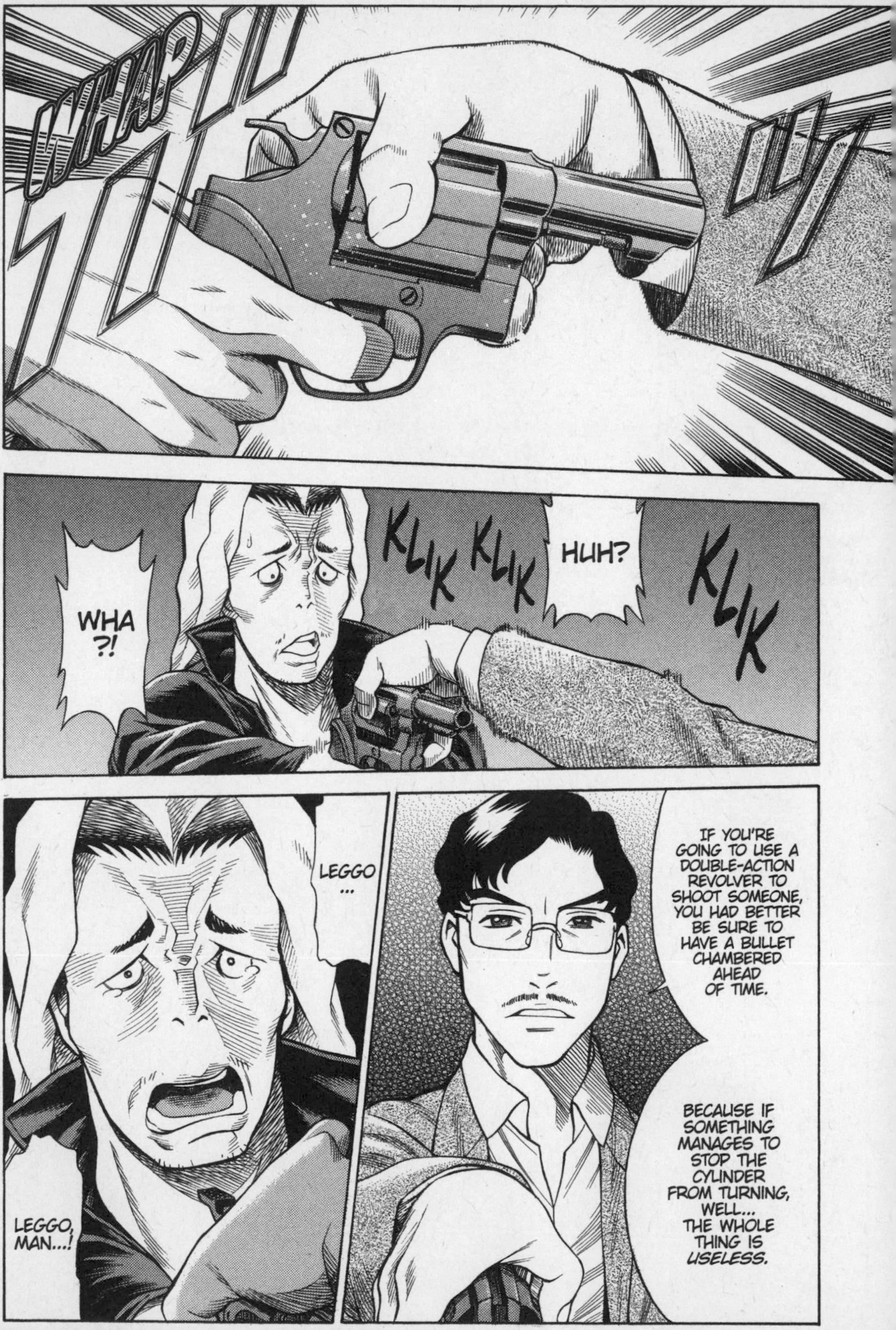
WHAP!!
KLIK
HUH?
KLIK KLIK
WHA ?!
IF YOU'RE GOING TO USE A DOUBLE-ACTION REVOLVER TO SHOOT SOMEONE, YOU HAD BETTER BE SURE TO HAVE A BULLET CHAMBERED AHEAD OF TIME.
BECAUSE IF SOMETHING MANAGES TO STOP THE CYLINDER FROM TURNING, WELL... THE WHOLE THING IS *USELESS.*
LEGGO ...
LEGGO, MAN...!

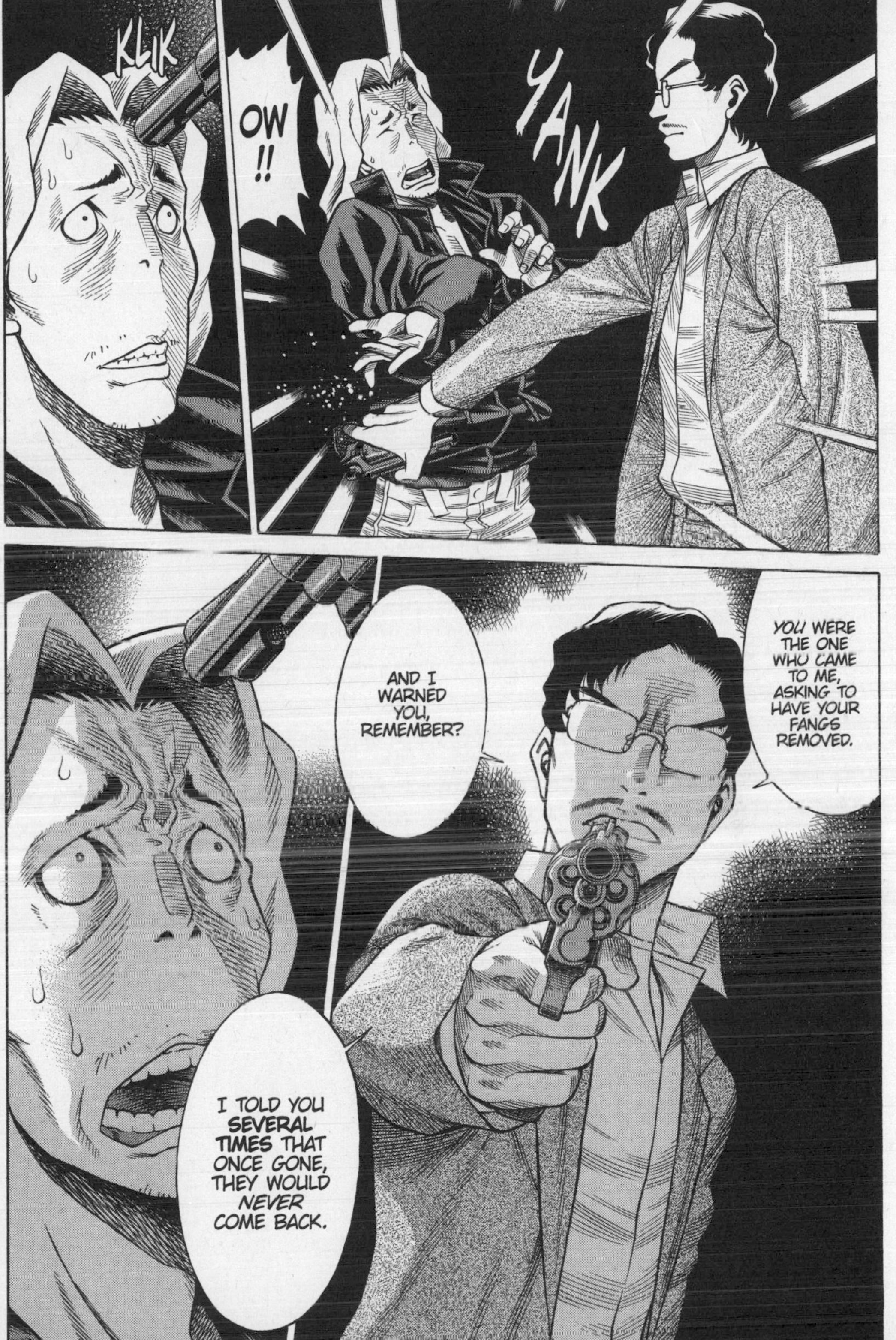
YANK
OW !!
KLIK
YOU WERE THE ONE WHO CAME TO ME, ASKING TO HAVE YOUR FANGS REMOVED.
AND I WARNED YOU, REMEMBER?
I TOLD YOU SEVERAL TIMES THAT ONCE GONE, THEY WOULD NEVER COME BACK.

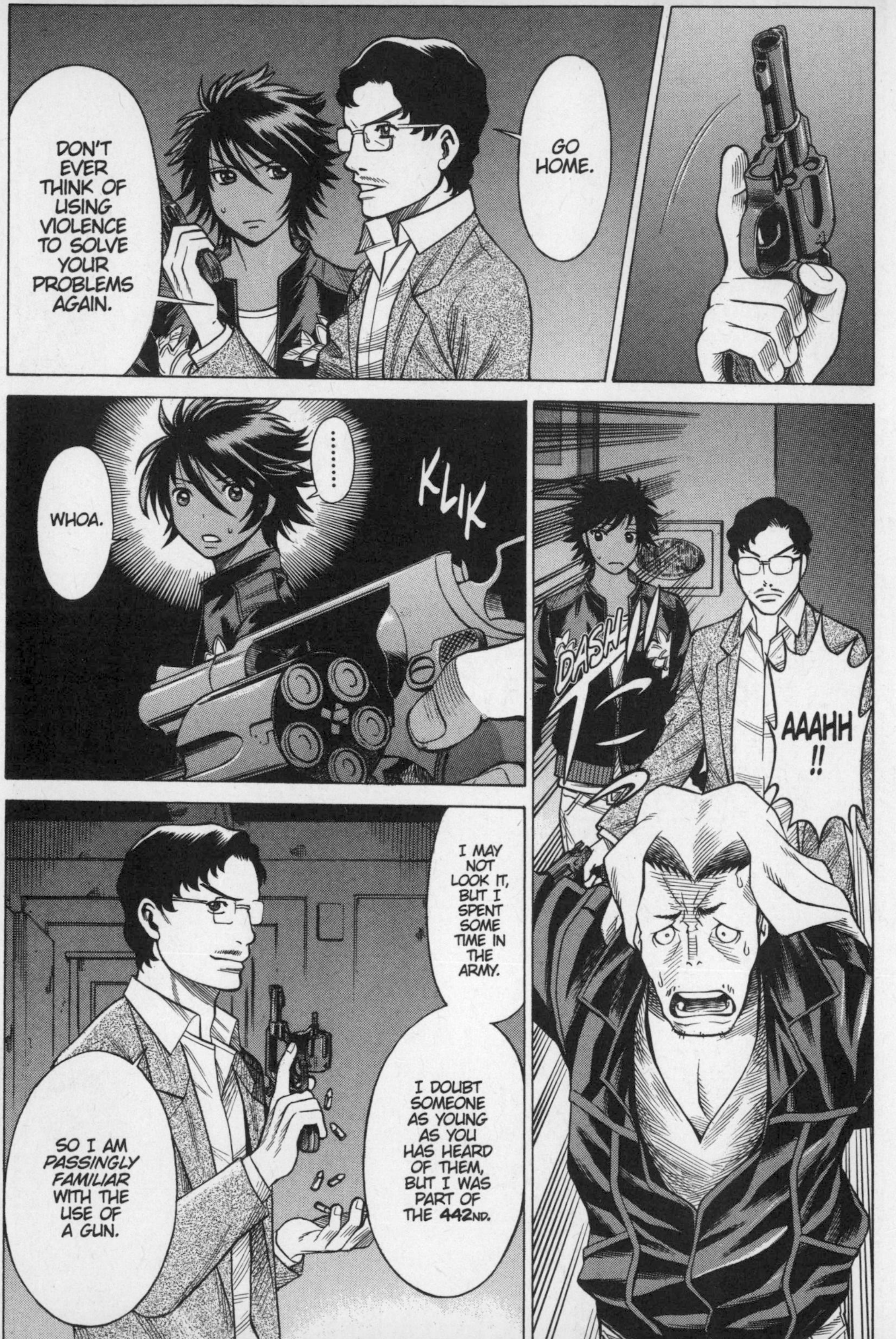
GO HOME.
DON'T EVER THINK OF USING VIOLENCE TO SOLVE YOUR PROBLEMS AGAIN.
DASH
AAAHH!!
......
KLIK
WHOA.
I MAY NOT LOOK IT, BUT I SPENT SOME TIME IN THE ARMY.
I DOUBT SOMEONE AS YOUNG AS YOU HAS HEARD OF THEM, BUT I WAS PART OF THE 442ND.
SO I AM *PASSINGLY FAMILIAR* WITH THE USE OF A GUN.

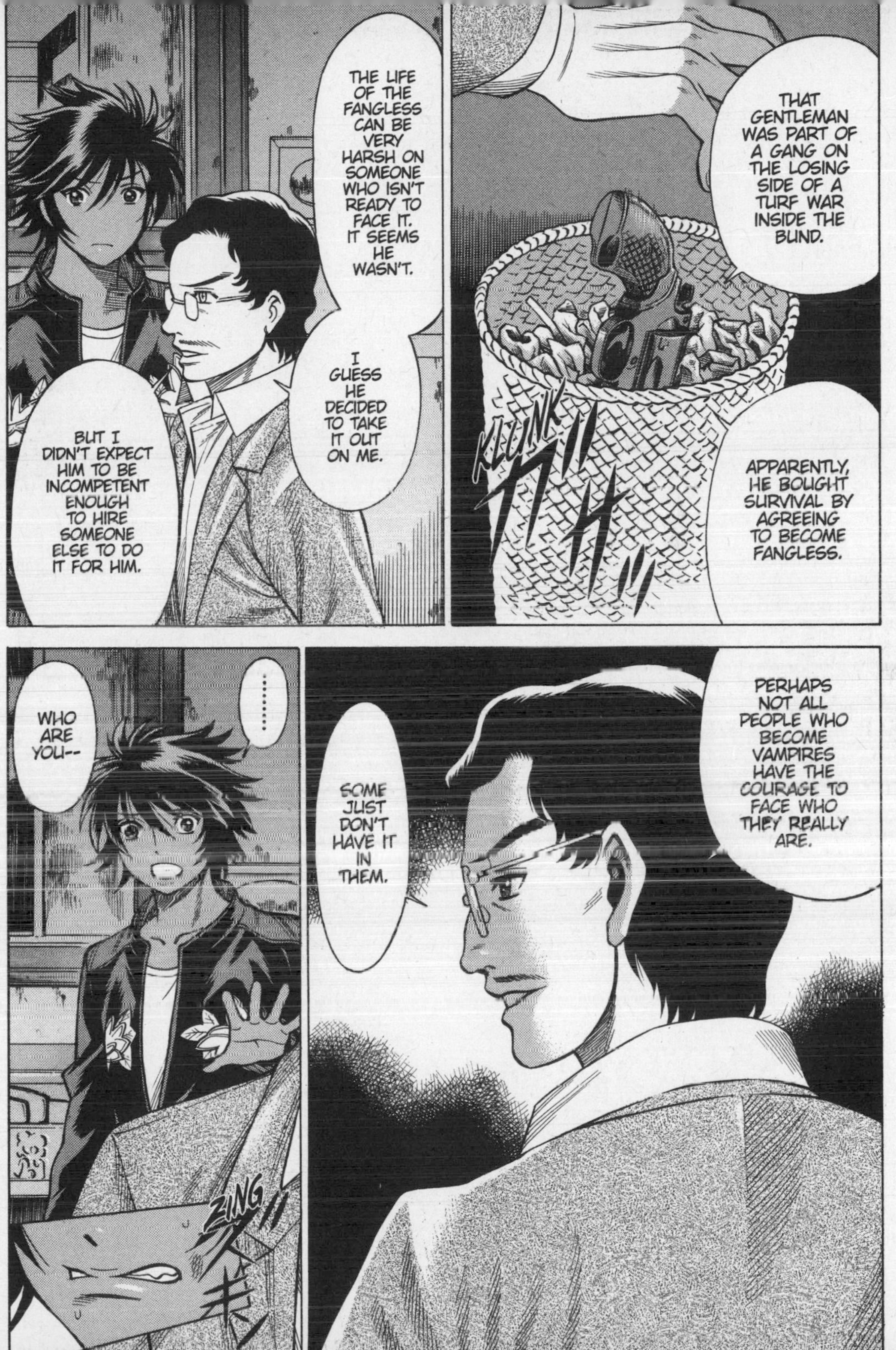
THAT GENTLEMAN WAS PART OF A GANG ON THE LOSING SIDE OF A TURF WAR INSIDE THE BUND.
KLUNK
APPARENTLY, HE BOUGHT SURVIVAL BY AGREEING TO BECOME FANGLESS.
THE LIFE OF THE FANGLESS CAN BE VERY HARSH ON SOMEONE WHO ISN'T READY TO FACE IT. IT SEEMS HE WASN'T.
I GUESS HE DECIDED TO TAKE IT OUT ON ME.
BUT I DIDN'T EXPECT HIM TO BE INCOMPETENT ENOUGH TO HIRE SOMEONE ELSE TO DO IT FOR HIM.
PERHAPS NOT ALL PEOPLE WHO BECOME VAMPIRES HAVE THE COURAGE TO FACE WHO THEY REALLY ARE.
SOME JUST DON'T HAVE IT IN THEM.
......
WHO ARE YOU--
ZING

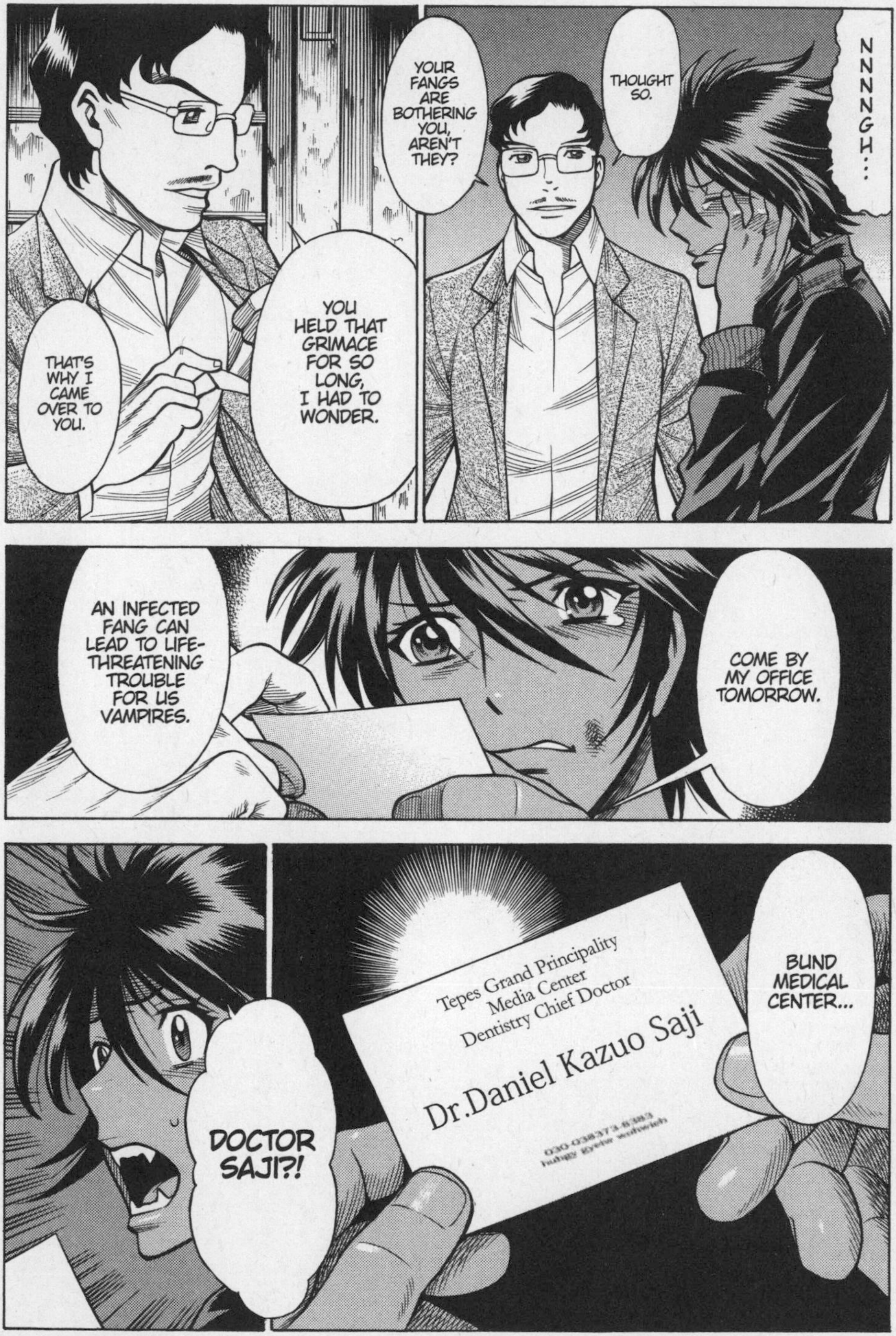
NNNNGH...
THOUGHT SO.
YOUR FANGS ARE BOTHERING YOU, AREN'T THEY?
YOU HELD THAT GRIMACE FOR SO LONG, I HAD TO WONDER.
THAT'S WHY I CAME OVER TO YOU.
COME BY MY OFFICE TOMORROW.
AN INFECTED FANG CAN LEAD TO LIFE-THREATENING TROUBLE FOR US VAMPIRES.
BUND MEDICAL CENTER...
Tepes Grand Principality
Media Center
Dentistry Chief Doctor
Dr.Daniel Kazuo Saji
DOCTOR SAJI?!

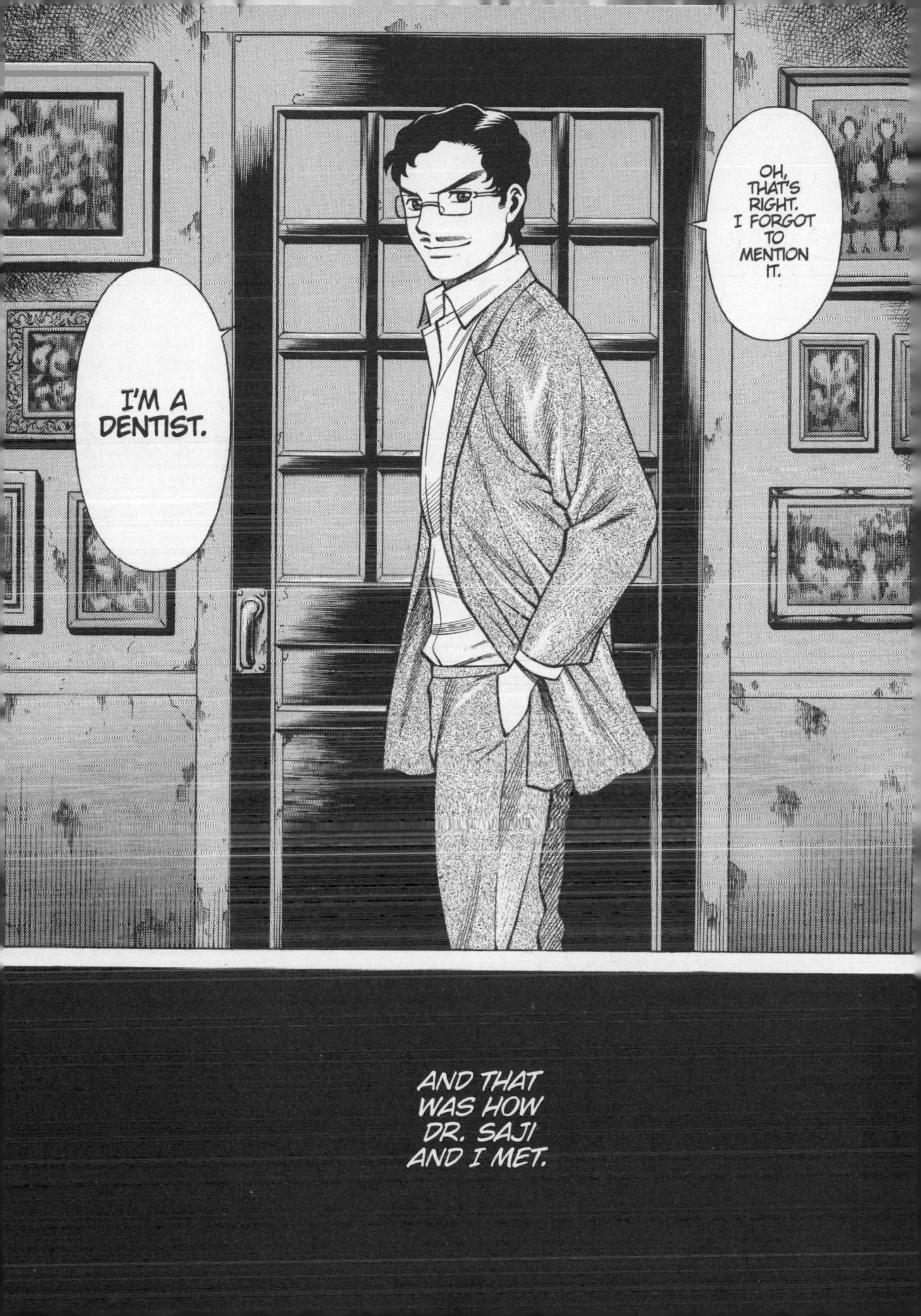
OH, THAT'S RIGHT. I FORGOT TO MENTION IT.
I'M A DENTIST.
AND THAT WAS HOW DR. SAJI AND I MET.

DOCTOR SAJI

Doctor Kazuo Daniel Saji is the Chief Dentist of the Bund. He first appeared in Volume 9, treating the wounded during Ivanovic's attack. In Volume 11, he appeared again as a valuable assistant to the two Akiras.

This past chapter was the tale of how (Vampire) Akira and Dr. Saji met. I had originally intended for this to be Dr. Saji's first appearance, and then to bring him into the main story later, but in the end, things wound up reversed.

JAPANESE-AMERICANS AND THE 442nd REGIMENTAL COMBAT TEAM

The history of Japanese-Americans begins at the end of the 19th century, when Japanese farmers immigrated to Hawaii to farm sugarcane and pineapples. These farmers started families, raised children, and eventually became a part of American society. However, everything changed when Japan bombed Pearl Harbor in 1941, resulting in immediate prejudice and discrimination against Japanese-Americans. The United States government labeled them "enemy aliens," confiscating the property of nearly 120,000 Japanese-Americans living on the West Coast and forcing them into internment camps.

Despite that, many second generation Japanese-Americans, who had been born and raised in the US, volunteered to join the army as a show of patriotism. These volunteers were all assigned together, forming the 442nd Regimental Combat Team, nicknamed the 442nd or the "Go For Broke" Regiment.

Dr. Saji was a med student at the University of Hawaii when he volunteered for the Army. He was made a combat medic of the 442nd and deployed with the regiment to the Italian front. Comprised entirely of Japanese-Americans, the 442nd faced the same discrimination issues as civilians did back home, but they still fought on with the highest distinction, earning a multitude of awards.

They showed special valor during the rescue of the 141st Regiment, the "Lost Battalion" that was cut off and entirely surrounded by German forces. The 442nd lost 800 soldiers while rescuing the 211 men of the 141st. (A famous scene later in the war has General Dahlquist demanding all of the regiment line up for a ceremony, and then chewing out the commander for having "too few men there." The commander replied calmly, saying that this was all their men. All the rest were dead or in the hospital.)

At the end of the war, the casualty rate for the 442nd was a staggering 314%. The average across the rest of the US Army was only 80%. However, their extreme valor was recognized, and today the 442nd is widely regarded as the most decorated infantry unit in the history of the US Army. They earned approximately 18,000 awards. The victory that the 442nd bought with their blood and sacrifice struck a chord with American civilians, going a long way towards helping to revive respect for Japanese-Americans as a whole after the war.

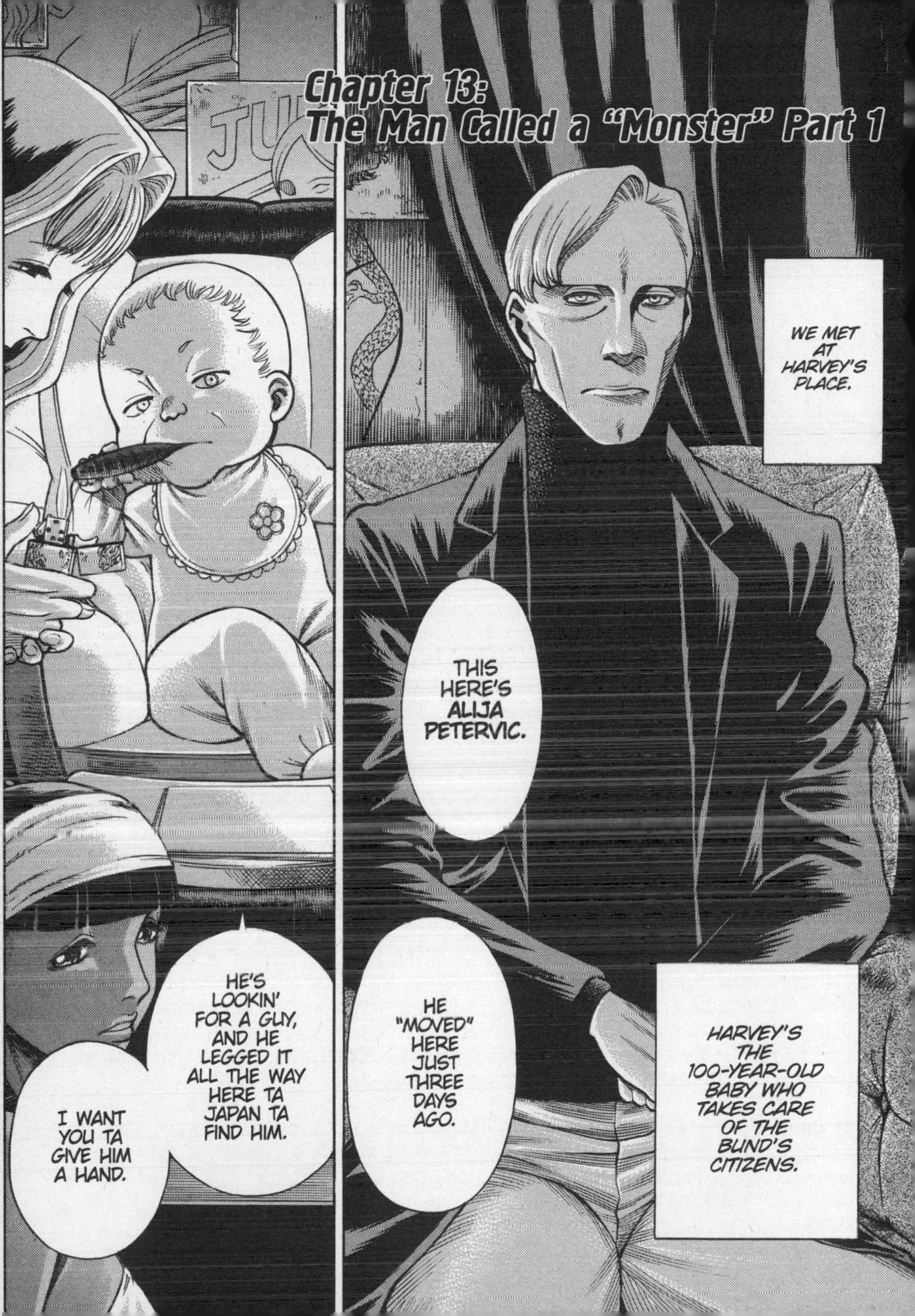
Chapter 13: The Man Called a "Monster" Part 1
WE MET AT HARVEY'S PLACE.
THIS HERE'S ALIJA PETERVIC.
HARVEY'S THE 100-YEAR-OLD BABY WHO TAKES CARE OF THE BUND'S CITIZENS.
HE "MOVED" HERE JUST THREE DAYS AGO.
HE'S LOOKIN' FOR A GUY, AND HE LEGGED IT ALL THE WAY HERE TA JAPAN TA FIND HIM.
I WANT YOU TA GIVE HIM A HAND.
JU

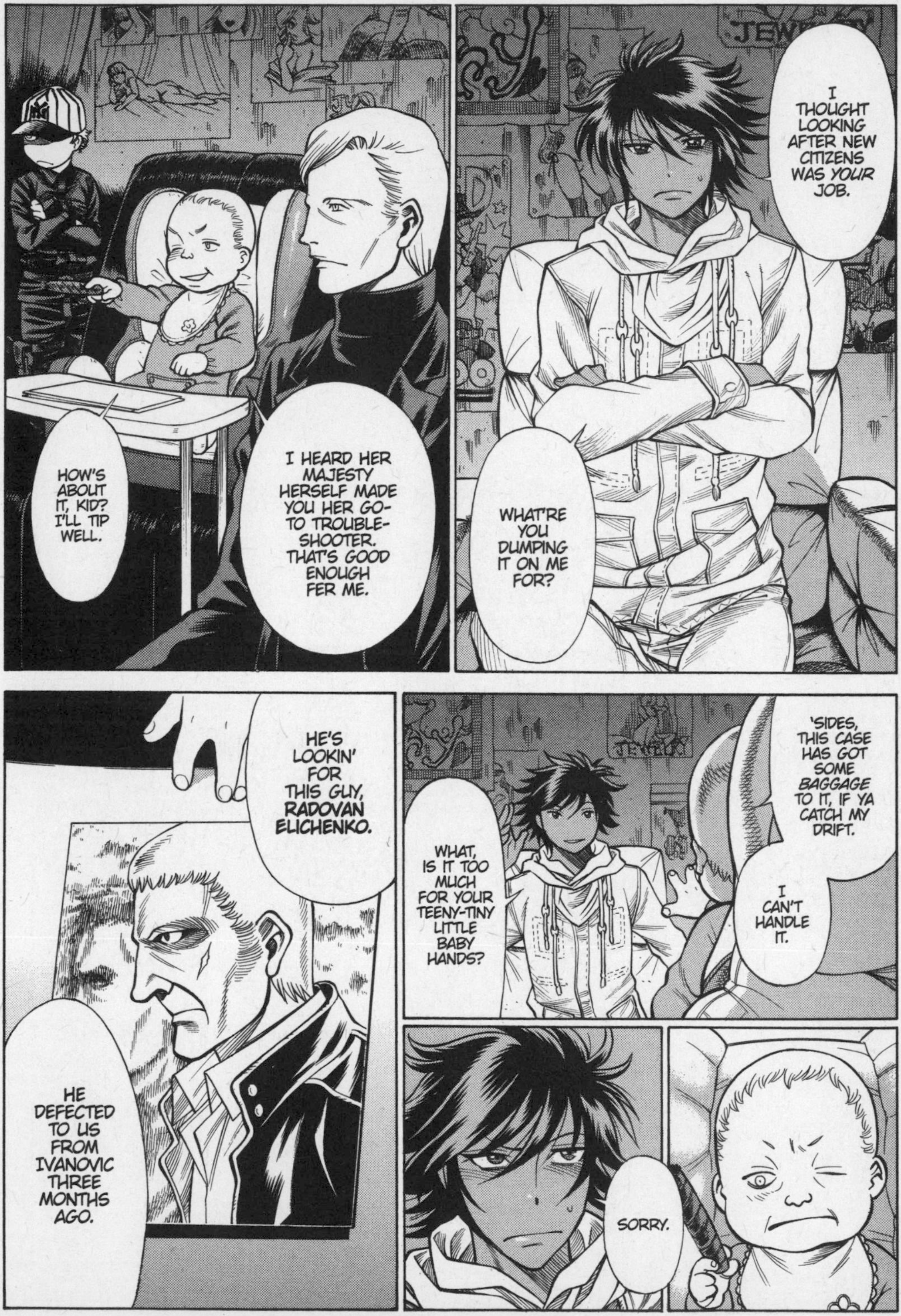
I THOUGHT LOOKING AFTER NEW CITIZENS WAS *YOUR* JOB.
WHAT'RE YOU DUMPING IT ON ME FOR?
I HEARD HER MAJESTY HERSELF MADE YOU HER GO-TO TROUBLE-SHOOTER. THAT'S GOOD ENOUGH FER ME.
HOW'S ABOUT IT, KID? I'LL TIP WELL.
'SIDES, THIS CASE HAS GOT SOME *BAGGAGE* TO IT, IF YA CATCH MY DRIFT.
I CAN'T HANDLE IT.
WHAT, IS IT TOO MUCH FOR YOUR TEENY-TINY LITTLE BABY HANDS?
SORRY.
HE'S LOOKIN' FOR THIS GUY, **RADOVAN ELICHENKO.**
HE DEFECTED TO US FROM IVANOVIC THREE MONTHS AGO.

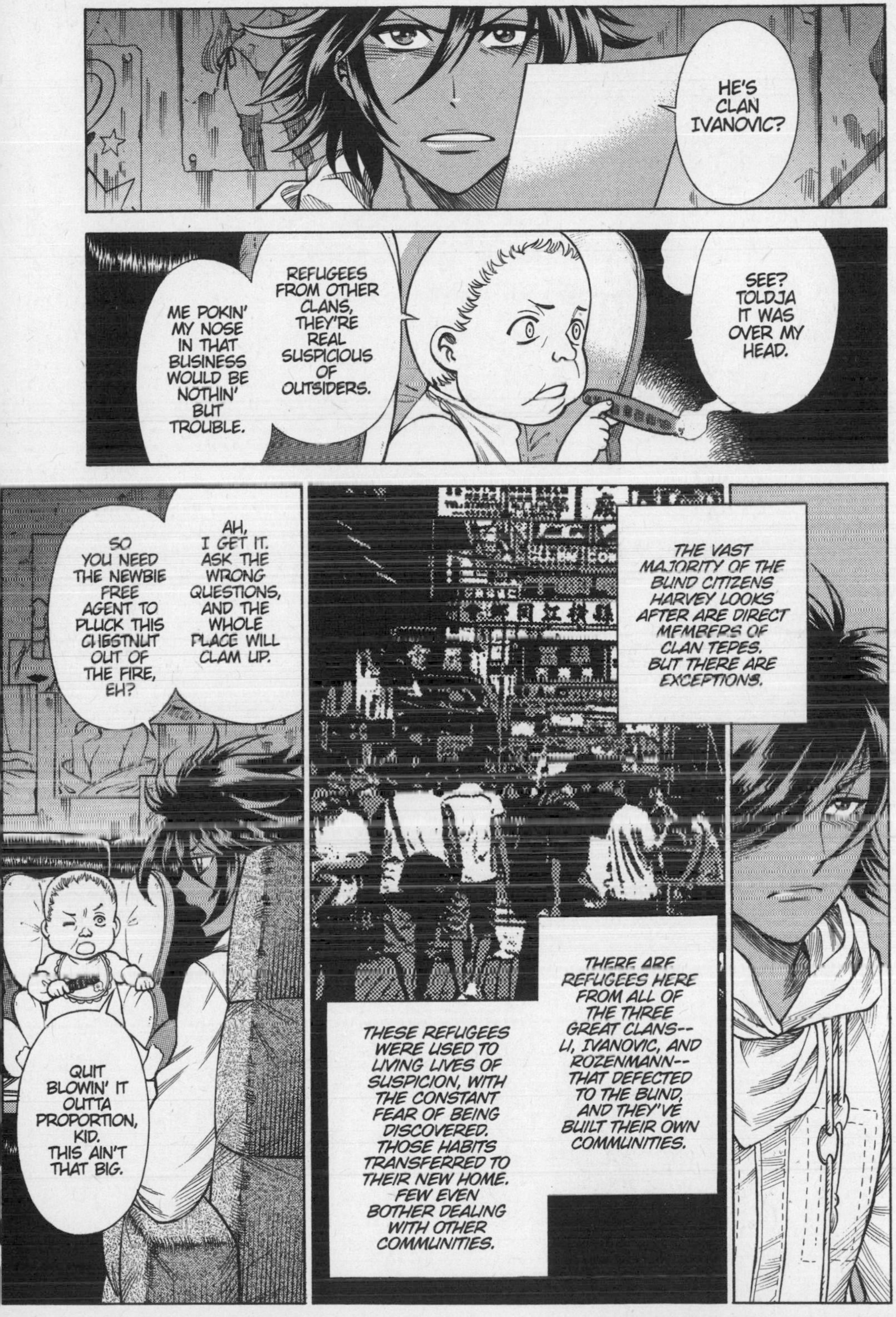
HE'S CLAN IVANOVIC?
SEE? TOLDJA IT WAS OVER MY HEAD.
REFUGEES FROM OTHER CLANS, THEY'RE REAL SUSPICIOUS OF OUTSIDERS.
ME POKIN' MY NOSE IN THAT BUSINESS WOULD BE NOTHIN' BUT TROUBLE.
THE VAST MAJORITY OF THE BUND CITIZENS HARVEY LOOKS AFTER ARE DIRECT MEMBERS OF CLAN TEPES. BUT THERE ARE EXCEPTIONS.
THERE ARE REFUGEES HERE FROM ALL OF THE THREE GREAT CLANS-- LI, IVANOVIC, AND ROZENMANN-- THAT DEFECTED TO THE BUND, AND THEY'VE BUILT THEIR OWN COMMUNITIES.
THESE REFUGEES WERE USED TO LIVING LIVES OF SUSPICION, WITH THE CONSTANT FEAR OF BEING DISCOVERED. THOSE HABITS TRANSFERRED TO THEIR NEW HOME. FEW EVEN BOTHER DEALING WITH OTHER COMMUNITIES.
AH, I GET IT. ASK THE WRONG QUESTIONS, AND THE WHOLE PLACE WILL CLAM UP.
SO YOU NEED THE NEWBIE FREE AGENT TO PLUCK THIS CHESTNUT OUT OF THE FIRE, EH?
QUIT BLOWIN' IT OUTTA PROPORTION, KID. THIS AIN'T THAT BIG.

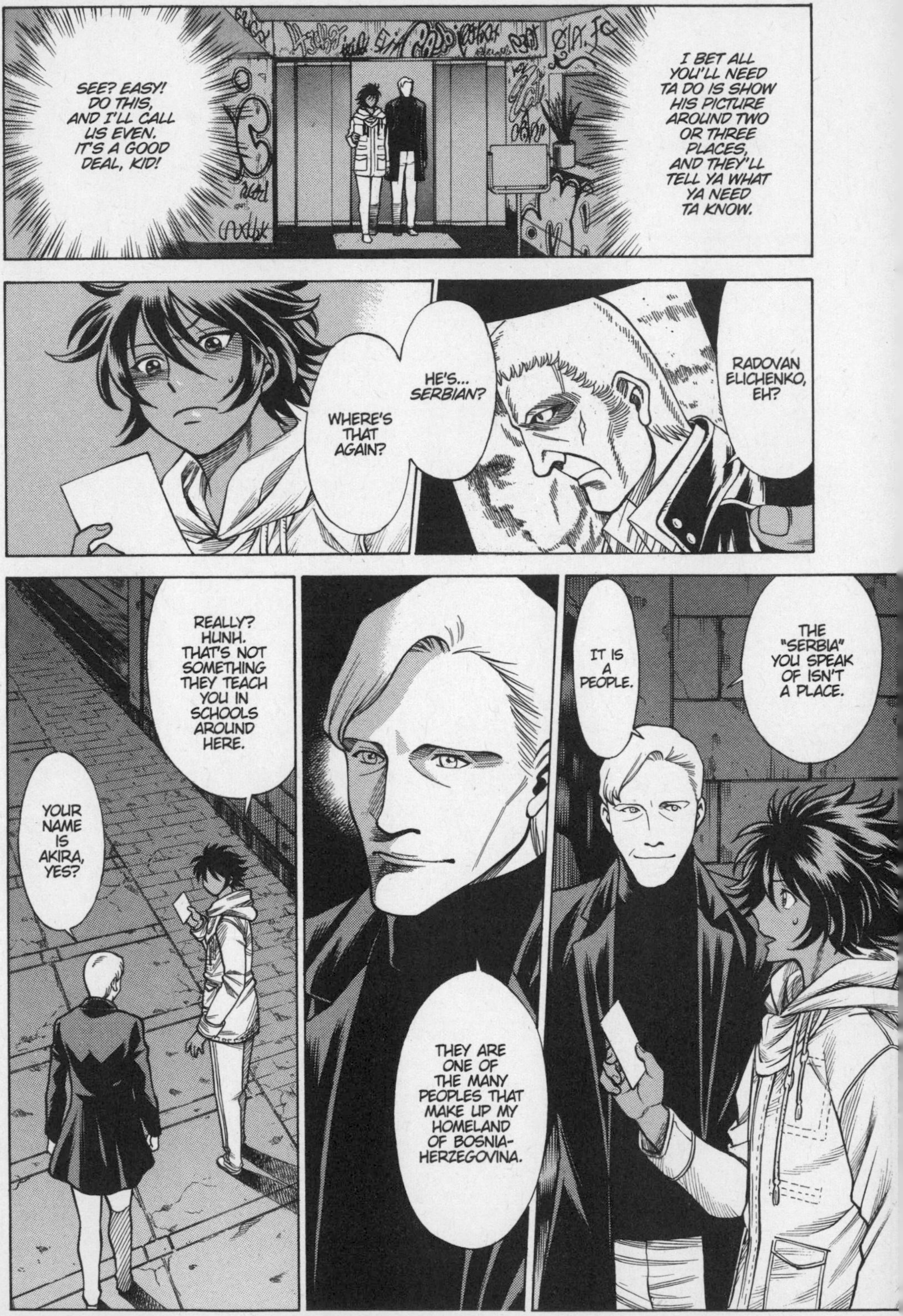
I BET ALL YOU'LL NEED TA DO IS SHOW HIS PICTURE AROUND TWO OR THREE PLACES, AND THEY'LL TELL YA WHAT YA NEED TA KNOW.
SEE? EASY! DO THIS, AND I'LL CALL US EVEN. IT'S A GOOD DEAL, KID!
RADOVAN ELICHENKO, EH?
HE'S... SERBIAN?
WHERE'S THAT AGAIN?
THE "SERBIA" YOU SPEAK OF ISN'T A PLACE.
IT IS A PEOPLE.
THEY ARE ONE OF THE MANY PEOPLES THAT MAKE UP MY HOMELAND OF BOSNIA-HERZEGOVINA.
REALLY? HUNH. THAT'S NOT SOMETHING THEY TEACH YOU IN SCHOOLS AROUND HERE.
YOUR NAME IS AKIRA, YES?

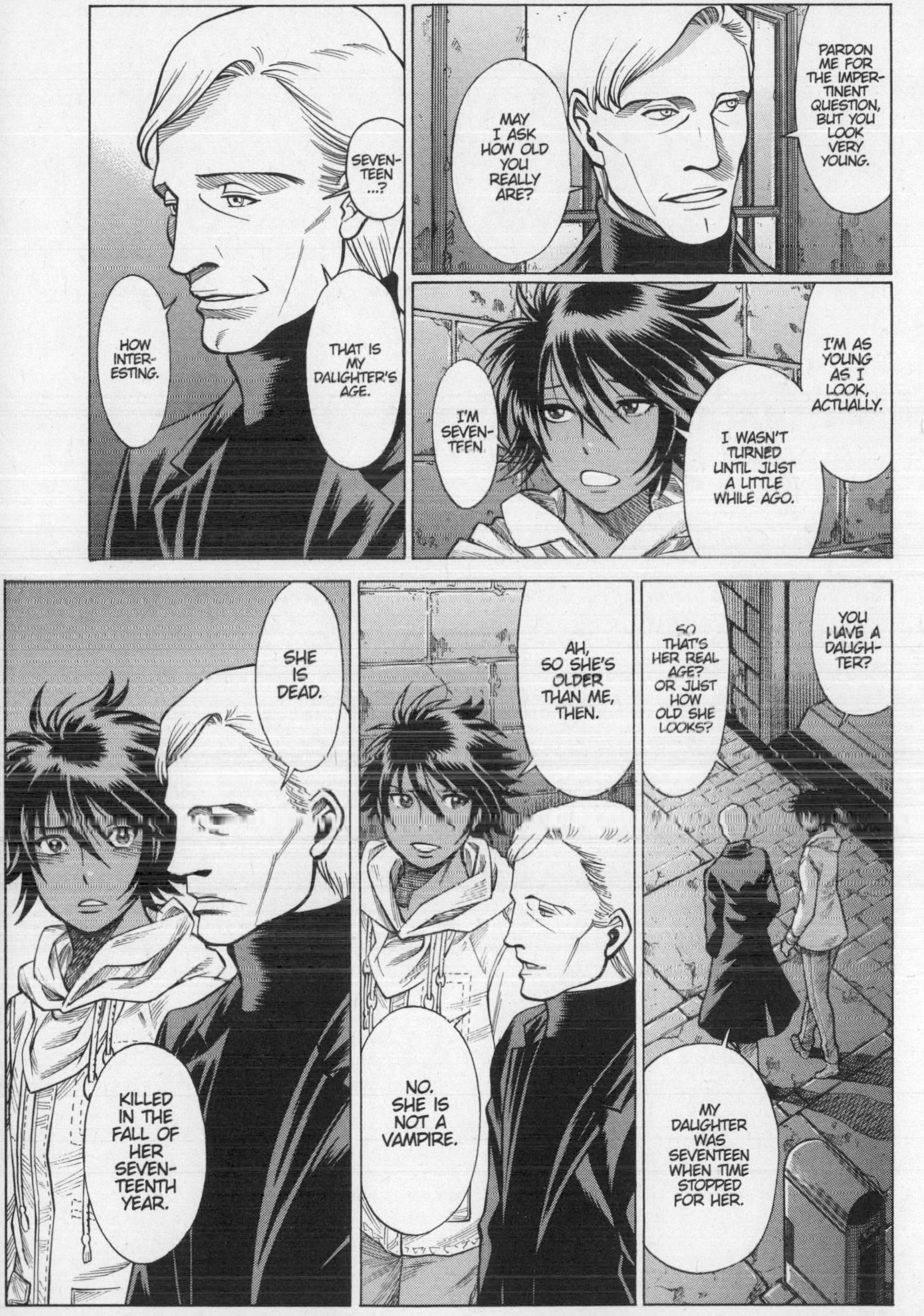
PARDON ME FOR THE IMPERTINENT QUESTION, BUT YOU LOOK VERY YOUNG.
MAY I ASK HOW OLD YOU REALLY ARE?
I'M AS YOUNG AS I LOOK, ACTUALLY.
I WASN'T TURNED UNTIL JUST A LITTLE WHILE AGO.
I'M SEVENTEEN.
SEVENTEEN ...?
THAT IS MY DAUGHTER'S AGE.
HOW INTERESTING.
YOU HAVE A DAUGHTER?
SO THAT'S HER REAL AGE? OR JUST HOW OLD SHE LOOKS?
MY DAUGHTER WAS SEVENTEEN WHEN TIME STOPPED FOR HER.
AH, SO SHE'S OLDER THAN ME, THEN.
NO. SHE IS NOT A VAMPIRE.
SHE IS DEAD.
KILLED IN THE FALL OF HER SEVENTEENTH YEAR.

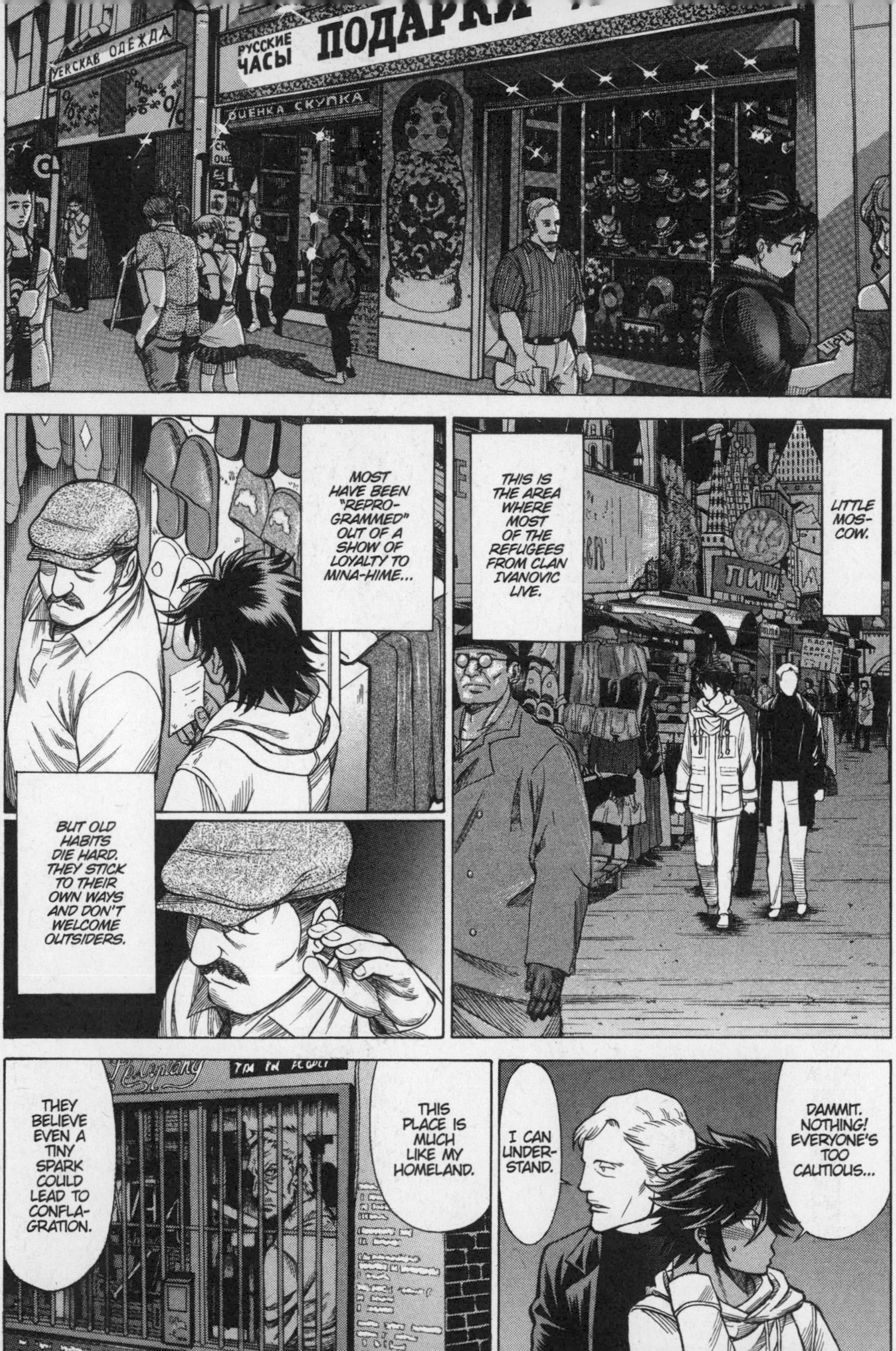
ПОДАРКИ
РУССКИЕ ЧАСЫ
ОЦЕНКА СКУПКА
LITTLE MOS-COW.
THIS IS THE AREA WHERE MOST OF THE REFUGEES FROM CLAN IVANOVIC LIVE.
MOST HAVE BEEN "REPRO-GRAMMED" OUT OF A SHOW OF LOYALTY TO MINA-HIME...
BUT OLD HABITS DIE HARD. THEY STICK TO THEIR OWN WAYS AND DON'T WELCOME OUTSIDERS.
DAMMIT. NOTHING! EVERYONE'S TOO CAUTIOUS...
I CAN UNDER-STAND.
THIS PLACE IS MUCH LIKE MY HOMELAND.
THEY BELIEVE EVEN A TINY SPARK COULD LEAD TO CONFLA-GRATION.

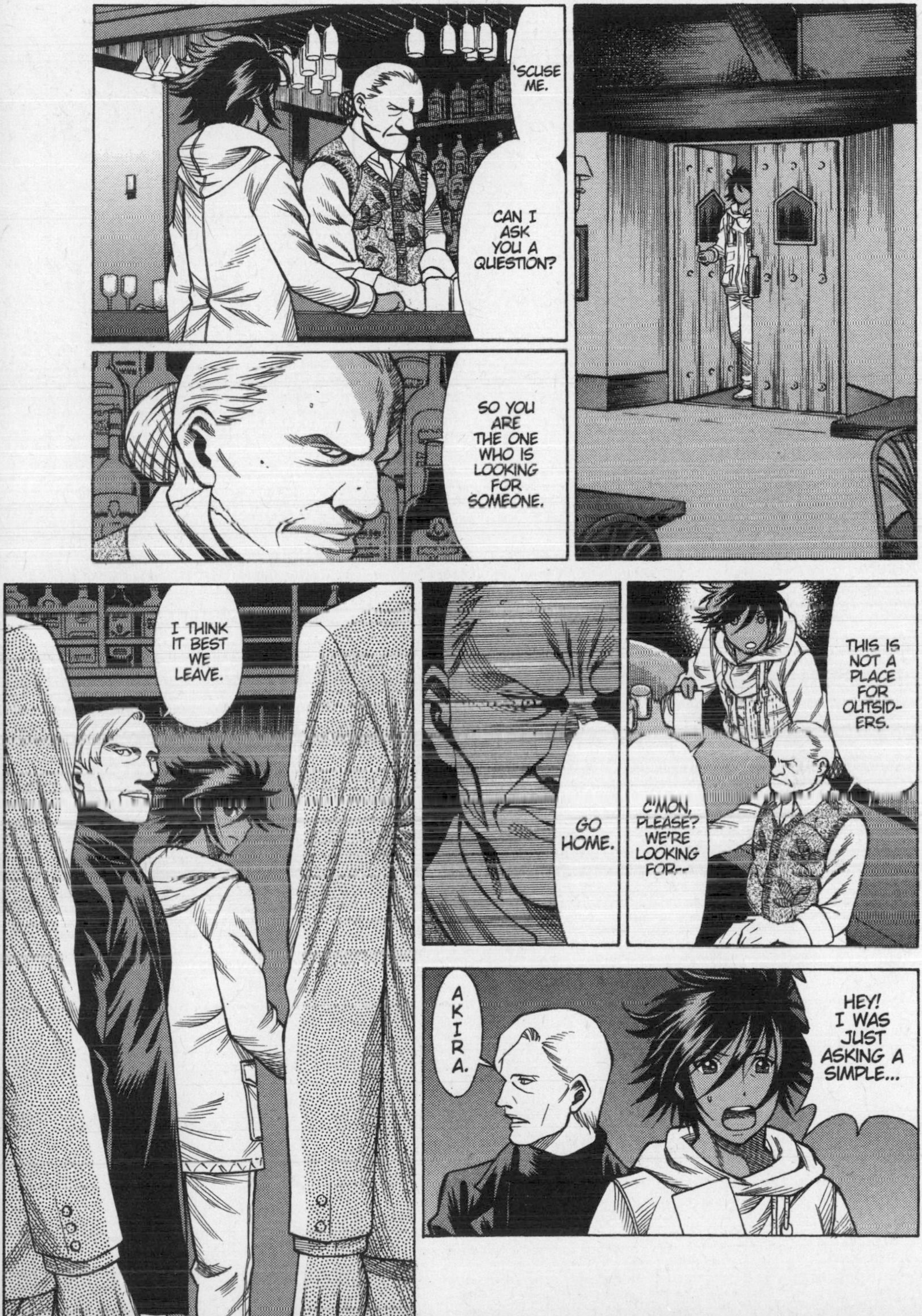
'SCUSE ME.
CAN I ASK YOU A QUESTION?
SO YOU ARE THE ONE WHO IS LOOKING FOR SOMEONE.
THIS IS NOT A PLACE FOR OUTSID-ERS.
C'MON, PLEASE? WE'RE LOOKING FOR--
GO HOME.
HEY! I WAS JUST ASKING A SIMPLE...
AKIRA.
I THINK IT BEST WE LEAVE.

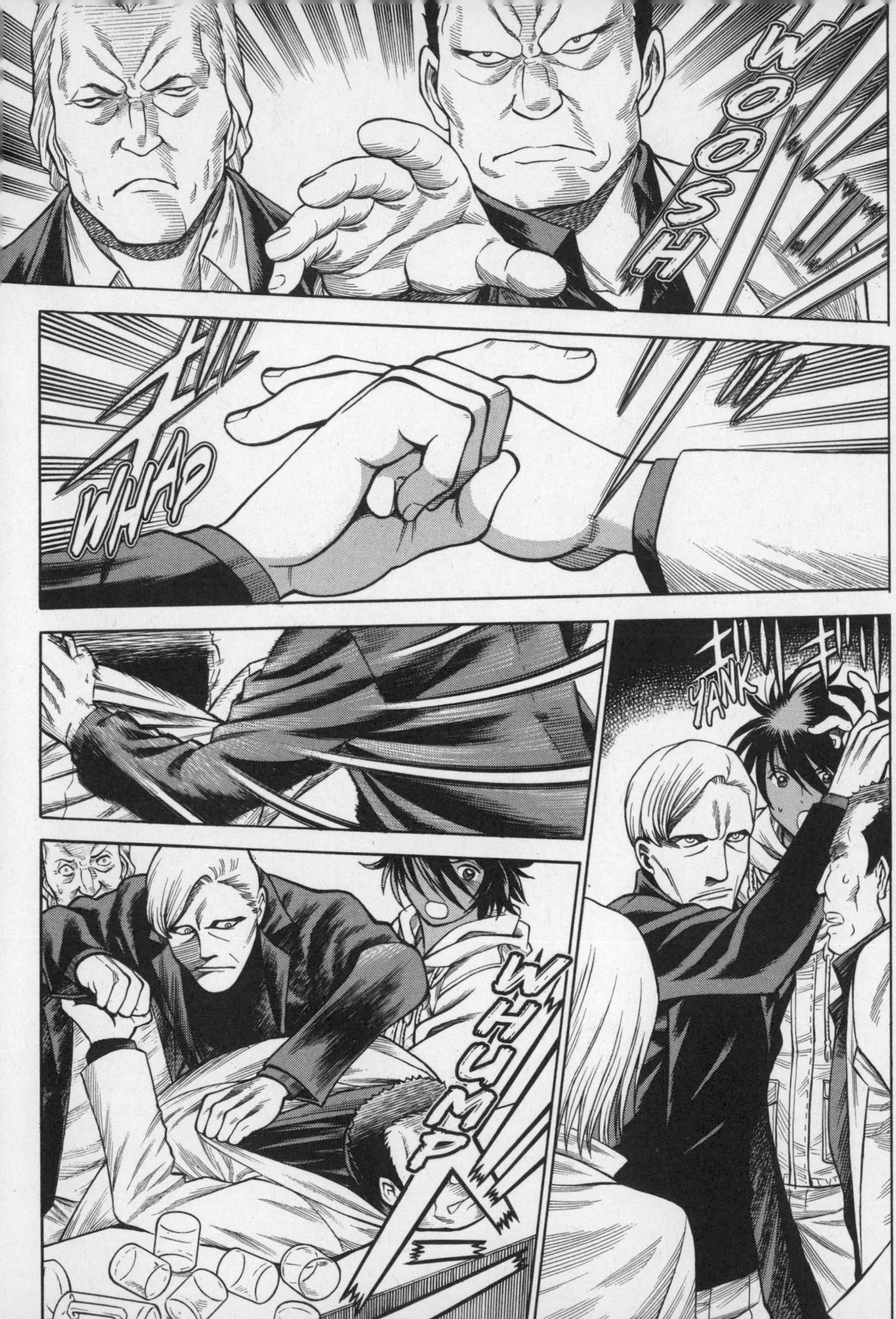
WOOSH
WHAP
YANK
WHUMP

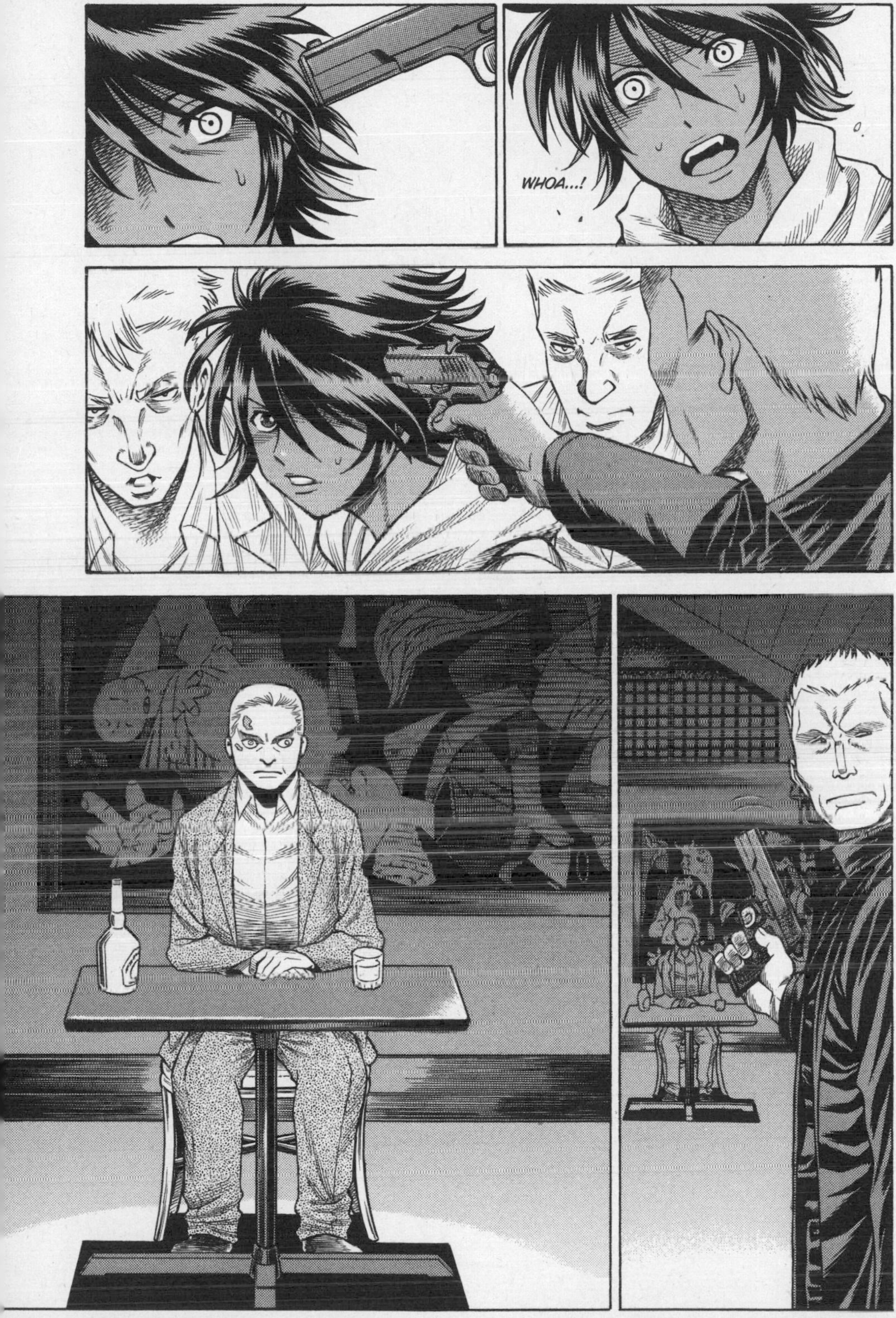
WHOA...!

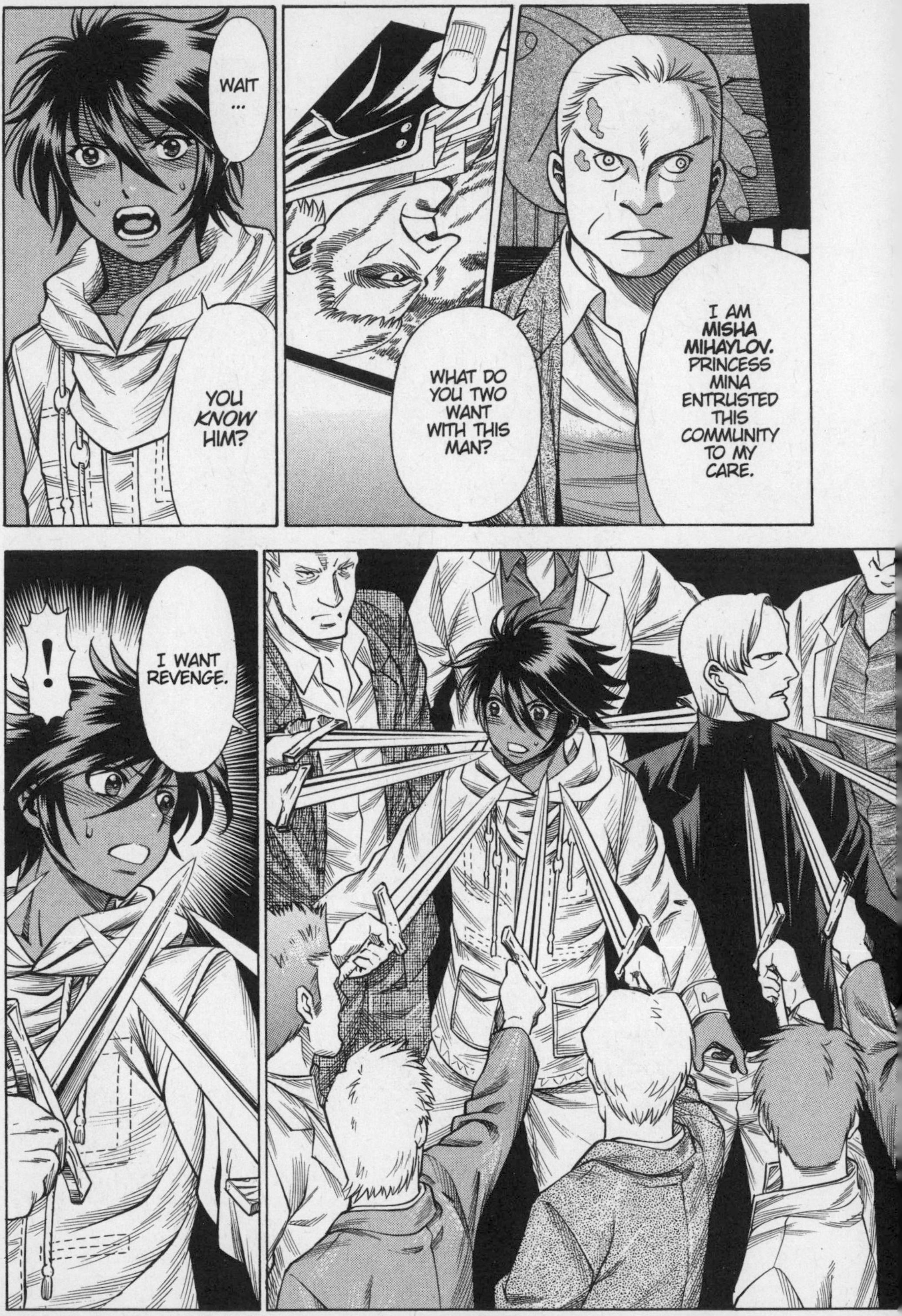
I AM MISHA MIHAYLOV. PRINCESS MINA ENTRUSTED THIS COMMUNITY TO MY CARE.
WHAT DO YOU TWO WANT WITH THIS MAN?
WAIT ...
YOU KNOW HIM?
I WANT REVENGE.
!

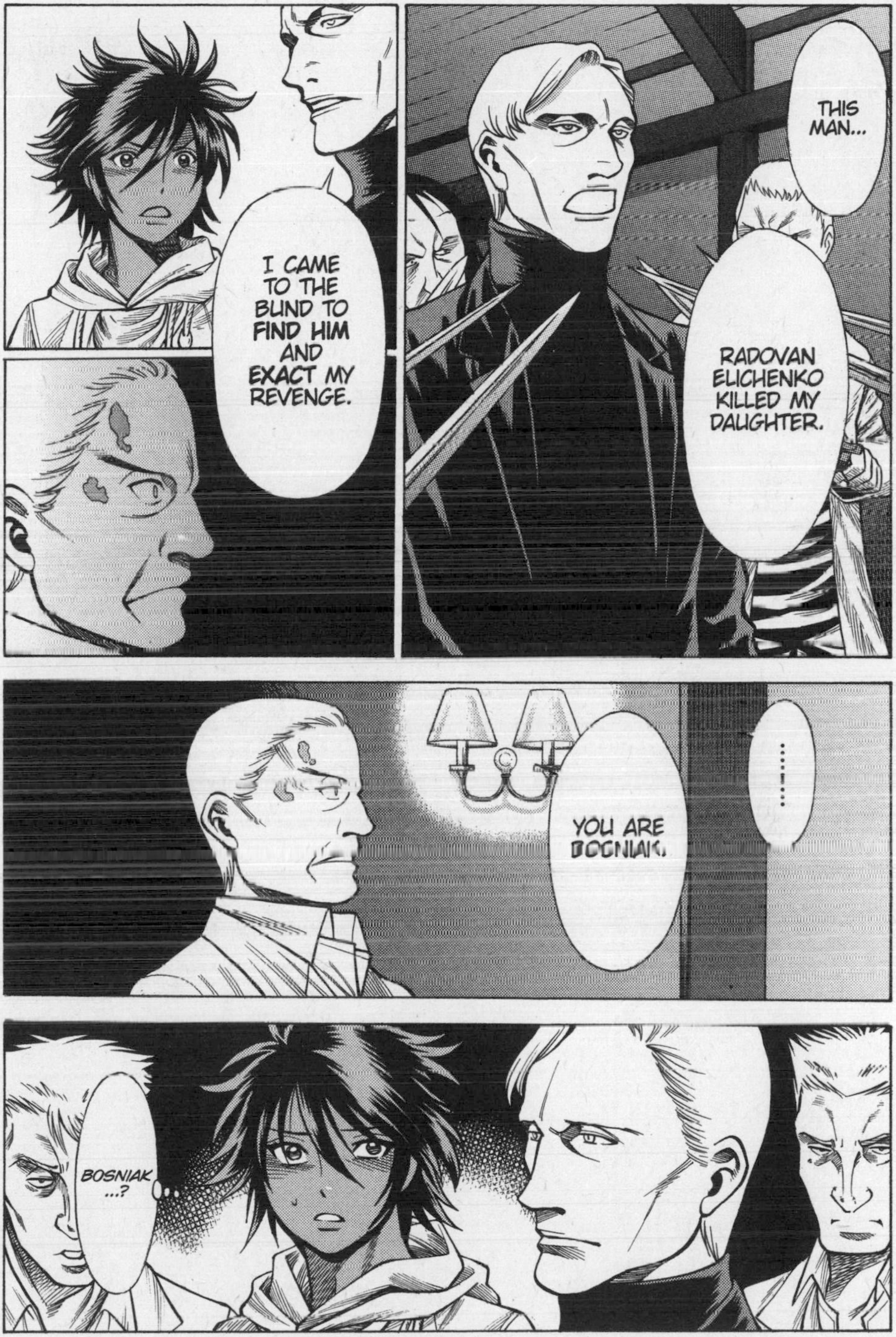
THIS MAN...
RADOVAN ELICHENKO KILLED MY DAUGHTER.
I CAME TO THE BUND TO FIND HIM AND EXACT MY REVENGE.
......!
YOU ARE BOSNIAK.
BOSNIAK ...?

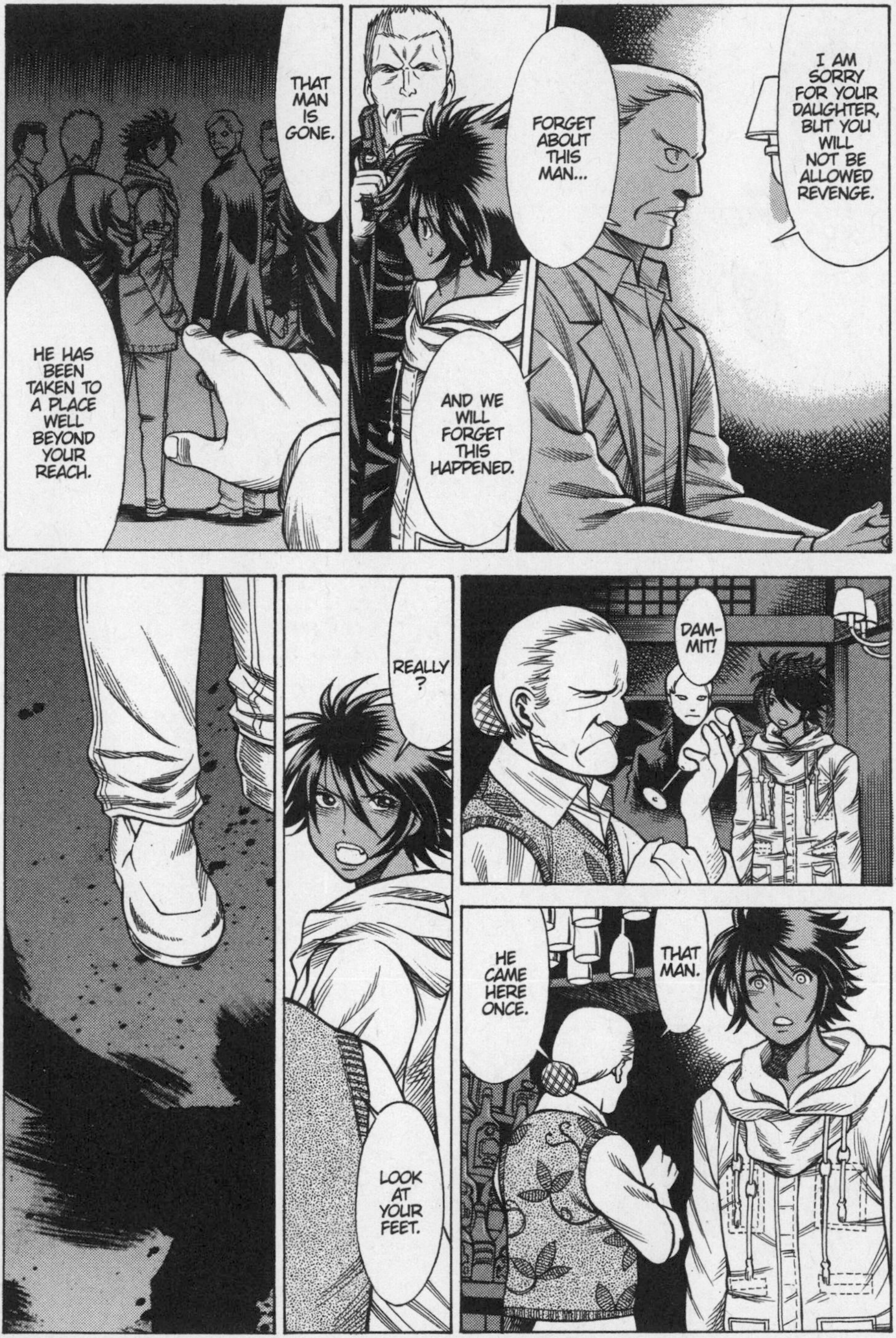
I AM SORRY FOR YOUR DAUGHTER, BUT YOU WILL NOT BE ALLOWED REVENGE.
FORGET ABOUT THIS MAN...
AND WE WILL FORGET THIS HAPPENED.
THAT MAN IS GONE.
HE HAS BEEN TAKEN TO A PLACE WELL BEYOND YOUR REACH.
DAM-MIT!
THAT MAN.
HE CAME HERE ONCE.
LOOK AT YOUR FEET.
REALLY?

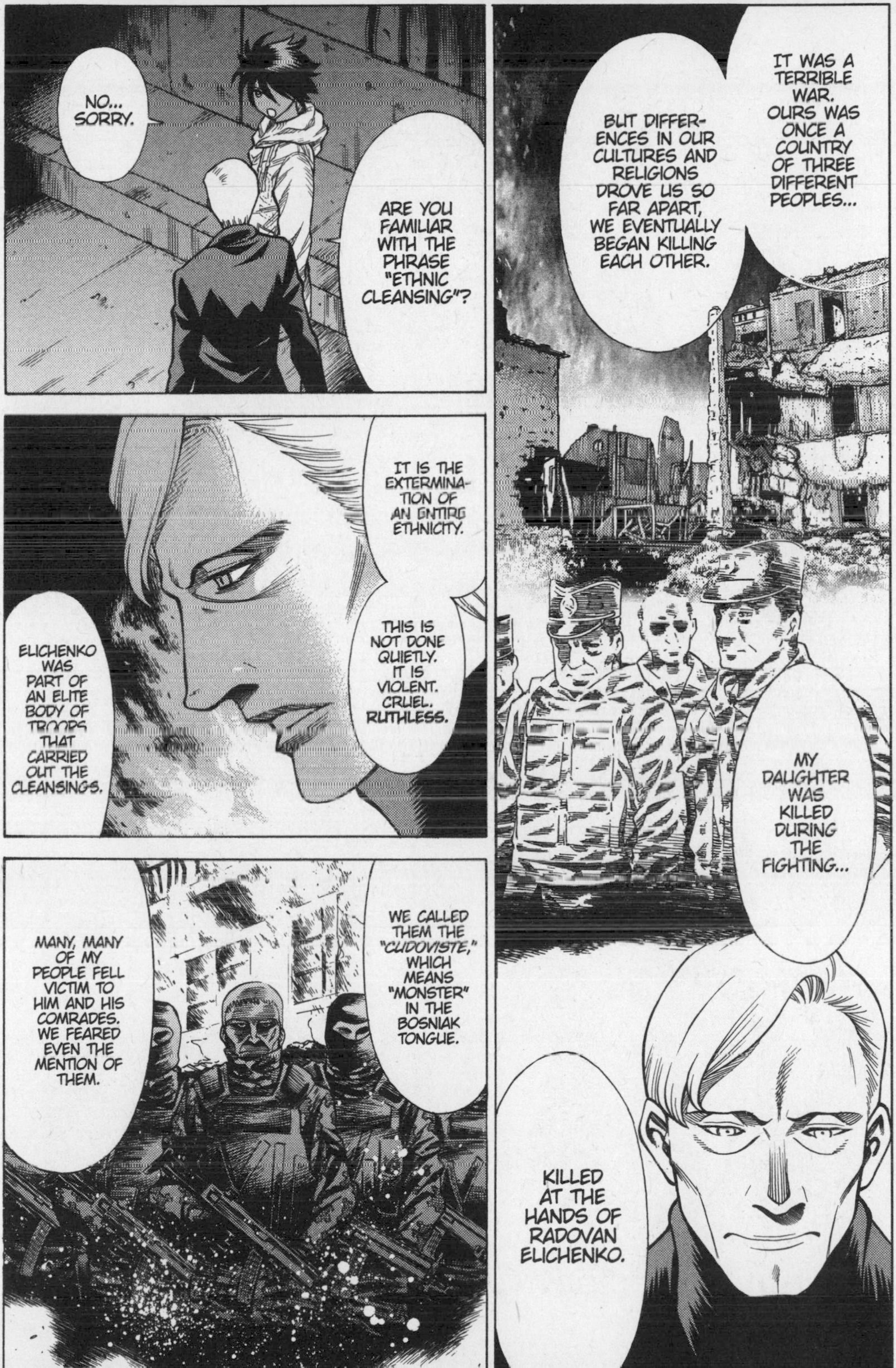
IT WAS A TERRIBLE WAR. OURS WAS ONCE A COUNTRY OF THREE DIFFERENT PEOPLES...
BUT DIFFERENCES IN OUR CULTURES AND RELIGIONS DROVE US SO FAR APART, WE EVENTUALLY BEGAN KILLING EACH OTHER.
MY DAUGHTER WAS KILLED DURING THE FIGHTING...
KILLED AT THE HANDS OF RADOVAN ELICHENKO.
ARE YOU FAMILIAR WITH THE PHRASE "ETHNIC CLEANSING"?
NO... SORRY.
IT IS THE EXTERMINATION OF AN ENTIRE ETHNICITY.
THIS IS NOT DONE QUIETLY. IT IS VIOLENT. CRUEL. RUTHLESS.
ELICHENKO WAS PART OF AN ELITE BODY OF TROOPS THAT CARRIED OUT THE CLEANSINGS.
WE CALLED THEM THE "CUDOVISTE," WHICH MEANS "MONSTER" IN THE BOSNIAK TONGUE.
MANY, MANY OF MY PEOPLE FELL VICTIM TO HIM AND HIS COMRADES. WE FEARED EVEN THE MENTION OF THEM.

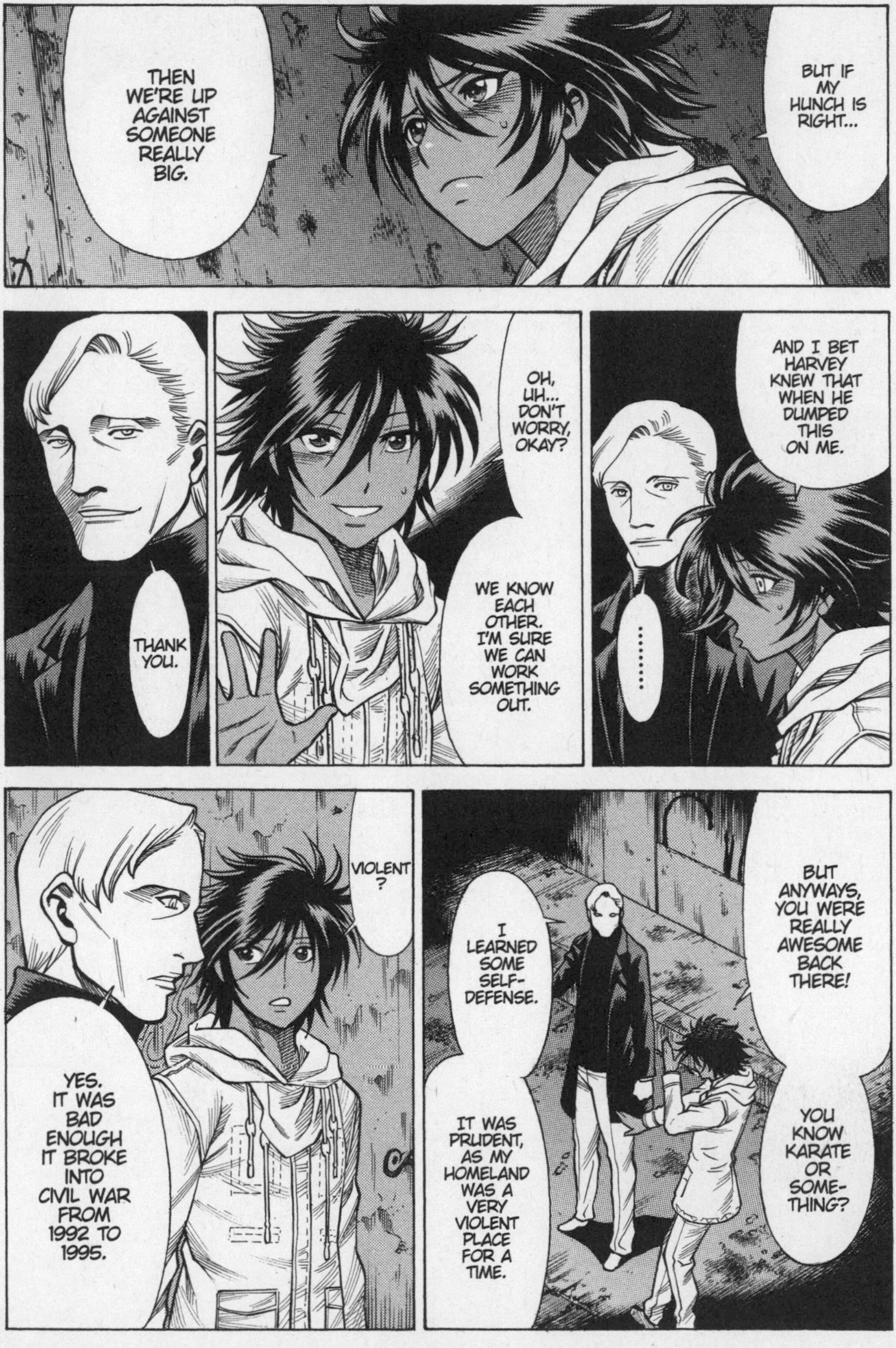
BUT IF MY HUNCH IS RIGHT...
THEN WE'RE UP AGAINST SOMEONE REALLY BIG.
AND I BET HARVEY KNEW THAT WHEN HE DUMPED THIS ON ME.
......
OH, UH... DON'T WORRY, OKAY?
WE KNOW EACH OTHER. I'M SURE WE CAN WORK SOMETHING OUT.
THANK YOU.
BUT ANYWAYS, YOU WERE REALLY AWESOME BACK THERE!
YOU KNOW KARATE OR SOME-THING?
I LEARNED SOME SELF-DEFENSE.
IT WAS PRUDENT, AS MY HOMELAND WAS A VERY VIOLENT PLACE FOR A TIME.
VIOLENT?
YES. IT WAS BAD ENOUGH IT BROKE INTO CIVIL WAR FROM 1992 TO 1995.

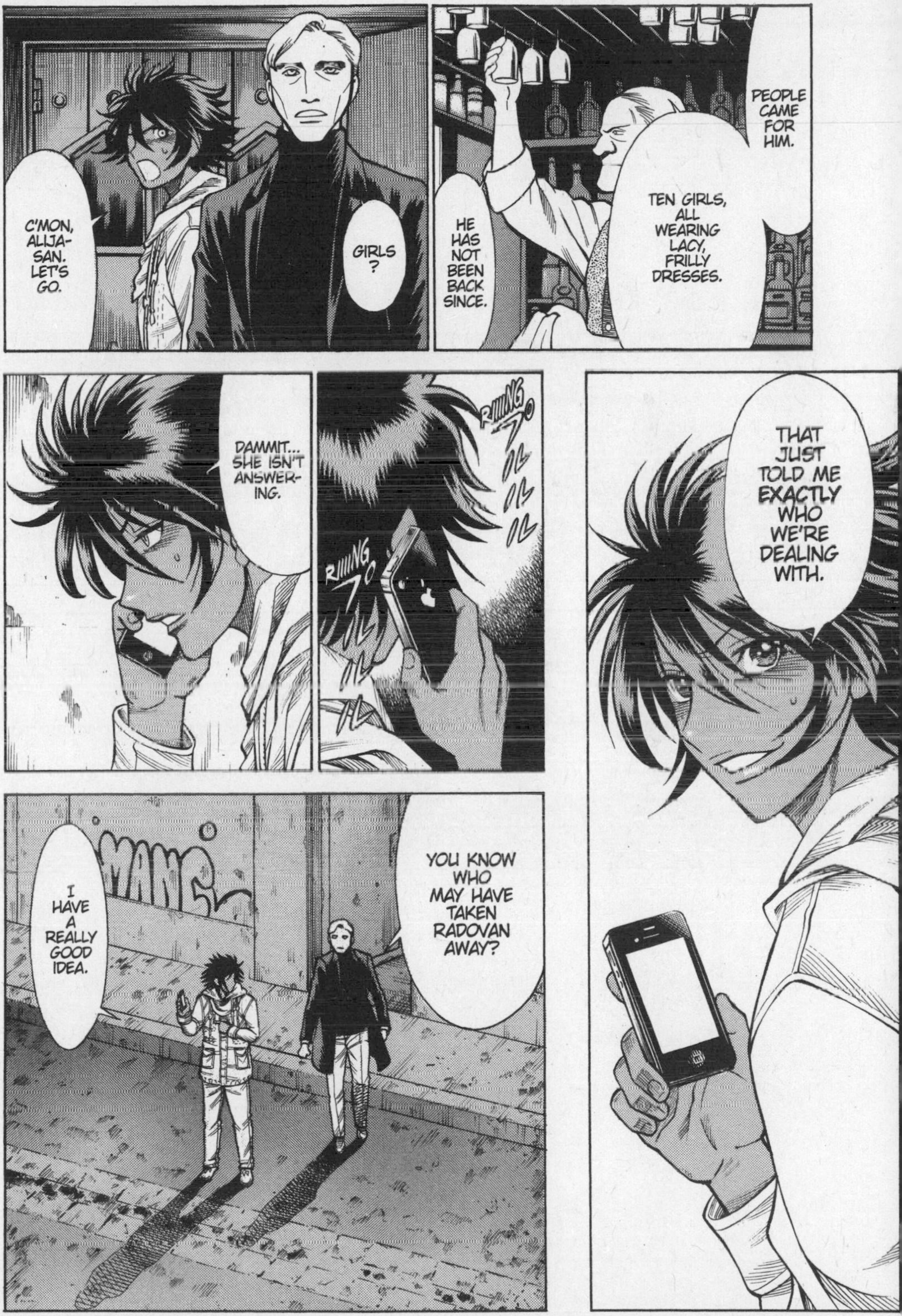
PEOPLE CAME FOR HIM.
TEN GIRLS, ALL WEARING LACY, FRILLY DRESSES.
HE HAS NOT BEEN BACK SINCE.
GIRLS?
C'MON, ALIJA-SAN. LET'S GO.
THAT JUST TOLD ME EXACTLY WHO WE'RE DEALING WITH.
RIIIING
RIIIING
DAMMIT... SHE ISN'T ANSWER-ING.
YOU KNOW WHO MAY HAVE TAKEN RADOVAN AWAY?
I HAVE A REALLY GOOD IDEA.
MANG

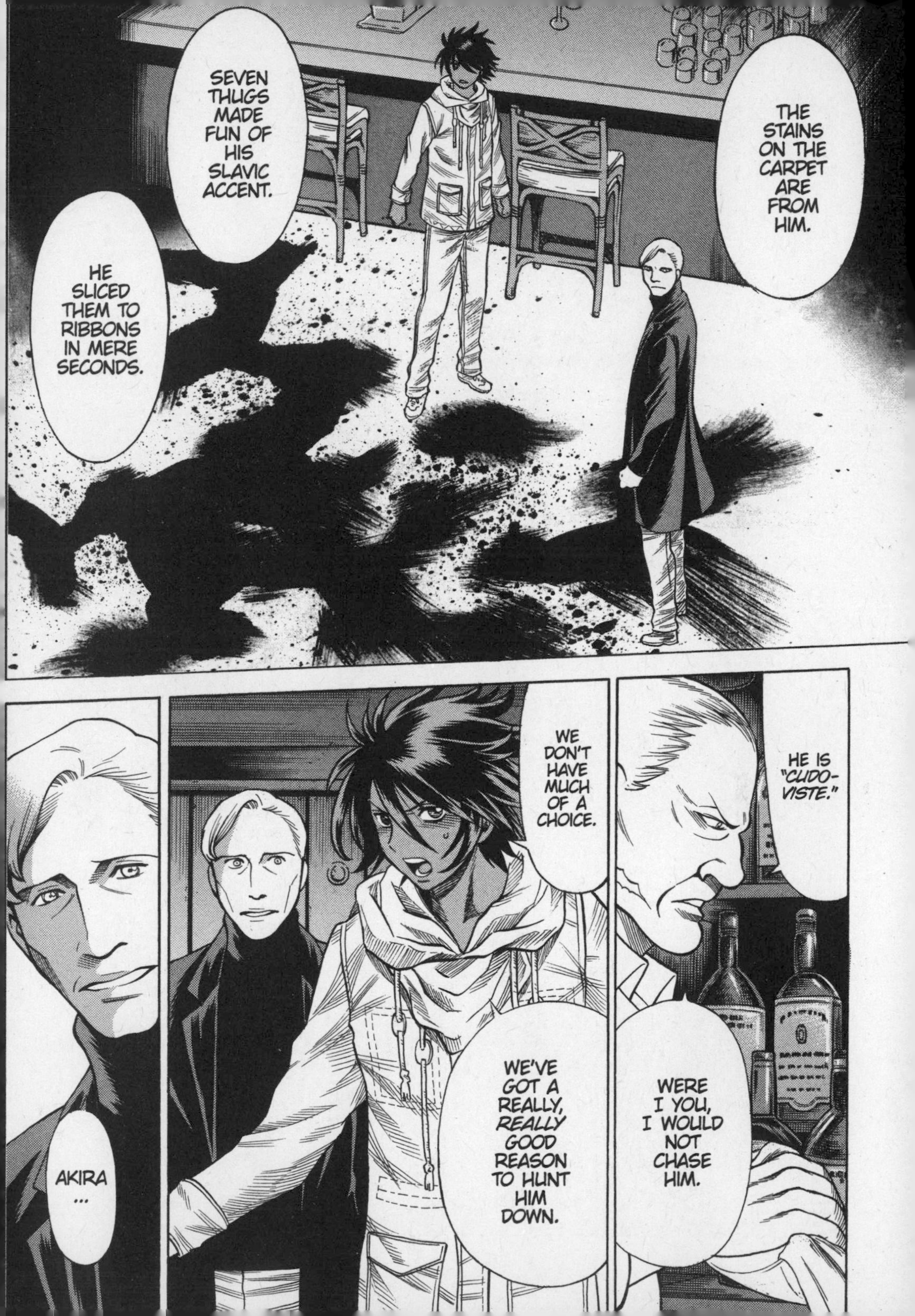
THE STAINS ON THE CARPET ARE FROM HIM.
SEVEN THUGS MADE FUN OF HIS SLAVIC ACCENT.
HE SLICED THEM TO RIBBONS IN MERE SECONDS.
HE IS "CUDO-VISTE."
WERE I YOU, I WOULD NOT CHASE HIM.
WE DON'T HAVE MUCH OF A CHOICE.
WE'VE GOT A REALLY, *REALLY* GOOD REASON TO HUNT HIM DOWN.
AKIRA ...

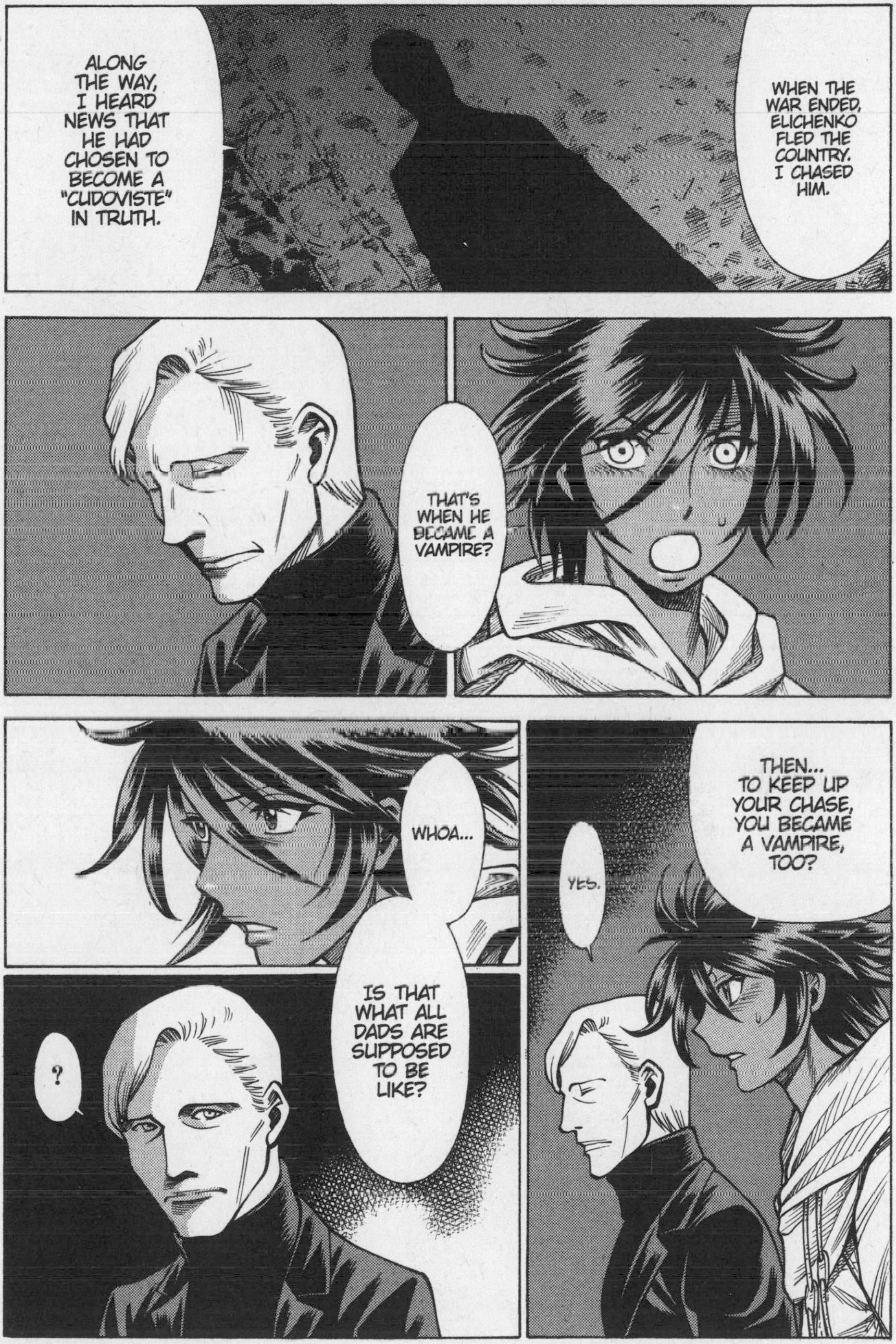
WHEN THE WAR ENDED, ELICHENKO FLED THE COUNTRY. I CHASED HIM.
ALONG THE WAY, I HEARD NEWS THAT HE HAD CHOSEN TO BECOME A "CUDOVISTE" IN TRUTH.
THAT'S WHEN HE BECAME A VAMPIRE?
THEN... TO KEEP UP YOUR CHASE, YOU BECAME A VAMPIRE, TOO?
YES.
WHOA...
IS THAT WHAT ALL DADS ARE SUPPOSED TO BE LIKE?
?

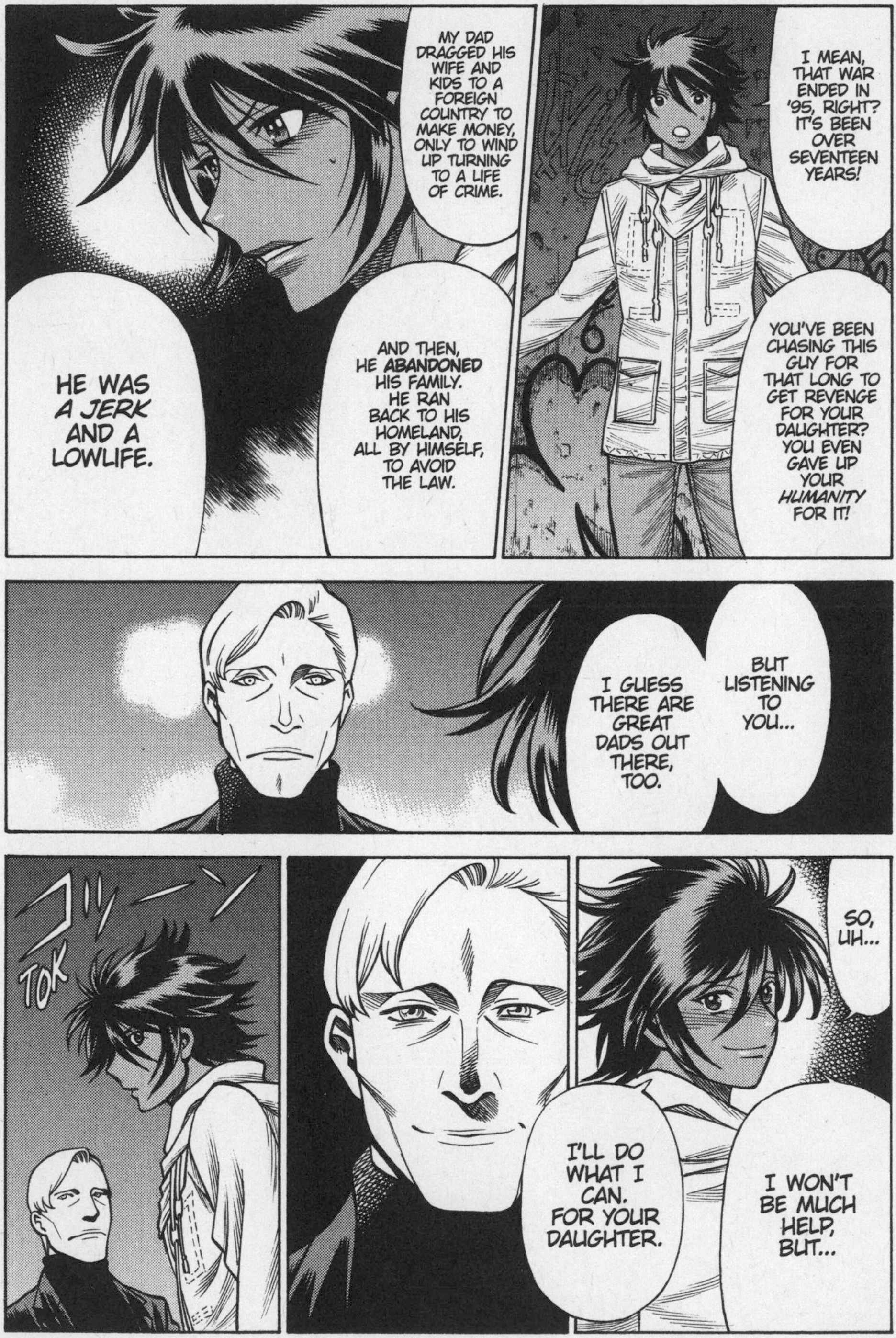

I MEAN, THAT WAR ENDED IN '95, RIGHT? IT'S BEEN OVER SEVENTEEN YEARS!
YOU'VE BEEN CHASING THIS GUY FOR THAT LONG TO GET REVENGE FOR YOUR DAUGHTER? YOU EVEN GAVE UP YOUR *HUMANITY* FOR IT!
MY DAD DRAGGED HIS WIFE AND KIDS TO A FOREIGN COUNTRY TO MAKE MONEY, ONLY TO WIND UP TURNING TO A LIFE OF CRIME.
AND THEN, HE **ABANDONED** HIS FAMILY. HE RAN BACK TO HIS HOMELAND, ALL BY HIMSELF, TO AVOID THE LAW.
HE WAS *A JERK* AND A LOWLIFE.
BUT LISTENING TO YOU...
I GUESS THERE ARE GREAT DADS OUT THERE, TOO.
SO, UH...
I WON'T BE MUCH HELP, BUT...
I'LL DO WHAT I CAN. FOR YOUR DAUGHTER.
コツーン
TOK

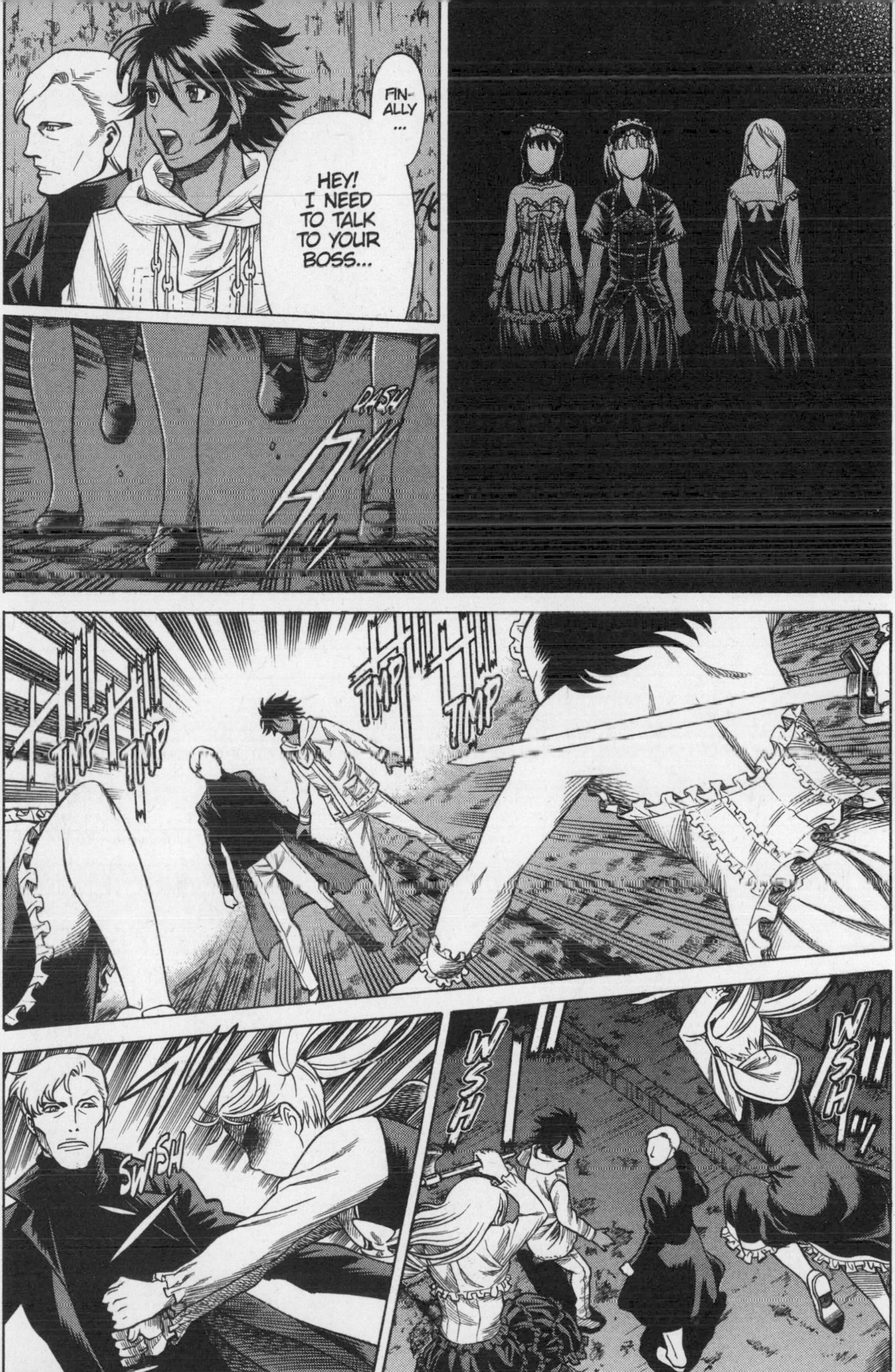
FIN-
ALLY
...
HEY! I NEED TO TALK TO YOUR BOSS...
DASH
TMP
TMP
TMP
TMP
WSH
WSH
SWISH

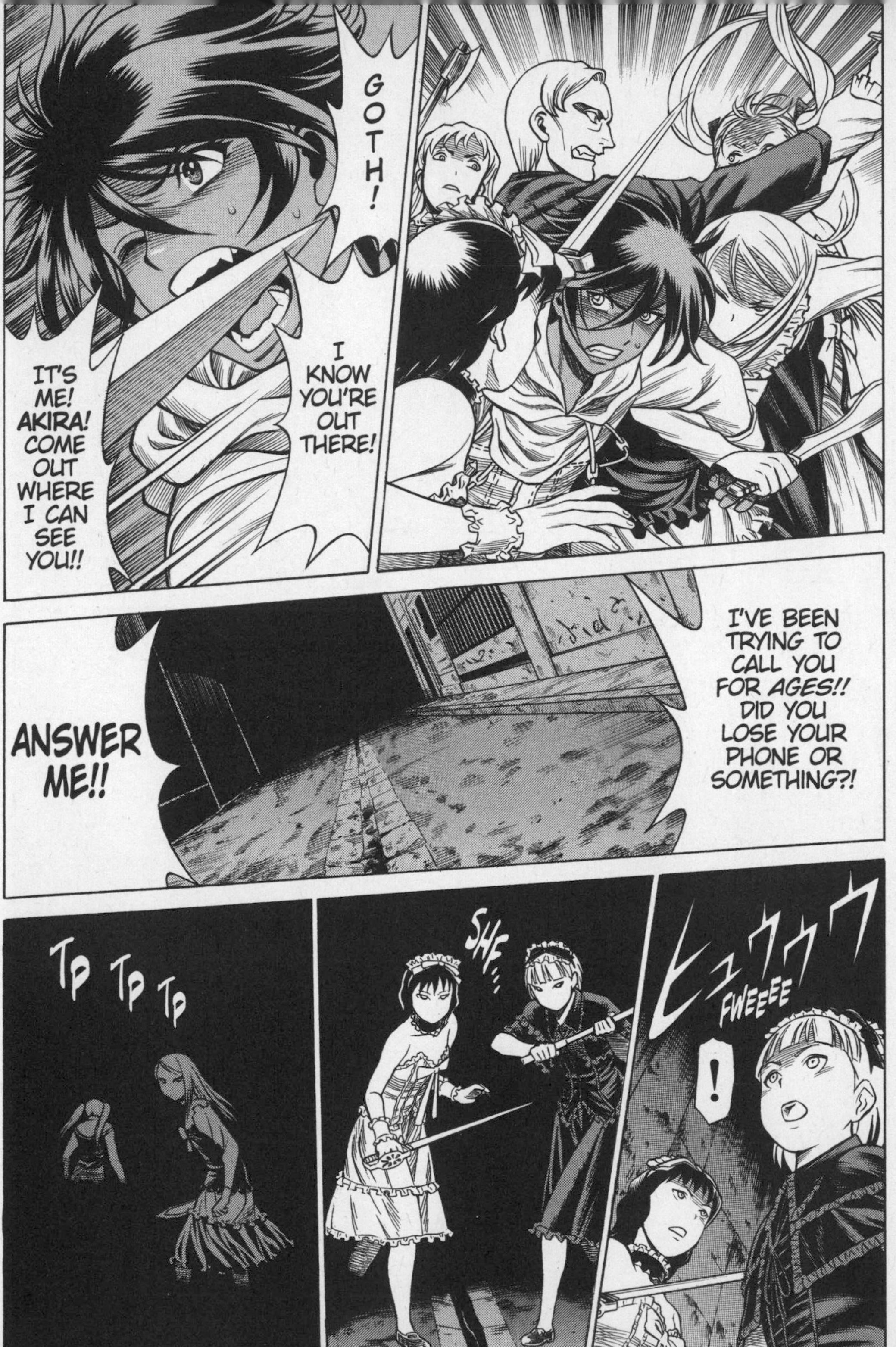
GOTH!
I KNOW YOU'RE OUT THERE!
IT'S ME! AKIRA! COME OUT WHERE I CAN SEE YOU!!
I'VE BEEN TRYING TO CALL YOU FOR AGES!! DID YOU LOSE YOUR PHONE OR SOMETHING?!
ANSWER ME!!
ヒュウウウ
FWEEEE
!
SHF...
Tp Tp Tp

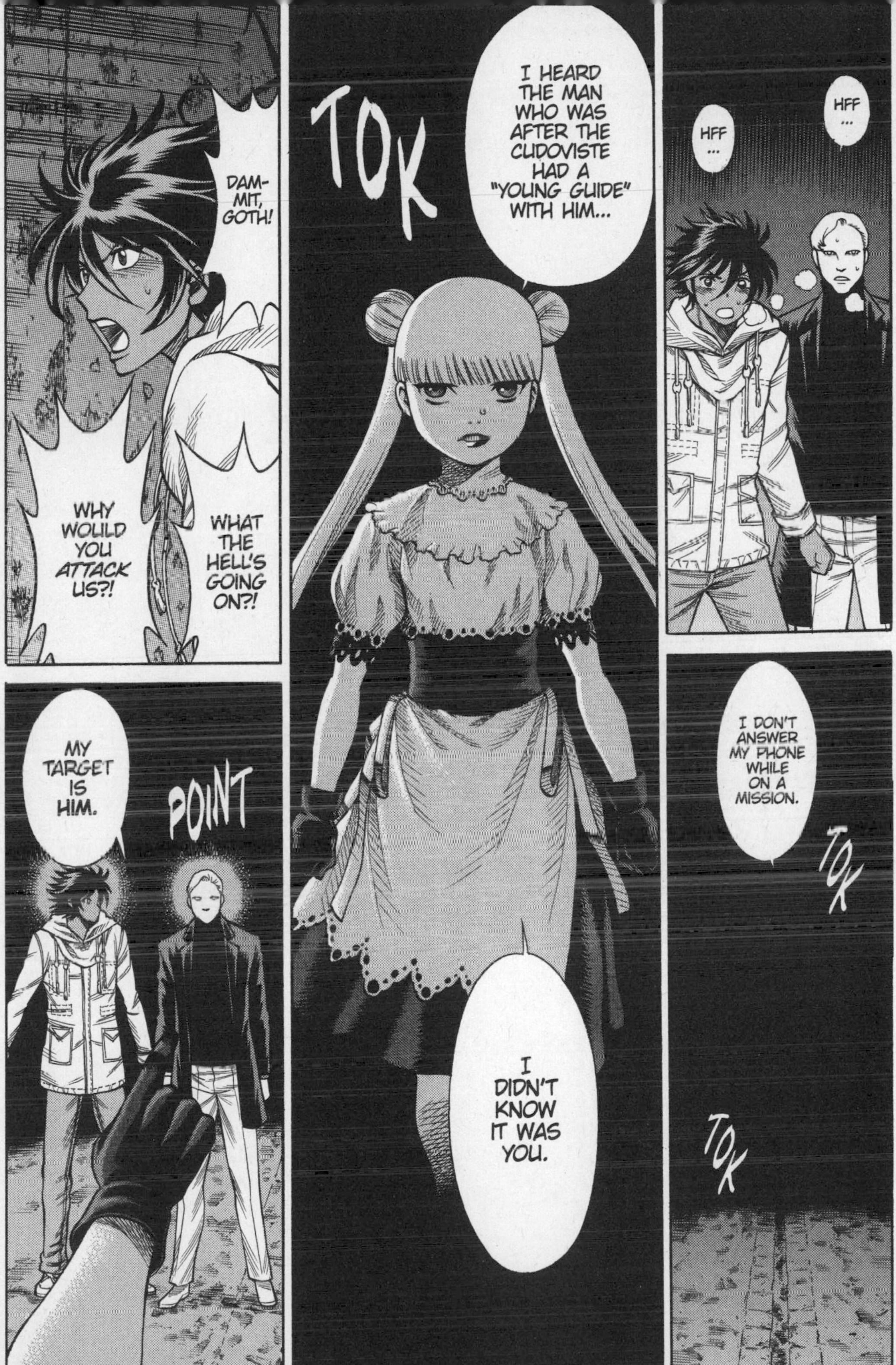
HFF ...
HFF ...
I DON'T ANSWER MY PHONE WHILE ON A MISSION.
TOK
TOK
TOK
I HEARD THE MAN WHO WAS AFTER THE CUDOVISTE HAD A "YOUNG GUIDE" WITH HIM...
I DIDN'T KNOW IT WAS YOU.
DAM-MIT, GOTH!
WHAT THE HELL'S GOING ON?!
WHY WOULD YOU ATTACK US?!
MY TARGET IS HIM.
POINT

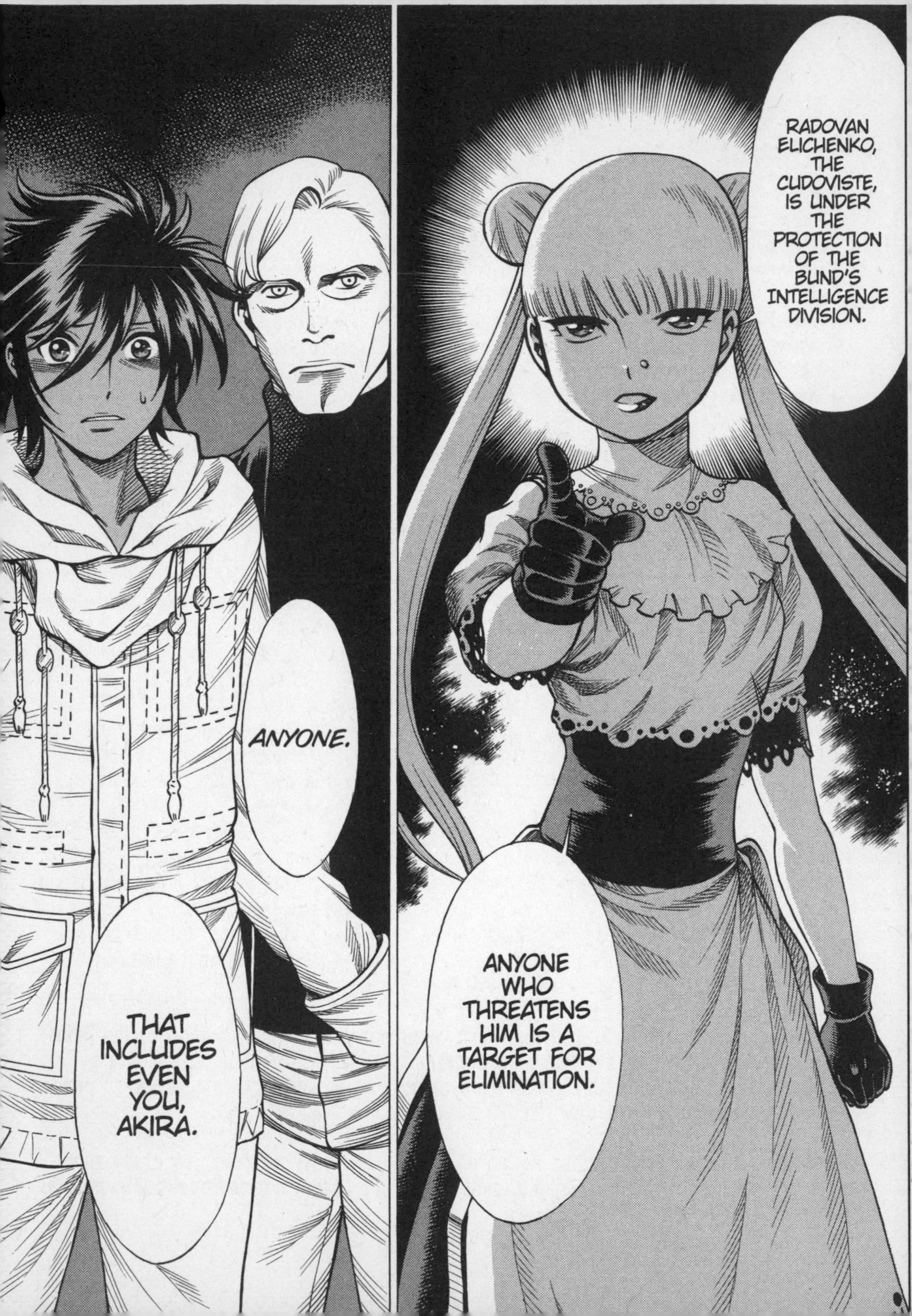
RADOVAN ELICHENKO, THE CUDOVISTE, IS UNDER THE PROTECTION OF THE BUND'S INTELLIGENCE DIVISION.
ANYONE WHO THREATENS HIM IS A TARGET FOR ELIMINATION.
ANYONE.
THAT INCLUDES EVEN YOU, AKIRA.

THE BOSNIAN WAR

Bosnia-Herzegovina is a small republic located on the northwestern side of the Balkan Peninsula in Eastern Europe. It was once a part of Democratic Federal Yugoslavia, but it successfully gained its independence during the Yugoslav Wars, which resulted in the total dissolution of Yugoslavia.

Yugoslavia was originally a country made up of multiple ethnicities, religions, and languages, and when Bosnia-Herzegovina split off, it too had many different peoples living together. The Bosniaks were the largest ethnicity, at 44% of the population. Next were the Serbs, with 33%. Third were the Croats at 17%, an ethnicity which isn't involved in the current story.

Though they were different ethnicities, they were essentially the same race. However, the Bosniaks are Muslims, while the Serbs and Croats are Orthodox Catholics. That created a large rift between their cultures.

The movement for independence from Yugoslavia began with the Bosniaks and the Croats, but the Serbs resisted it, intending to secure independence for themselves. A month after the declaration of the independence of Bosnia-Herzegovina, there was military conflict between the armies of Bosnia-Herzegovina and Serbia over territory, and the civil war began.

At first, the war went back and forth, as Bosnia-Herzegovina had the larger army, but Serbia had better equipment. However, as the war dragged on, dissidence between the Bosniaks and the Croats rose to the surface, and the advantage shifted to the Serbian side. Eventually, the Croats signed an alliance with the Serbs, putting the Bosniaks at an extreme disadvantage. They were killed in large numbers until American intervention in 1994 helped to reverse their position.

Air strikes by the United States and NATO weakened the Serbian position to the point of ceasefire. However, a decisive blow could not be struck. The war turned into a quagmire that took three and a half years to end. When Serbia finally agreed to peace, over 200,000 people were dead, and 2 million were left as refugees.

Today, the Bosniak and Croatian nation of Bosnia-Herzegovina exists peacefully along-side the Serbian Republic of Srpska, both recognized by the international community as independent nations.

DIVE IN THE VAMPIRE BUND

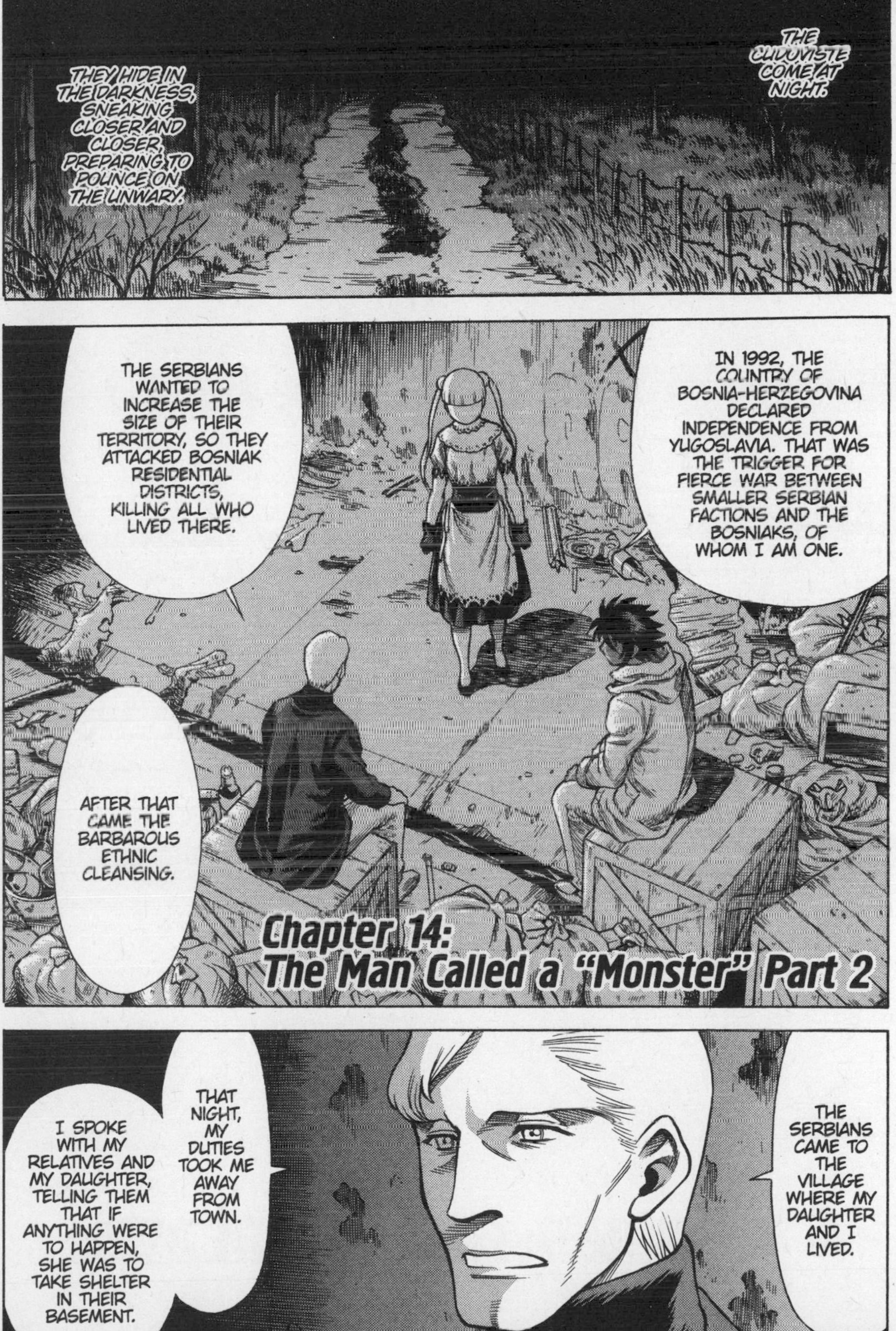
THE CUDOVISTE COME AT NIGHT.
THEY HIDE IN THE DARKNESS, SNEAKING CLOSER AND CLOSER, PREPARING TO POUNCE ON THE UNWARY.
IN 1992, THE COUNTRY OF BOSNIA-HERZEGOVINA DECLARED INDEPENDENCE FROM YUGOSLAVIA. THAT WAS THE TRIGGER FOR FIERCE WAR BETWEEN SMALLER SERBIAN FACTIONS AND THE BOSNIAKS, OF WHOM I AM ONE.
THE SERBIANS WANTED TO INCREASE THE SIZE OF THEIR TERRITORY, SO THEY ATTACKED BOSNIAK RESIDENTIAL DISTRICTS, KILLING ALL WHO LIVED THERE.
AFTER THAT CAME THE BARBAROUS ETHNIC CLEANSING.
Chapter 14: The Man Called a "Monster" Part 2
THE SERBIANS CAME TO THE VILLAGE WHERE MY DAUGHTER AND I LIVED.
THAT NIGHT, MY DUTIES TOOK ME AWAY FROM TOWN.
I SPOKE WITH MY RELATIVES AND MY DAUGHTER, TELLING THEM THAT IF ANYTHING WERE TO HAPPEN, SHE WAS TO TAKE SHELTER IN THEIR BASEMENT.

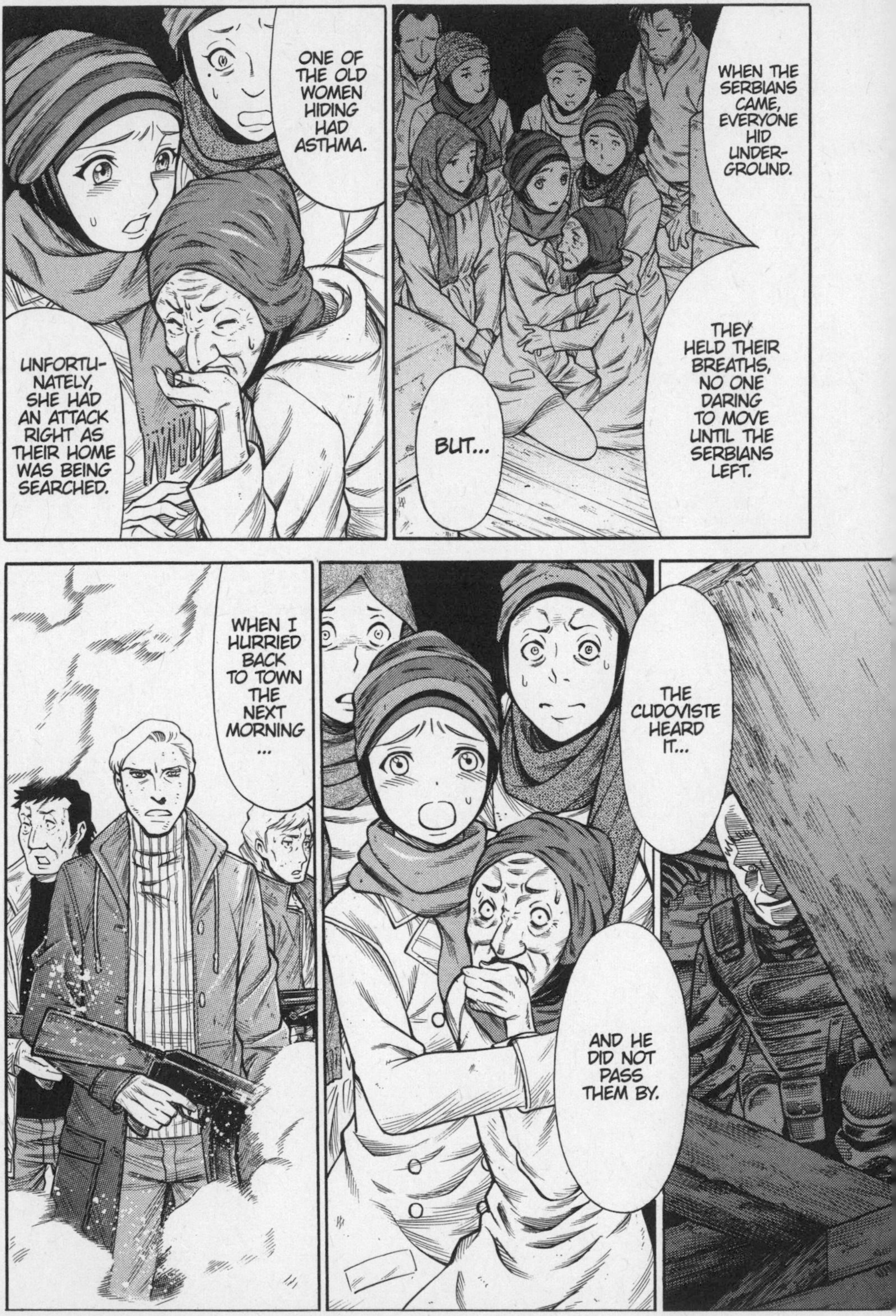
WHEN THE SERBIANS CAME, EVERYONE HID UNDERGROUND.
THEY HELD THEIR BREATHS, NO ONE DARING TO MOVE UNTIL THE SERBIANS LEFT.
BUT...
ONE OF THE OLD WOMEN HIDING HAD ASTHMA.
UNFORTUNATELY, SHE HAD AN ATTACK RIGHT AS THEIR HOME WAS BEING SEARCHED.
THE CUDOVISTE HEARD IT...
AND HE DID NOT PASS THEM BY.
WHEN I HURRIED BACK TO TOWN THE NEXT MORNING ...

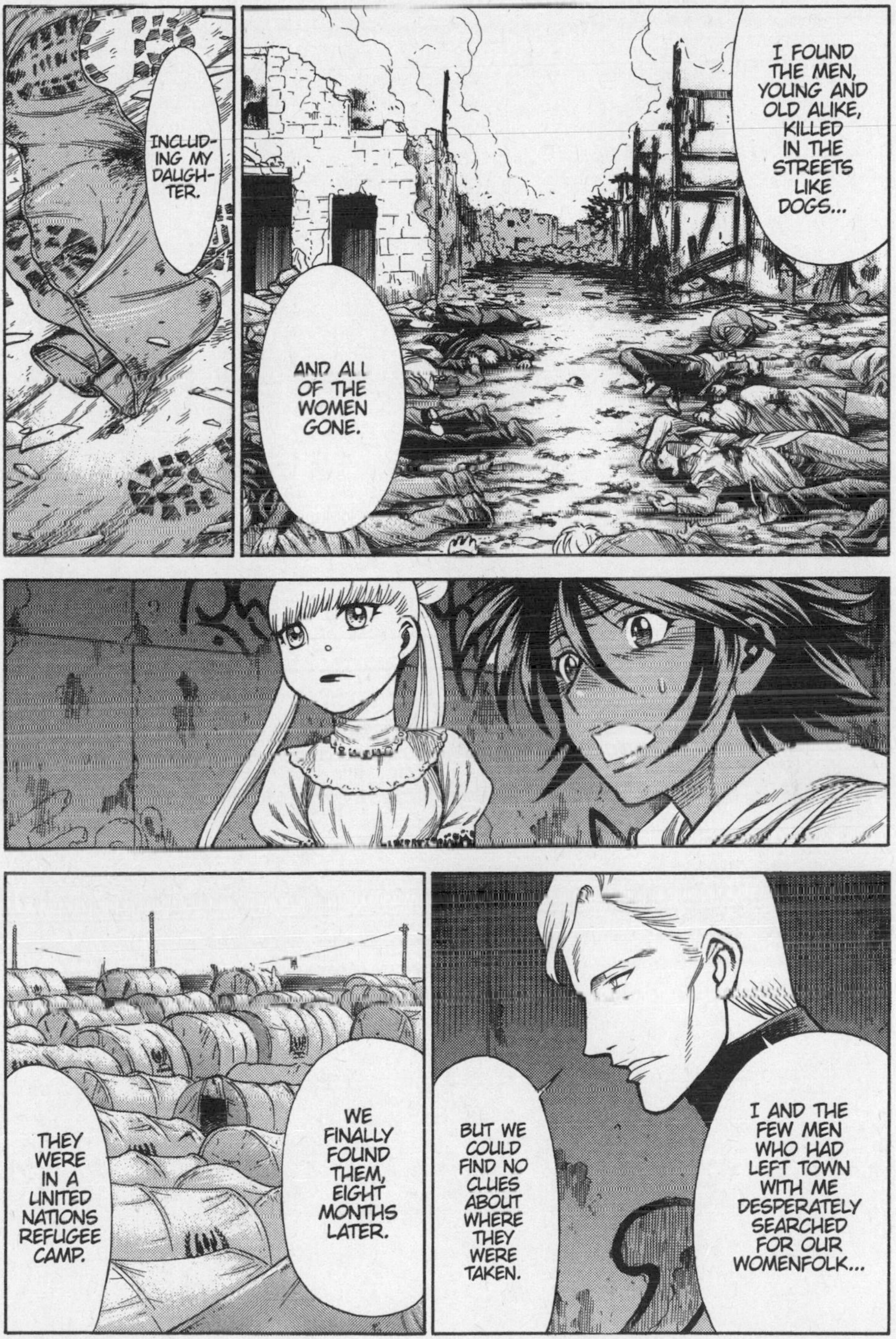
I FOUND THE MEN, YOUNG AND OLD ALIKE, KILLED IN THE STREETS LIKE DOGS...
AND ALL OF THE WOMEN GONE.
INCLUDING MY DAUGHTER.
I AND THE FEW MEN WHO HAD LEFT TOWN WITH ME DESPERATELY SEARCHED FOR OUR WOMENFOLK...
BUT WE COULD FIND NO CLUES ABOUT WHERE THEY WERE TAKEN.
WE FINALLY FOUND THEM, EIGHT MONTHS LATER.
THEY WERE IN A UNITED NATIONS REFUGEE CAMP.

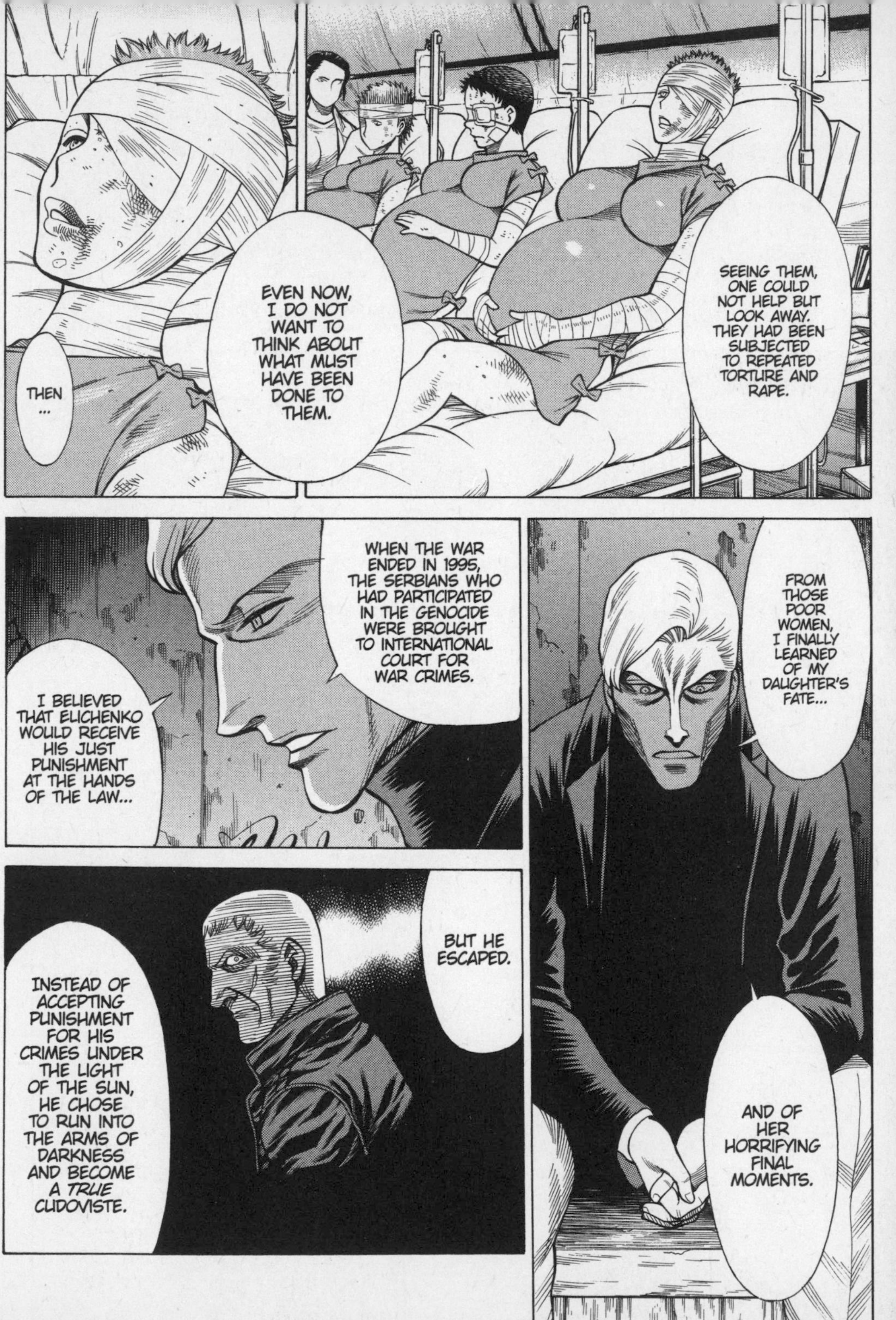
SEEING THEM, ONE COULD NOT HELP BUT LOOK AWAY. THEY HAD BEEN SUBJECTED TO REPEATED TORTURE AND RAPE.
EVEN NOW, I DO NOT WANT TO THINK ABOUT WHAT MUST HAVE BEEN DONE TO THEM.
THEN ...
FROM THOSE POOR WOMEN, I FINALLY LEARNED OF MY DAUGHTER'S FATE...
AND OF HER HORRIFYING FINAL MOMENTS.
WHEN THE WAR ENDED IN 1995, THE SERBIANS WHO HAD PARTICIPATED IN THE GENOCIDE WERE BROUGHT TO INTERNATIONAL COURT FOR WAR CRIMES.
I BELIEVED THAT ELICHENKO WOULD RECEIVE HIS JUST PUNISHMENT AT THE HANDS OF THE LAW...
BUT HE ESCAPED.
INSTEAD OF ACCEPTING PUNISHMENT FOR HIS CRIMES UNDER THE LIGHT OF THE SUN, HE CHOSE TO RUN INTO THE ARMS OF DARKNESS AND BECOME A *TRUE* CUDOVISTE.

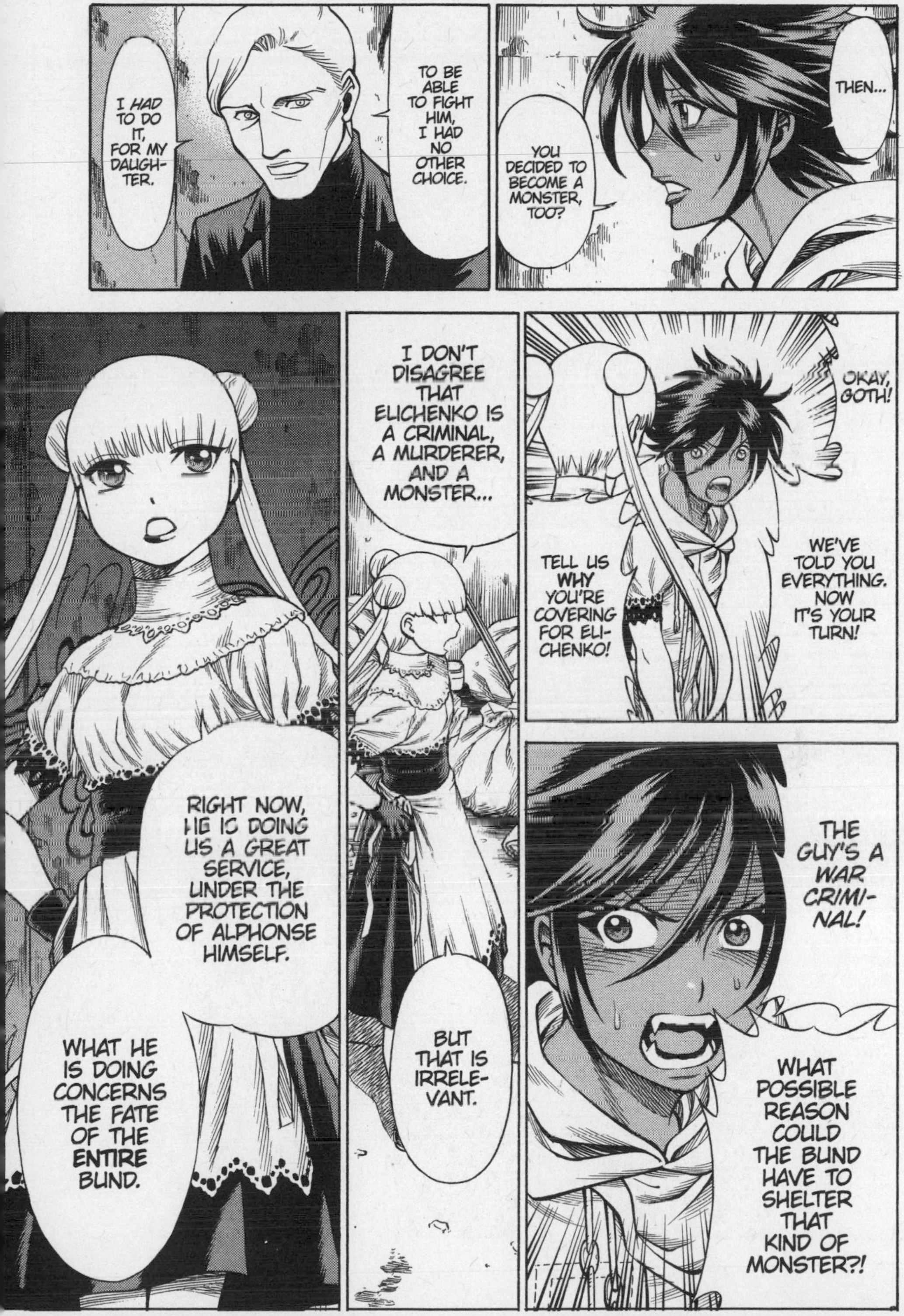
THEN...
YOU DECIDED TO BECOME A MONSTER, TOO?
TO BE ABLE TO FIGHT HIM, I HAD NO OTHER CHOICE.
I *HAD* TO DO IT, FOR MY DAUGHTER.
OKAY, GOTH!
WE'VE TOLD YOU EVERYTHING. NOW IT'S YOUR TURN!
TELL US WHY YOU'RE COVERING FOR ELICHENKO!
THE GUY'S A *WAR CRIMINAL!*
WHAT POSSIBLE REASON COULD THE BUND HAVE TO SHELTER THAT KIND OF MONSTER?!
I DON'T DISAGREE THAT ELICHENKO IS A CRIMINAL, A MURDERER, AND A MONSTER...
BUT THAT IS IRRELEVANT.
RIGHT NOW, HE IS DOING US A GREAT SERVICE, UNDER THE PROTECTION OF ALPHONSE HIMSELF.
WHAT HE IS DOING CONCERNS THE FATE OF THE ENTIRE BUND.

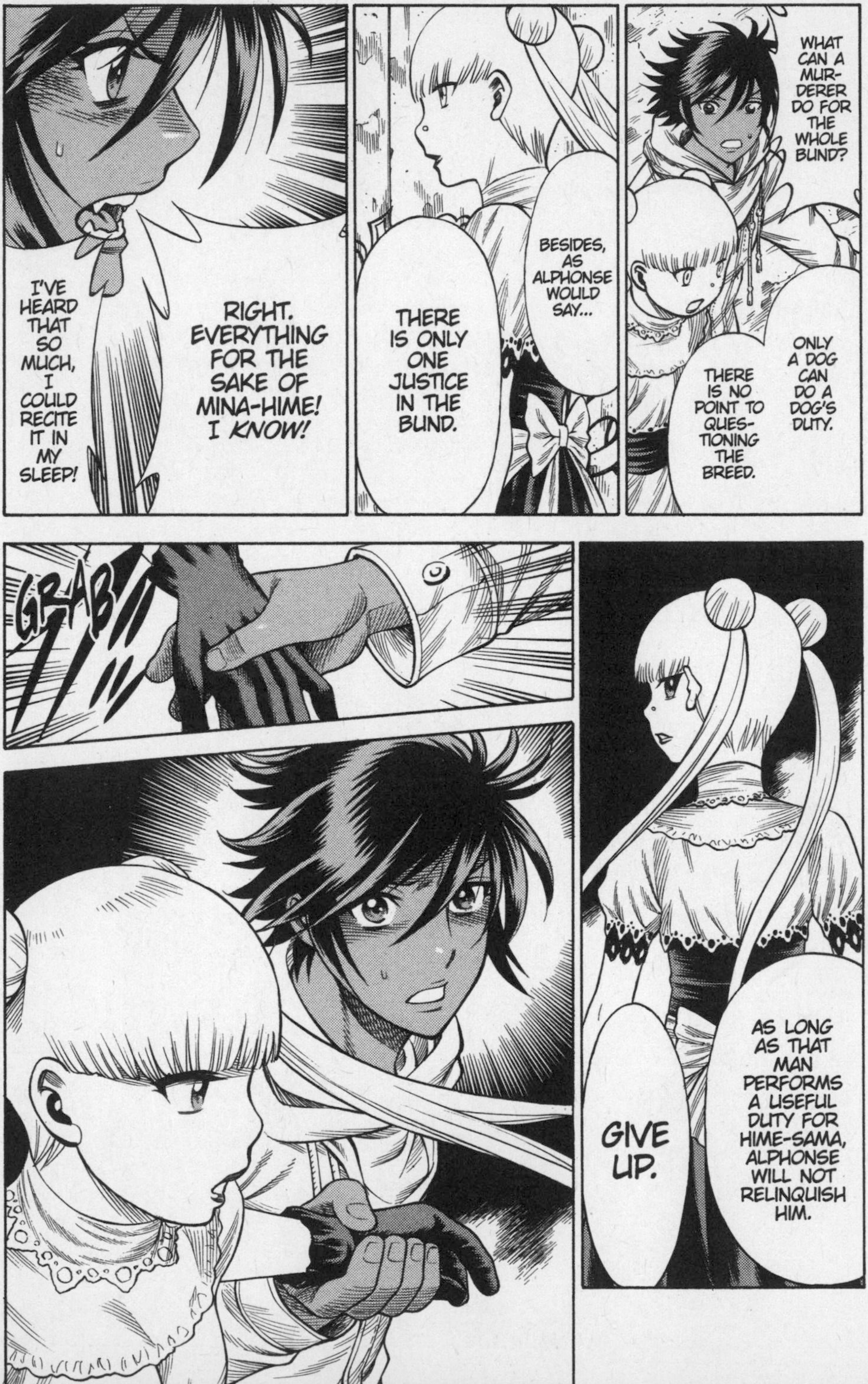
WHAT CAN A MURDERER DO FOR THE WHOLE BUND?
ONLY A DOG CAN DO A DOG'S DUTY.
THERE IS NO POINT TO QUESTIONING THE BREED.
BESIDES, AS ALPHONSE WOULD SAY...
THERE IS ONLY ONE JUSTICE IN THE BUND.
RIGHT. EVERYTHING FOR THE SAKE OF MINA-HIME! I *KNOW!*
I'VE HEARD THAT SO MUCH, I COULD RECITE IT IN MY SLEEP!
AS LONG AS THAT MAN PERFORMS A USEFUL DUTY FOR HIME-SAMA, ALPHONSE WILL NOT RELINQUISH HIM.
GIVE UP.
GRAB

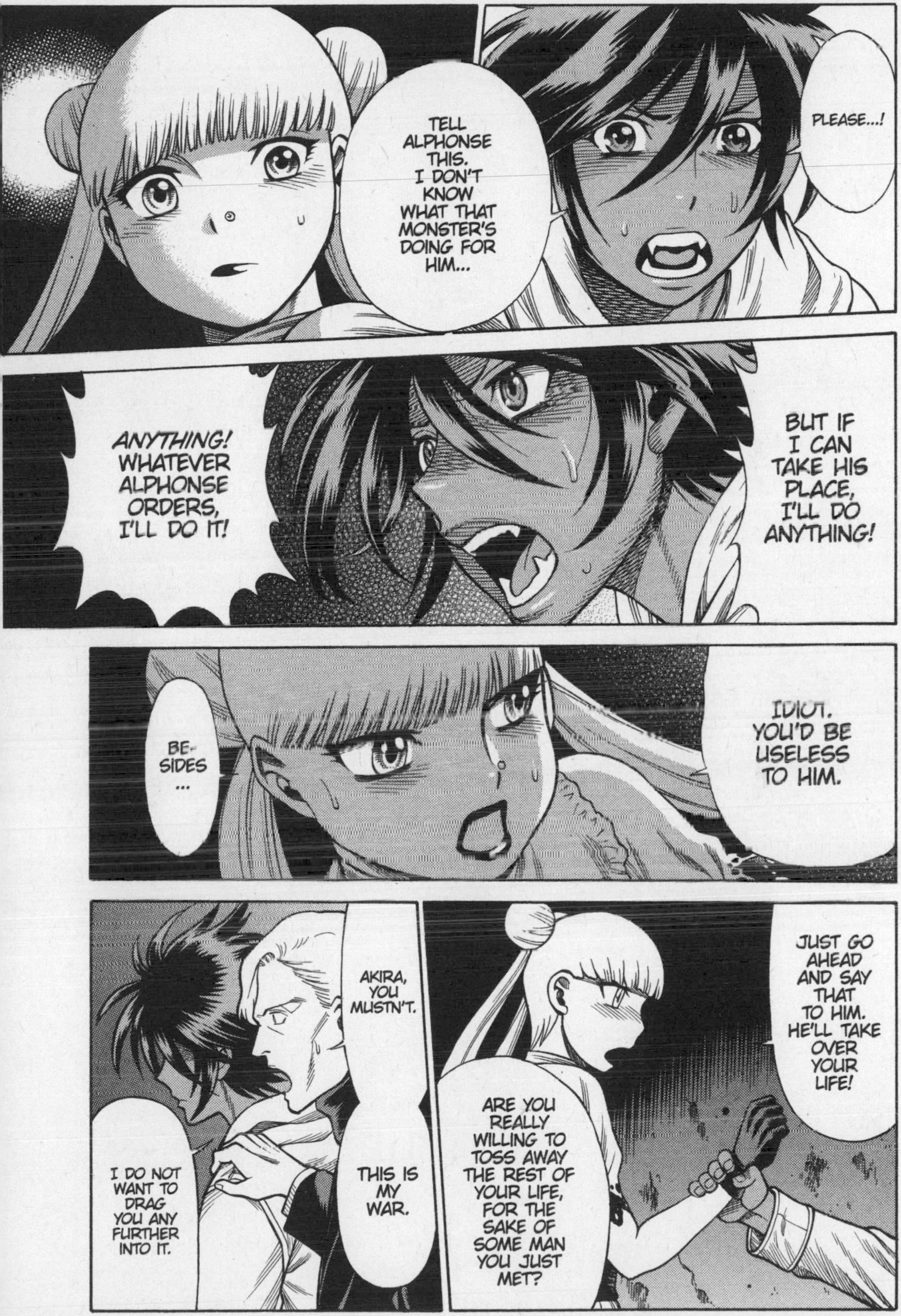
PLEASE...!
TELL ALPHONSE THIS. I DON'T KNOW WHAT THAT MONSTER'S DOING FOR HIM...
BUT IF I CAN TAKE HIS PLACE, I'LL DO ANYTHING!
ANYTHING! WHATEVER ALPHONSE ORDERS, I'LL DO IT!
IDIOT. YOU'D BE USELESS TO HIM.
BE-SIDES...
JUST GO AHEAD AND SAY THAT TO HIM. HE'LL TAKE OVER YOUR LIFE!
ARE YOU REALLY WILLING TO TOSS AWAY THE REST OF YOUR LIFE, FOR THE SAKE OF SOME MAN YOU JUST MET?
AKIRA, YOU MUSTN'T.
THIS IS MY WAR.
I DO NOT WANT TO DRAG YOU ANY FURTHER INTO IT.

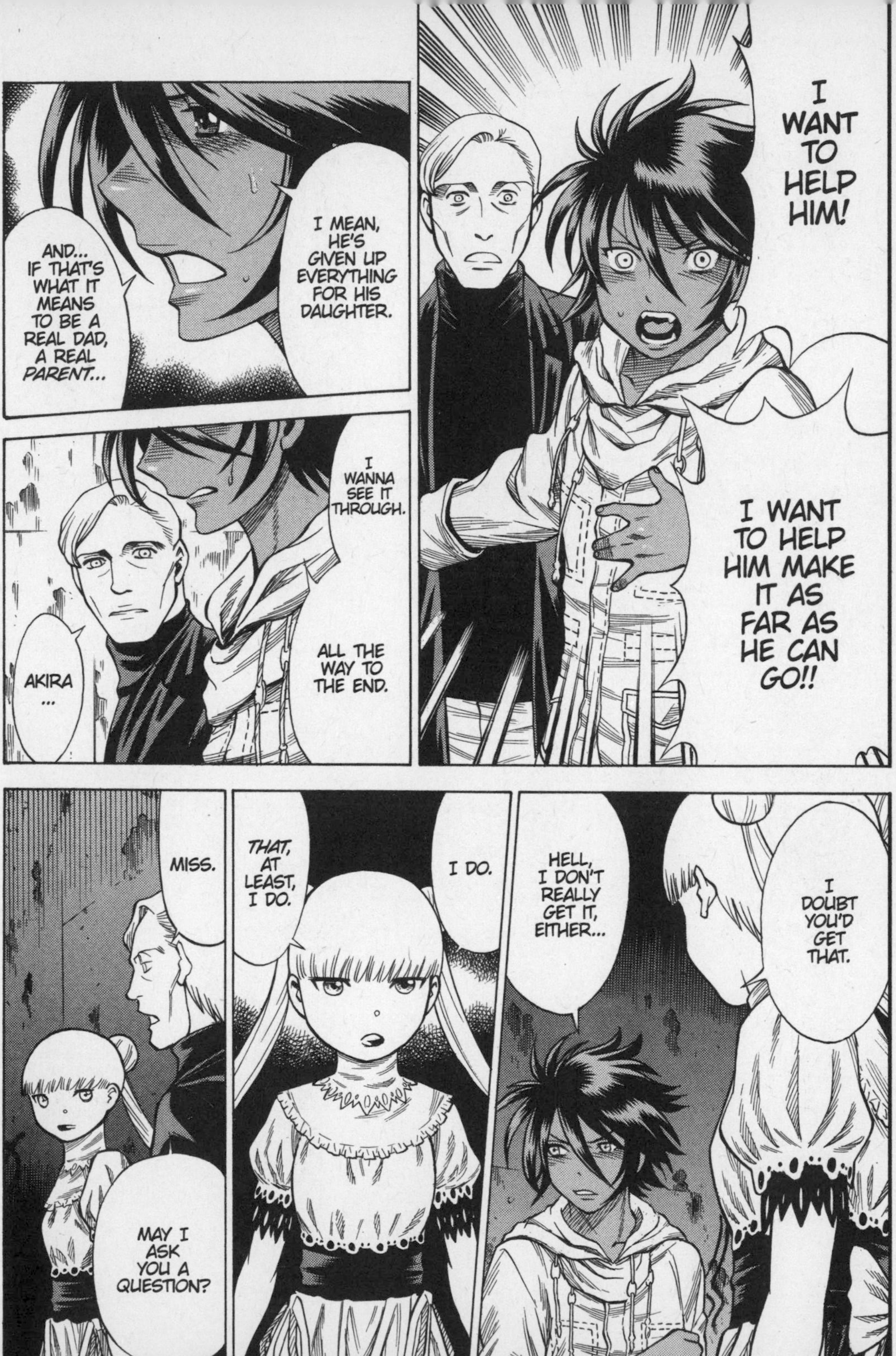
I WANT TO HELP HIM!
I WANT TO HELP HIM MAKE IT AS FAR AS HE CAN GO!!
I MEAN, HE'S GIVEN UP EVERYTHING FOR HIS DAUGHTER.
AND... IF THAT'S WHAT IT MEANS TO BE A REAL DAD, A REAL *PARENT*...
I WANNA SEE IT THROUGH.
ALL THE WAY TO THE END.
AKIRA ...
I DOUBT YOU'D GET THAT.
HELL, I DON'T REALLY GET IT, EITHER...
I DO.
THAT, AT LEAST, I DO.
MISS.
MAY I ASK YOU A QUESTION?

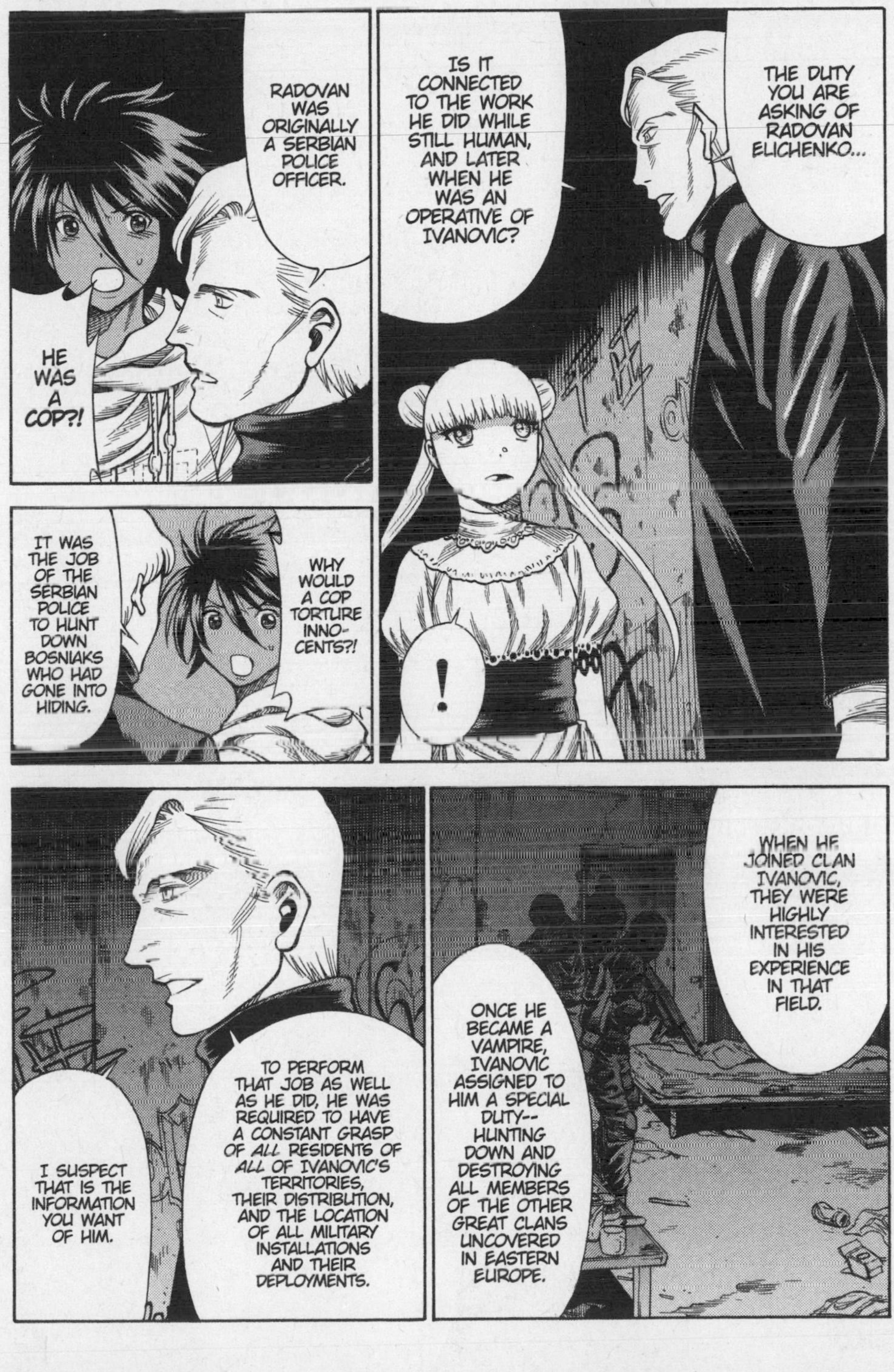
THE DUTY YOU ARE ASKING OF RADOVAN ELICHENKO...
IS IT CONNECTED TO THE WORK HE DID WHILE STILL HUMAN, AND LATER WHEN HE WAS AN OPERATIVE OF IVANOVIC?
!
RADOVAN WAS ORIGINALLY A SERBIAN POLICE OFFICER.
HE WAS A COP?!
WHY WOULD A COP TORTURE INNO-CENTS?!
IT WAS THE JOB OF THE SERBIAN POLICE TO HUNT DOWN BOSNIAKS WHO HAD GONE INTO HIDING.
WHEN HE JOINED CLAN IVANOVIC, THEY WERE HIGHLY INTERESTED IN HIS EXPERIENCE IN THAT FIELD.
ONCE HE BECAME A VAMPIRE, IVANOVIC ASSIGNED TO HIM A SPECIAL DUTY-- HUNTING DOWN AND DESTROYING ALL MEMBERS OF THE OTHER GREAT CLANS UNCOVERED IN EASTERN EUROPE.
TO PERFORM THAT JOB AS WELL AS HE DID, HE WAS REQUIRED TO HAVE A CONSTANT GRASP OF *ALL* RESIDENTS OF *ALL* OF IVANOVIC'S TERRITORIES, THEIR DISTRIBUTION, AND THE LOCATION OF ALL MILITARY INSTALLATIONS AND THEIR DEPLOYMENTS.
I SUSPECT THAT IS THE INFORMATION YOU WANT OF HIM.

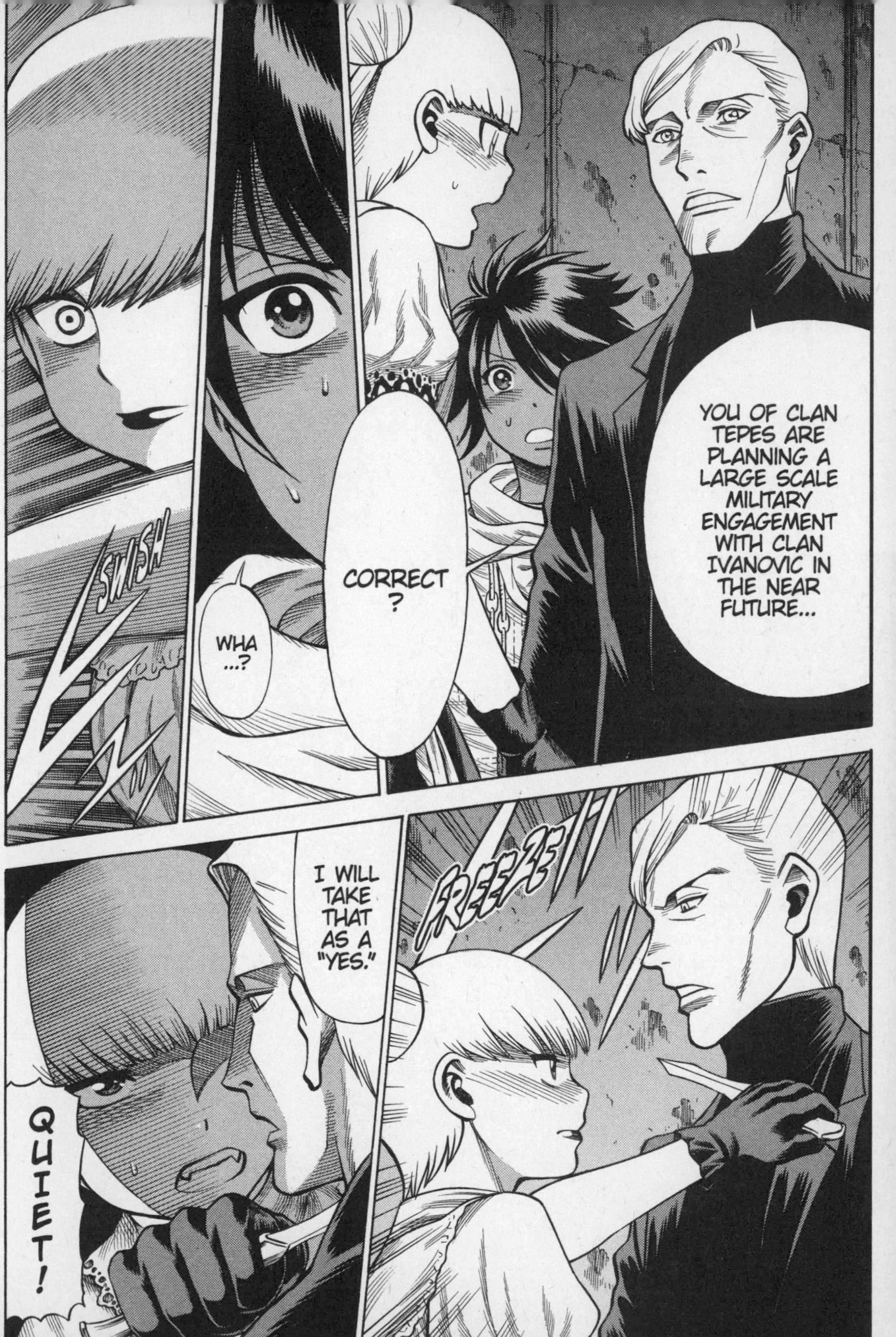
YOU OF CLAN TEPES ARE PLANNING A LARGE SCALE MILITARY ENGAGEMENT WITH CLAN IVANOVIC IN THE NEAR FUTURE...
CORRECT?
WHA...?
SWISH
FREEZE
I WILL TAKE THAT AS A "YES."
QUIET!

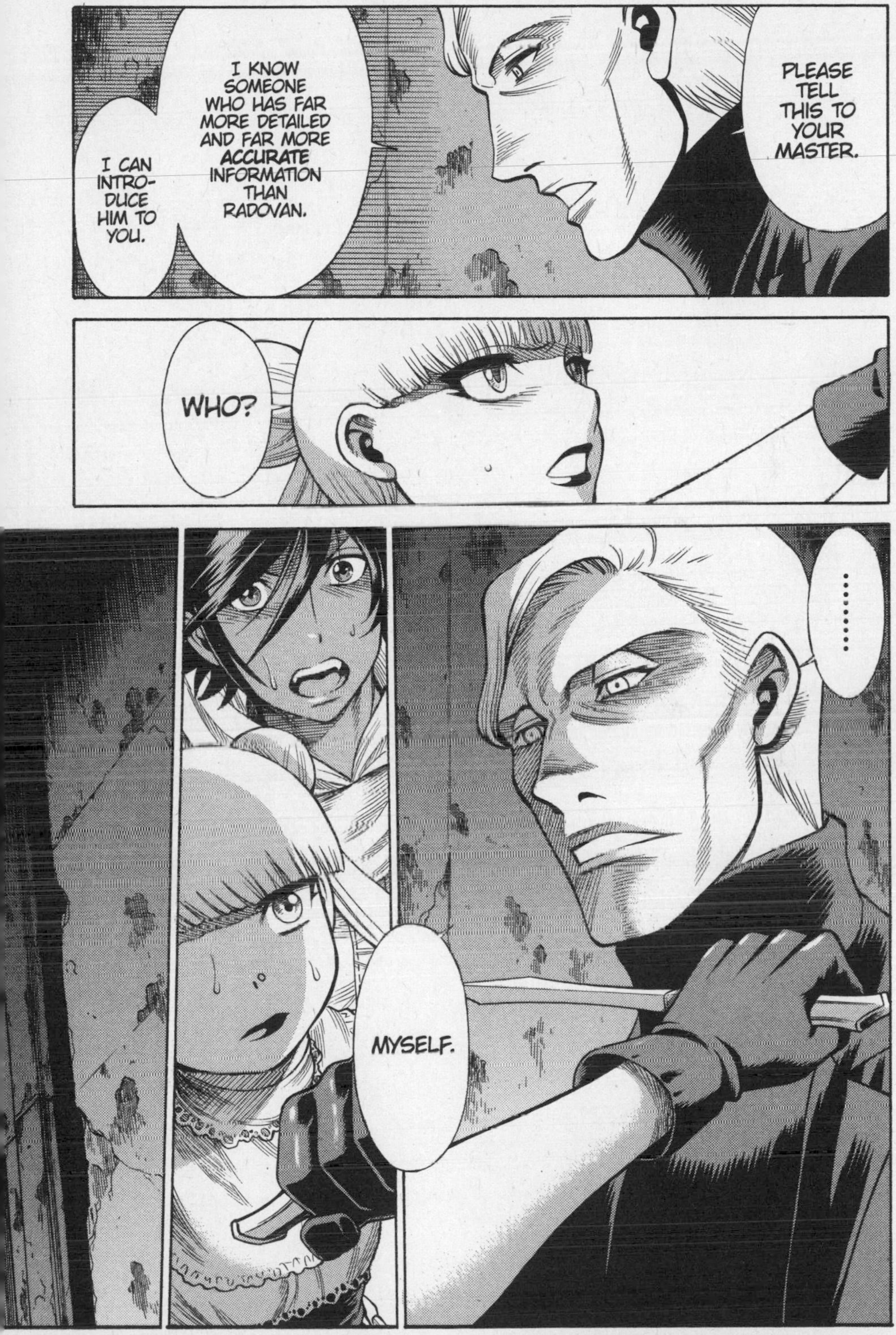
PLEASE TELL THIS TO YOUR MASTER.
I KNOW SOMEONE WHO HAS FAR MORE DETAILED AND FAR MORE ACCURATE INFORMATION THAN RADOVAN.
I CAN INTRO-DUCE HIM TO YOU.
WHO?
......
MYSELF.

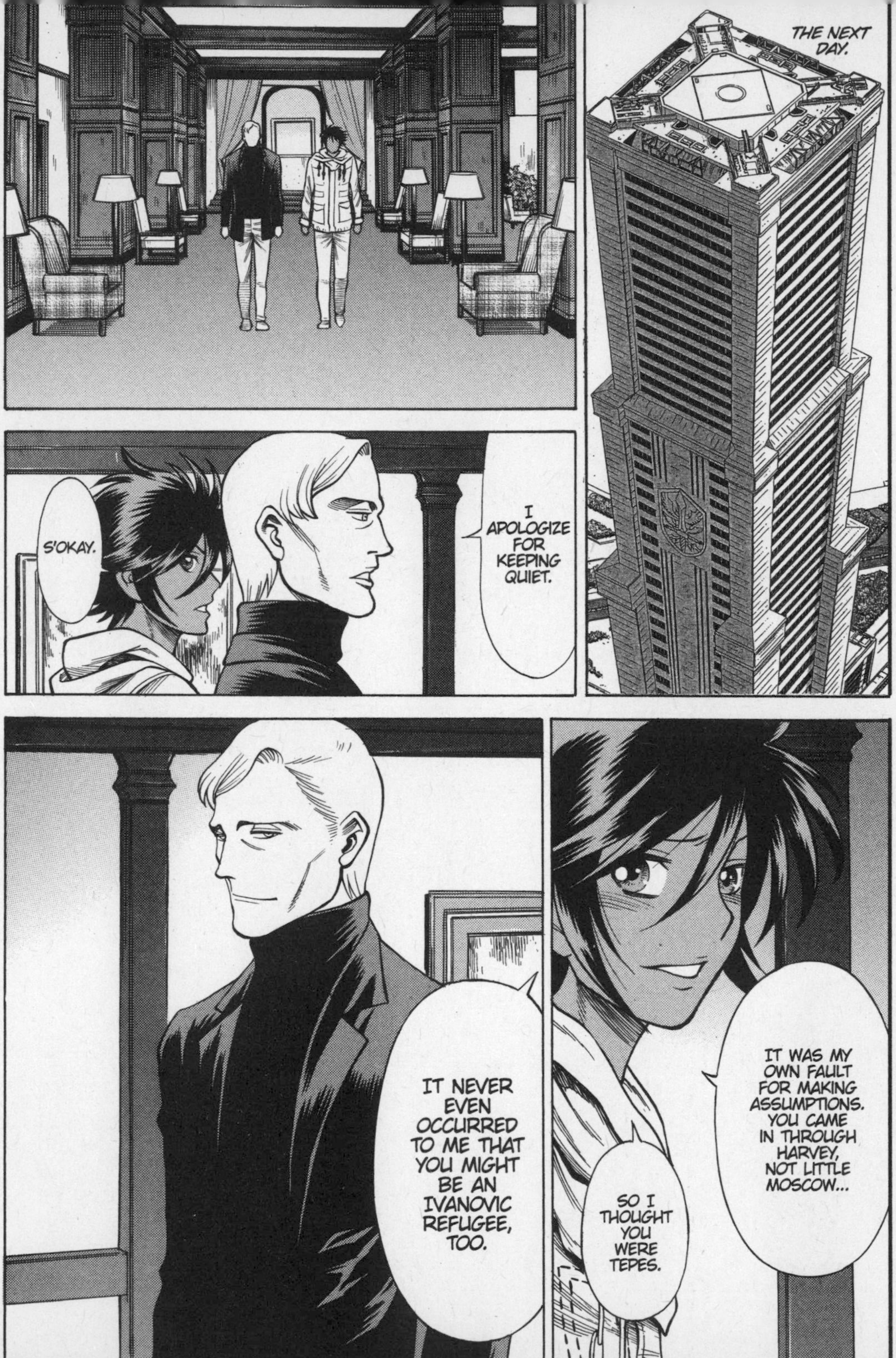
THE NEXT DAY.
I APOLOGIZE FOR KEEPING QUIET.
S'OKAY.
IT WAS MY OWN FAULT FOR MAKING ASSUMPTIONS. YOU CAME IN THROUGH HARVEY, NOT LITTLE MOSCOW...
SO I THOUGHT YOU WERE TEPES.
IT NEVER EVEN OCCURRED TO ME THAT YOU MIGHT BE AN IVANOVIC REFUGEE, TOO.

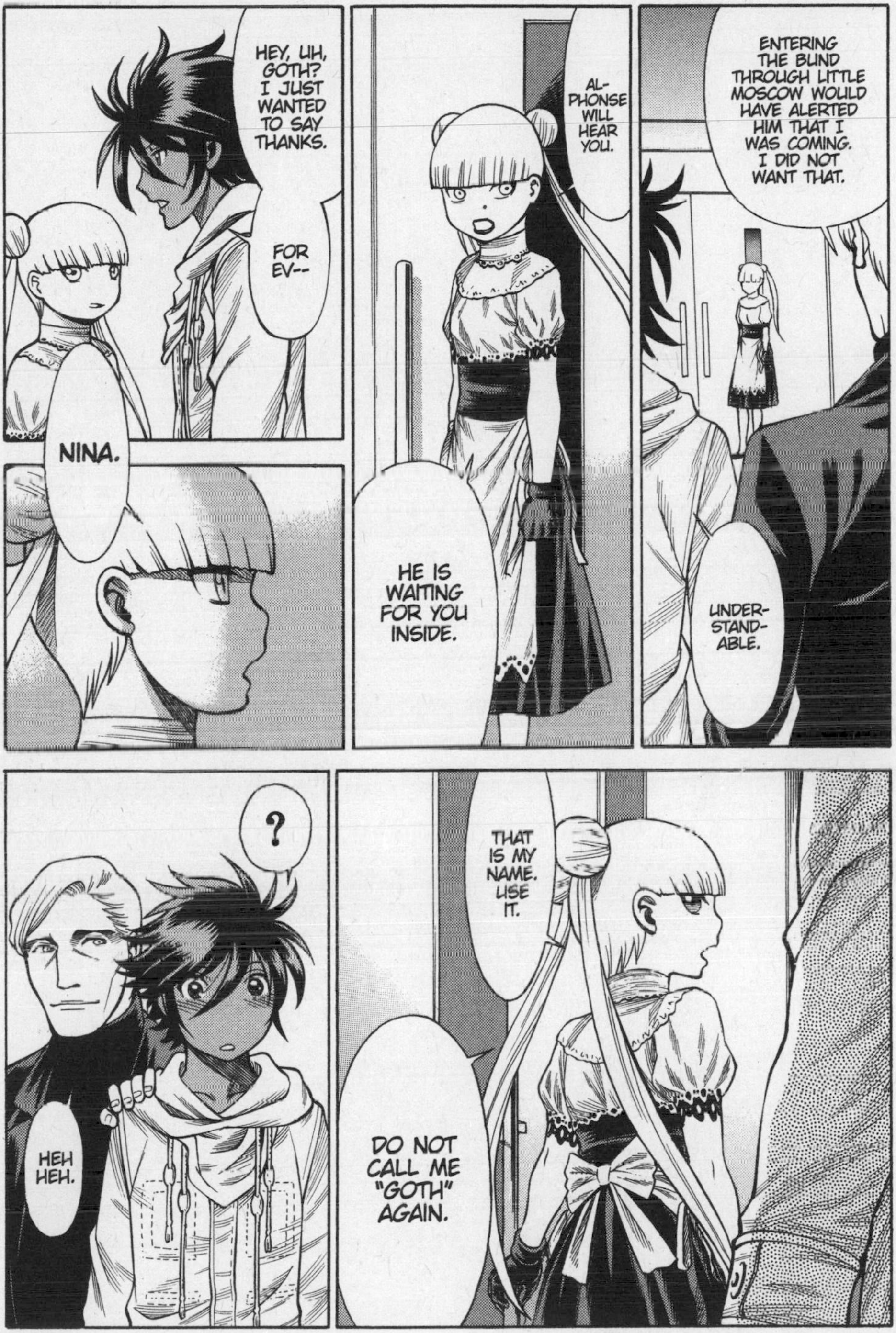
ENTERING THE BUND THROUGH LITTLE MOSCOW WOULD HAVE ALERTED HIM THAT I WAS COMING. I DID NOT WANT THAT.
UNDER-STAND-ABLE.
AL-PHONSE WILL HEAR YOU.
HE IS WAITING FOR YOU INSIDE.
HEY, UH, GOTH? I JUST WANTED TO SAY THANKS.
FOR EV--
NINA.
THAT IS MY NAME. USE IT.
DO NOT CALL ME "GOTH" AGAIN.
?
HEH HEH.

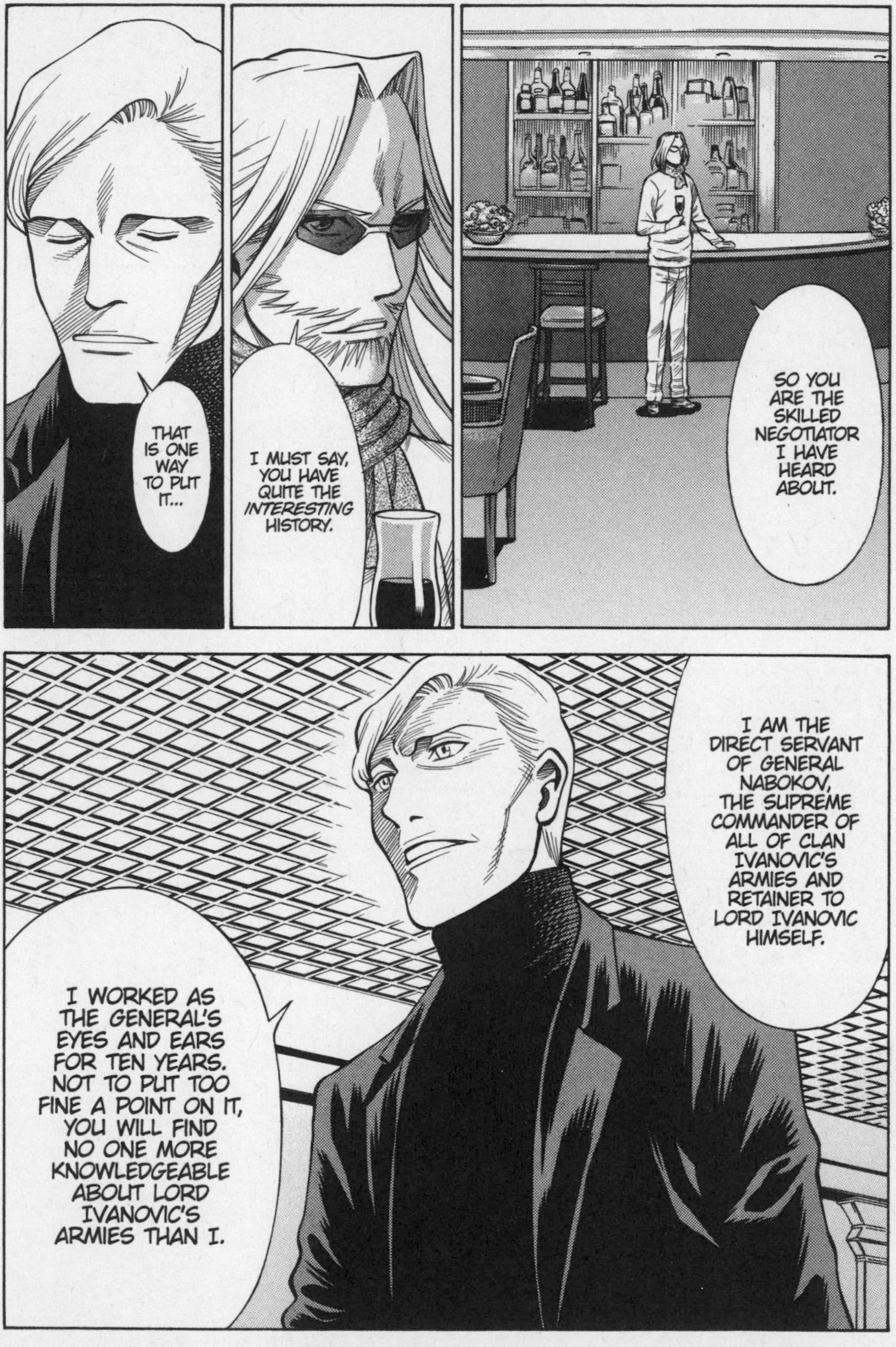
SO YOU ARE THE SKILLED NEGOTIATOR I HAVE HEARD ABOUT.
I MUST SAY, YOU HAVE QUITE THE *INTERESTING* HISTORY.
THAT IS ONE WAY TO PUT IT...
I AM THE DIRECT SERVANT OF GENERAL NABOKOV, THE SUPREME COMMANDER OF ALL OF CLAN IVANOVIC'S ARMIES AND RETAINER TO LORD IVANOVIC HIMSELF.
I WORKED AS THE GENERAL'S EYES AND EARS FOR TEN YEARS. NOT TO PUT TOO FINE A POINT ON IT, YOU WILL FIND NO ONE MORE KNOWLEDGEABLE ABOUT LORD IVANOVIC'S ARMIES THAN I.

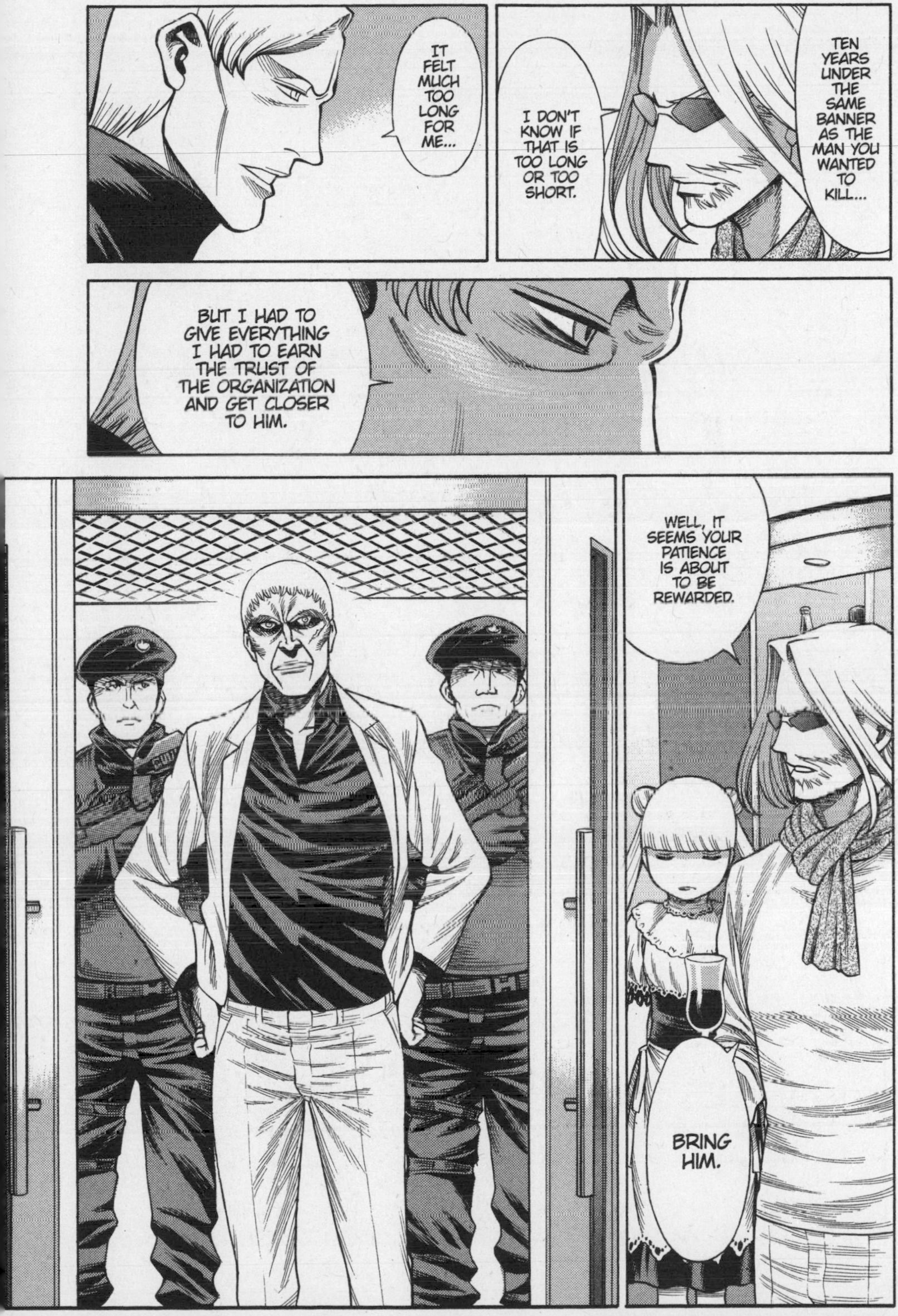
TEN YEARS UNDER THE SAME BANNER AS THE MAN YOU WANTED TO KILL...
I DON'T KNOW IF THAT IS TOO LONG OR TOO SHORT.
IT FELT MUCH TOO LONG FOR ME...
BUT I HAD TO GIVE EVERYTHING I HAD TO EARN THE TRUST OF THE ORGANIZATION AND GET CLOSER TO HIM.
WELL, IT SEEMS YOUR PATIENCE IS ABOUT TO BE REWARDED.
BRING HIM.

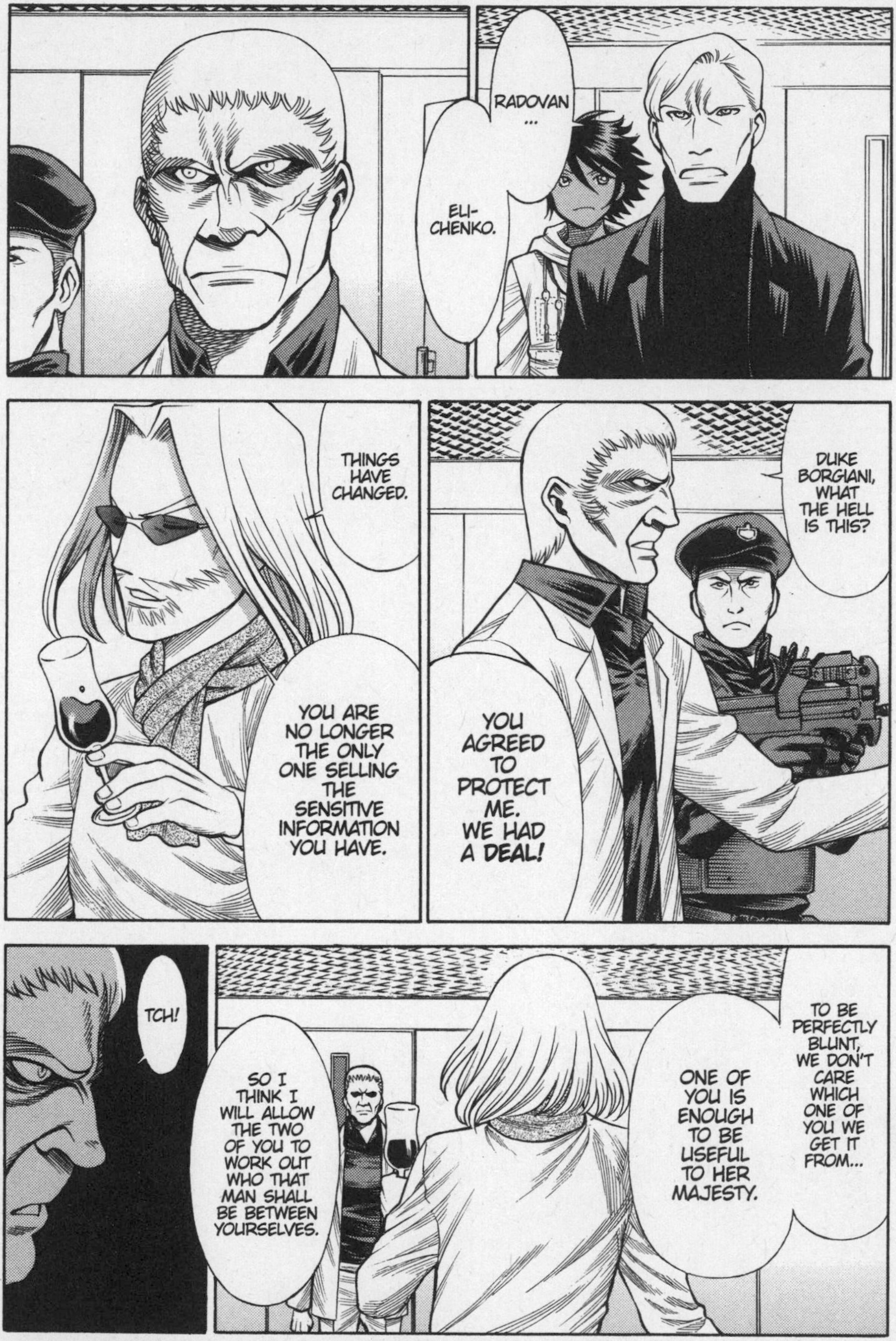
RADOVAN ...
ELI-CHENKO.
DUKE BORGIANI, WHAT THE HELL IS THIS?
YOU AGREED TO PROTECT ME. WE HAD A DEAL!
THINGS HAVE CHANGED.
YOU ARE NO LONGER THE ONLY ONE SELLING THE SENSITIVE INFORMATION YOU HAVE.
TO BE PERFECTLY BLUNT, WE DON'T CARE WHICH ONE OF YOU WE GET IT FROM...
ONE OF YOU IS ENOUGH TO BE USEFUL TO HER MAJESTY.
SO I THINK I WILL ALLOW THE TWO OF YOU TO WORK OUT WHO THAT MAN SHALL BE BETWEEN YOURSELVES.
TCH!

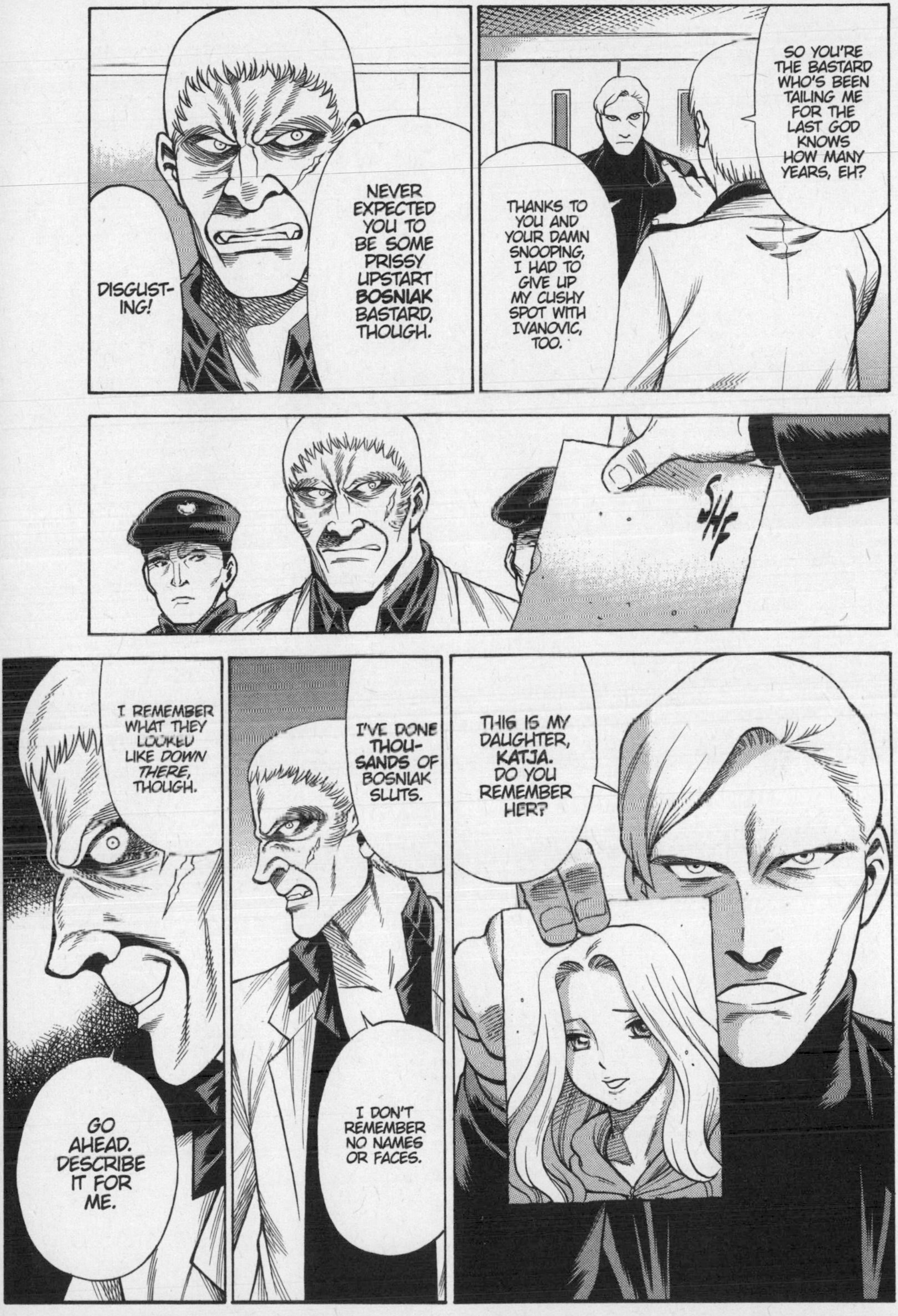
SO YOU'RE THE BASTARD WHO'S BEEN TAILING ME FOR THE LAST GOD KNOWS HOW MANY YEARS, EH?
THANKS TO YOU AND YOUR DAMN SNOOPING, I HAD TO GIVE UP MY CUSHY SPOT WITH IVANOVIC, TOO.
NEVER EXPECTED YOU TO BE SOME PRISSY UPSTART **BOSNIAK** BASTARD, THOUGH.
DISGUSTING!
SHF
THIS IS MY DAUGHTER, **KATJA**. DO YOU REMEMBER HER?
I'VE DONE **THOUSANDS** OF BOSNIAK SLUTS.
I DON'T REMEMBER NO NAMES OR FACES.
I REMEMBER WHAT THEY LOOKED LIKE *DOWN THERE*, THOUGH.
GO AHEAD. DESCRIBE IT FOR ME.

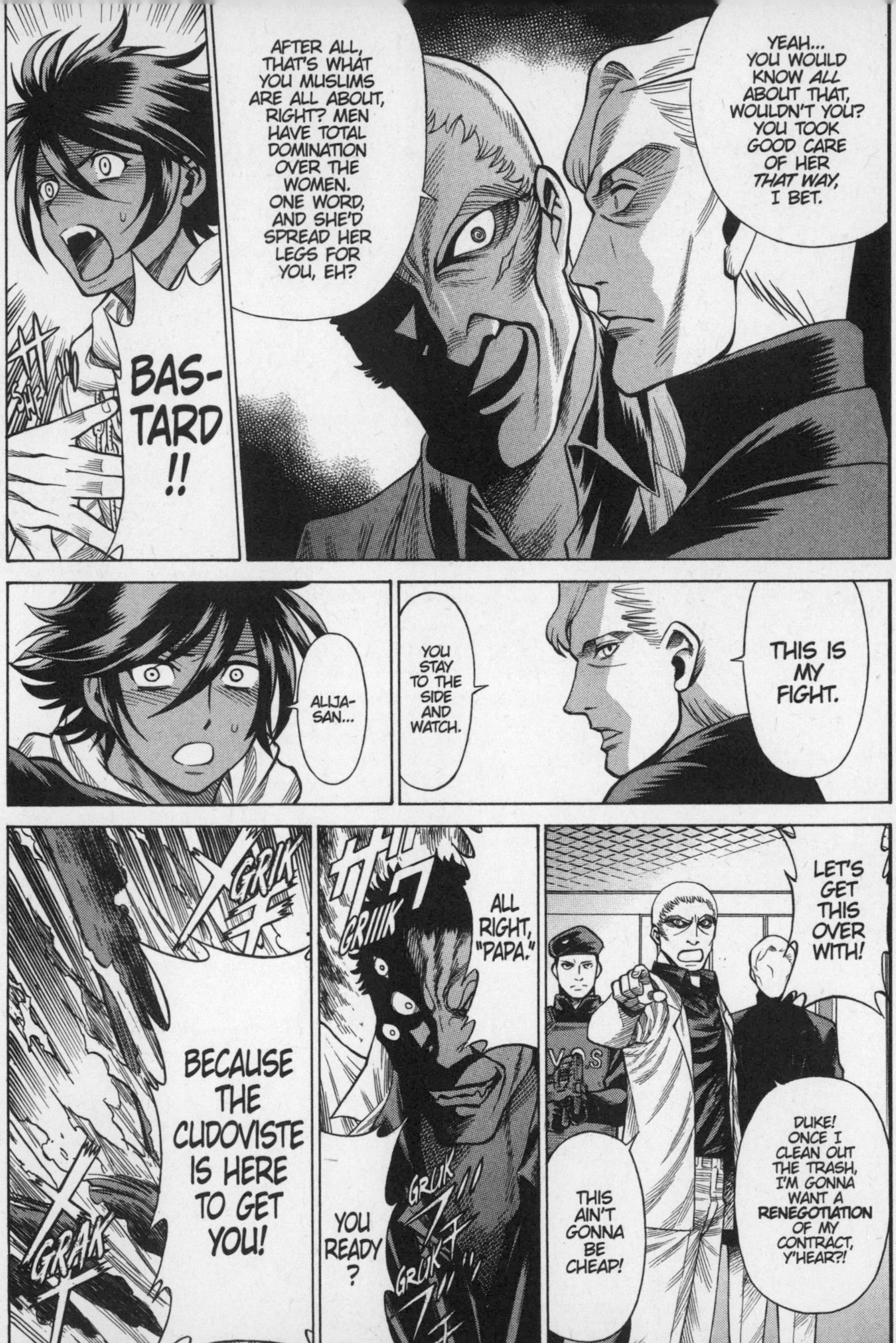
YEAH... YOU WOULD KNOW ALL ABOUT THAT, WOULDN'T YOU? YOU TOOK GOOD CARE OF HER THAT WAY, I BET.
AFTER ALL, THAT'S WHAT YOU MUSLIMS ARE ALL ABOUT, RIGHT? MEN HAVE TOTAL DOMINATION OVER THE WOMEN. ONE WORD, AND SHE'D SPREAD HER LEGS FOR YOU, EH?
BAS-TARD!!
SHA
THIS IS MY FIGHT.
YOU STAY TO THE SIDE AND WATCH.
ALIJA-SAN...
LET'S GET THIS OVER WITH!
DUKE! ONCE I CLEAN OUT THE TRASH, I'M GONNA WANT A RENEGOTIATION OF MY CONTRACT, Y'HEAR?!
THIS AIN'T GONNA BE CHEAP!
ALL RIGHT, "PAPA."
GRIIIK
YOU READY?
GRUK
GRUK
GRIK
BECAUSE THE CUDOVISTE IS HERE TO GET YOU!
GRAK

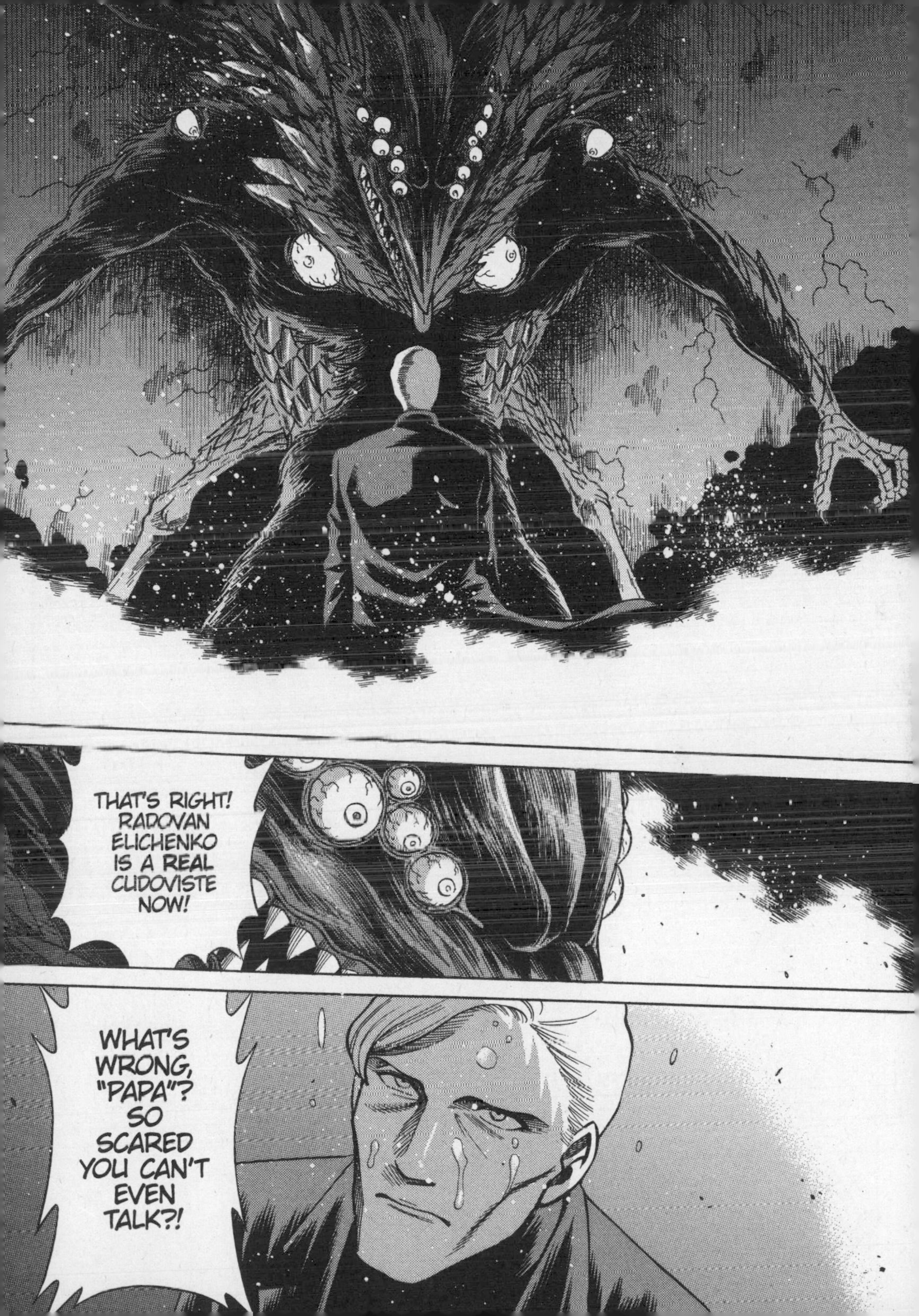
THAT'S RIGHT! RADOVAN ELICHENKO IS A REAL CUDOVISTE NOW!
WHAT'S WRONG, "PAPA"? SO SCARED YOU CAN'T EVEN TALK?!

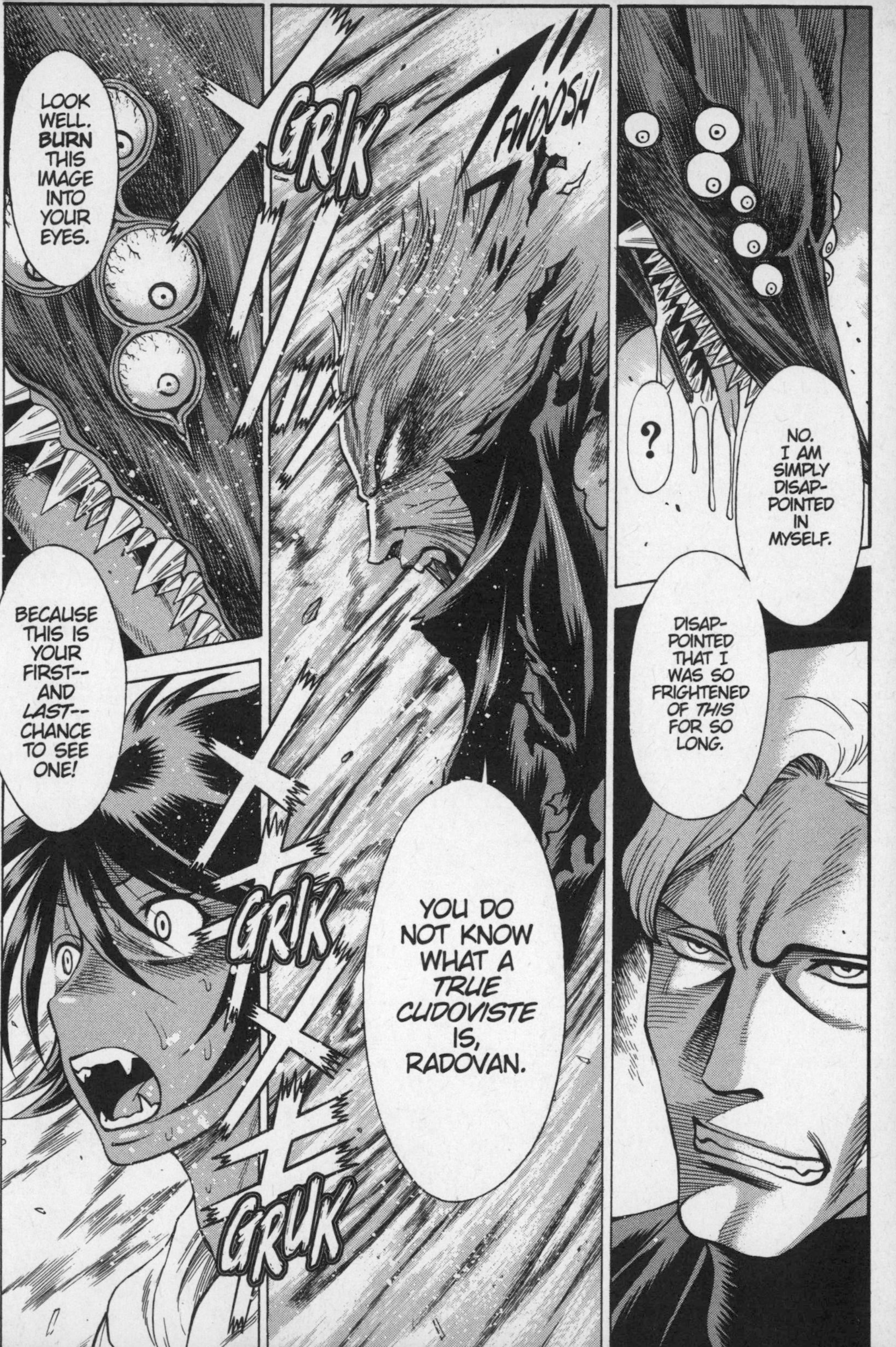
NO. I AM SIMPLY DISAP-POINTED IN MYSELF.
?
DISAP-POINTED THAT I WAS SO FRIGHTENED OF *THIS* FOR SO LONG.
FWOOSH
GRIK
YOU DO NOT KNOW WHAT A *TRUE* CUDOVISTE IS, RADOVAN.
GRIK
GRUK
LOOK WELL. BURN THIS IMAGE INTO YOUR EYES.
BECAUSE THIS IS YOUR FIRST-- AND *LAST*-- CHANCE TO SEE ONE!

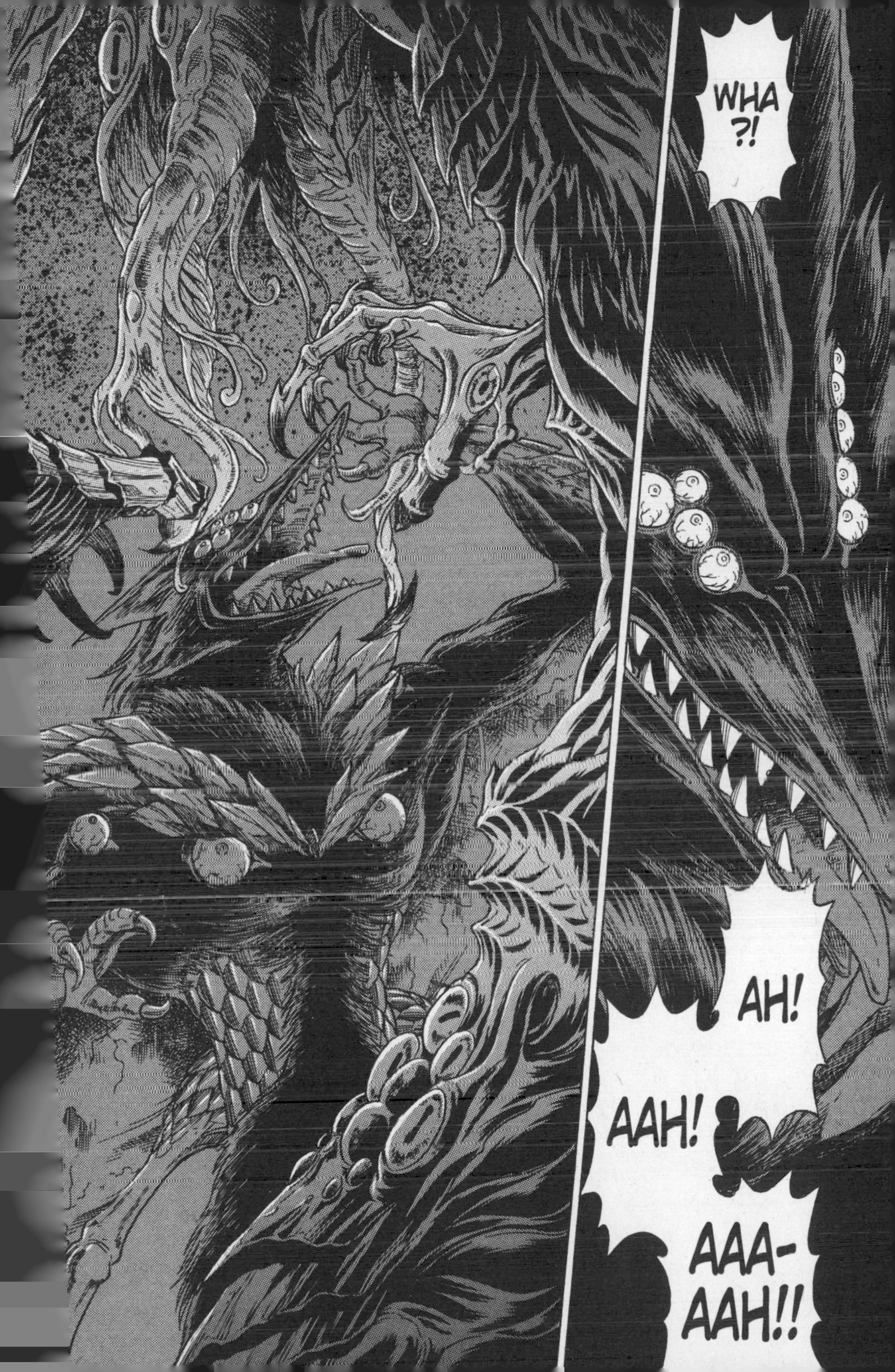
WHA ?!
AH!
AAH!
AAA-AAH!!

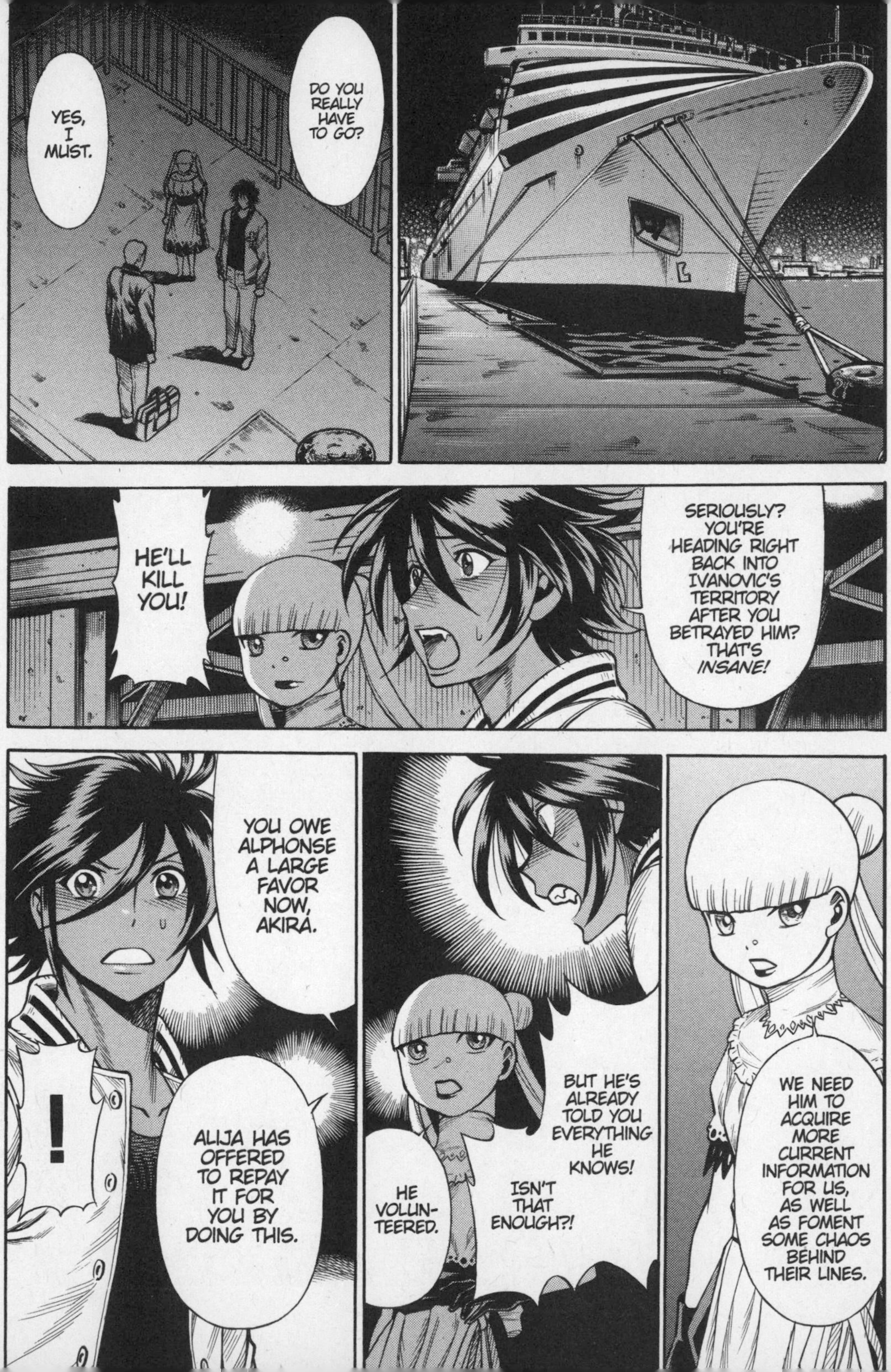
DO YOU REALLY HAVE TO GO?
YES, I MUST.
SERIOUSLY? YOU'RE HEADING RIGHT BACK INTO IVANOVIC'S TERRITORY AFTER YOU BETRAYED HIM? THAT'S *INSANE!*
HE'LL KILL YOU!
WE NEED HIM TO ACQUIRE MORE CURRENT INFORMATION FOR US, AS WELL AS FOMENT SOME CHAOS BEHIND THEIR LINES.
BUT HE'S ALREADY TOLD YOU EVERYTHING HE KNOWS!
ISN'T THAT ENOUGH?!
HE VOLUN-TEERED.
YOU OWE ALPHONSE A LARGE FAVOR NOW, AKIRA.
!
ALIJA HAS OFFERED TO REPAY IT FOR YOU BY DOING THIS.

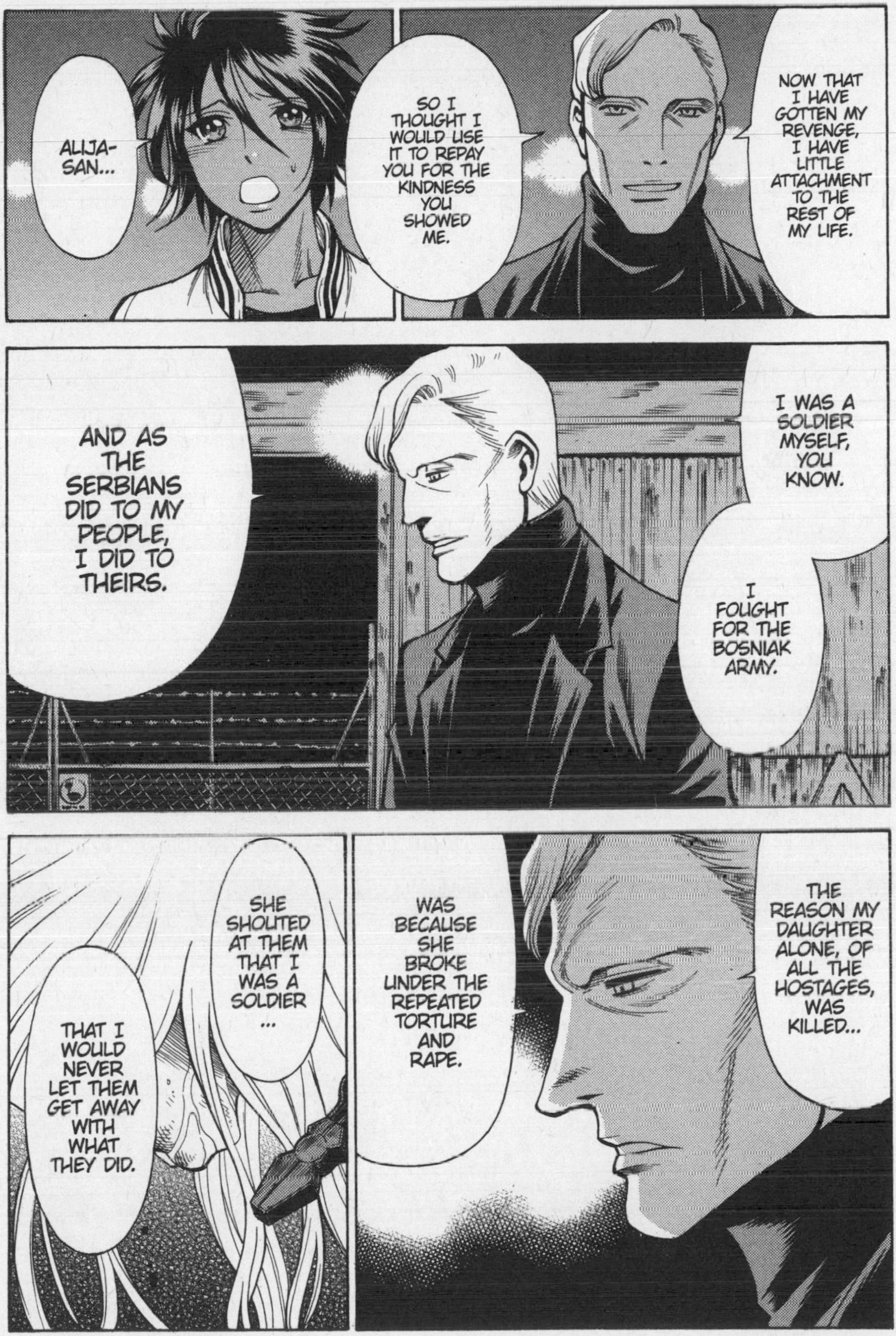
NOW THAT I HAVE GOTTEN MY REVENGE, I HAVE LITTLE ATTACHMENT TO THE REST OF MY LIFE.
SO I THOUGHT I WOULD USE IT TO REPAY YOU FOR THE KINDNESS YOU SHOWED ME.
ALIJA-SAN...
I WAS A SOLDIER MYSELF, YOU KNOW.
I FOUGHT FOR THE BOSNIAK ARMY.
AND AS THE SERBIANS DID TO MY PEOPLE, I DID TO THEIRS.
THE REASON MY DAUGHTER ALONE, OF ALL THE HOSTAGES, WAS KILLED...
WAS BECAUSE SHE BROKE UNDER THE REPEATED TORTURE AND RAPE.
SHE SHOUTED AT THEM THAT I WAS A SOLDIER...
THAT I WOULD NEVER LET THEM GET AWAY WITH WHAT THEY DID.

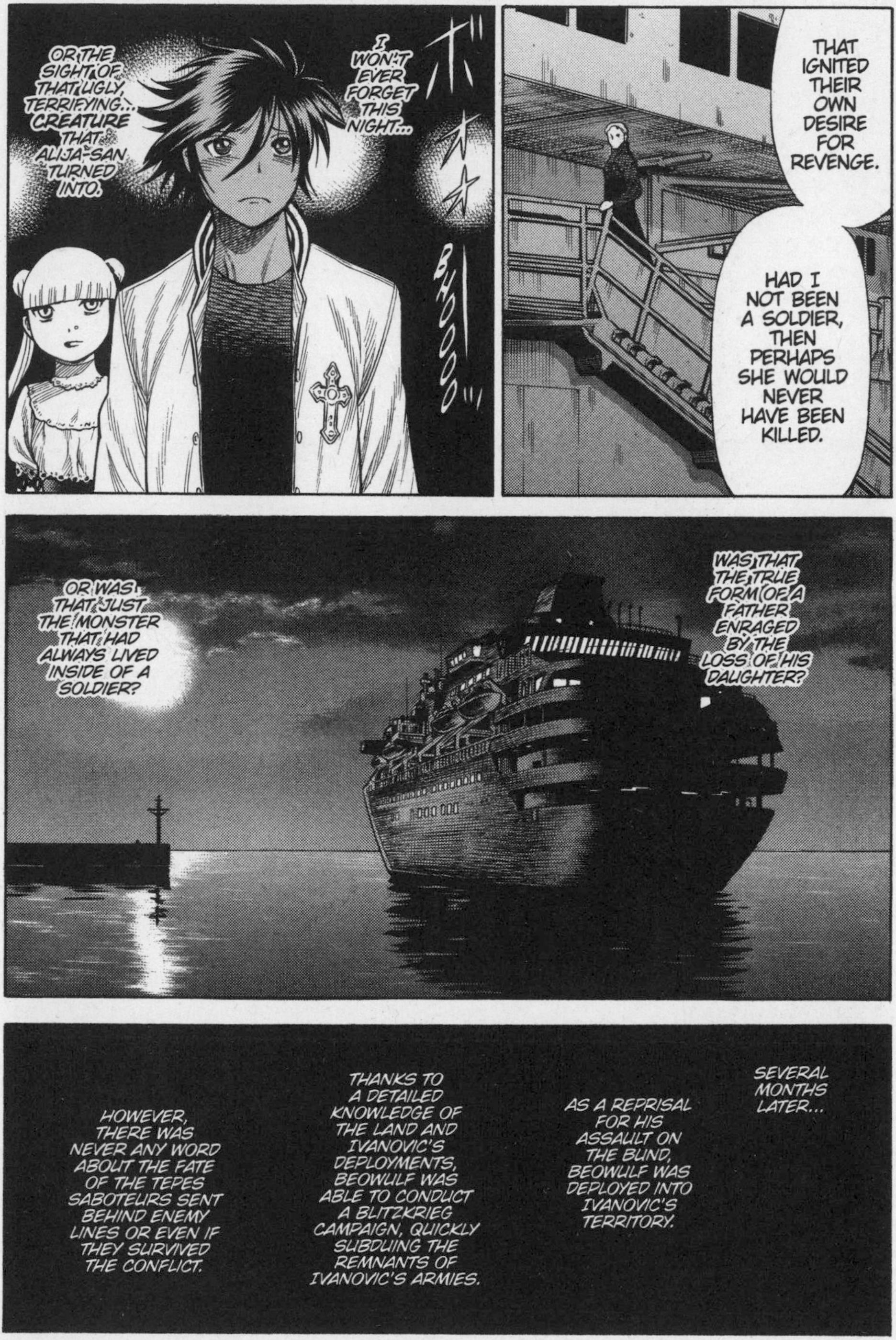
THAT IGNITED THEIR OWN DESIRE FOR REVENGE.
HAD I NOT BEEN A SOLDIER, THEN PERHAPS SHE WOULD NEVER HAVE BEEN KILLED.
BHOOOOO!!
I WON'T EVER FORGET THIS NIGHT...
OR THE SIGHT OF THAT UGLY, TERRIFYING... CREATURE THAT ALIJA-SAN TURNED INTO.
WAS THAT THE TRUE FORM OF A FATHER ENRAGED BY THE LOSS OF HIS DAUGHTER?
OR WAS THAT JUST THE MONSTER THAT HAD ALWAYS LIVED INSIDE OF A SOLDIER?
SEVERAL MONTHS LATER...
AS A REPRISAL FOR HIS ASSAULT ON THE BUND, BEOWULF WAS DEPLOYED INTO IVANOVIC'S TERRITORY.
THANKS TO A DETAILED KNOWLEDGE OF THE LAND AND IVANOVIC'S DEPLOYMENTS, BEOWULF WAS ABLE TO CONDUCT A BLITZKRIEG CAMPAIGN, QUICKLY SUBDUING THE REMNANTS OF IVANOVIC'S ARMIES.
HOWEVER, THERE WAS NEVER ANY WORD ABOUT THE FATE OF THE TEPES SABOTEURS SENT BEHIND ENEMY LINES OR EVEN IF THEY SURVIVED THE CONFLICT.

ETHNIC CLEANSING

Bosnia-Herzegovina was a country where many different ethnicities lived, jumbled together in the same areas. If the Bosniaks and the Serbs had lived in concentrated groups separate from each other, they would have been able to form their own separate countries unhindered, and their bloody civil war might never have taken place. During the war, each side was doing as much as they could to increase their own territory, at the expense of the others. They also tried to homogenize their territories by getting rid of any people of the other ethnic groups still living there. The method the various new governments turned to most often to accomplish this was "ethnic cleansing."

"Ethnic cleansing" means oppression and violent persecution of foreign ethnicities, usually by government or military forces, giving the foreign ethnicities no choice but to leave. As it escalates, it can lead to forced relocations of large populations, mass confiscation of property, and genocide. The Holocaust is a prime example of ethnic cleansing on that level.

During the Bosnian War, Serbian persecution of the Bosniaks was rampant. Thousands upon thousands of young Bosniak men were killed, while the young women were kidnapped, beaten, and raped. They were raped with the intention of getting them pregnant, and then confined until shortly before they were due, so that the women could not have the children aborted. They would be forced to bear them. Bosniaks are devout followers of Islam, and their society is a heavily patriarchal one. Menfolk have complete control of the household, and their women are expected to be docile. The thought of their wives and daughters being subjected to torture at the hands of Serbians was too much for many Bosniaks to take. They quickly began seeking refuge elsewhere, letting the Serbians move in and easily take over their territories.

The most terrifying aspect of the ethnic cleansing during the Bosnian War was how organized and efficient it was, and how it was conducted publicly by government officials. Like Radovan in the main storyline, there were many Serbians who participated in the cleansings because they were police officers who were ordered to do so.

After the end of the war, many of those who participated in the cleansings were brought before international court as war criminals. However, few were ever punished. Most escaped, and their whereabouts are still unknown to this day.

Later, in 1998, during the Kosovo War, the Serbians were persecuted at the hands of the Albanians, much as the Serbians had earlier persecuted the Bosniaks. Though they were the same ethnicity, being in a different country drastically changed their position.

These wars are truly an example of conflicts where no one was innocent, and everyone had blood on their hands.

DIVE IN THE VAMPIRE BUND

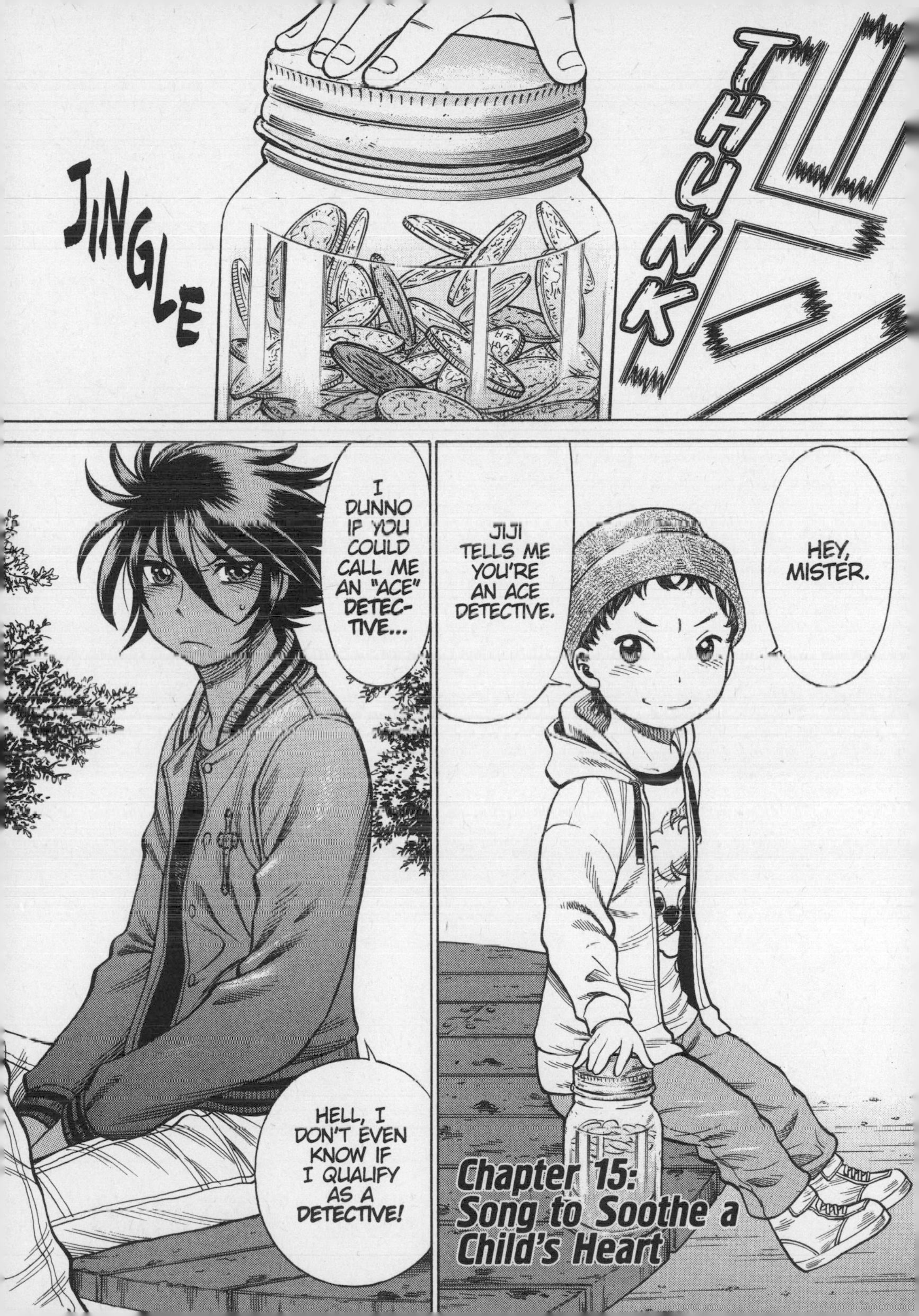
THUNK
JINGLE
HEY, MISTER.
JIJI TELLS ME YOU'RE AN ACE DETECTIVE.
Chapter 15: Song to Soothe a Child's Heart
I DUNNO IF YOU COULD CALL ME AN "ACE" DETEC-TIVE...
HELL, I DON'T EVEN KNOW IF I QUALIFY AS A DETECTIVE!

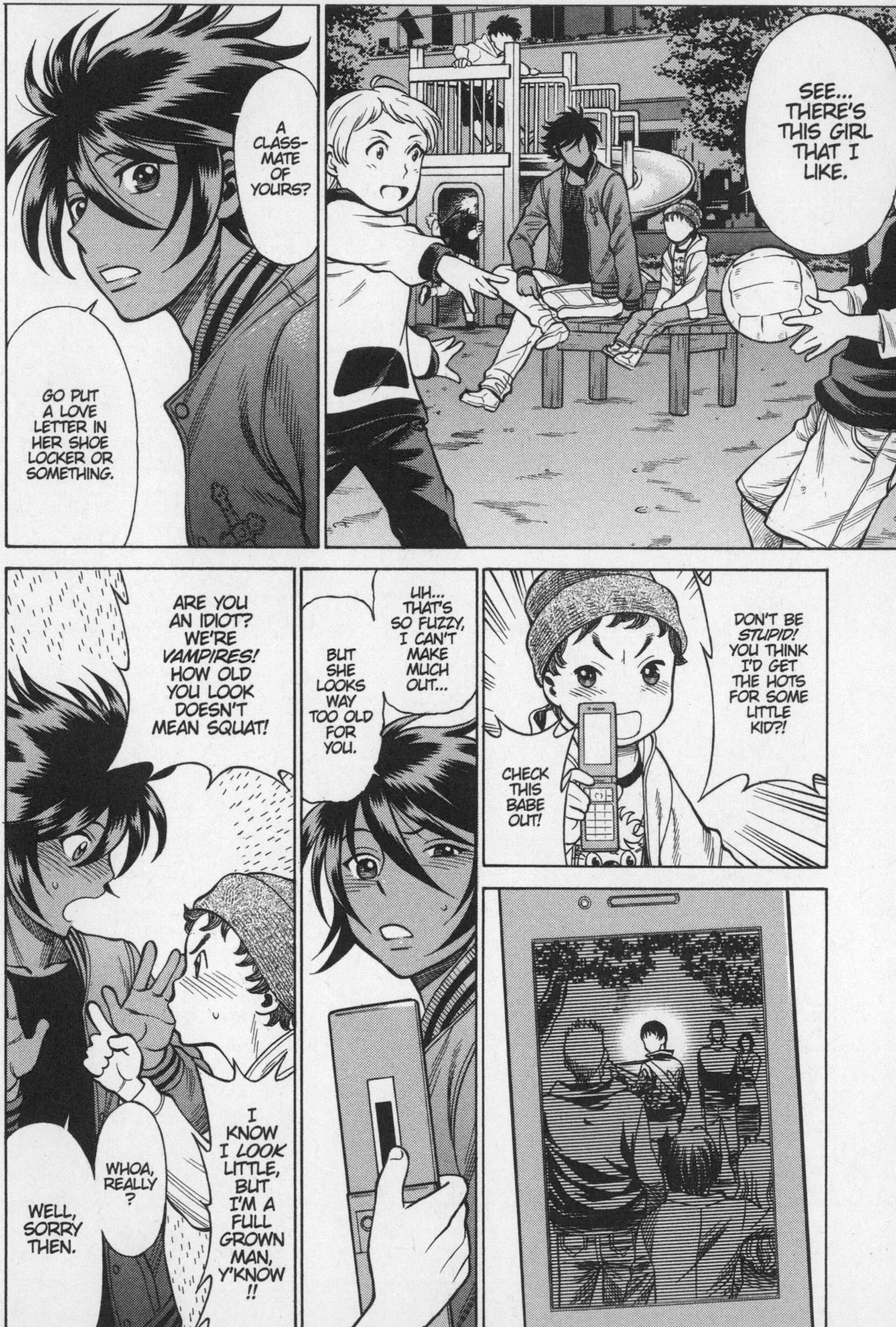
SEE... THERE'S THIS GIRL THAT I LIKE.
A CLASS-MATE OF YOURS?
GO PUT A LOVE LETTER IN HER SHOE LOCKER OR SOMETHING.
DON'T BE *STUPID!* YOU THINK I'D GET THE HOTS FOR SOME LITTLE KID?!
CHECK THIS BABE OUT!
UH... THAT'S SO FUZZY, I CAN'T MAKE MUCH OUT...
BUT SHE LOOKS WAY TOO OLD FOR YOU.
ARE YOU AN IDIOT? WE'RE *VAMPIRES!* HOW OLD YOU LOOK DOESN'T MEAN SQUAT!
I KNOW I *LOOK* LITTLE, BUT I'M A FULL GROWN MAN, Y'KNOW!!
WHOA, REALLY?
WELL, SORRY THEN.

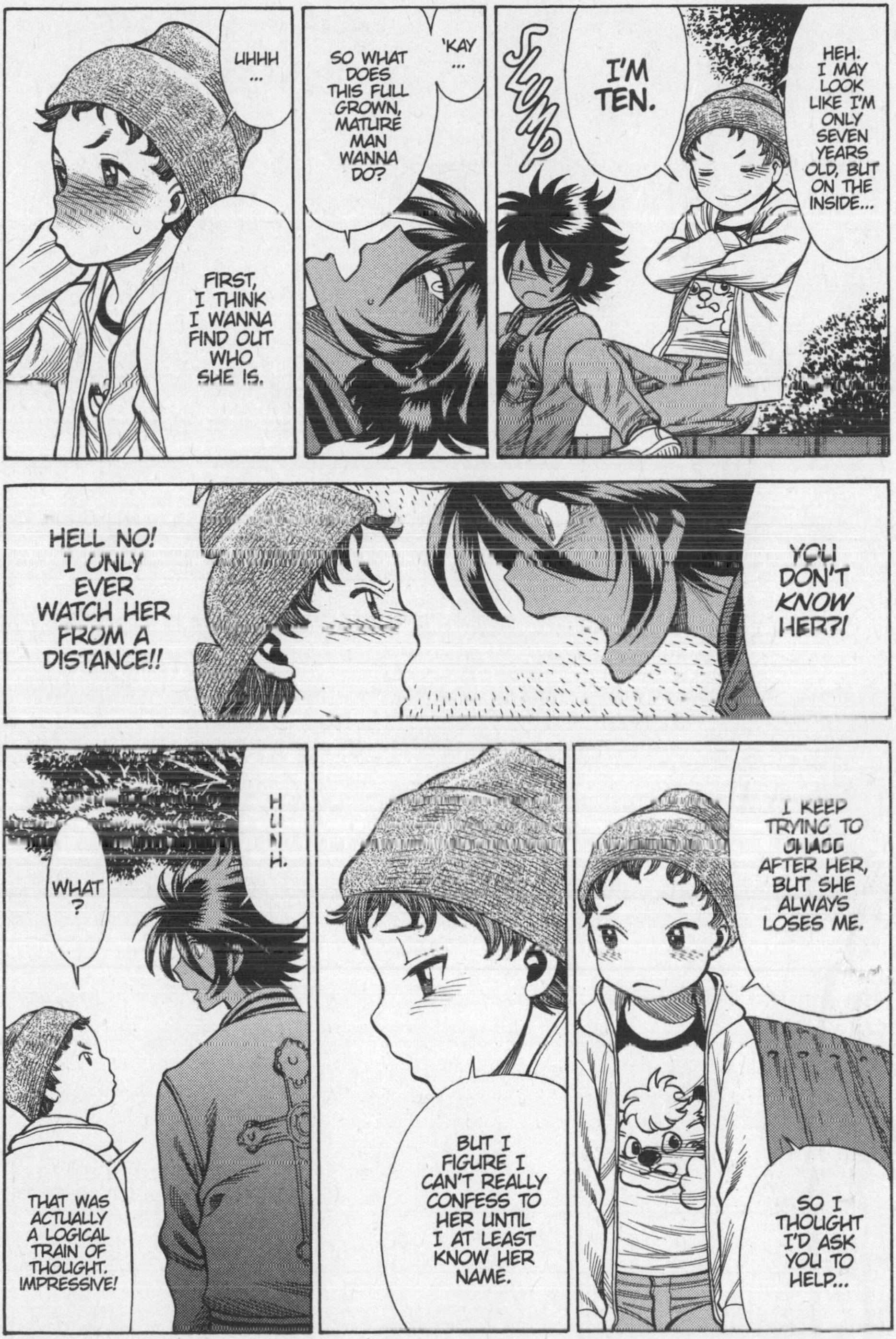
HEH. I MAY LOOK LIKE I'M ONLY SEVEN YEARS OLD, BUT ON THE INSIDE...
I'M TEN.
SLUMP
'KAY ...
SO WHAT DOES THIS FULL GROWN, MATURE MAN WANNA DO?
UHHH ...
FIRST, I THINK I WANNA FIND OUT WHO SHE IS.
YOU DON'T KNOW HER?!
HELL NO! I ONLY EVER WATCH HER FROM A DISTANCE!!
I KEEP TRYING TO CHASE AFTER HER, BUT SHE ALWAYS LOSES ME.
SO I THOUGHT I'D ASK YOU TO HELP...
BUT I FIGURE I CAN'T REALLY CONFESS TO HER UNTIL I AT LEAST KNOW HER NAME.
HUNH.
WHAT ?
THAT WAS ACTUALLY A LOGICAL TRAIN OF THOUGHT. IMPRESSIVE!

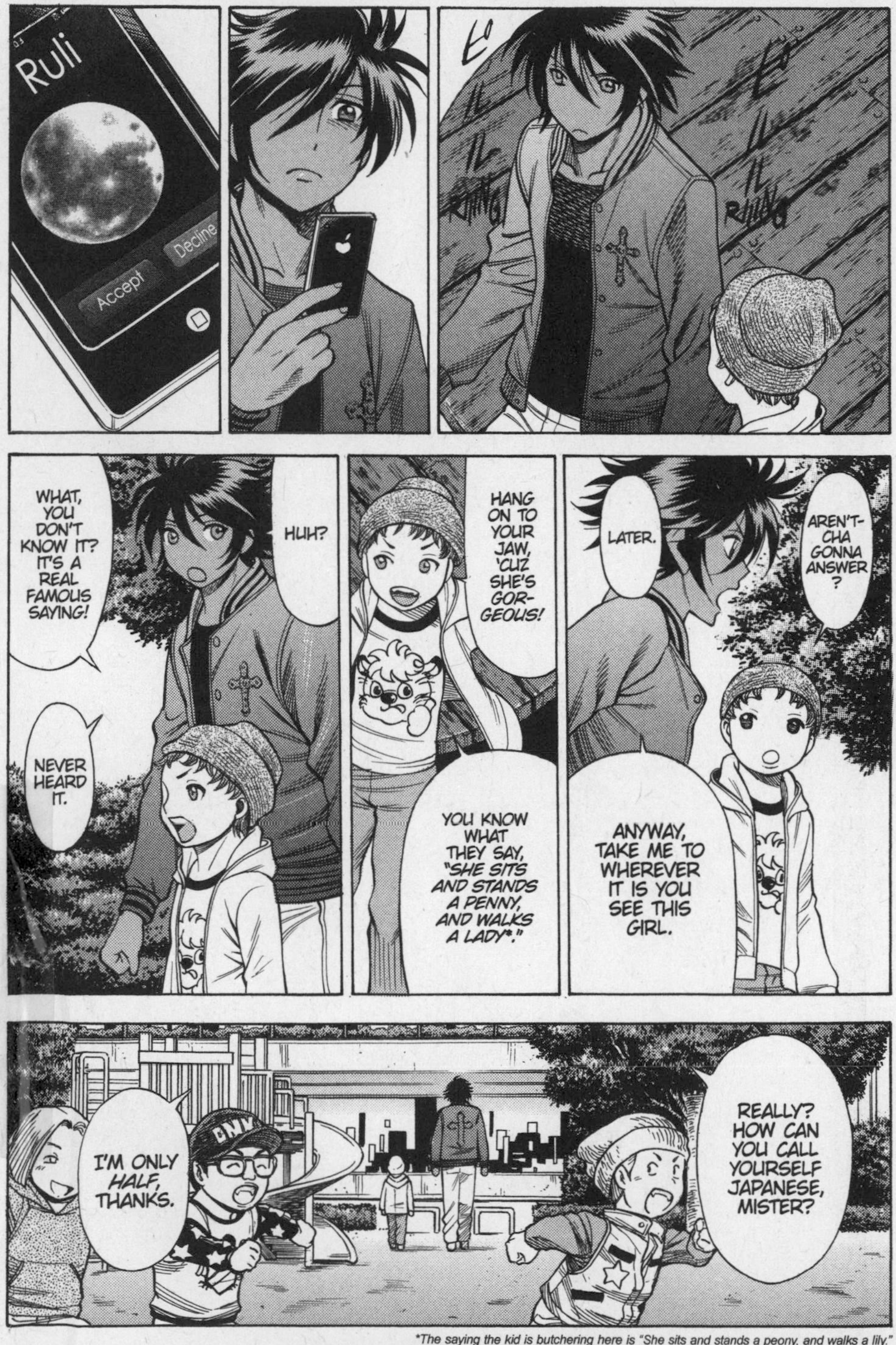
RIIING
RIIING
Ruli
Decline
Accept
AREN'T-CHA GONNA ANSWER?
LATER.
ANYWAY, TAKE ME TO WHEREVER IT IS YOU SEE THIS GIRL.
HANG ON TO YOUR JAW, 'CUZ SHE'S GORGEOUS!
YOU KNOW WHAT THEY SAY, "SHE SITS AND STANDS A PENNY, AND WALKS A LADY*."
HUH?
WHAT, YOU DON'T KNOW IT? IT'S A REAL FAMOUS SAYING!
NEVER HEARD IT.
REALLY? HOW CAN YOU CALL YOURSELF JAPANESE, MISTER?
I'M ONLY HALF, THANKS.

*The saying the kid is butchering here is "She sits and stands a peony, and walks a lily." Its meaning is that a woman is as beautiful as a flower, no matter what she is doing.

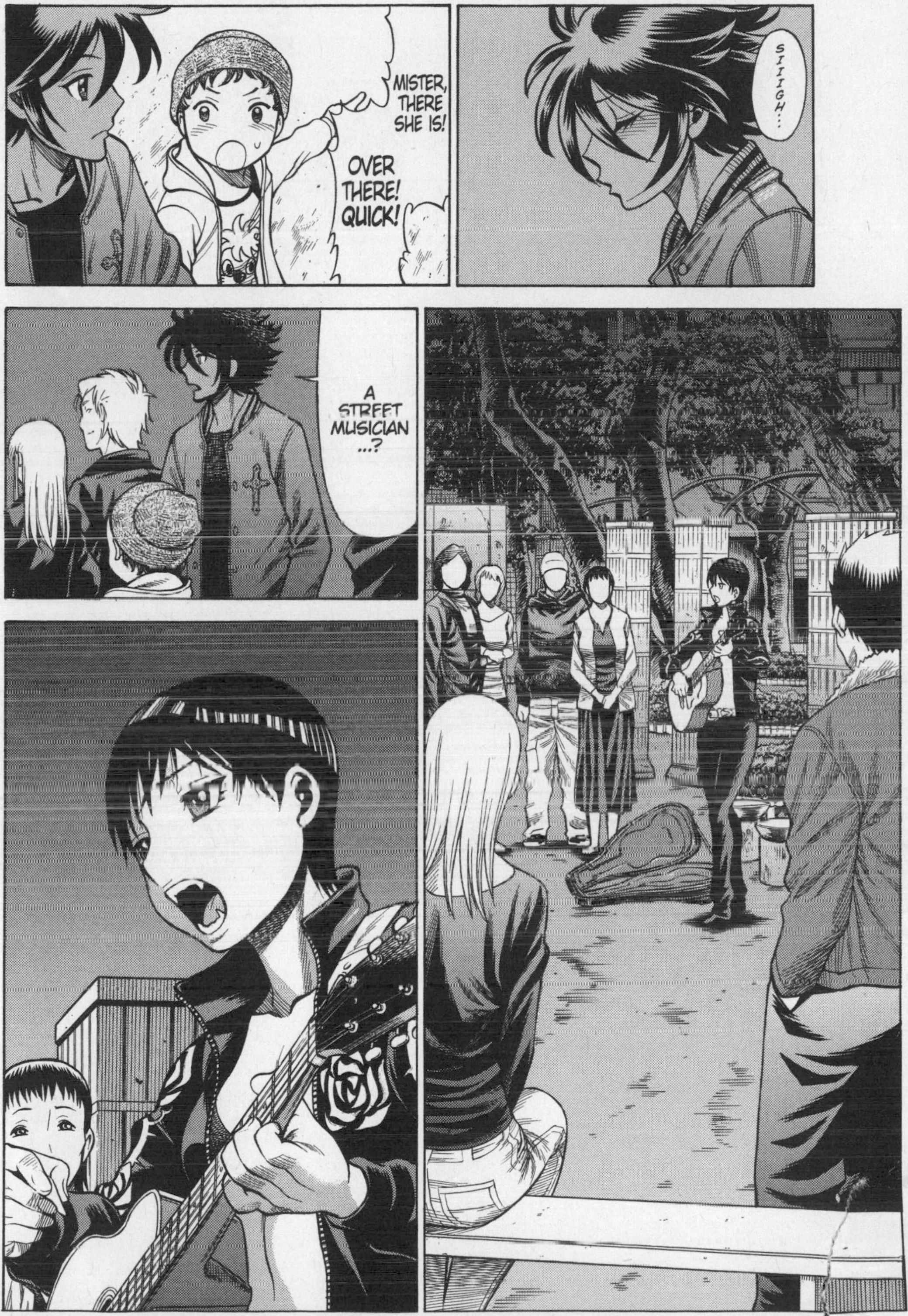
SIIIGH...
MISTER, THERE SHE IS!
OVER THERE! QUICK!
A STREET MUSICIAN ...?

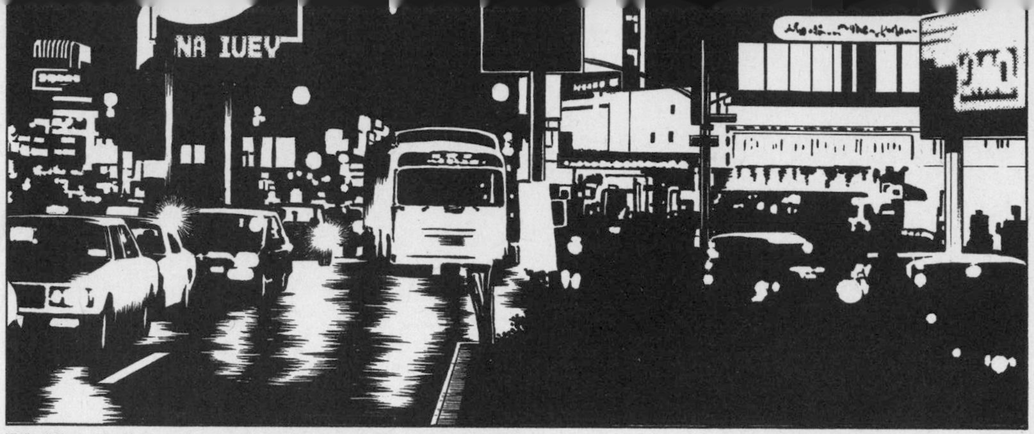

*Feijoada is a stew of beans, with pork and beef. It's considered the national dish of Brazil.

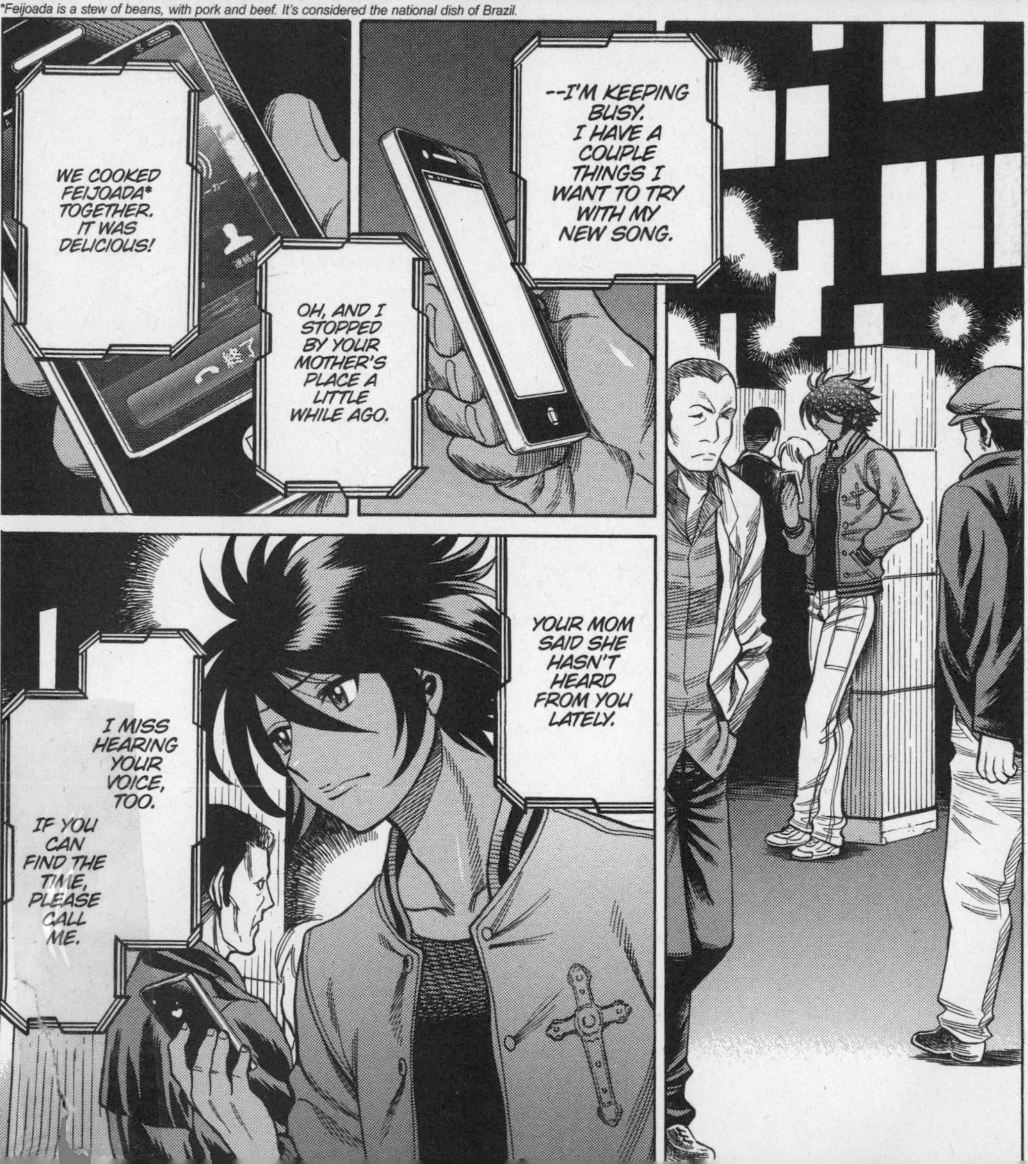
--I'M KEEPING BUSY. I HAVE A COUPLE THINGS I WANT TO TRY WITH MY NEW SONG.
OH, AND I STOPPED BY YOUR MOTHER'S PLACE A LITTLE WHILE AGO.
WE COOKED FEIJOADA* TOGETHER. IT WAS DELICIOUS!
YOUR MOM SAID SHE HASN'T HEARD FROM YOU LATELY.
I MISS HEARING YOUR VOICE, TOO.
IF YOU CAN FIND THE TIME, PLEASE CALL ME.

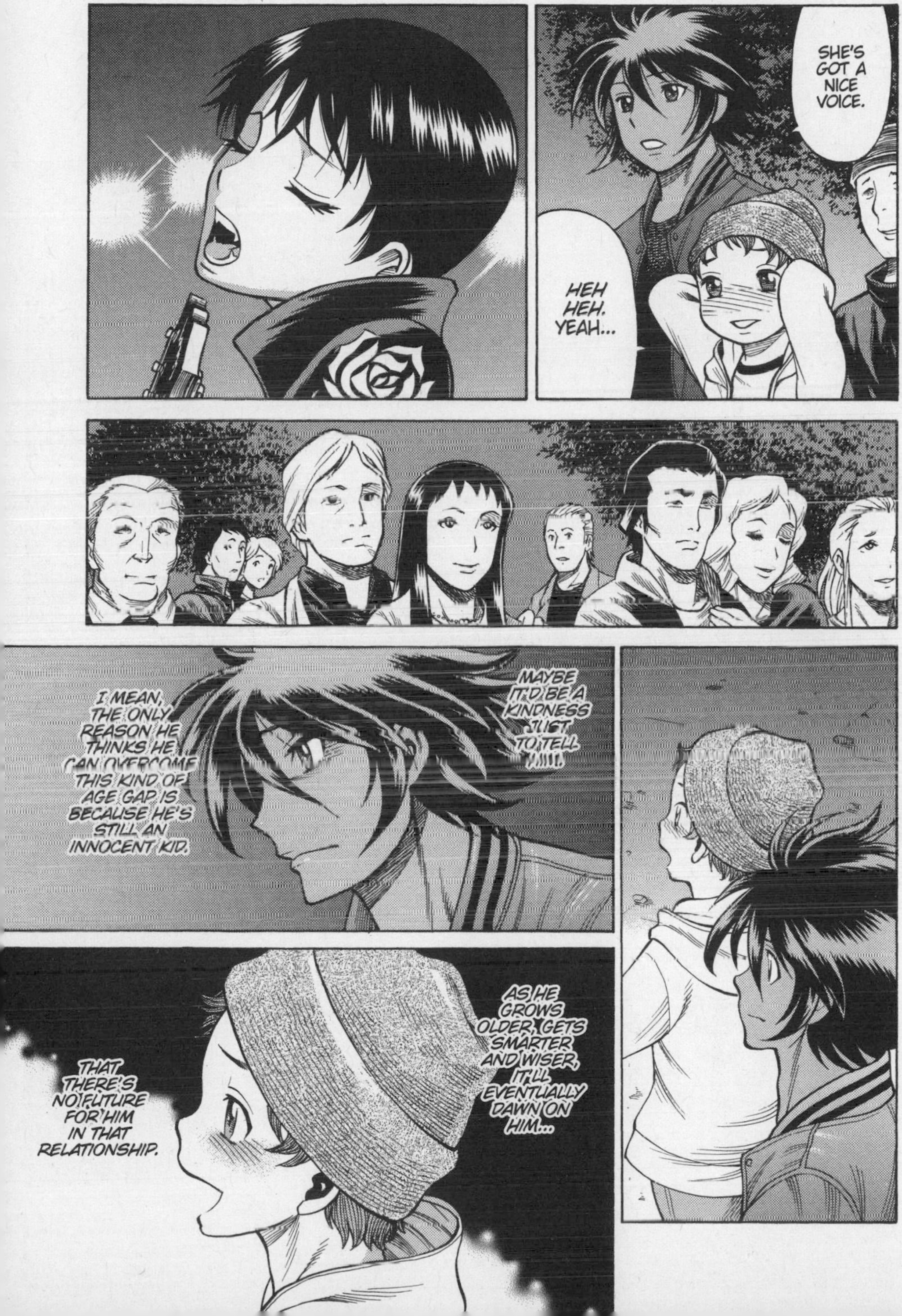
SHE'S GOT A NICE VOICE.
HEH HEH. YEAH...
MAYBE IT'D BE A KINDNESS JUST TO TELL HIM.
I MEAN, THE ONLY REASON HE THINKS HE CAN OVERCOME THIS KIND OF AGE GAP IS BECAUSE HE'S STILL AN INNOCENT KID.
AS HE GROWS OLDER, GETS SMARTER AND WISER, IT'LL EVENTUALLY DAWN ON HIM...
THAT THERE'S NO FUTURE FOR HIM IN THAT RELATIONSHIP.

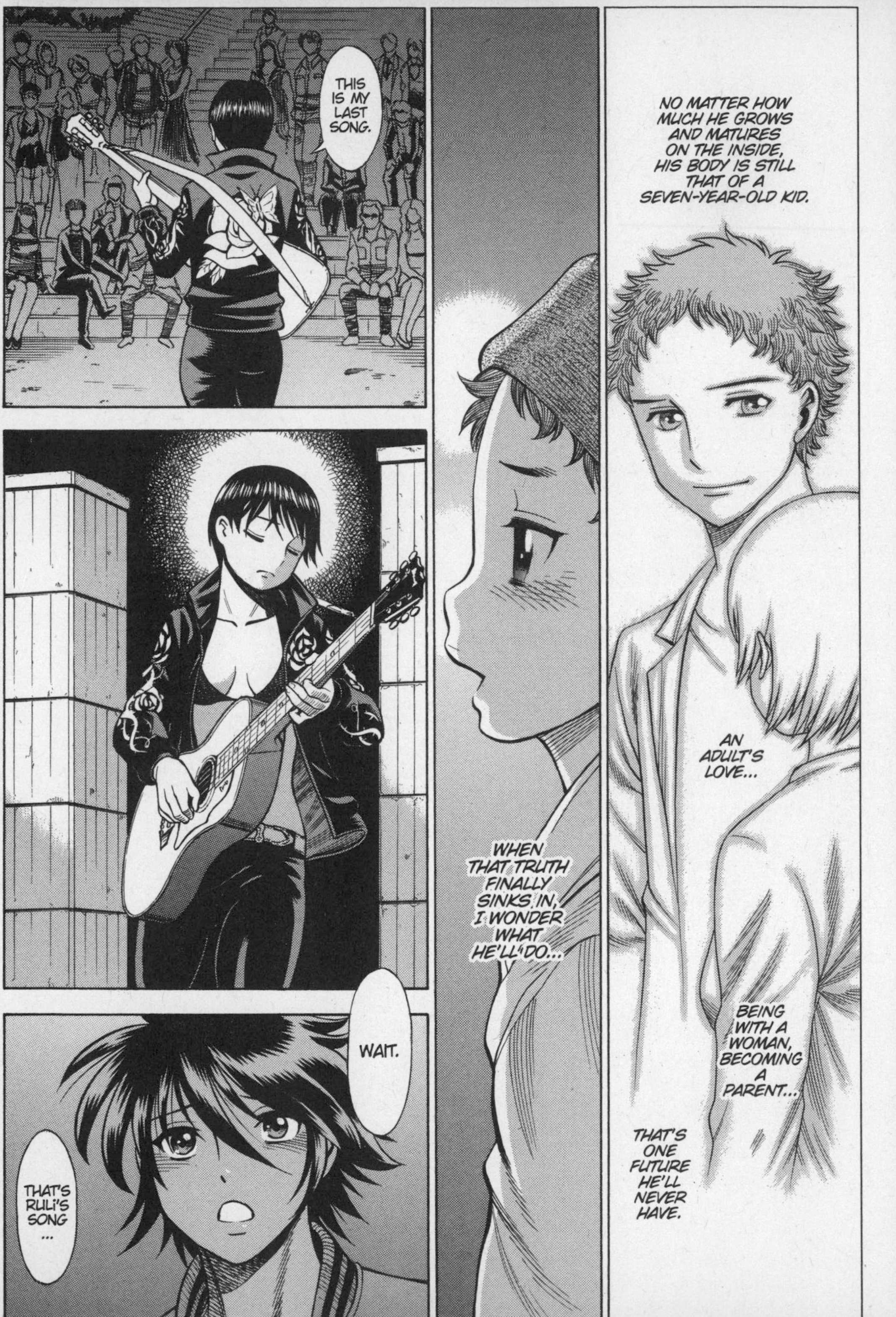

NO MATTER HOW MUCH HE GROWS AND MATURES ON THE INSIDE, HIS BODY IS STILL THAT OF A SEVEN-YEAR-OLD KID.
AN ADULT'S LOVE...
BEING WITH A WOMAN, BECOMING A PARENT...
THAT'S ONE FUTURE HE'LL NEVER HAVE.
WHEN THAT TRUTH FINALLY SINKS IN, I WONDER WHAT HE'LL DO...
THIS IS MY LAST SONG.
WAIT.
THAT'S RULi's SONG...

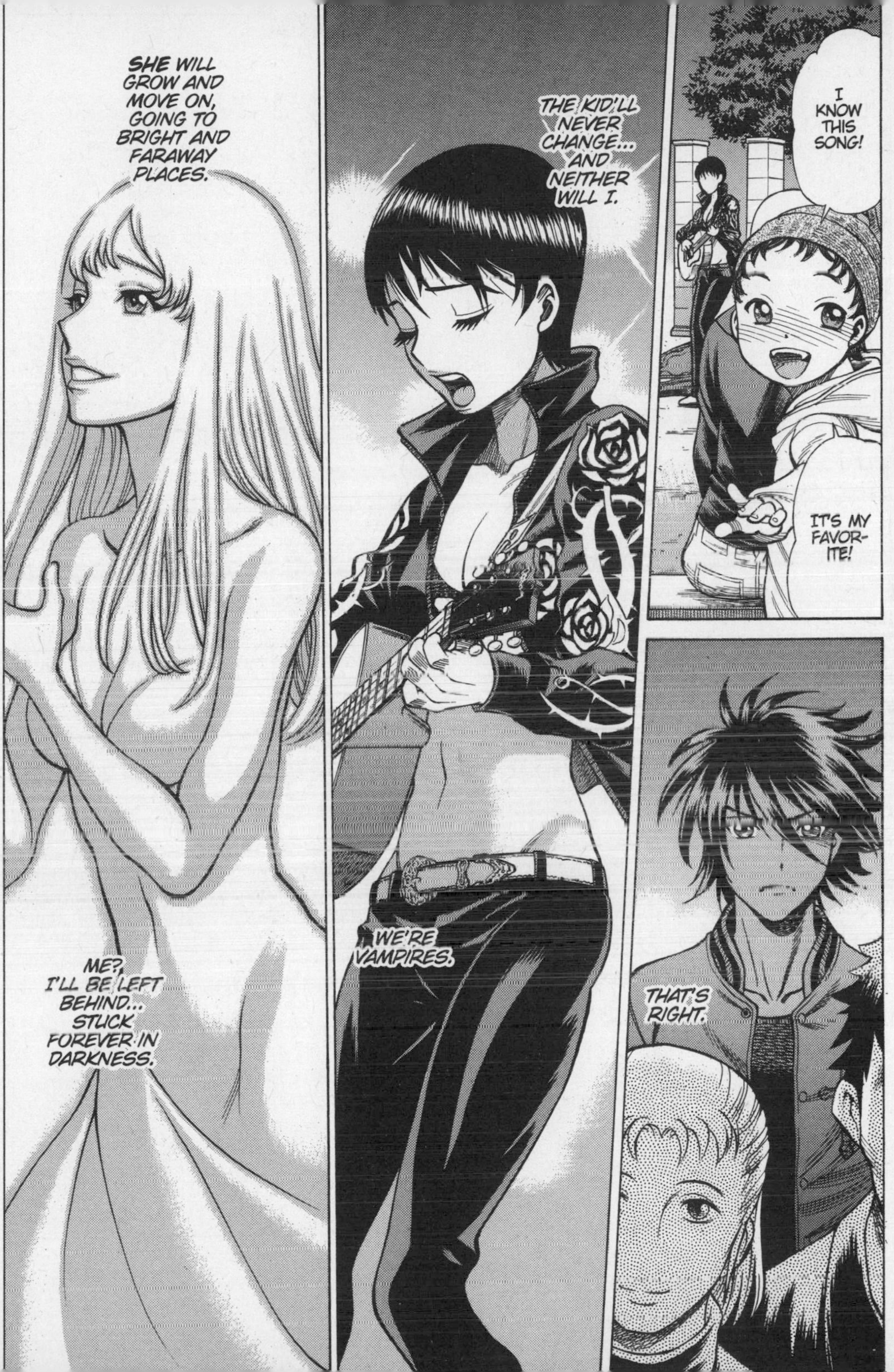
I KNOW THIS SONG!
IT'S MY FAVOR-ITE!
THAT'S RIGHT.
THE KID'LL NEVER CHANGE... AND NEITHER WILL I.
WE'RE VAMPIRES.
SHE WILL GROW AND MOVE ON, GOING TO BRIGHT AND FARAWAY PLACES.
ME?, I'LL BE LEFT BEHIND... STUCK FOREVER IN DARKNESS.

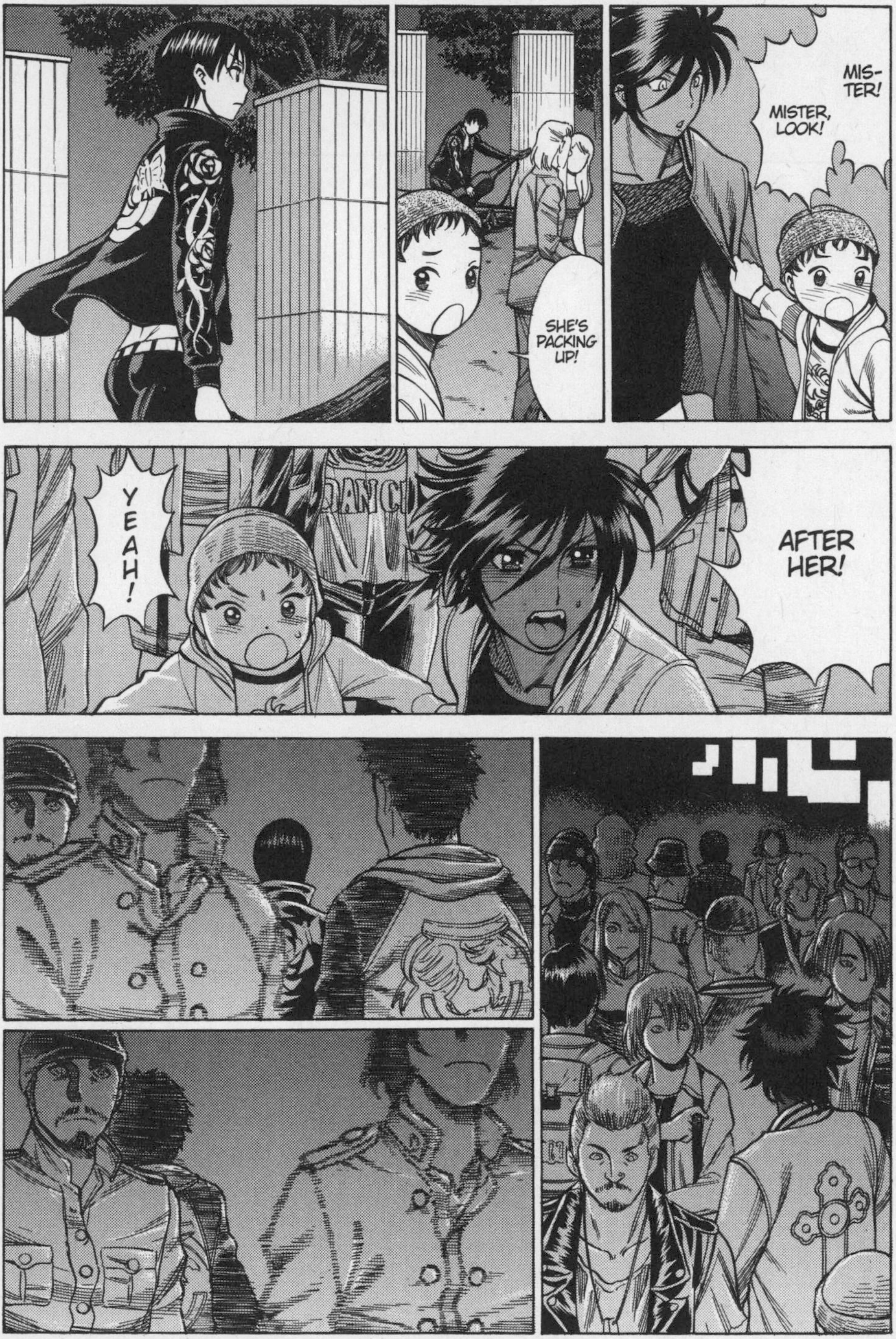
MIS-TER!
MISTER, LOOK!
SHE'S PACKING UP!
AFTER HER!
YEAH!

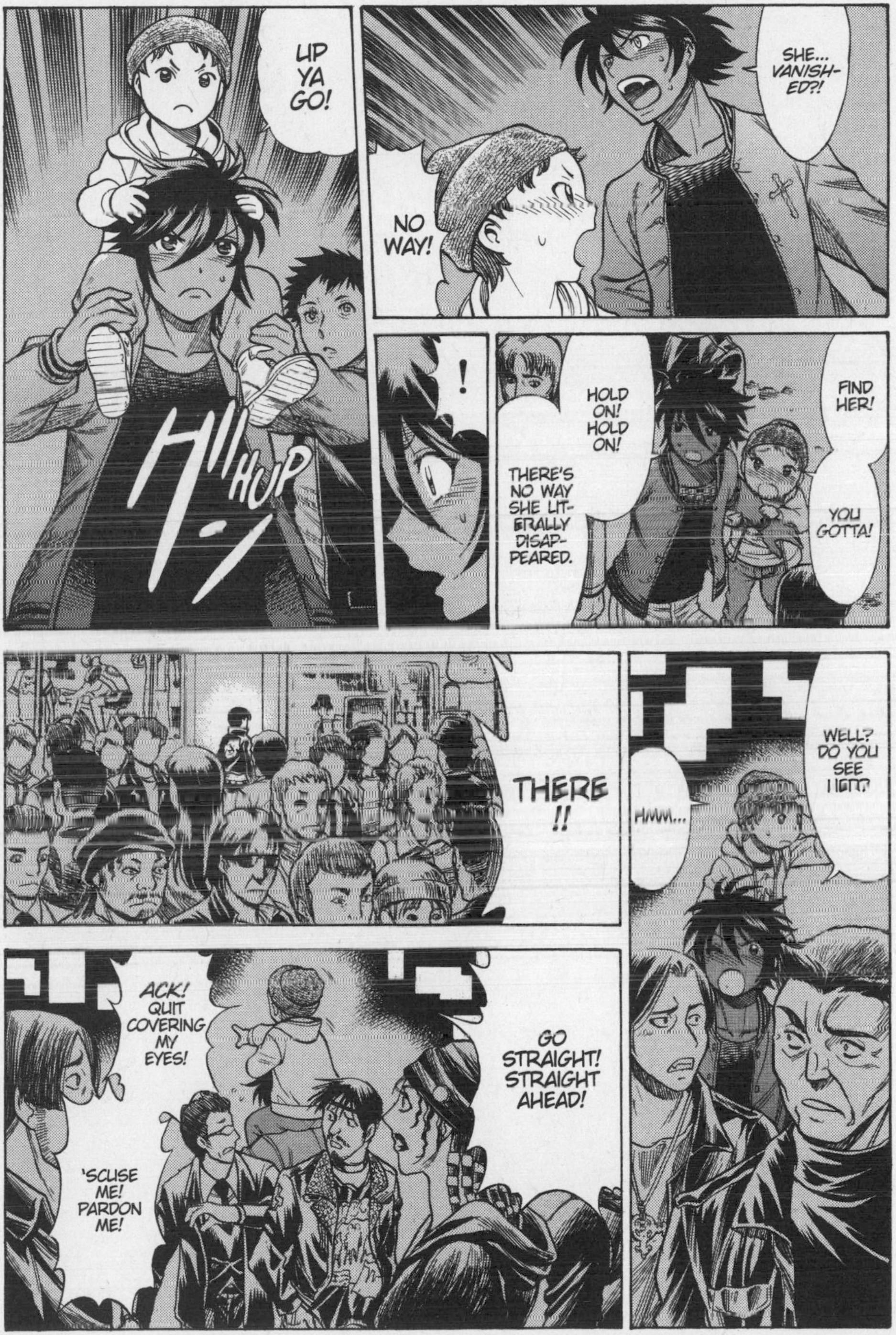
SHE... VANISH-ED?!
NO WAY!
FIND HER!
YOU GOTTA!
HOLD ON! HOLD ON!
THERE'S NO WAY SHE LIT-ERALLY DISAP-PEARED.
!
UP YA GO!
HUP
WELL? DO YOU SEE HER?
HMM...
THERE!!
GO STRAIGHT! STRAIGHT AHEAD!
ACK! QUIT COVERING MY EYES!
'SCUSE ME! PARDON ME!

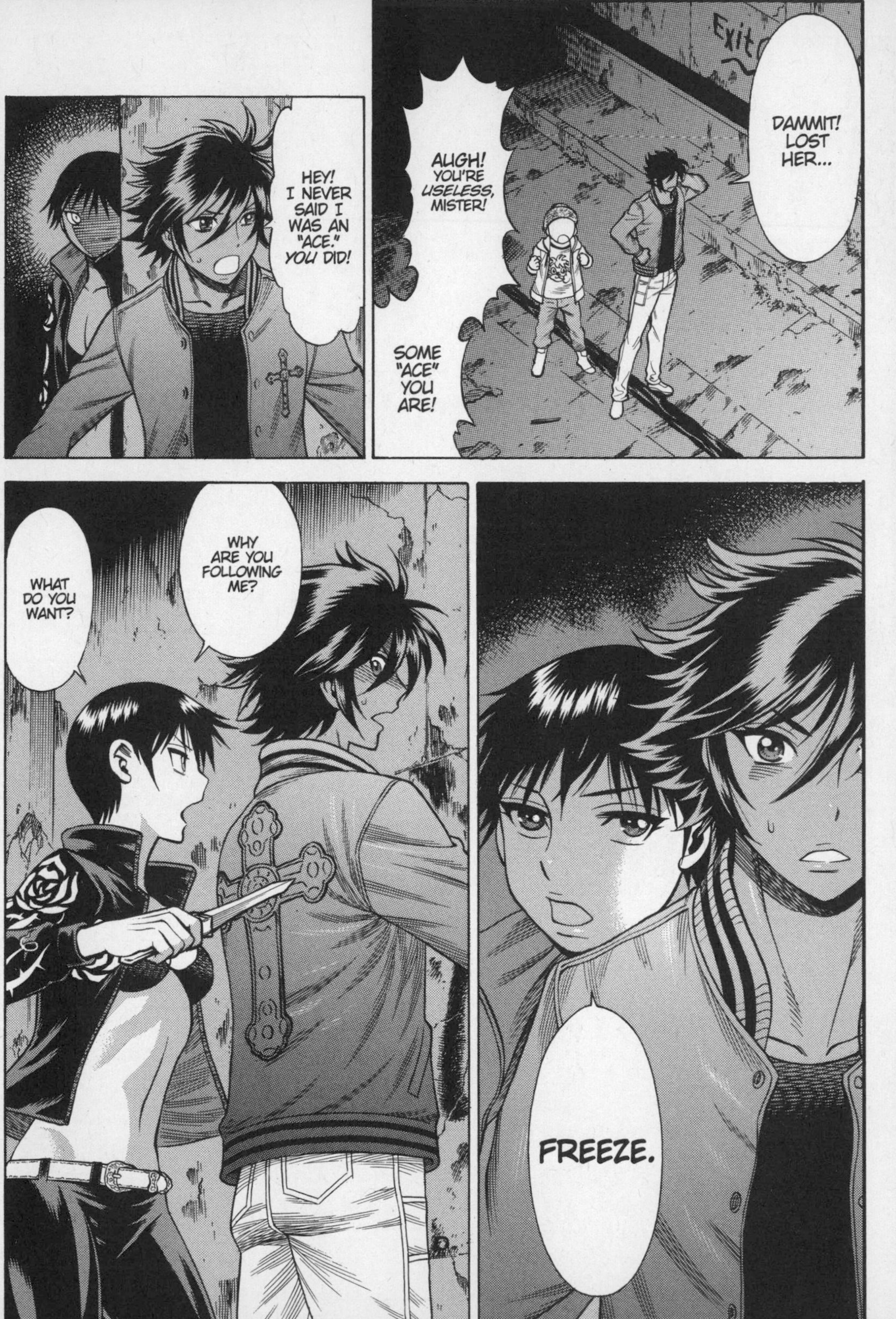
DAMMIT! LOST HER...
AUGH! YOU'RE *USELESS,* MISTER!
SOME "ACE" YOU ARE!
HEY! I NEVER SAID I WAS AN "ACE." *YOU* DID!
FREEZE.
WHY ARE YOU FOLLOWING ME?
WHAT DO YOU WANT?

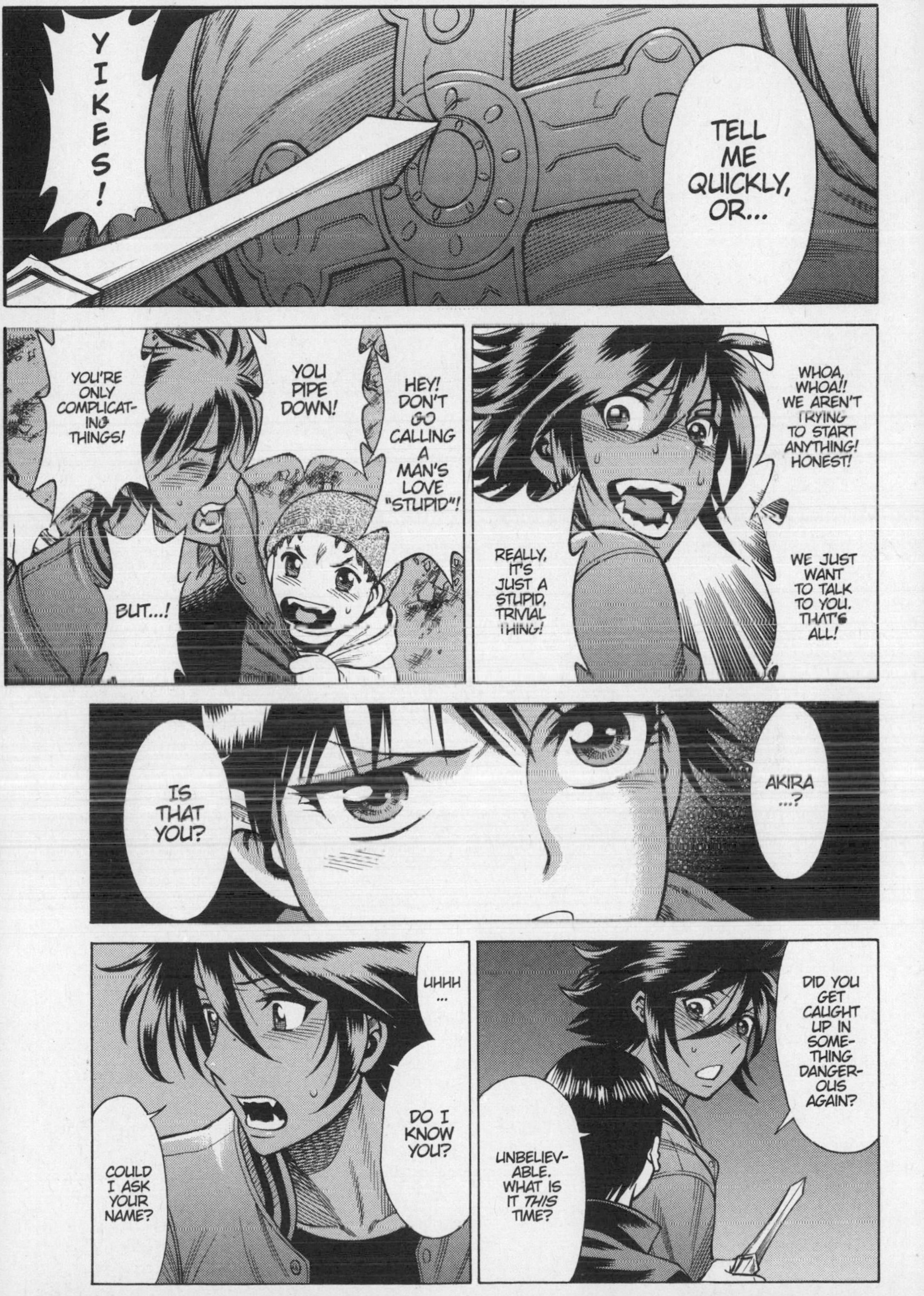
TELL ME QUICKLY, OR...
YIKES!
WHOA, WHOA!! WE AREN'T TRYING TO START ANYTHING! HONEST!
WE JUST WANT TO TALK TO YOU. THAT'S ALL!
REALLY, IT'S JUST A STUPID, TRIVIAL THING!
HEY! DON'T GO CALLING A MAN'S LOVE "STUPID"!
YOU PIPE DOWN!
YOU'RE ONLY COMPLICATING THINGS!
BUT...!
AKIRA ...?
IS THAT YOU?
DID YOU GET CAUGHT UP IN SOMETHING DANGEROUS AGAIN?
UNBELIEVABLE. WHAT IS IT *THIS* TIME?
UHHH ...
DO I KNOW YOU?
COULD I ASK YOUR NAME?

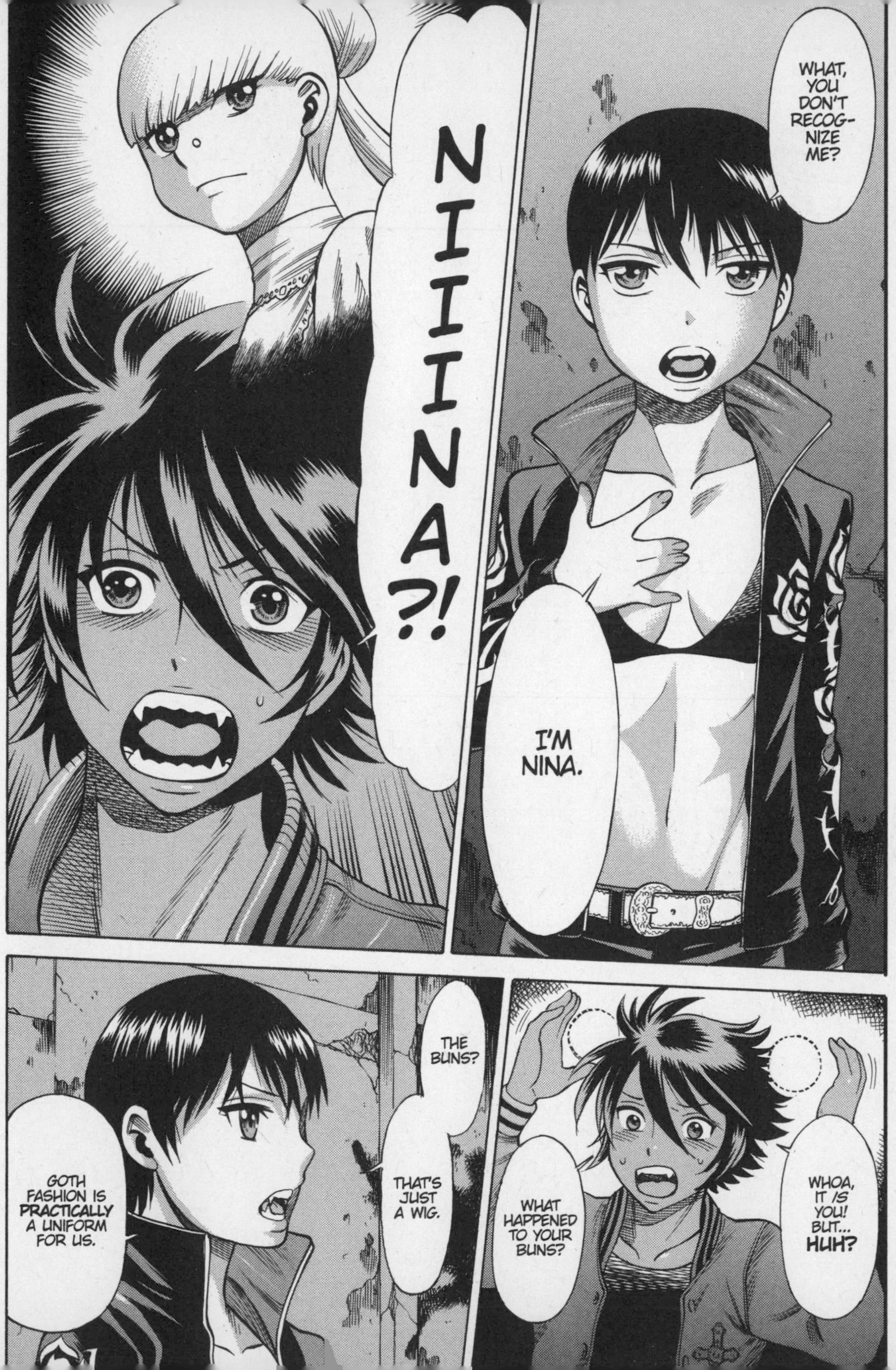
WHAT, YOU DON'T RECOG-NIZE ME?
I'M NINA.
NIIINA?!
WHOA, IT IS YOU! BUT... HUH?
WHAT HAPPENED TO YOUR BUNS?
THE BUNS?
THAT'S JUST A WIG.
GOTH FASHION IS PRACTICALLY A UNIFORM FOR US.

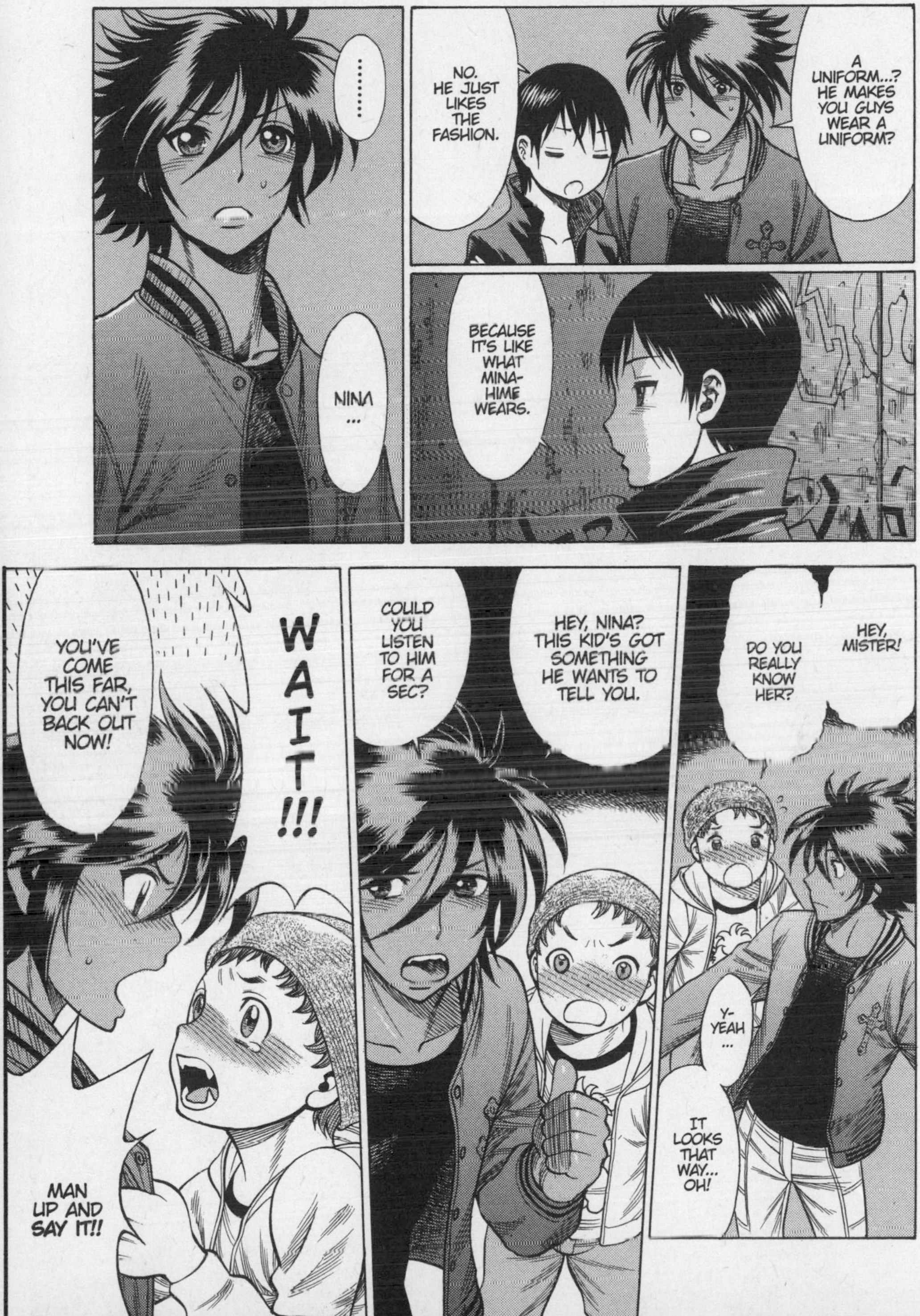
A UNIFORM...? HE MAKES YOU GUYS WEAR A UNIFORM?
NO. HE JUST LIKES THE FASHION.
BECAUSE IT'S LIKE WHAT MINA-HIME WEARS.
....
NINA ...
HEY, MISTER!
DO YOU REALLY KNOW HER?
Y-YEAH ...
IT LOOKS THAT WAY... OH!
HEY, NINA? THIS KID'S GOT SOMETHING HE WANTS TO TELL YOU.
COULD YOU LISTEN TO HIM FOR A SEC?
WAIT!!!
YOU'VE COME THIS FAR, YOU CAN'T BACK OUT NOW!
MAN UP AND SAY IT!!

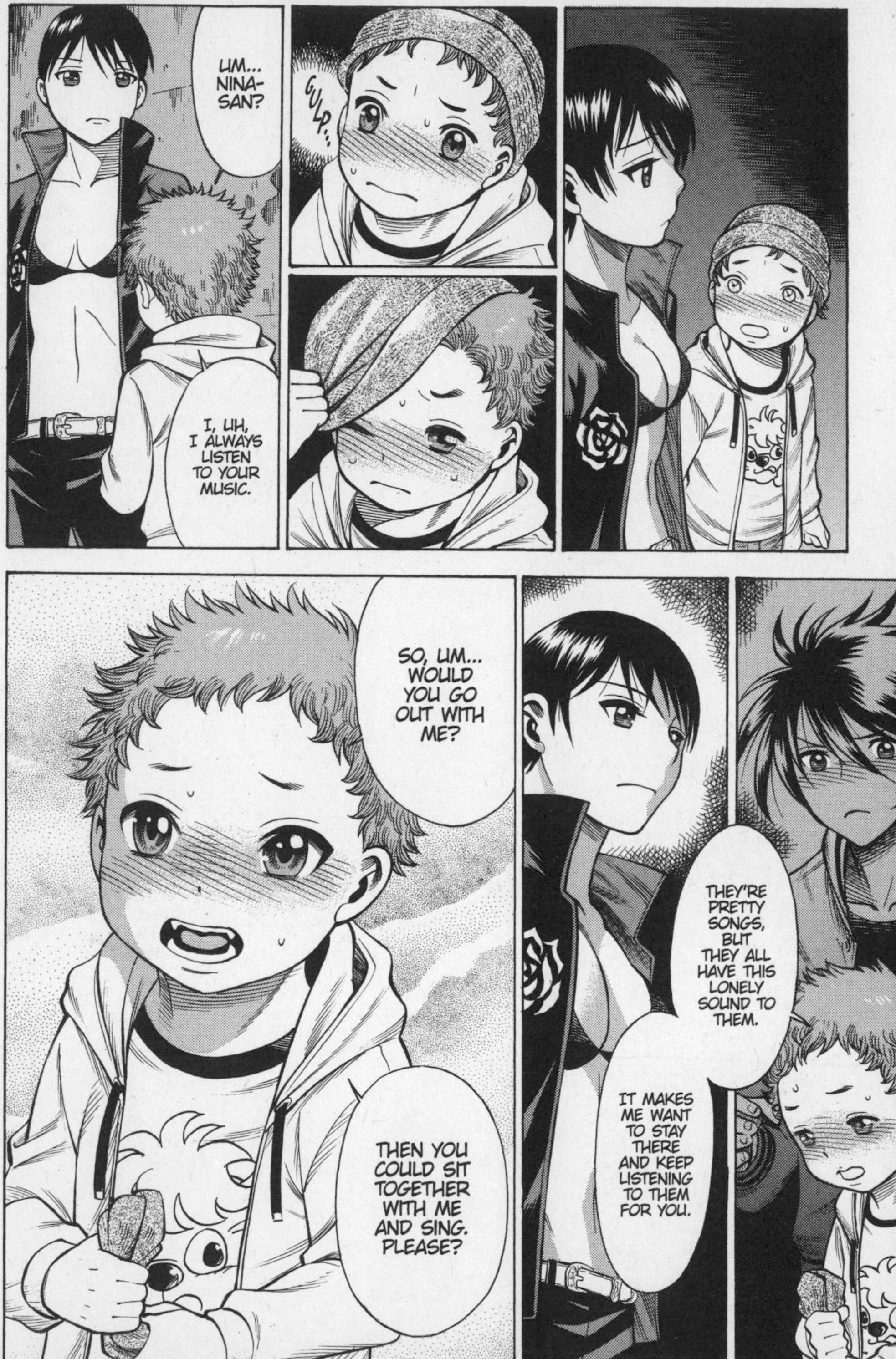
GULP...
UM... NINA-SAN?
I, UH, I ALWAYS LISTEN TO YOUR MUSIC.
THEY'RE PRETTY SONGS, BUT THEY ALL HAVE THIS LONELY SOUND TO THEM.
IT MAKES ME WANT TO STAY THERE AND KEEP LISTENING TO THEM FOR YOU.
SO, UM... WOULD YOU GO OUT WITH ME?
THEN YOU COULD SIT TOGETHER WITH ME AND SING. PLEASE?

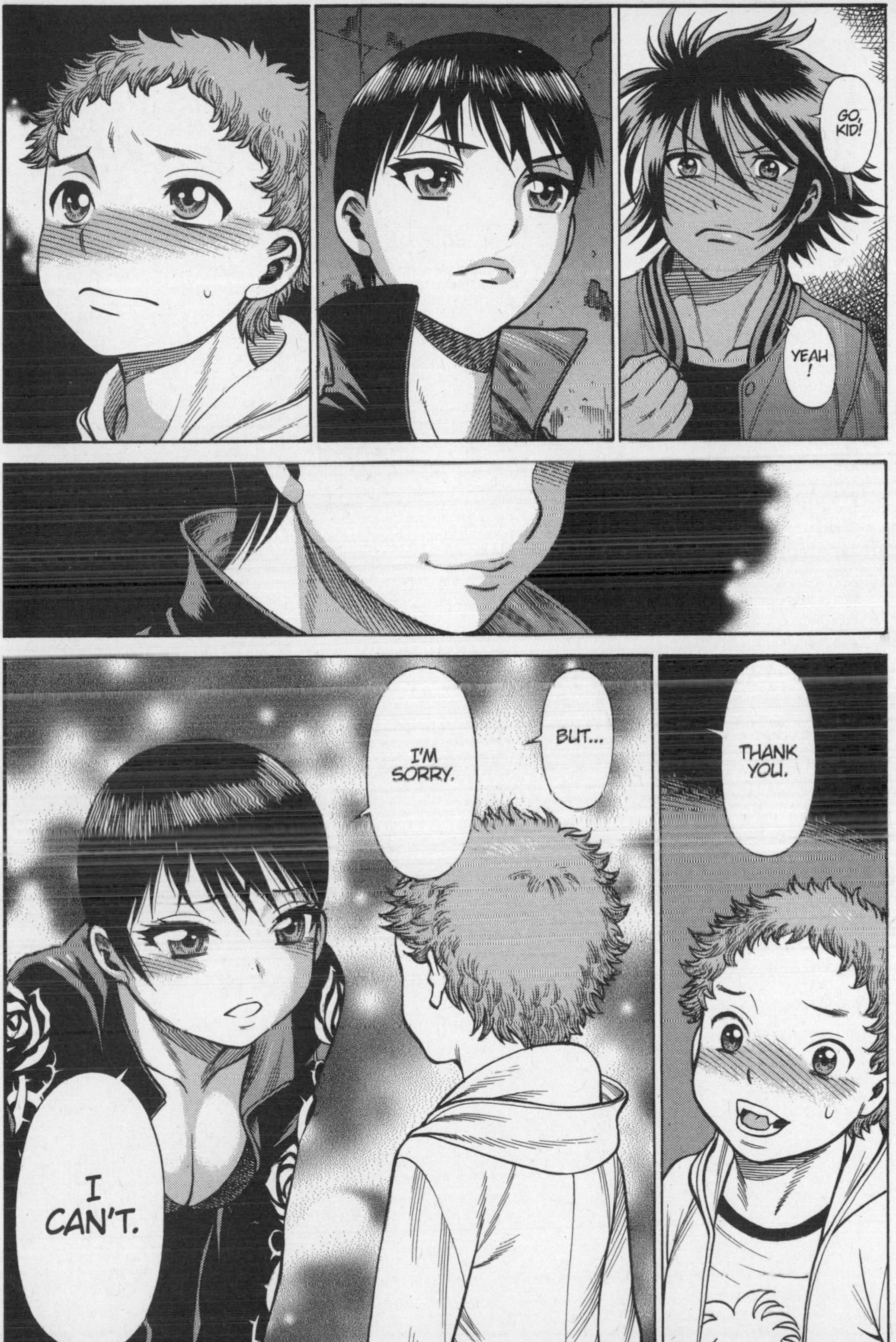
GO, KID!
YEAH!
THANK YOU.
BUT...
I'M SORRY.
I CAN'T.

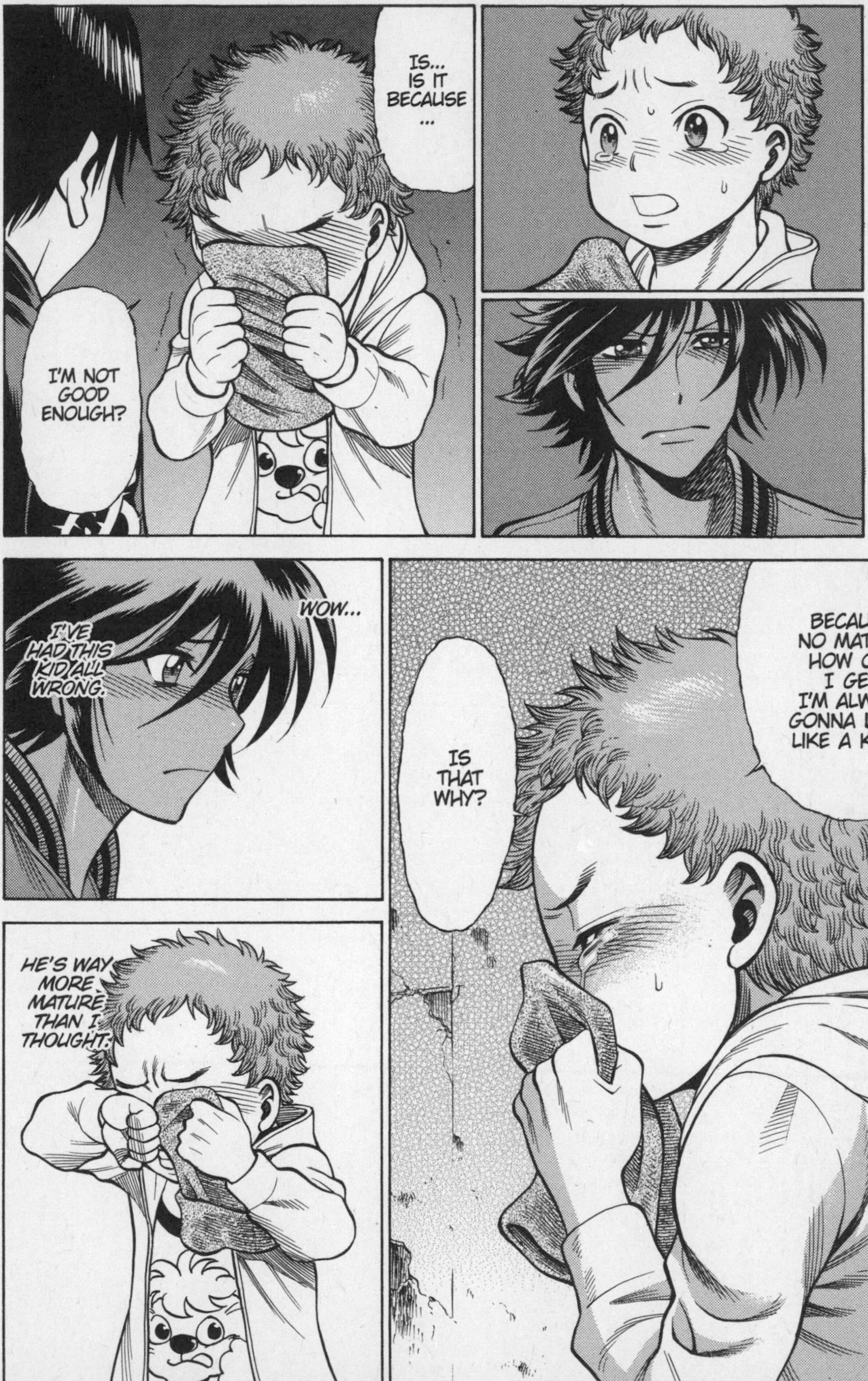
IS... IS IT BECAUSE ...
I'M NOT GOOD ENOUGH?
BECAUSE NO MATTER HOW OLD I GET, I'M ALWAYS GONNA LOOK LIKE A KID...?
IS THAT WHY?
WOW...
I'VE HAD THIS KID ALL WRONG.
HE'S WAY MORE MATURE THAN I THOUGHT.

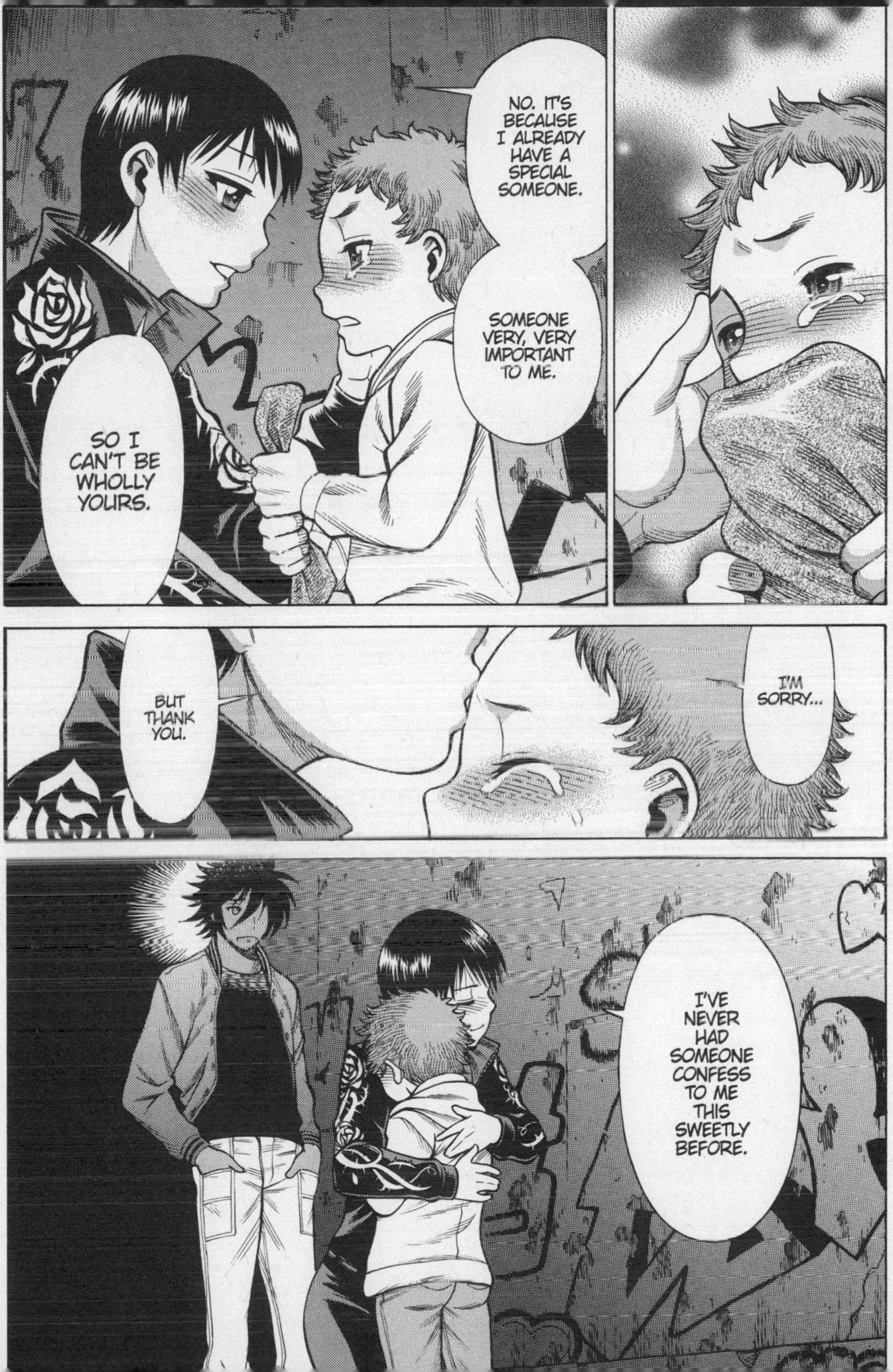
NO. IT'S BECAUSE I ALREADY HAVE A SPECIAL SOMEONE.
SOMEONE VERY, VERY IMPORTANT TO ME.
SO I CAN'T BE WHOLLY YOURS.
I'M SORRY...
BUT THANK YOU.
I'VE NEVER HAD SOMEONE CONFESS TO ME THIS SWEETLY BEFORE.

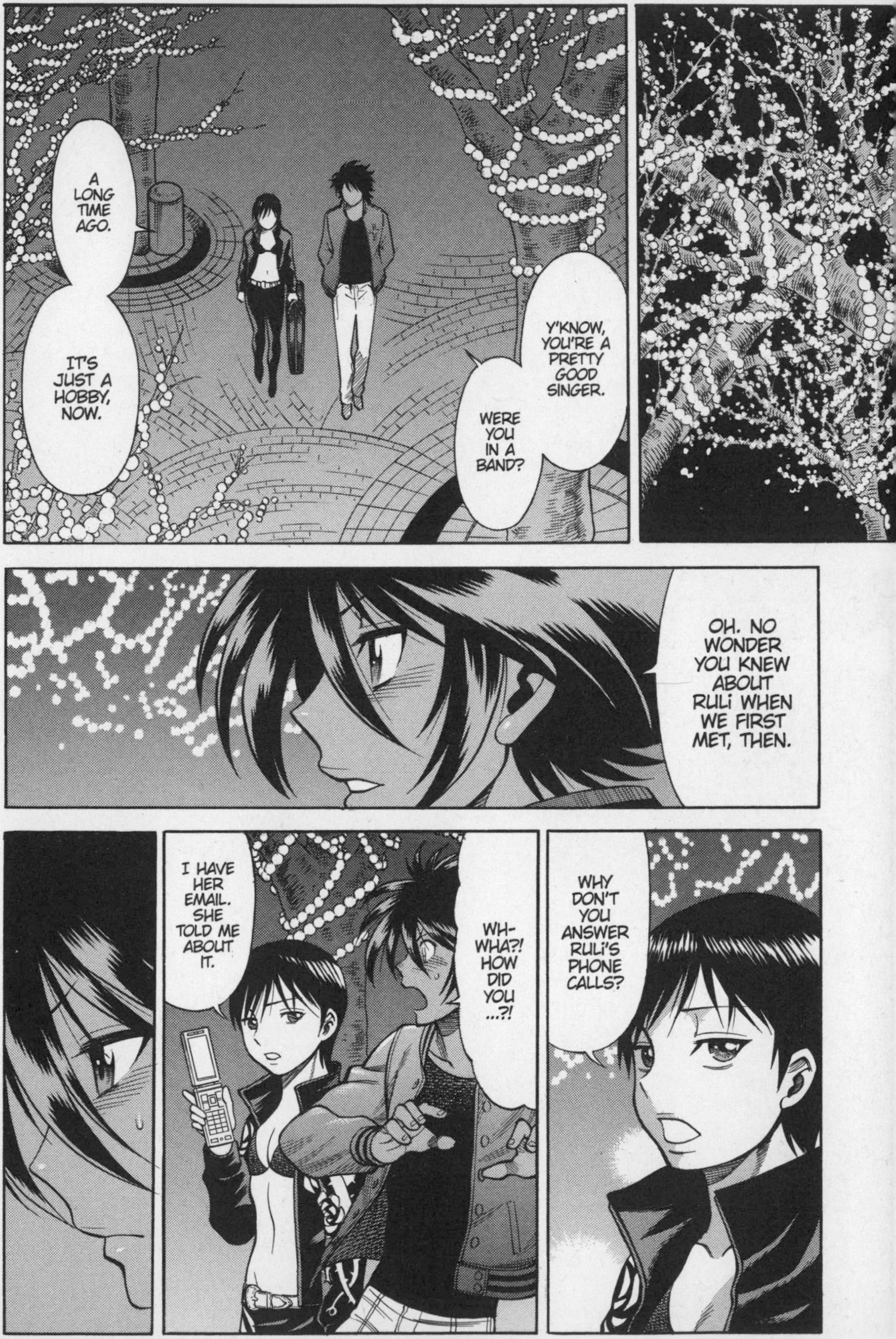
Y'KNOW, YOU'RE A PRETTY GOOD SINGER.
WERE YOU IN A BAND?
A LONG TIME AGO.
IT'S JUST A HOBBY, NOW.
OH. NO WONDER YOU KNEW ABOUT RULi WHEN WE FIRST MET, THEN.
WHY DON'T YOU ANSWER RULi'S PHONE CALLS?
WH-WHA?! HOW DID YOU ...?!
I HAVE HER EMAIL. SHE TOLD ME ABOUT IT.

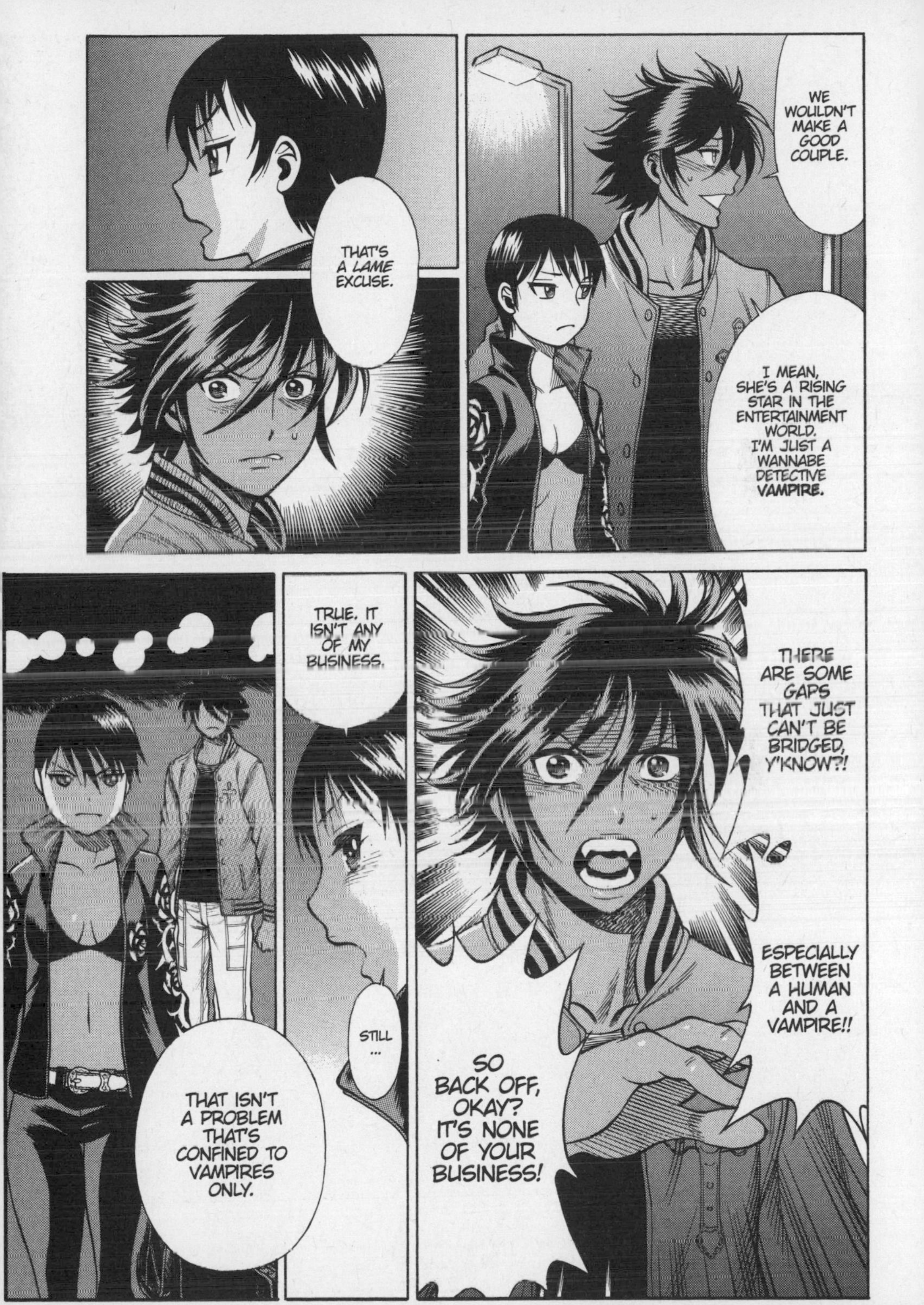
WE WOULDN'T MAKE A GOOD COUPLE.
I MEAN, SHE'S A RISING STAR IN THE ENTERTAINMENT WORLD. I'M JUST A WANNABE DETECTIVE **VAMPIRE.**
THAT'S A *LAME* EXCUSE.
THERE ARE SOME GAPS THAT JUST CAN'T BE BRIDGED, Y'KNOW?!
ESPECIALLY BETWEEN A HUMAN AND A VAMPIRE!!
SO BACK OFF, OKAY? IT'S NONE OF YOUR BUSINESS!
TRUE. IT ISN'T ANY OF MY BUSINESS.
STILL ...
THAT ISN'T A PROBLEM THAT'S CONFINED TO VAMPIRES ONLY.

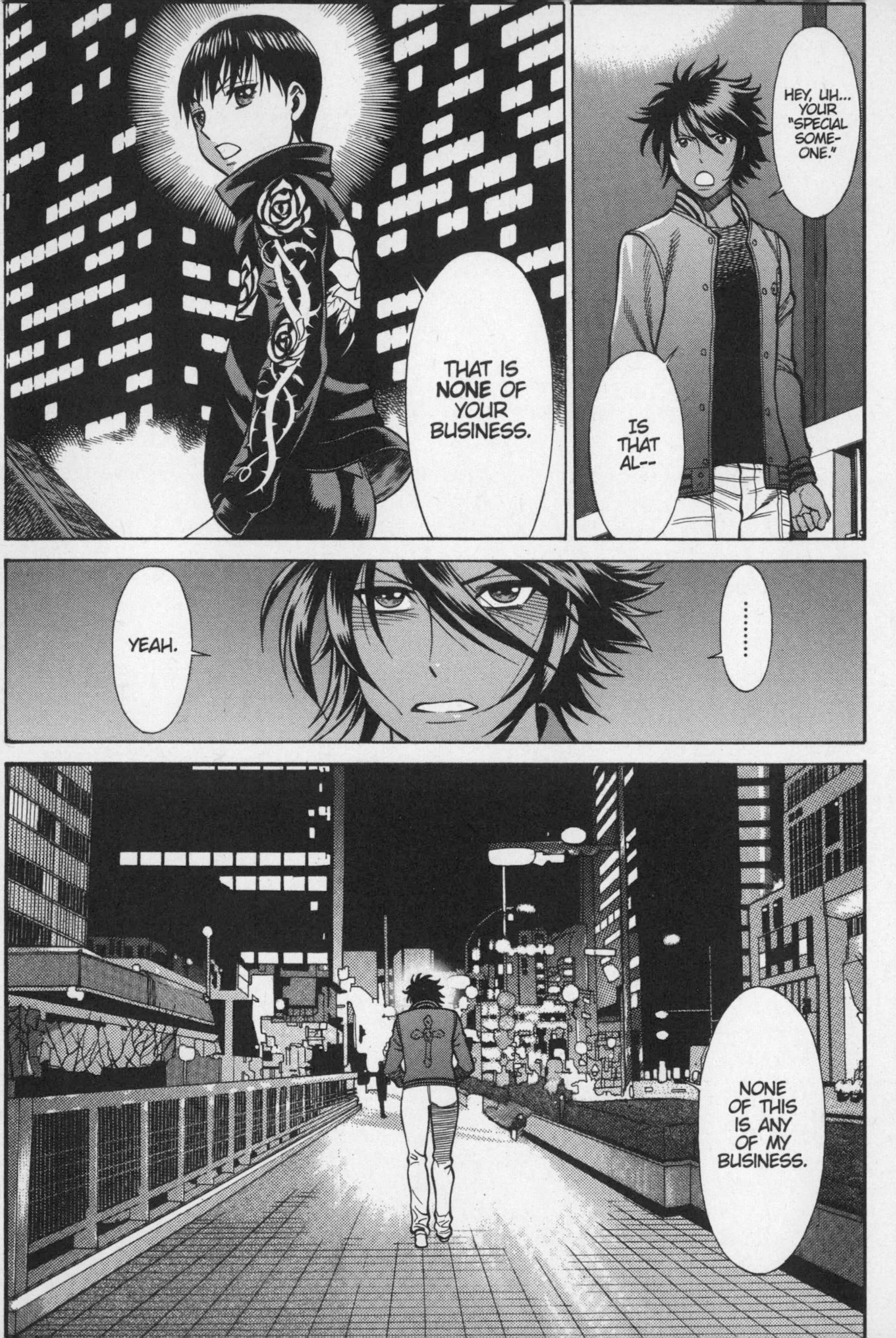
HEY, UH... YOUR "SPECIAL SOME-ONE."
IS THAT AL--
THAT IS NONE OF YOUR BUSINESS.
......
YEAH.
NONE OF THIS IS ANY OF MY BUSINESS.

NINA THE "GOTH"

Nina is the leader of the band of "Gothic-Lolitas" who work in the shadows of the Bund at Alphonse's orders. An elite fighting squad, they are part of House Tepes' intelligence Division.

Simply called "Goth" by both Akiras, she's been a character shrouded in mystery. However, in this past chapter, we pulled back a corner of the curtain hiding her. Also, as an interesting note, of all the characters from *Dance in the Vampire Bund* appearing in *Dive*, she's the one who was introduced first. Her first appearance was in Vampire Bund Volume 1, Chapter 5, a few pages before Alphonse.

She had several other minor appearances after that, and then was given a slot in the main cast of *Dive*. Now she finally has a name. It only took, what... 7 years?

Seeing how she is a street musician, it's obvious that she has a taste for indie music. That's how she knew who RULi was in Volume 1, even though she hadn't made her official debut yet.

There are still many mysteries surrounding Nina, though. I'm looking forward to showing more and more about her as the story progresses.

DIVE IN THE VAMPIRE BUND

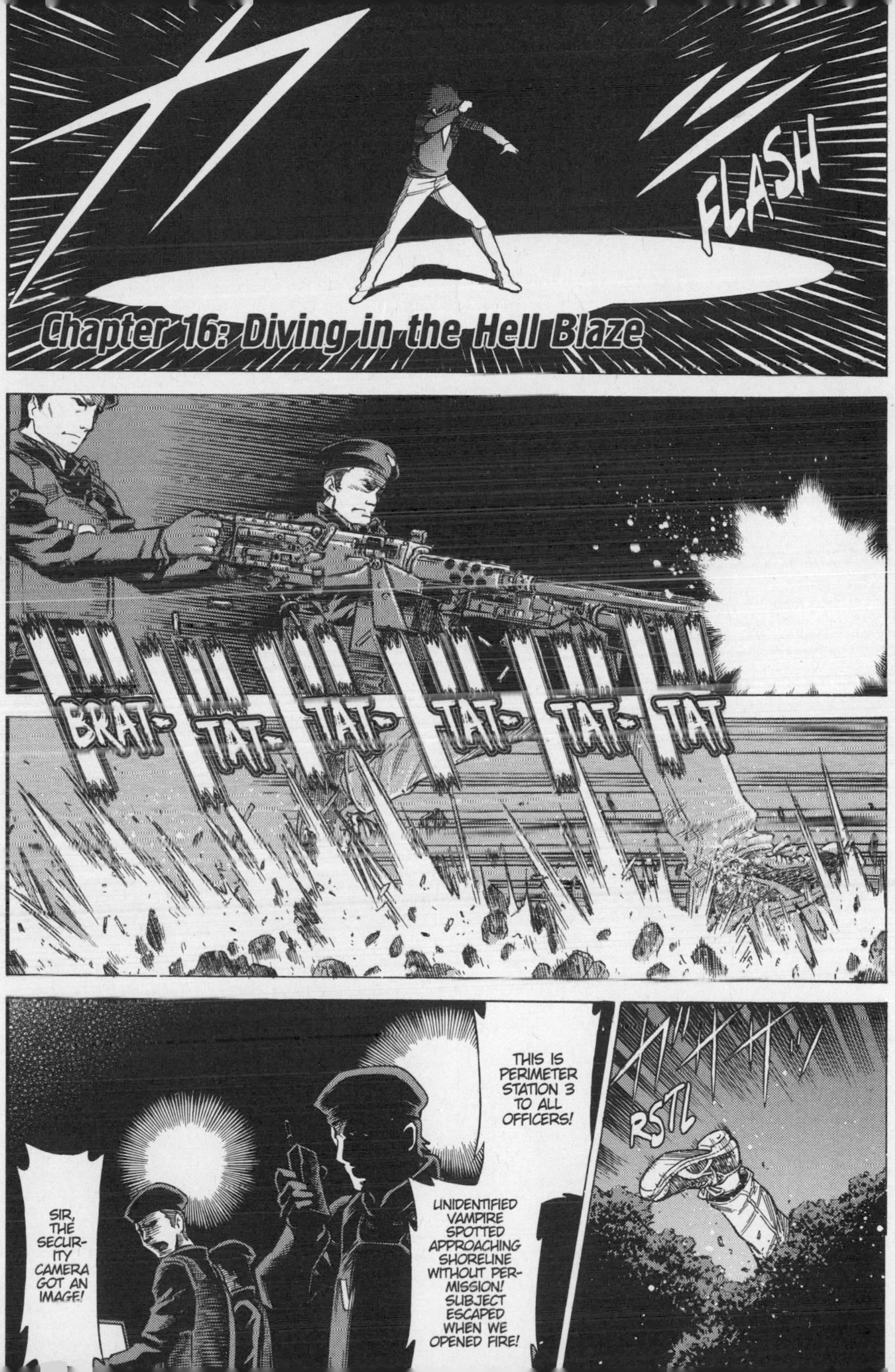
FLASH
Chapter 16: Diving in the Hell Blaze
BRAT-TAT-TAT-TAT-TAT-TAT
RSTL
THIS IS PERIMETER STATION 3 TO ALL OFFICERS!
UNIDENTIFIED VAMPIRE SPOTTED APPROACHING SHORELINE WITHOUT PERMISSION! SUBJECT ESCAPED WHEN WE OPENED FIRE!
SIR, THE SECURITY CAMERA GOT AN IMAGE!

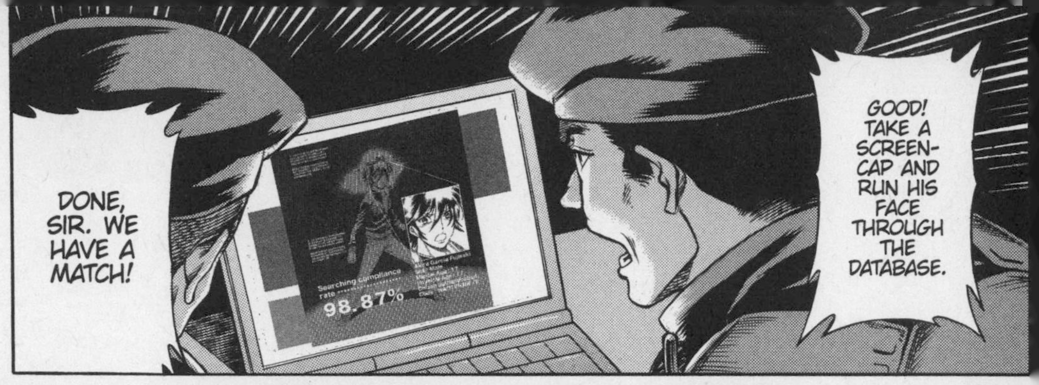
GOOD! TAKE A SCREEN-CAP AND RUN HIS FACE THROUGH THE DATABASE.
DONE, SIR. WE HAVE A MATCH!

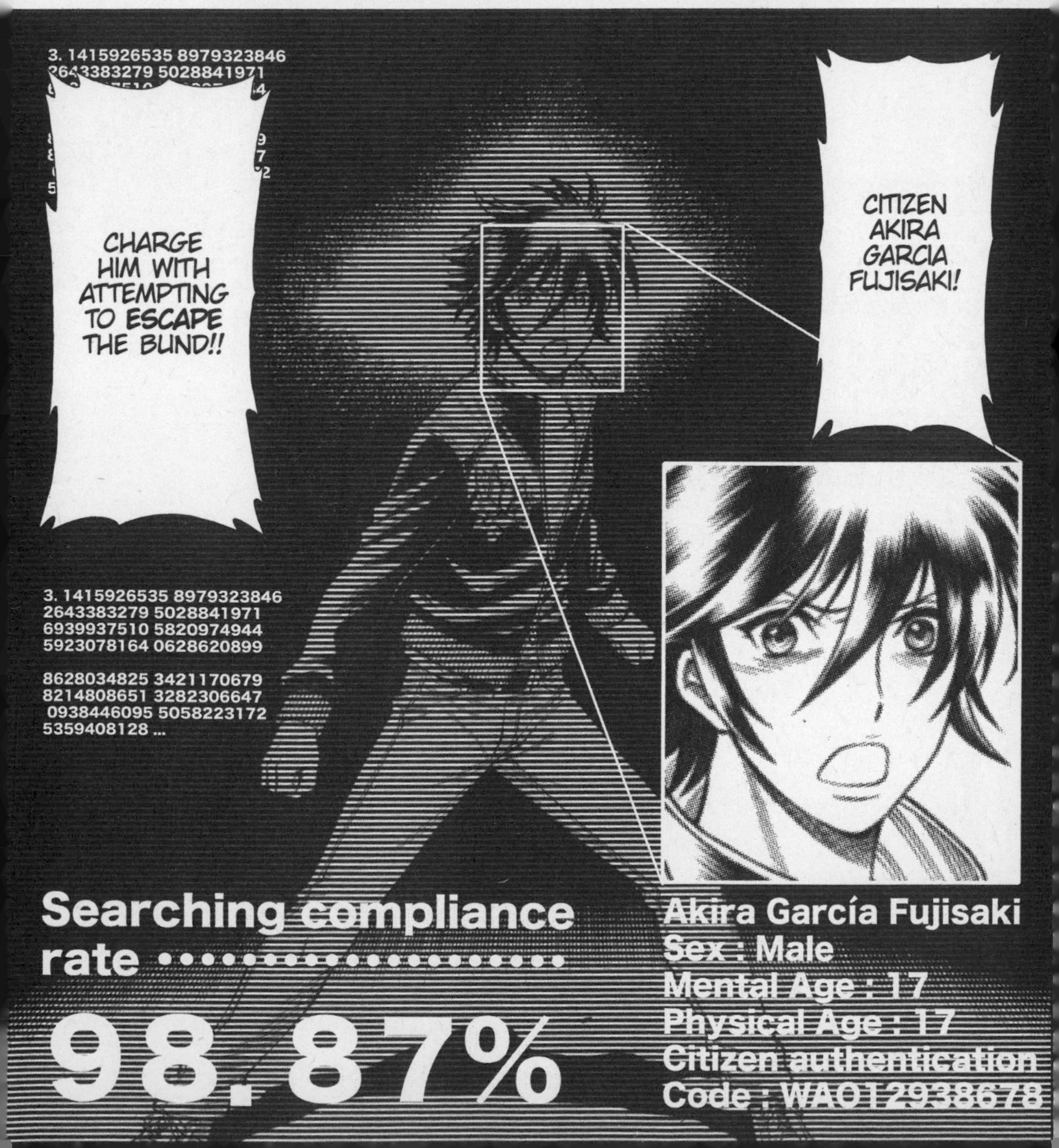
CITIZEN AKIRA GARCIA FUJISAKI!
3. 1415926535 8979323846
2643383279 5028841971
CHARGE HIM WITH ATTEMPTING TO ESCAPE THE BUND!!
3. 1415926535 8979323846
2643383279 5028841971
6939937510 5820974944
5923078164 0628620899
8628034825 3421170679
8214808651 3282306647
0938446095 5058223172
5359408128 ...
Akira García Fujisaki
Sex : Male
Mental Age : 17
Physical Age : 17
Citizen authentication
Code : WAO12938678
Searching compliance rate ••••••••••••••••••••
98.87%

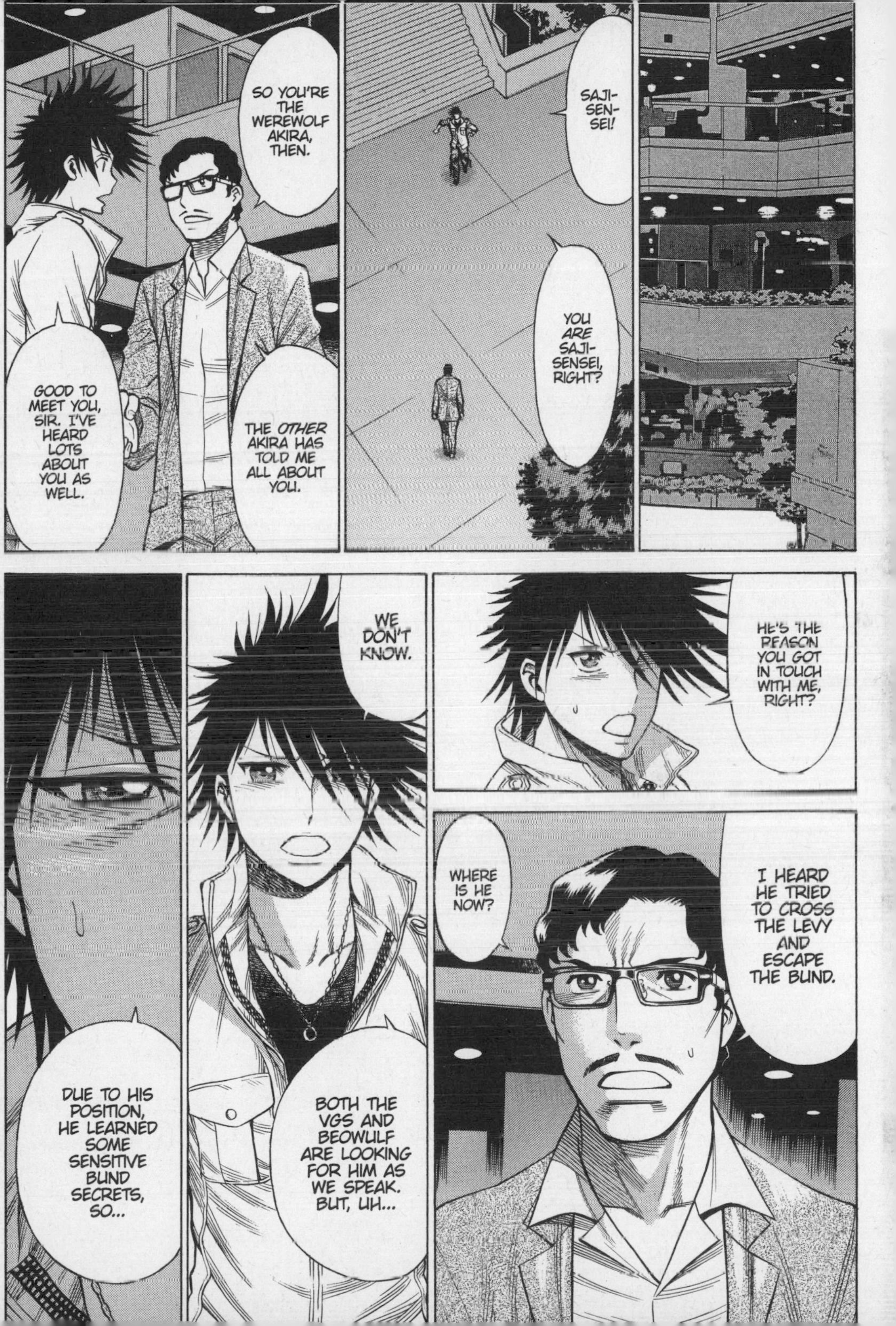
SAJI-SEN-SEI!
YOU ARE SAJI-SENSEI, RIGHT?
SO YOU'RE THE WEREWOLF AKIRA, THEN.
THE *OTHER* AKIRA HAS TOLD ME ALL ABOUT YOU.
GOOD TO MEET YOU, SIR. I'VE HEARD LOTS ABOUT YOU AS WELL.
HE'S THE REASON YOU GOT IN TOUCH WITH ME, RIGHT?
I HEARD HE TRIED TO CROSS THE LEVY AND ESCAPE THE BUND.
WHERE IS HE NOW?
WE DON'T KNOW.
BOTH THE VGS AND BEOWULF ARE LOOKING FOR HIM AS WE SPEAK. BUT, UH...
DUE TO HIS POSITION, HE LEARNED SOME SENSITIVE BUND SECRETS, SO...

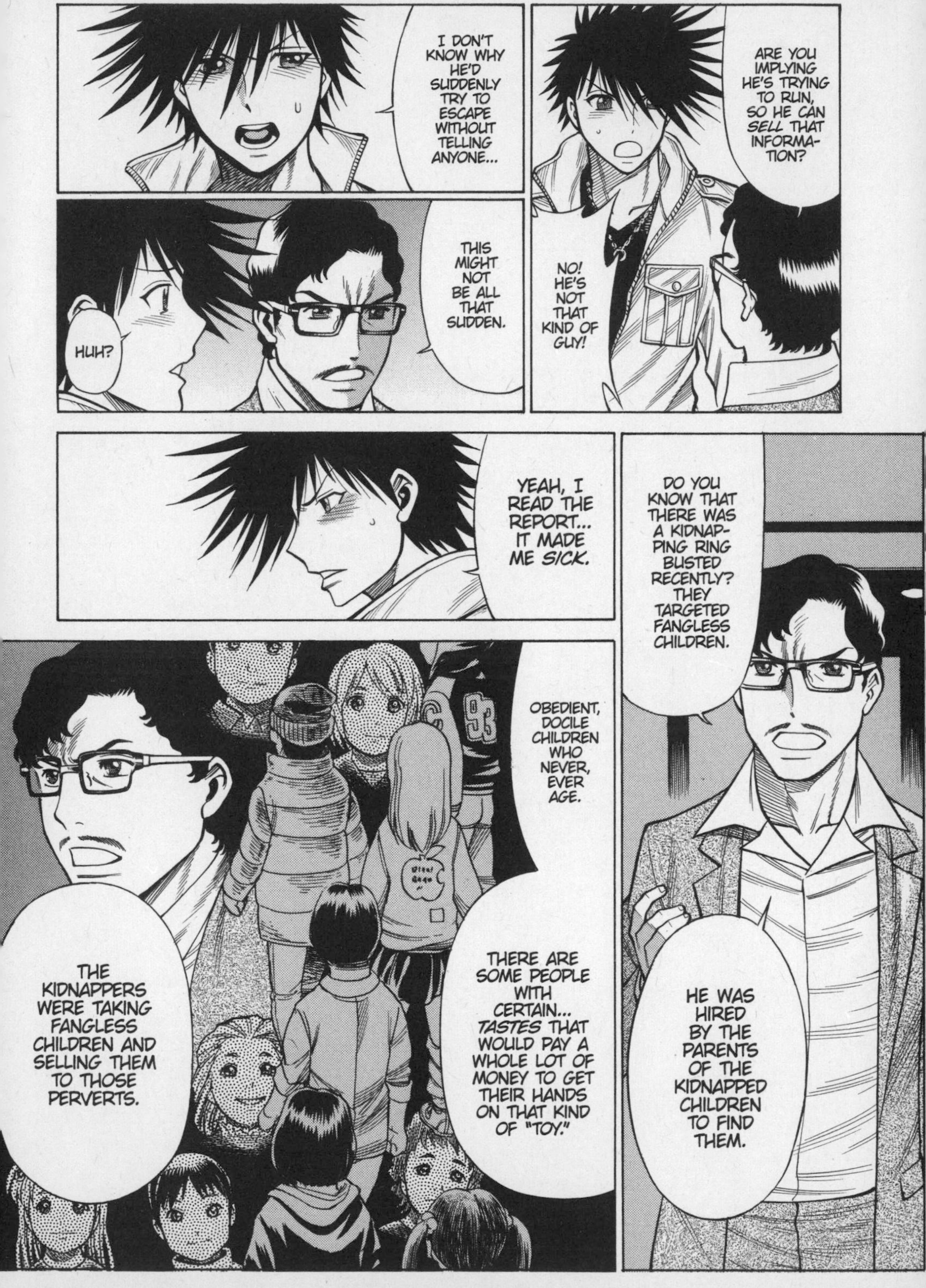
ARE YOU IMPLYING HE'S TRYING TO RUN, SO HE CAN *SELL* THAT INFORMATION?
NO! HE'S NOT THAT KIND OF GUY!
I DON'T KNOW WHY HE'D SUDDENLY TRY TO ESCAPE WITHOUT TELLING ANYONE...
THIS MIGHT NOT BE ALL THAT SUDDEN.
HUH?
DO YOU KNOW THAT THERE WAS A KIDNAPPING RING BUSTED RECENTLY? THEY TARGETED FANGLESS CHILDREN.
HE WAS HIRED BY THE PARENTS OF THE KIDNAPPED CHILDREN TO FIND THEM.
YEAH, I READ THE REPORT... IT MADE ME *SICK*.
OBEDIENT, DOCILE CHILDREN WHO NEVER, EVER AGE.
THERE ARE SOME PEOPLE WITH CERTAIN... *TASTES* THAT WOULD PAY A WHOLE LOT OF MONEY TO GET THEIR HANDS ON THAT KIND OF "TOY."
THE KIDNAPPERS WERE TAKING FANGLESS CHILDREN AND SELLING THEM TO THOSE PERVERTS.

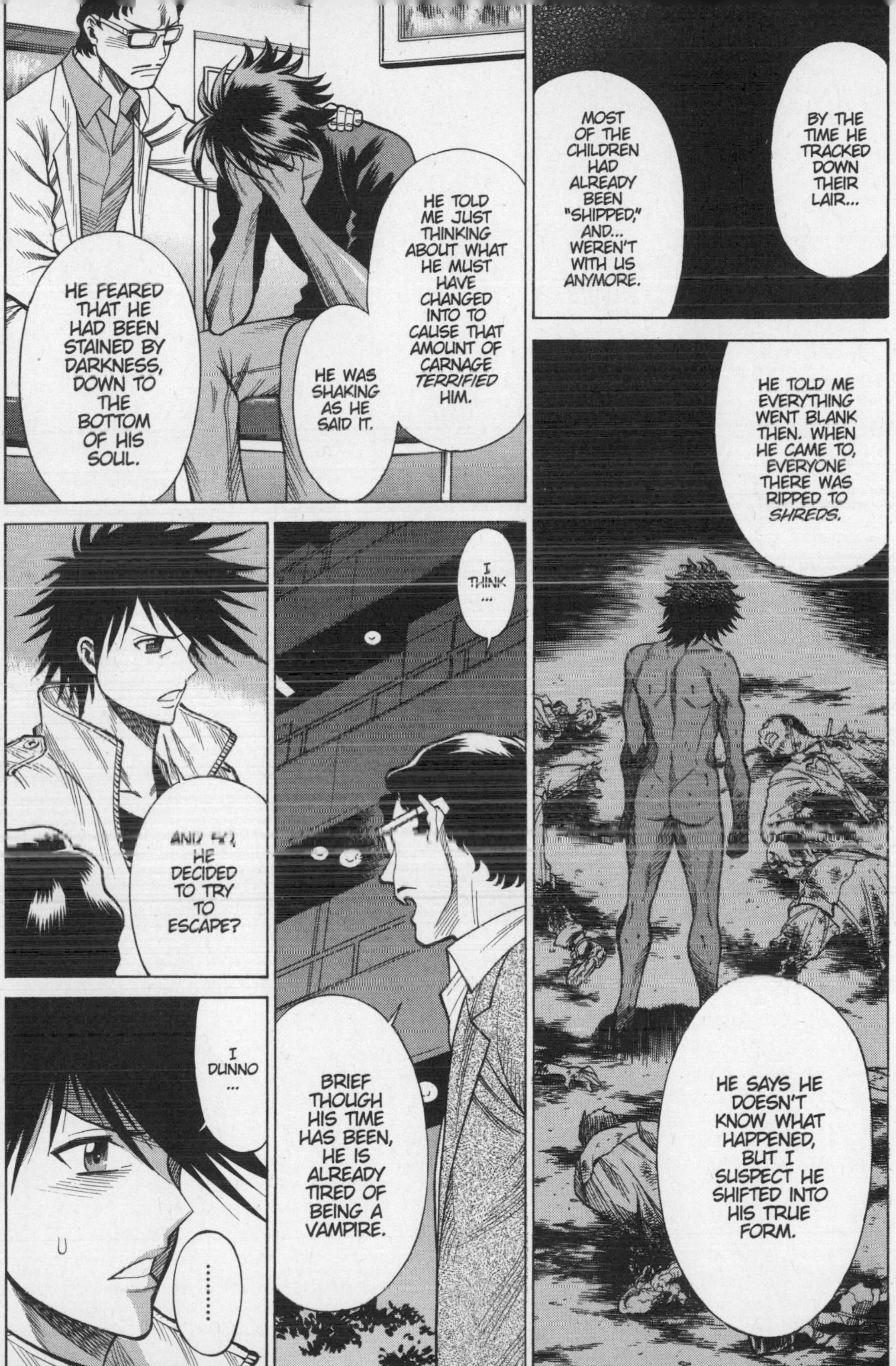

BY THE TIME HE TRACKED DOWN THEIR LAIR...
MOST OF THE CHILDREN HAD ALREADY BEEN "SHIPPED," AND... WEREN'T WITH US ANYMORE.
HE TOLD ME EVERYTHING WENT BLANK THEN. WHEN HE CAME TO, EVERYONE THERE WAS RIPPED TO *SHREDS.*
HE SAYS HE DOESN'T KNOW WHAT HAPPENED, BUT I SUSPECT HE SHIFTED INTO HIS TRUE FORM.
HE TOLD ME JUST THINKING ABOUT WHAT HE MUST HAVE CHANGED INTO TO CAUSE THAT AMOUNT OF CARNAGE *TERRIFIED* HIM.
HE WAS SHAKING AS HE SAID IT.
HE FEARED THAT HE HAD BEEN STAINED BY DARKNESS, DOWN TO THE BOTTOM OF HIS SOUL.
I THINK...
BRIEF THOUGH HIS TIME HAS BEEN, HE IS ALREADY TIRED OF BEING A VAMPIRE.
AND SO, HE DECIDED TO TRY TO ESCAPE?
I DUNNO...
....

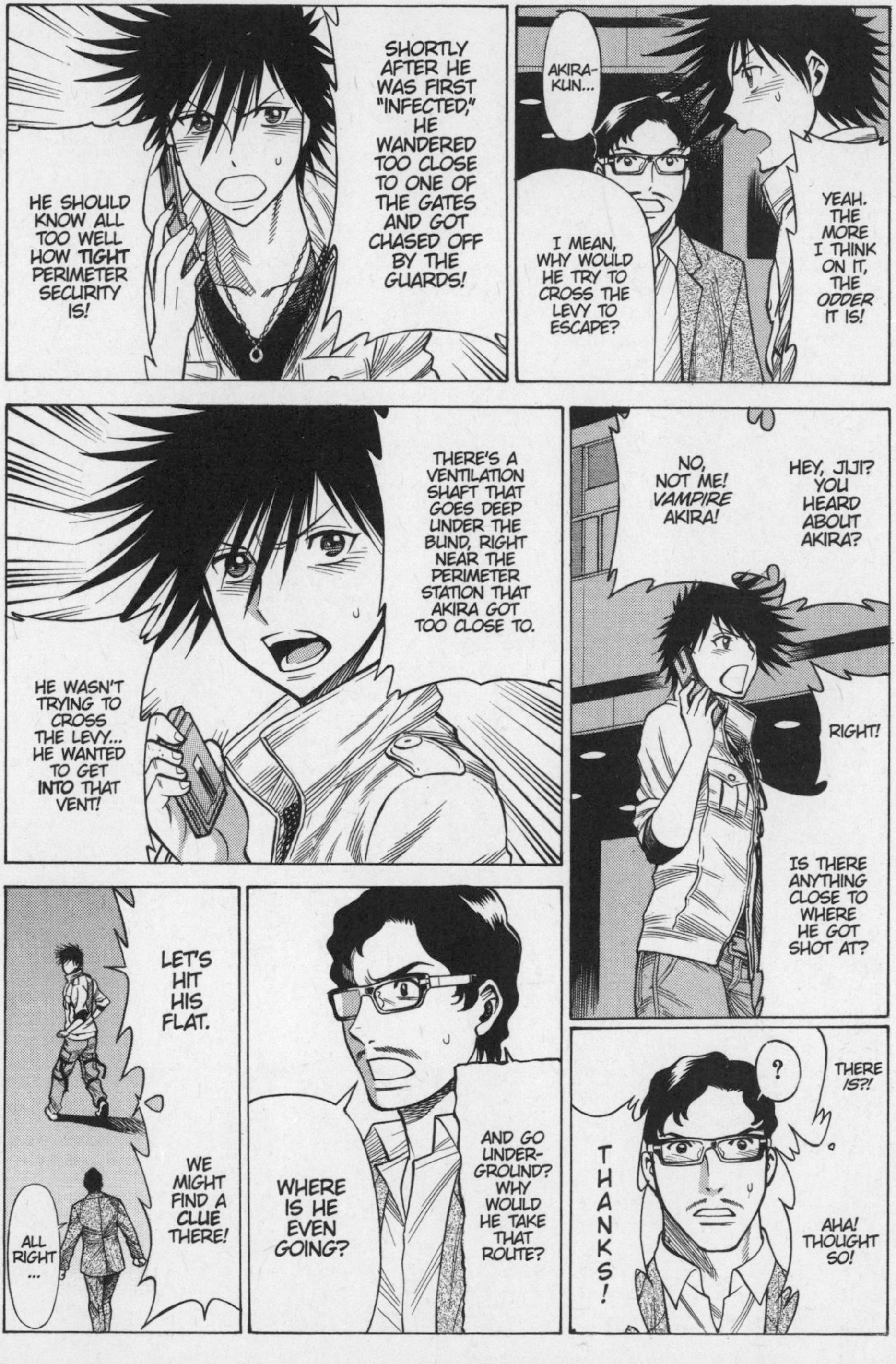
AKIRA-KUN...
YEAH. THE MORE I THINK ON IT, THE *ODDER* IT IS!
I MEAN, WHY WOULD HE TRY TO CROSS THE LEVY TO ESCAPE?
SHORTLY AFTER HE WAS FIRST "INFECTED," HE WANDERED TOO CLOSE TO ONE OF THE GATES AND GOT CHASED OFF BY THE GUARDS!
HE SHOULD KNOW ALL TOO WELL HOW **TIGHT** PERIMETER SECURITY IS!
HEY, JIJI? YOU HEARD ABOUT AKIRA?
NO, NOT ME! *VAMPIRE* AKIRA!
RIGHT!
IS THERE ANYTHING CLOSE TO WHERE HE GOT SHOT AT?
THERE'S A VENTILATION SHAFT THAT GOES DEEP UNDER THE BUND, RIGHT NEAR THE PERIMETER STATION THAT AKIRA GOT TOO CLOSE TO.
HE WASN'T TRYING TO CROSS THE LEVY... HE WANTED TO GET **INTO** THAT VENT!
THERE *IS*?!
?
AHA! THOUGHT SO!
THANKS!
AND GO UNDERGROUND? WHY WOULD HE TAKE THAT ROUTE?
WHERE IS HE EVEN GOING?
LET'S HIT HIS FLAT.
WE MIGHT FIND A **CLUE** THERE!
ALL RIGHT...

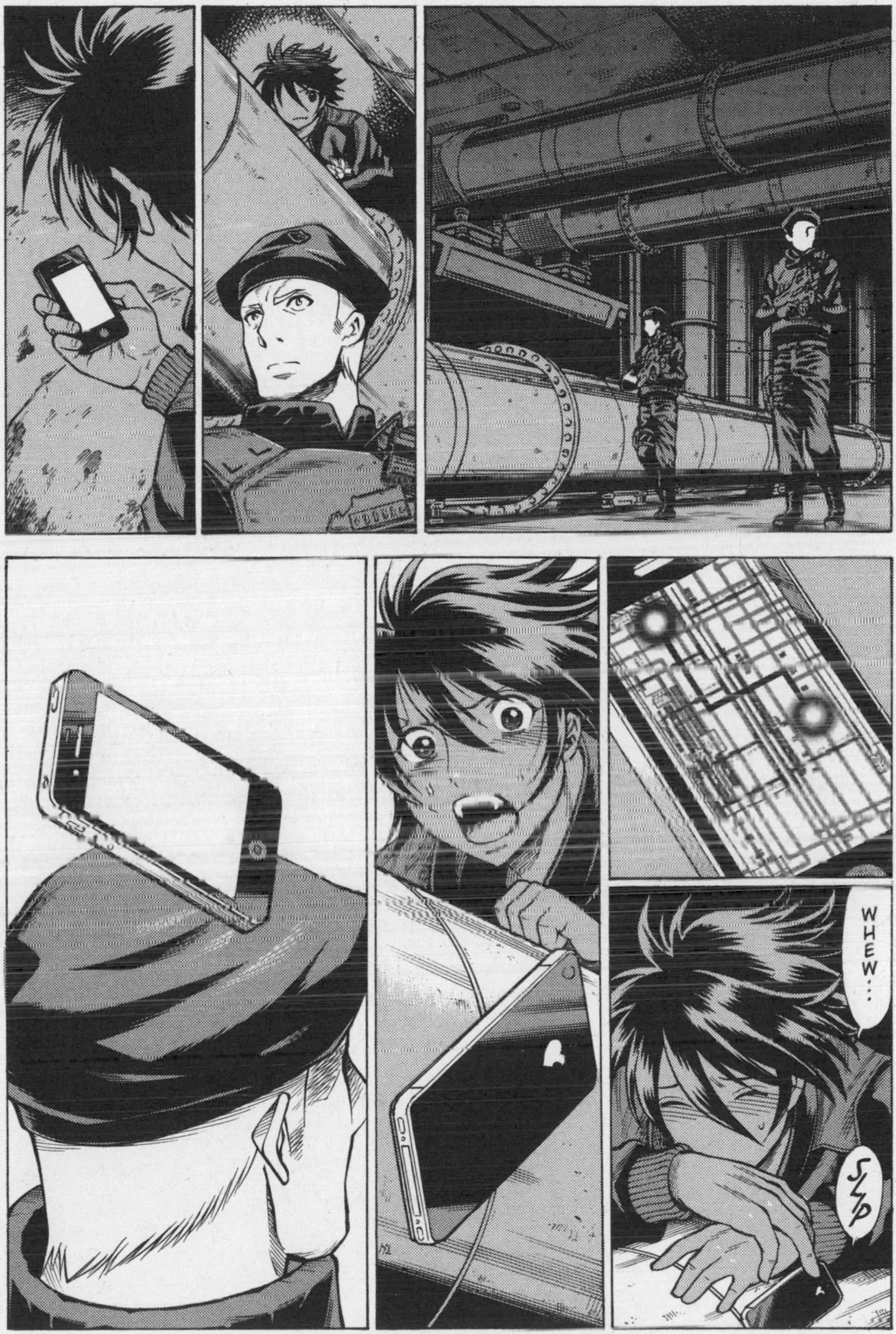
WHEW...
SLIP

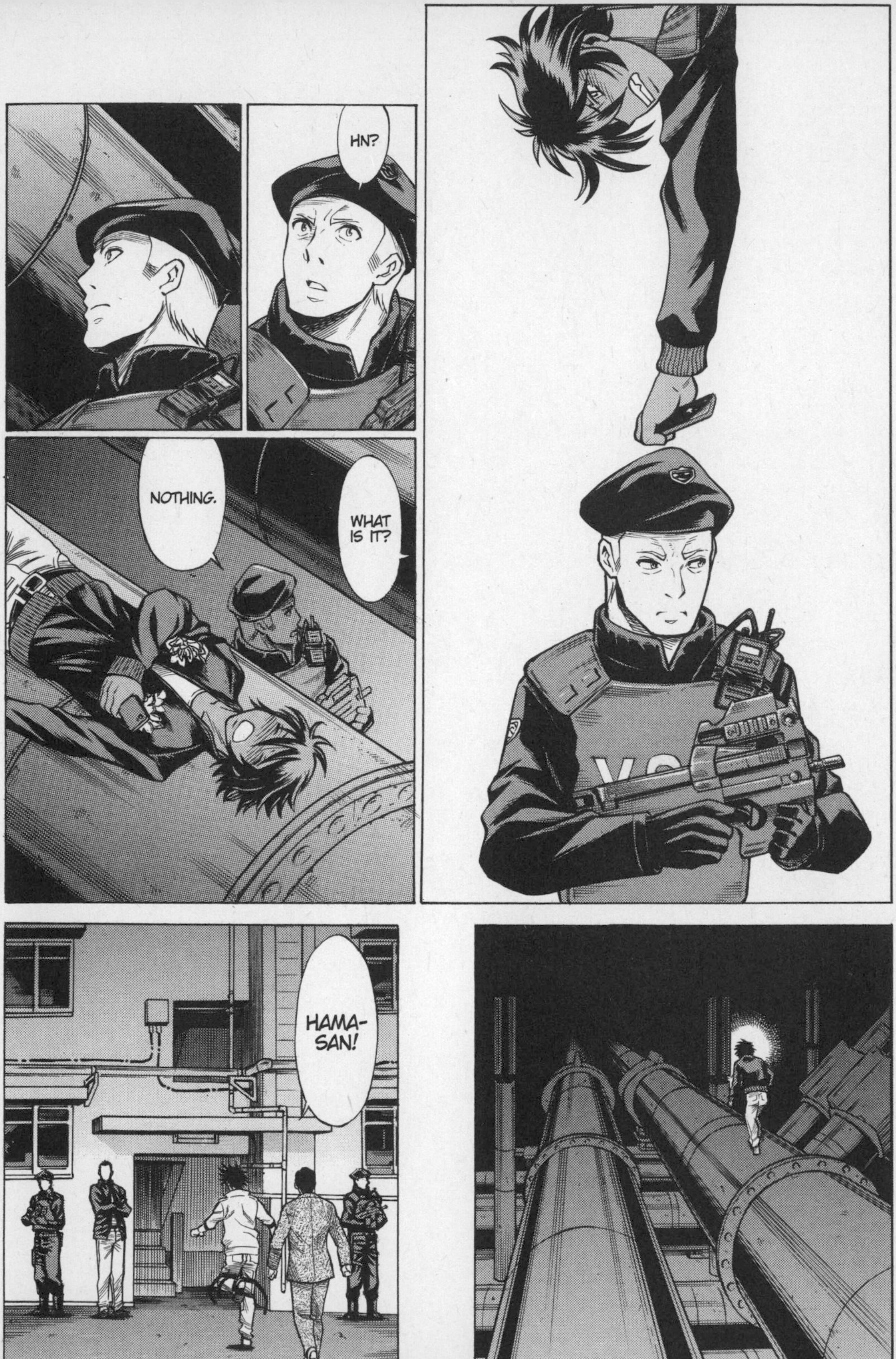
HN?
WHAT IS IT?
NOTHING.
HAMA-SAN!

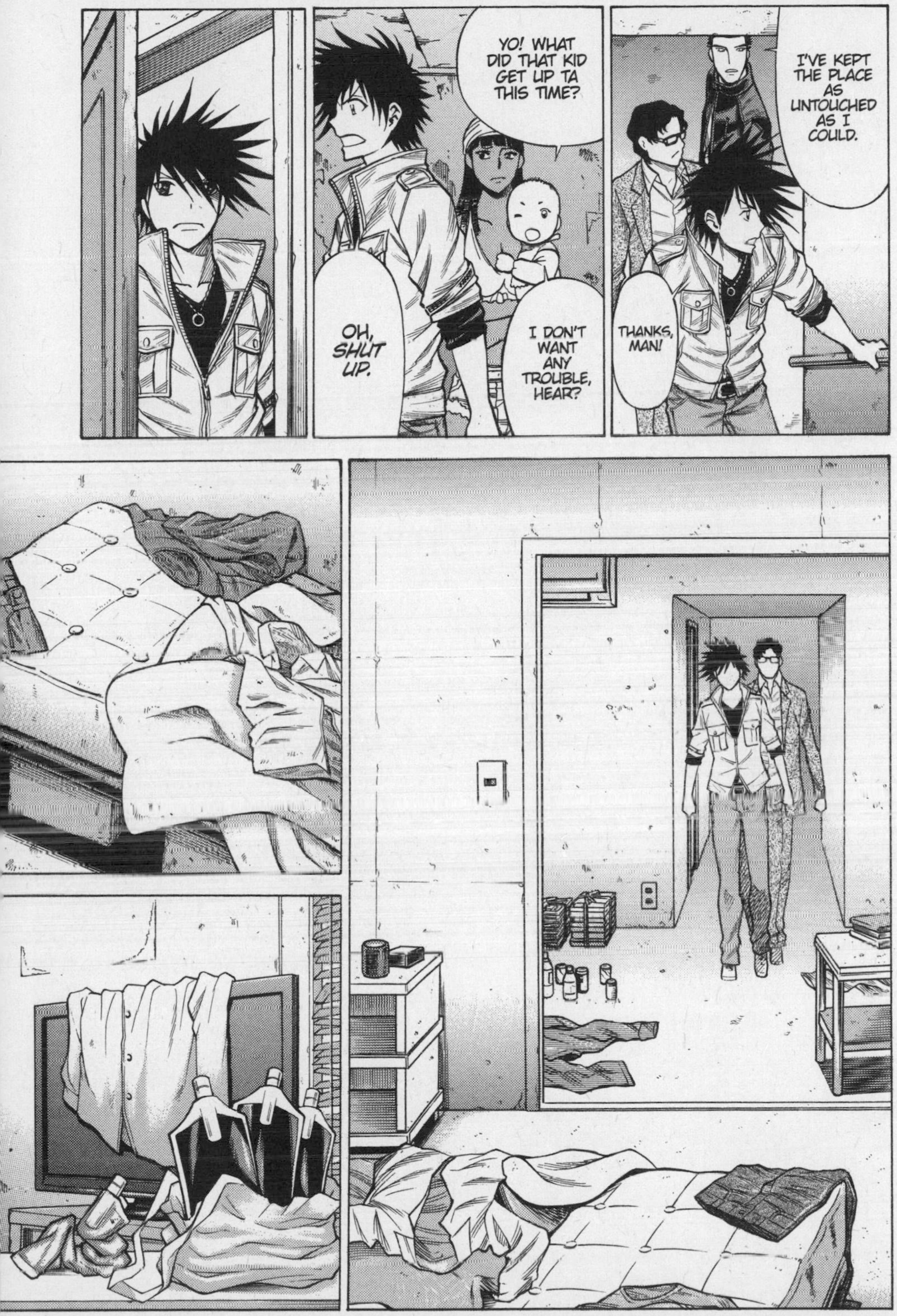
I'VE KEPT THE PLACE AS UNTOUCHED AS I COULD.
THANKS, MAN!
YO! WHAT DID THAT KID GET UP TA THIS TIME?
I DON'T WANT ANY TROUBLE, HEAR?
OH, SHUT UP.

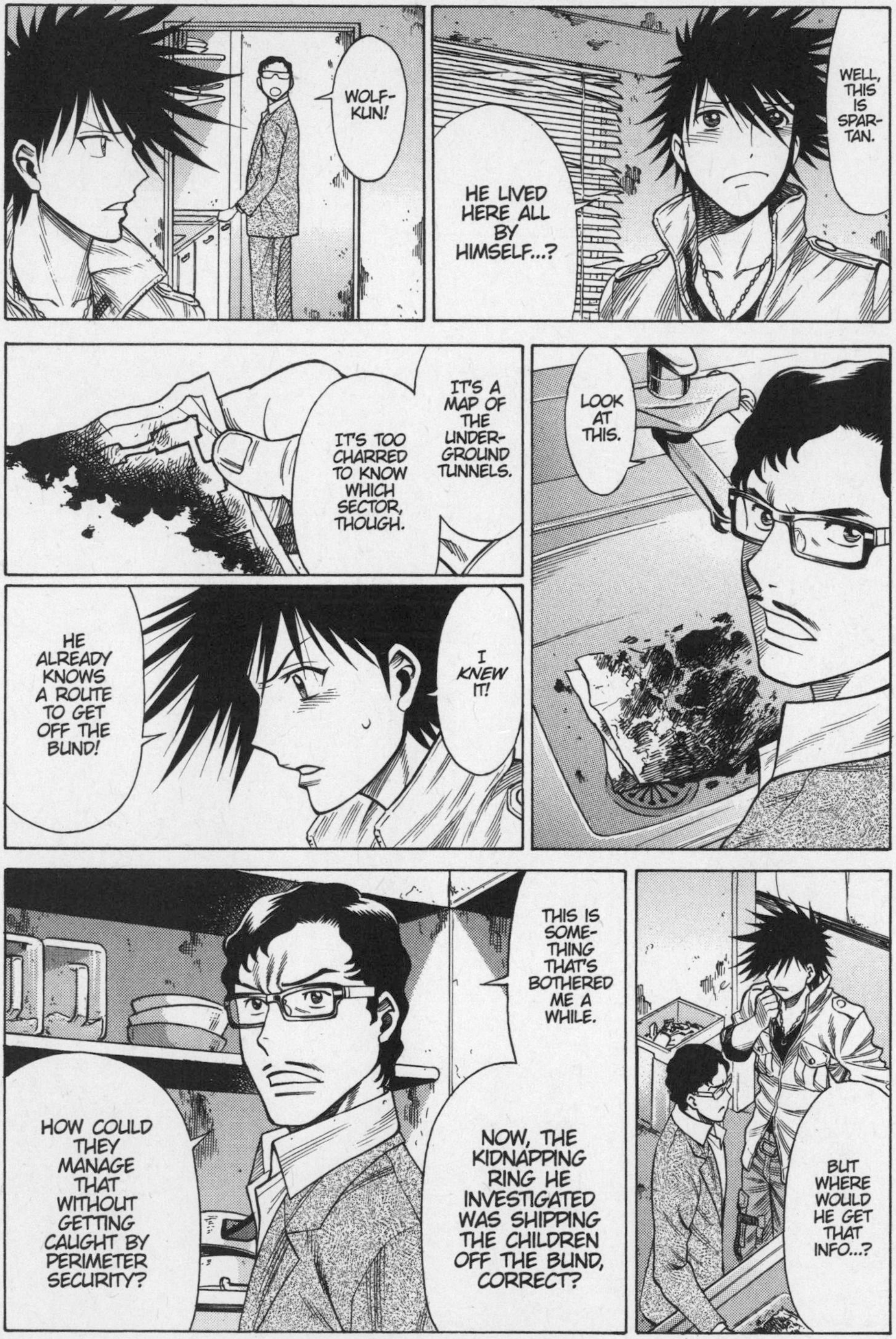
WELL, THIS IS SPAR-TAN.
HE LIVED HERE ALL BY HIMSELF...?
WOLF-KUN!
LOOK AT THIS.
IT'S A MAP OF THE UNDER-GROUND TUNNELS.
IT'S TOO CHARRED TO KNOW WHICH SECTOR, THOUGH.
I *KNEW* IT!
HE ALREADY KNOWS A ROUTE TO GET OFF THE BUND!
BUT WHERE WOULD HE GET THAT INFO...?
THIS IS SOME-THING THAT'S BOTHERED ME A WHILE.
NOW, THE KIDNAPPING RING HE INVESTIGATED WAS SHIPPING THE CHILDREN OFF THE BUND, CORRECT?
HOW COULD THEY MANAGE THAT WITHOUT GETTING CAUGHT BY PERIMETER SECURITY?

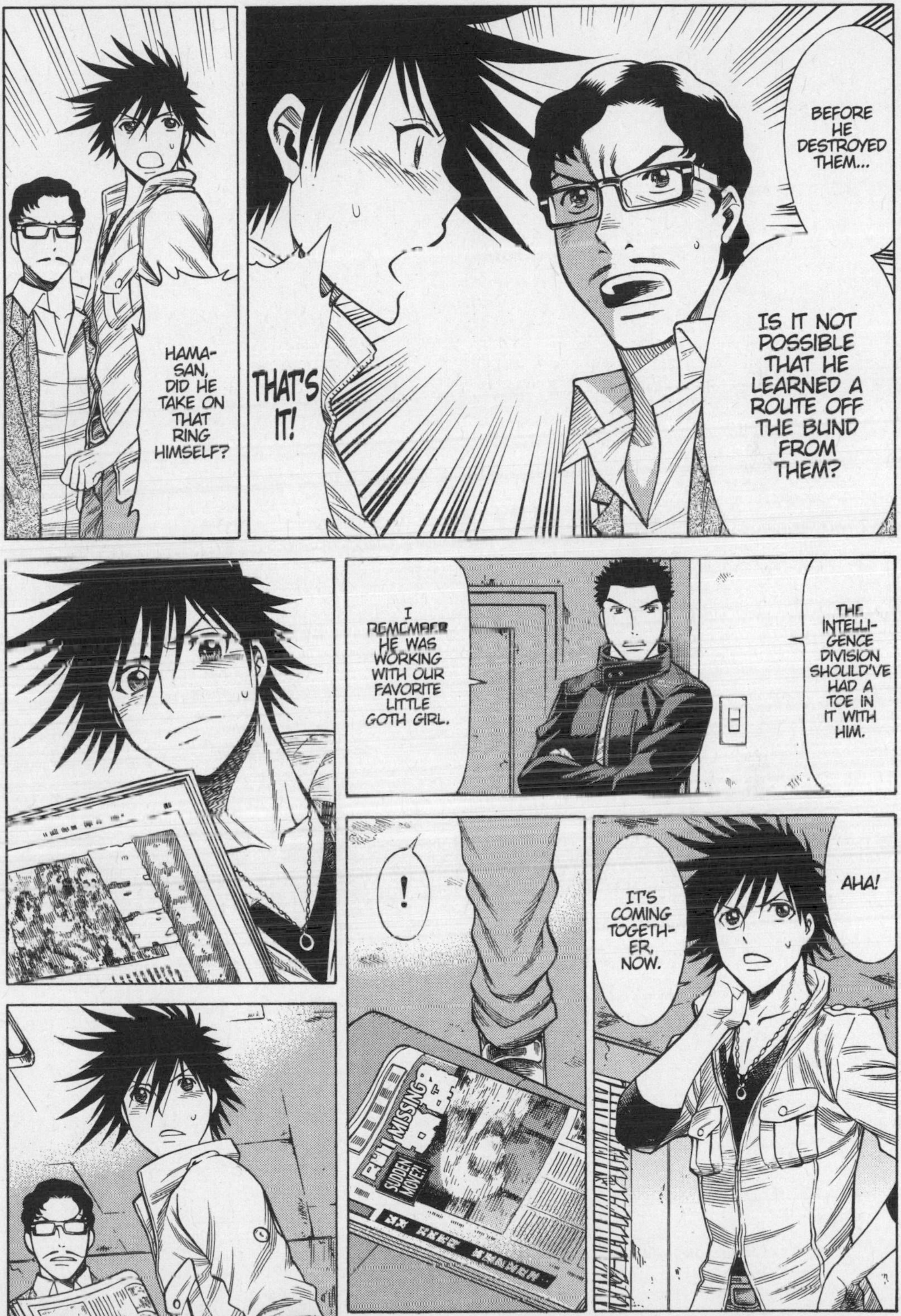
BEFORE HE DESTROYED THEM...
IS IT NOT POSSIBLE THAT HE LEARNED A ROUTE OFF THE BUND FROM THEM?
THAT'S IT!
HAMA-SAN, DID HE TAKE ON THAT RING HIMSELF?
THE INTELLI-GENCE DIVISION SHOULD'VE HAD A TOE IN IT WITH HIM.
I REMEMBER HE WAS WORKING WITH OUR FAVORITE LITTLE GOTH GIRL.
AHA!
IT'S COMING TOGETH-ER, NOW.
!
MISSING
SUDDEN MOVE?!

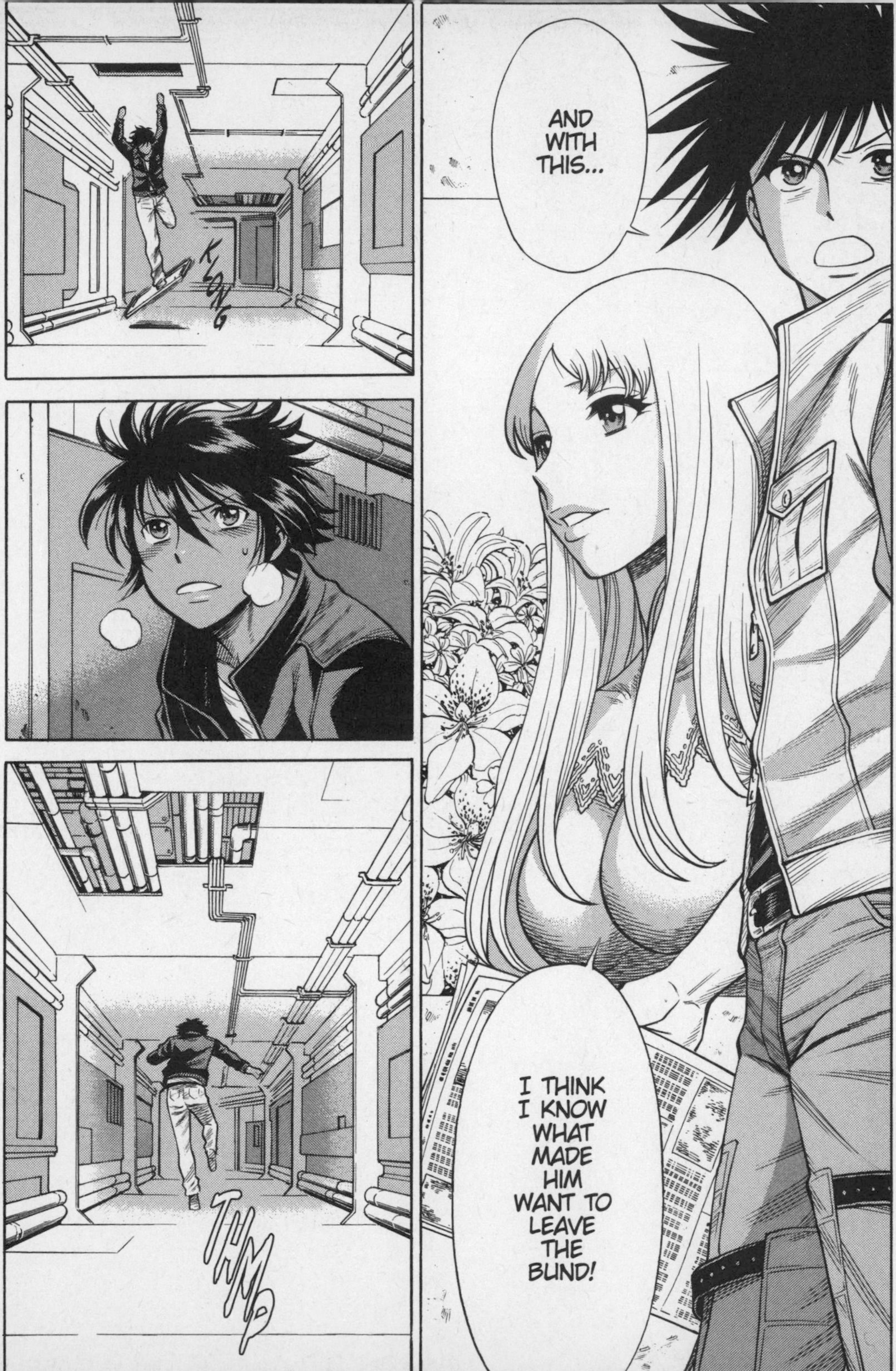
AND WITH THIS...
I THINK I KNOW WHAT MADE HIM WANT TO LEAVE THE BLIND!
KLONG
THMP

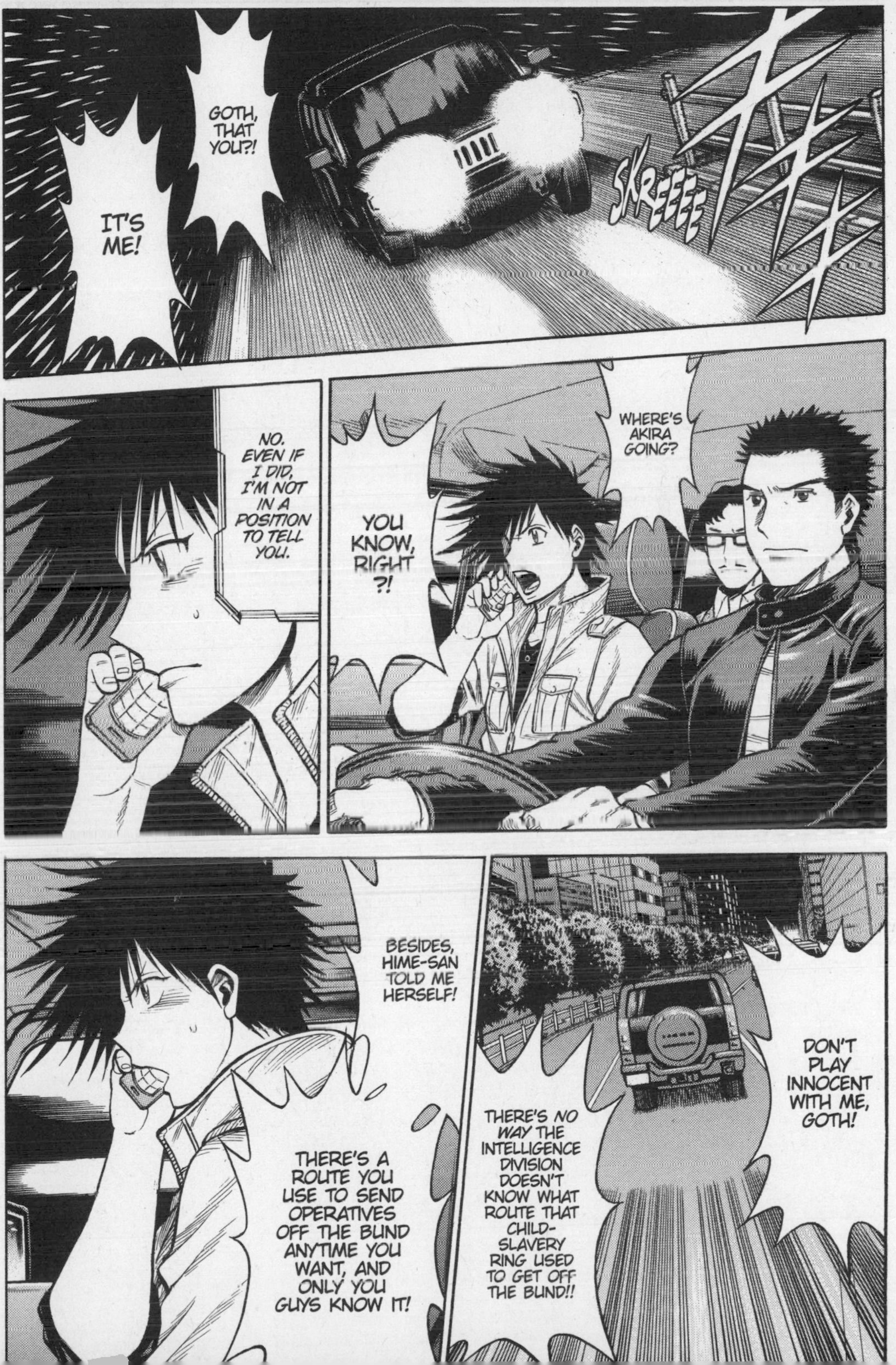
SKREEEEE
GOTH, THAT YOU?!
IT'S ME!
WHERE'S AKIRA GOING?
YOU KNOW, RIGHT?!
NO. EVEN IF I DID, I'M NOT IN A POSITION TO TELL YOU.
DON'T PLAY INNOCENT WITH ME, GOTH!
THERE'S NO WAY THE INTELLIGENCE DIVISION DOESN'T KNOW WHAT ROUTE THAT CHILD-SLAVERY RING USED TO GET OFF THE BUND!!
BESIDES, HIME-SAN TOLD ME HERSELF!
THERE'S A ROUTE YOU USE TO SEND OPERATIVES OFF THE BUND ANYTIME YOU WANT, AND ONLY YOU GUYS KNOW IT!

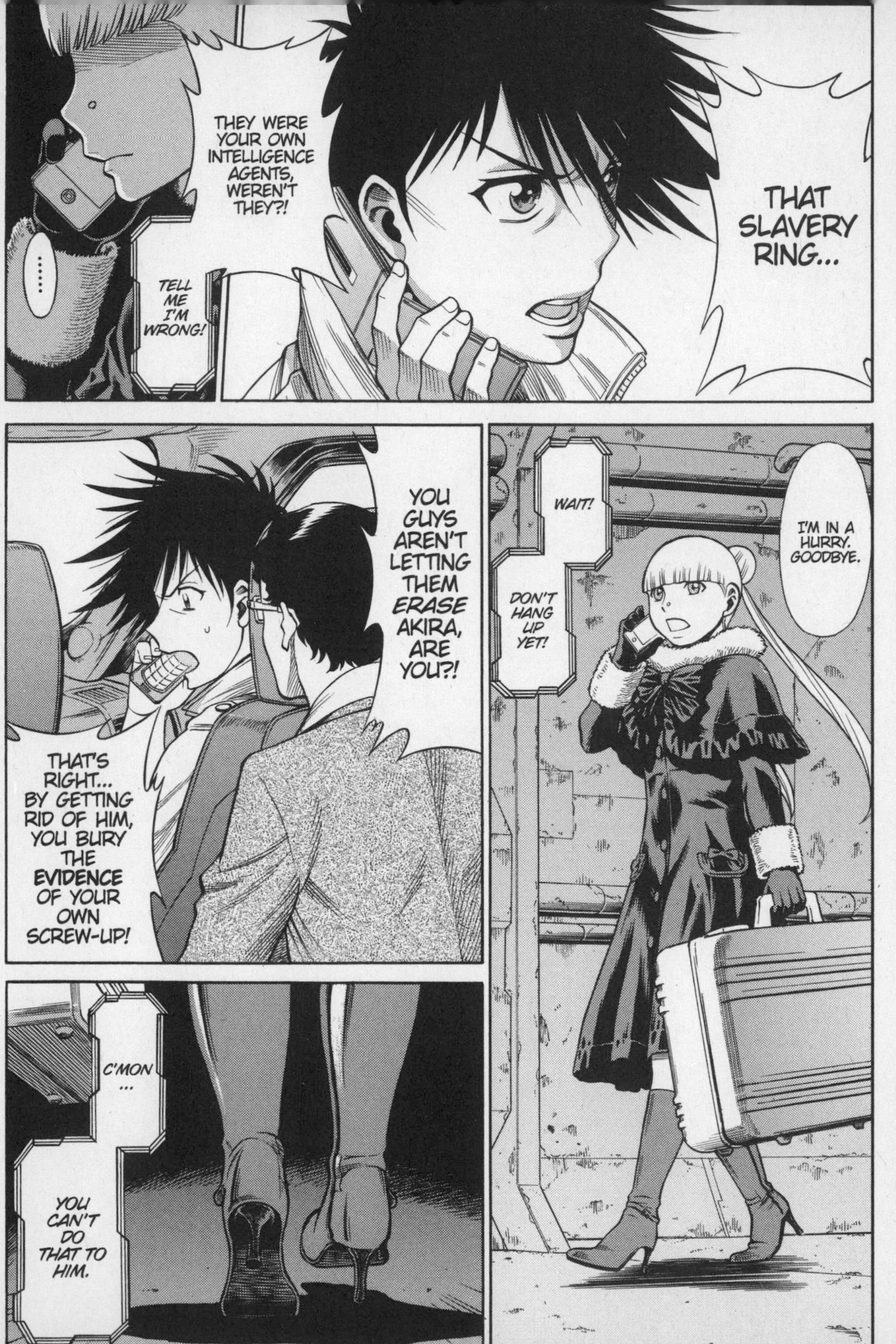
THAT SLAVERY RING...
THEY WERE YOUR OWN INTELLIGENCE AGENTS, WEREN'T THEY?!
TELL ME I'M WRONG!
......
I'M IN A HURRY. GOODBYE.
WAIT!
DON'T HANG UP YET!
YOU GUYS AREN'T LETTING THEM ERASE AKIRA, ARE YOU?!
THAT'S RIGHT... BY GETTING RID OF HIM, YOU BURY THE EVIDENCE OF YOUR OWN SCREW-UP!
C'MON...
YOU CAN'T DO THAT TO HIM.

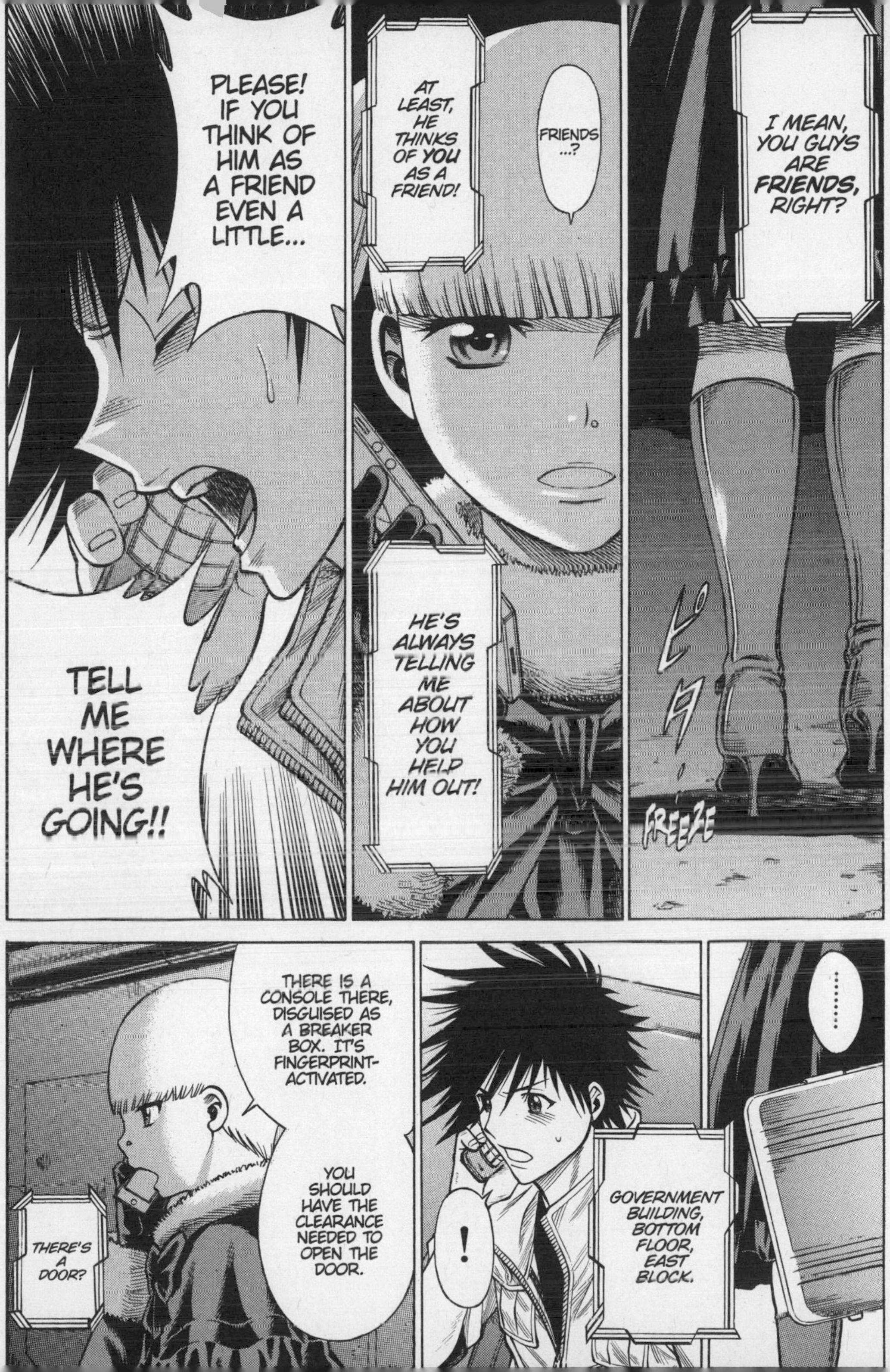
I MEAN, YOU GUYS ARE FRIENDS, RIGHT?
FREEZE
FRIENDS ...?
AT LEAST, HE THINKS OF YOU AS A FRIEND!
HE'S ALWAYS TELLING ME ABOUT HOW YOU HELP HIM OUT!
PLEASE! IF YOU THINK OF HIM AS A FRIEND EVEN A LITTLE...
TELL ME WHERE HE'S GOING!!
......
GOVERNMENT BUILDING, BOTTOM FLOOR, EAST BLOCK.
!
THERE IS A CONSOLE THERE, DISGUISED AS A BREAKER BOX. IT'S FINGERPRINT-ACTIVATED.
YOU SHOULD HAVE THE CLEARANCE NEEDED TO OPEN THE DOOR.
THERE'S A DOOR?

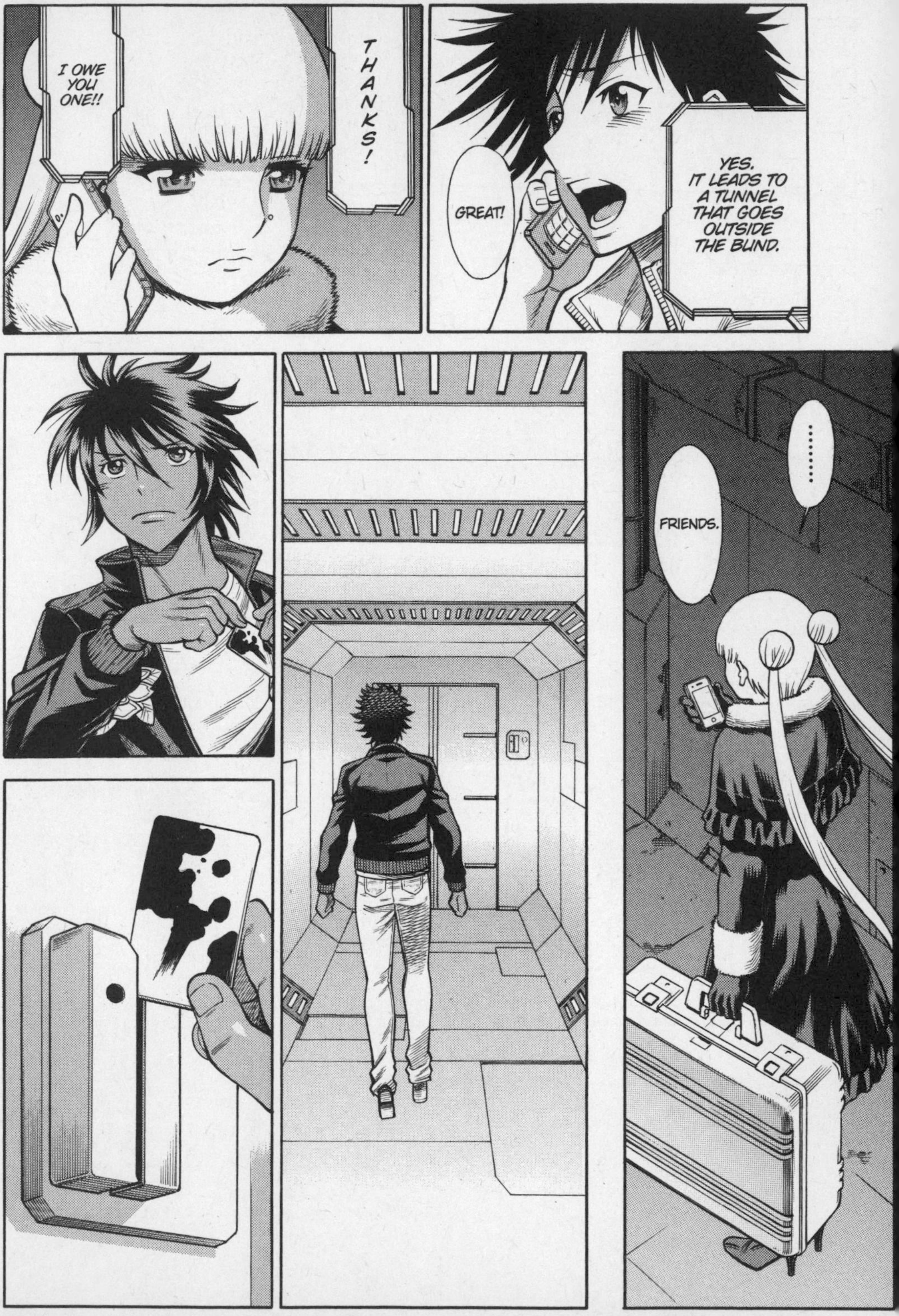
YES. IT LEADS TO A TUNNEL THAT GOES OUTSIDE THE BUND.
GREAT!
THANKS!
I OWE YOU ONE!!
......
FRIENDS.

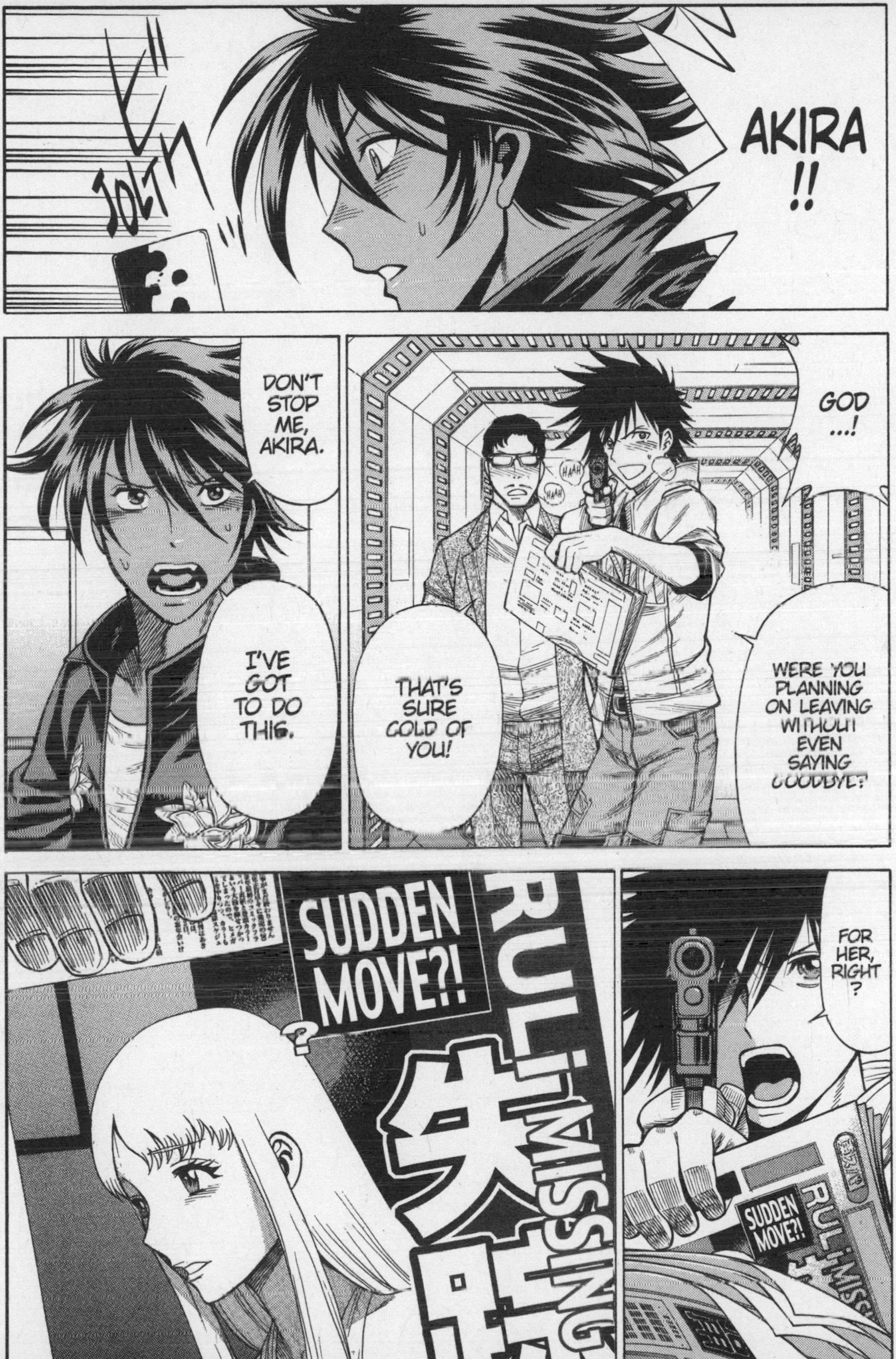
AKIRA !!
JOLT
GOD ...!
HAAH
HAAH
WERE YOU PLANNING ON LEAVING WITHOUT EVEN SAYING GOODBYE?
THAT'S SURE COLD OF YOU!
DON'T STOP ME, AKIRA.
I'VE GOT TO DO THIS.
FOR HER, RIGHT?
SUDDEN MOVE?!
RUL MISSING
SUDDEN MOVE?!
RUL MISSING
?

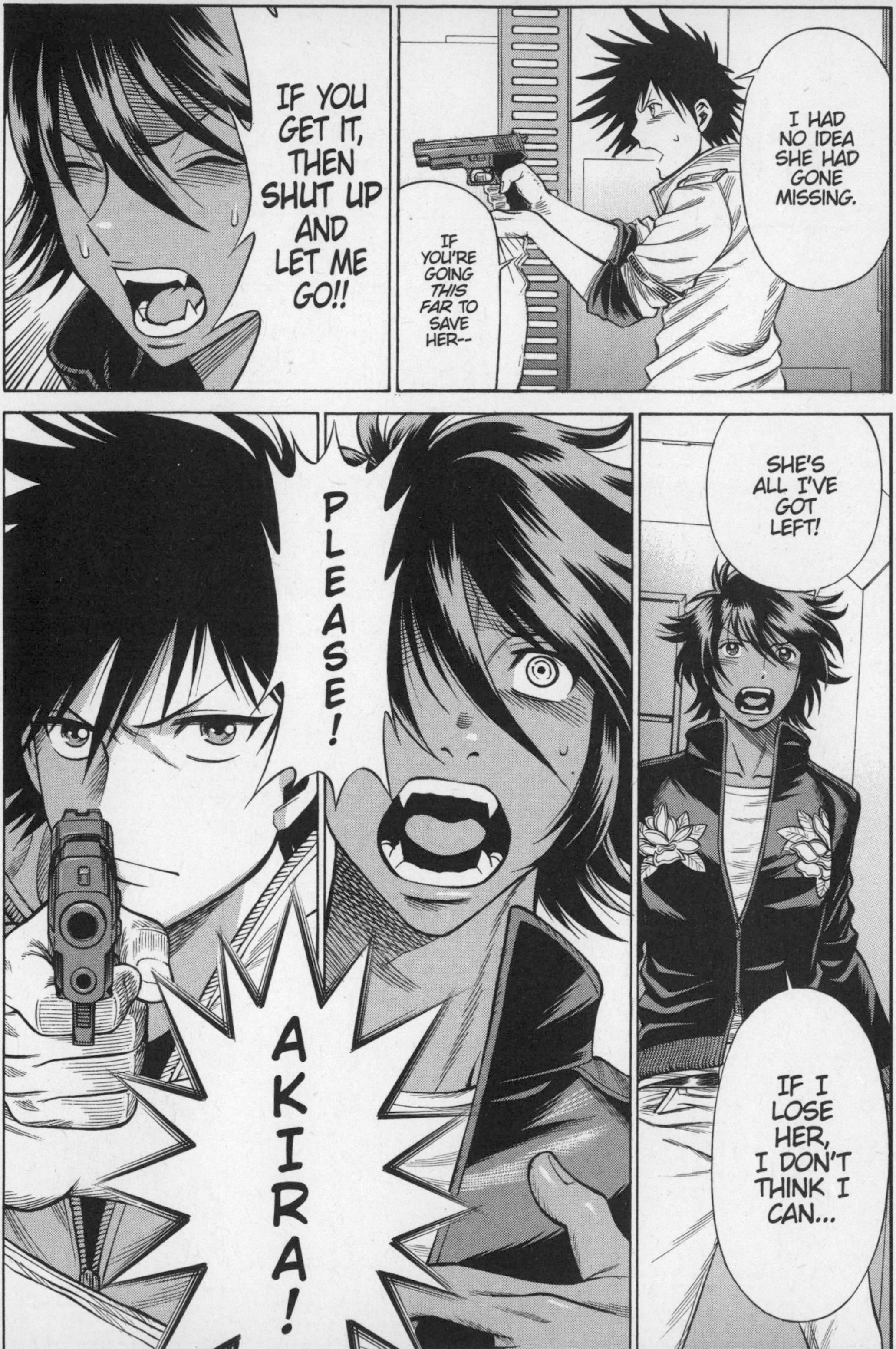
I HAD NO IDEA SHE HAD GONE MISSING.
IF YOU'RE GOING THIS FAR TO SAVE HER--
IF YOU GET IT, THEN SHUT UP AND LET ME GO!!
SHE'S ALL I'VE GOT LEFT!
IF I LOSE HER, I DON'T THINK I CAN...
PLEASE!
AKIRA!

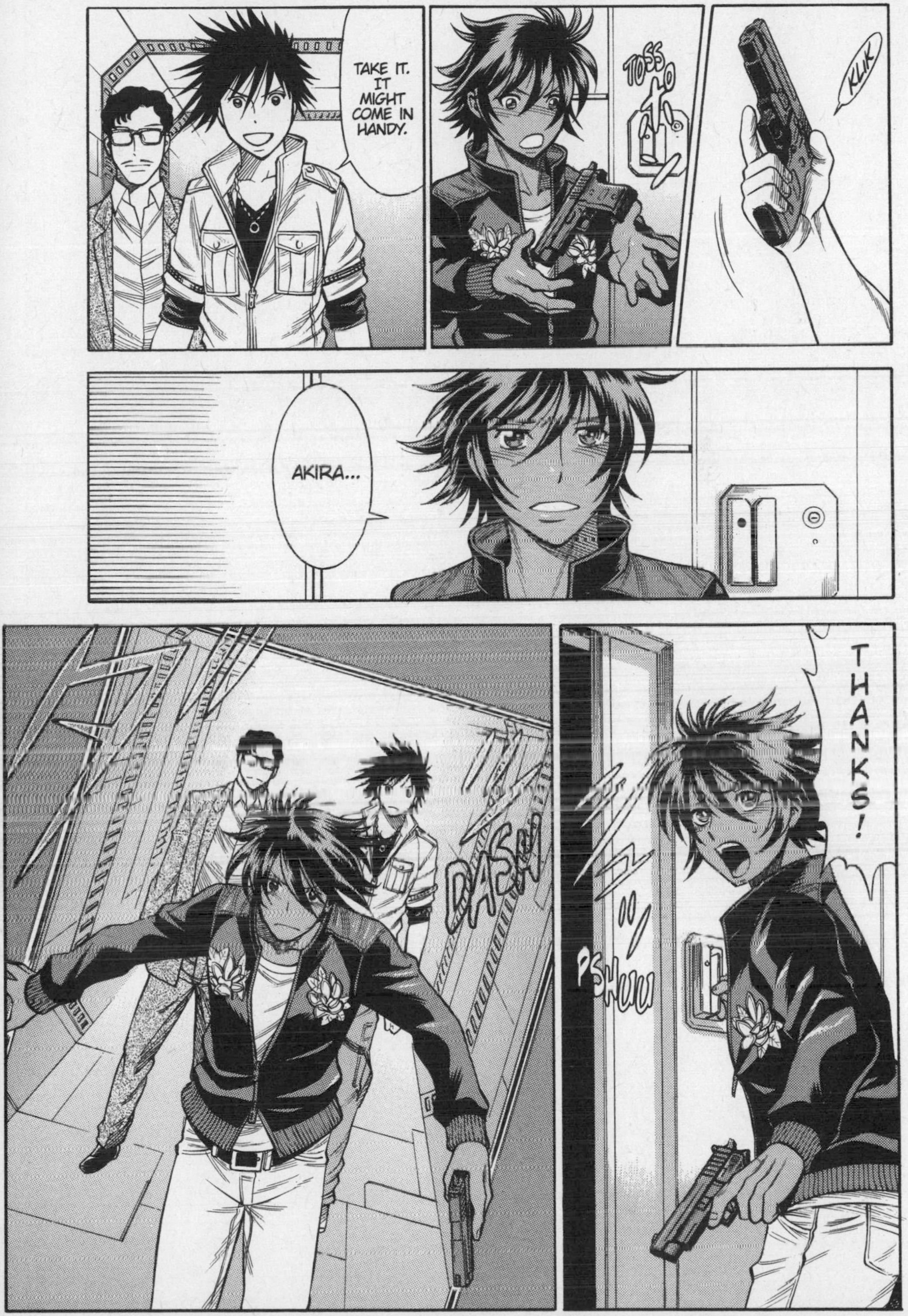
KLIK
TOSS
TAKE IT. IT MIGHT COME IN HANDY.
AKIRA...
THANKS!
PSHUU
DASH

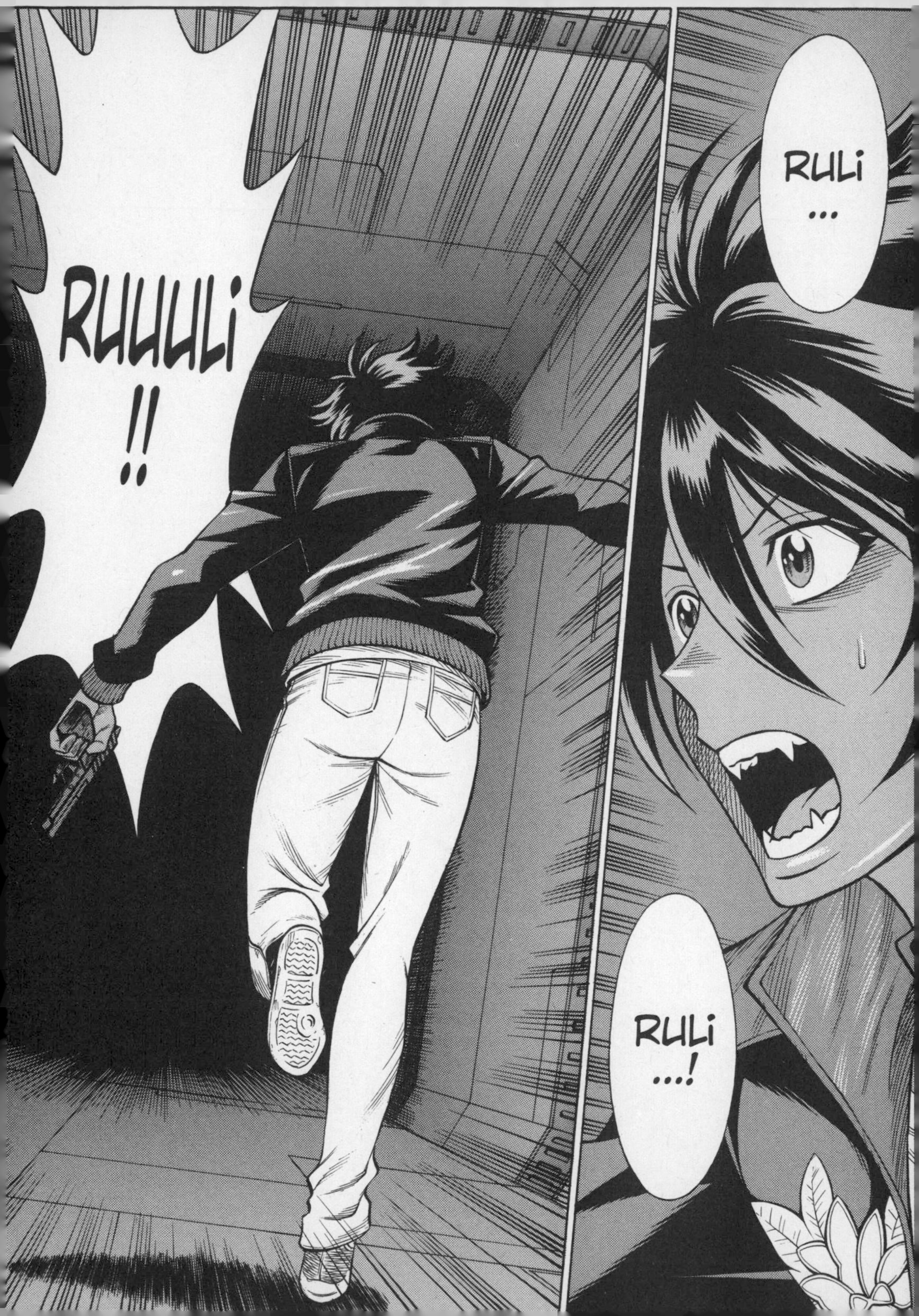
RULI ...
RULI ...!
RUUULI !!

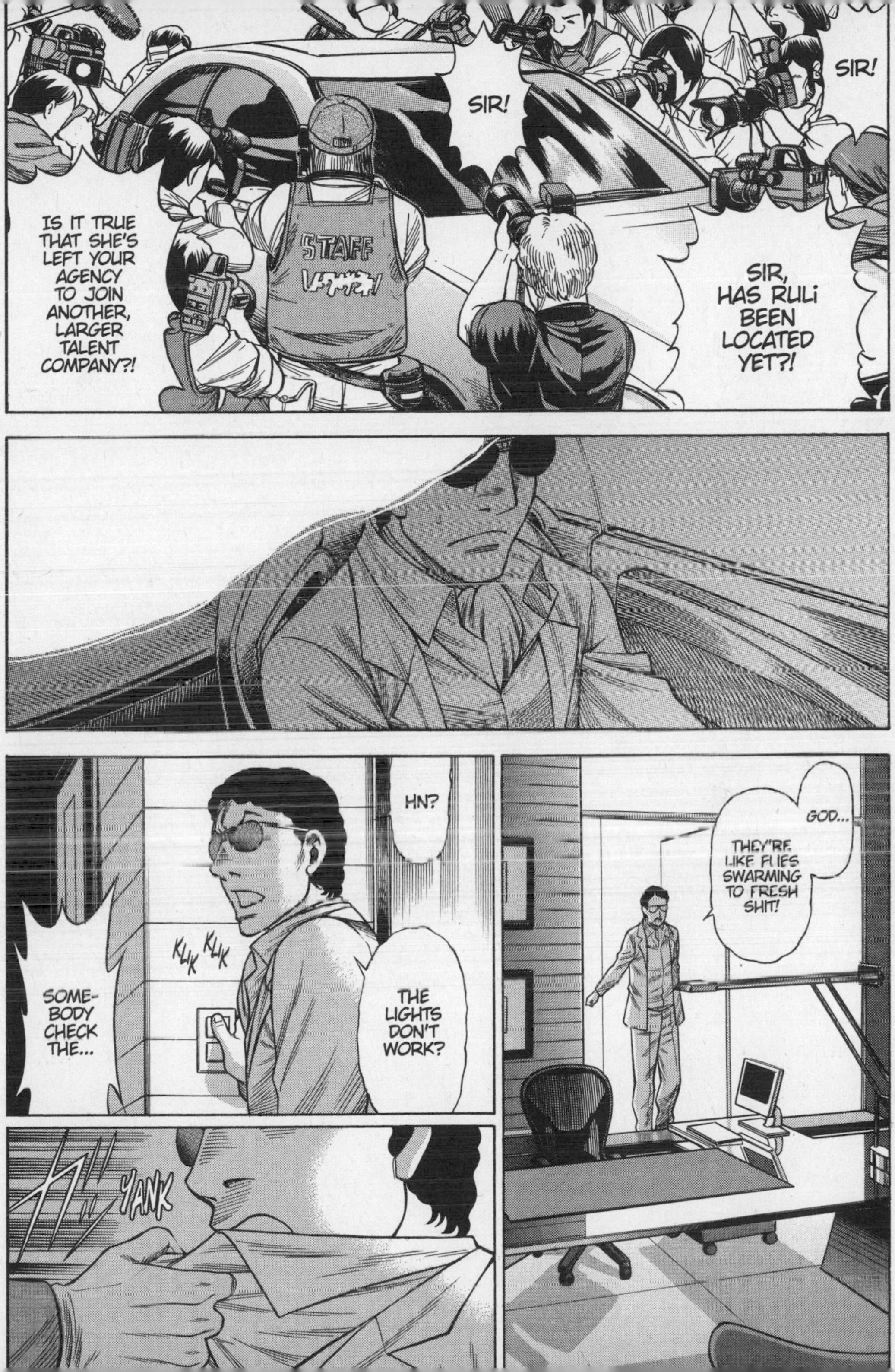
SIR!
SIR!
SIR, HAS RULi BEEN LOCATED YET?!
STAFF
IS IT TRUE THAT SHE'S LEFT YOUR AGENCY TO JOIN ANOTHER, LARGER TALENT COMPANY?!
GOD...
THEY'RE LIKE FLIES SWARMING TO FRESH SHIT!
HN?
KLIK KLIK
THE LIGHTS DON'T WORK?
SOME-BODY CHECK THE...
YANK

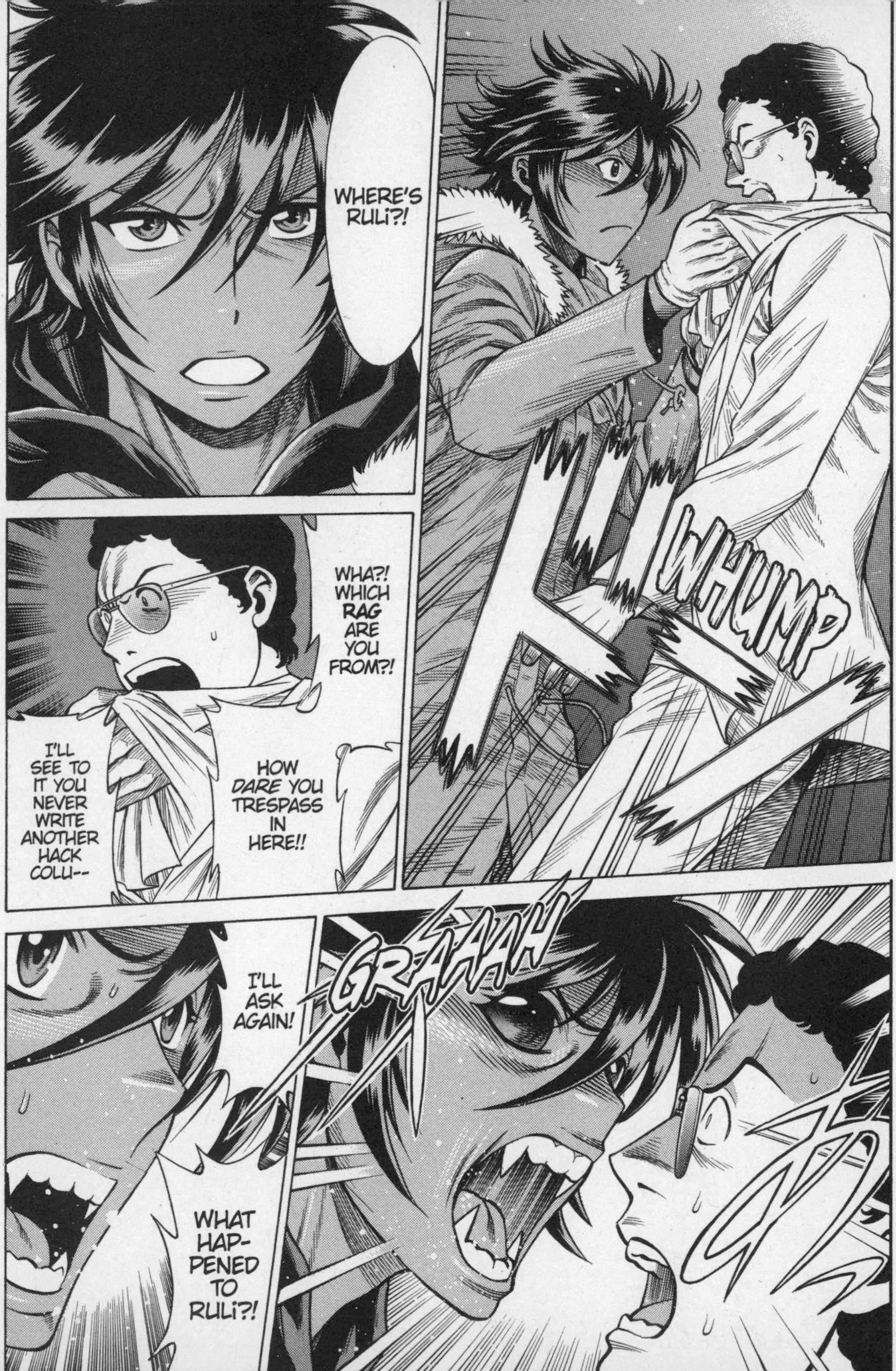
WHUMP
WHERE'S RULi?!
WHA?! WHICH RAG ARE YOU FROM?!
HOW DARE YOU TRESPASS IN HERE!!
I'LL SEE TO IT YOU NEVER WRITE ANOTHER HACK COLU--
GRAAAH
I'LL ASK AGAIN!
WHAT HAP-PENED TO RULi?!

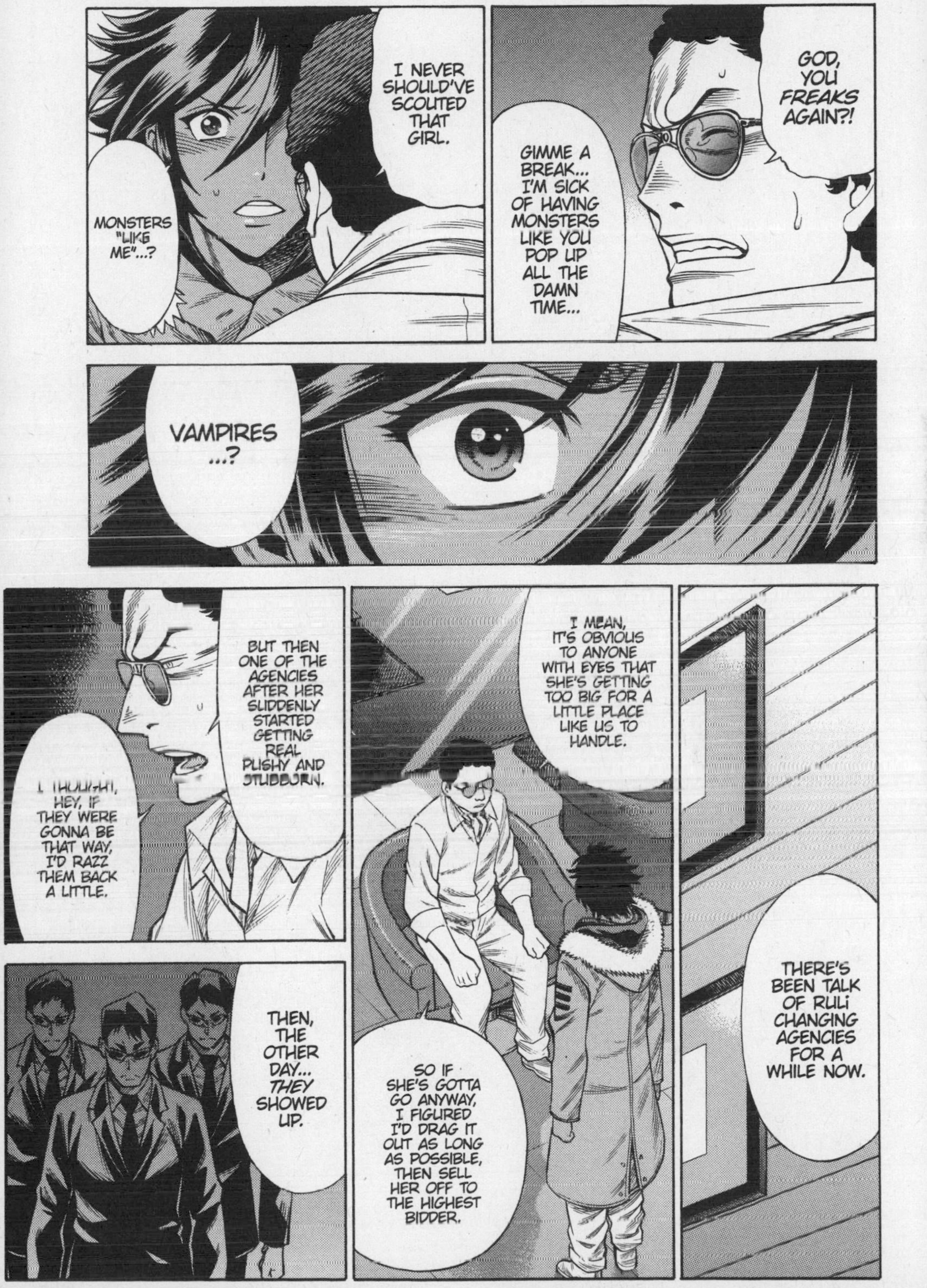
GOD, YOU FREAKS AGAIN?!
GIMME A BREAK... I'M SICK OF HAVING MONSTERS LIKE YOU POP UP ALL THE DAMN TIME...
I NEVER SHOULD'VE SCOUTED THAT GIRL.
MONSTERS "LIKE ME"...?
VAMPIRES ...?
THERE'S BEEN TALK OF RULi CHANGING AGENCIES FOR A WHILE NOW.
I MEAN, IT'S OBVIOUS TO ANYONE WITH EYES THAT SHE'S GETTING TOO BIG FOR A LITTLE PLACE LIKE US TO HANDLE.
SO IF SHE'S GOTTA GO ANYWAY, I FIGURED I'D DRAG IT OUT AS LONG AS POSSIBLE, THEN SELL HER OFF TO THE HIGHEST BIDDER.
BUT THEN ONE OF THE AGENCIES AFTER HER SUDDENLY STARTED GETTING REAL PUSHY AND STUBBORN.
I THOUGHT, HEY, IF THEY WERE GONNA BE THAT WAY, I'D RAZZ THEM BACK A LITTLE.
THEN, THE OTHER DAY... *THEY* SHOWED UP.

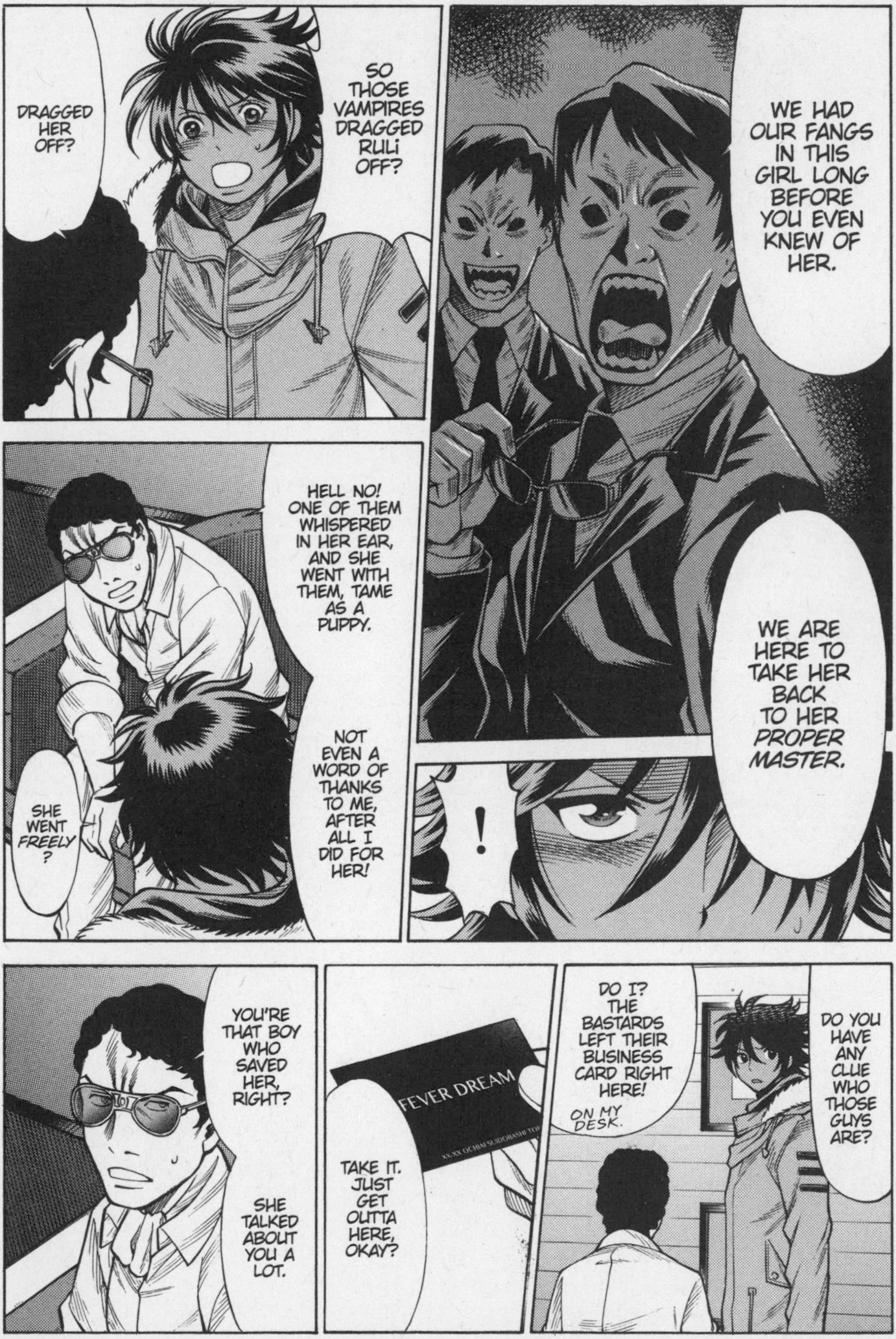
WE HAD OUR FANGS IN THIS GIRL LONG BEFORE YOU EVEN KNEW OF HER.
WE ARE HERE TO TAKE HER BACK TO HER *PROPER MASTER.*
!
SO THOSE VAMPIRES DRAGGED RULi OFF?
DRAGGED HER OFF?
HELL NO! ONE OF THEM WHISPERED IN HER EAR, AND SHE WENT WITH THEM, TAME AS A PUPPY.
NOT EVEN A WORD OF THANKS TO ME, AFTER ALL I DID FOR HER!
SHE WENT *FREELY*?
DO YOU HAVE ANY CLUE WHO THOSE GUYS ARE?
DO I? THE BASTARDS LEFT THEIR BUSINESS CARD RIGHT HERE!
ON MY DESK.
FEVER DREAM
TAKE IT. JUST GET OUTTA HERE, OKAY?
YOU'RE THAT BOY WHO SAVED HER, RIGHT?
SHE TALKED ABOUT YOU A LOT.

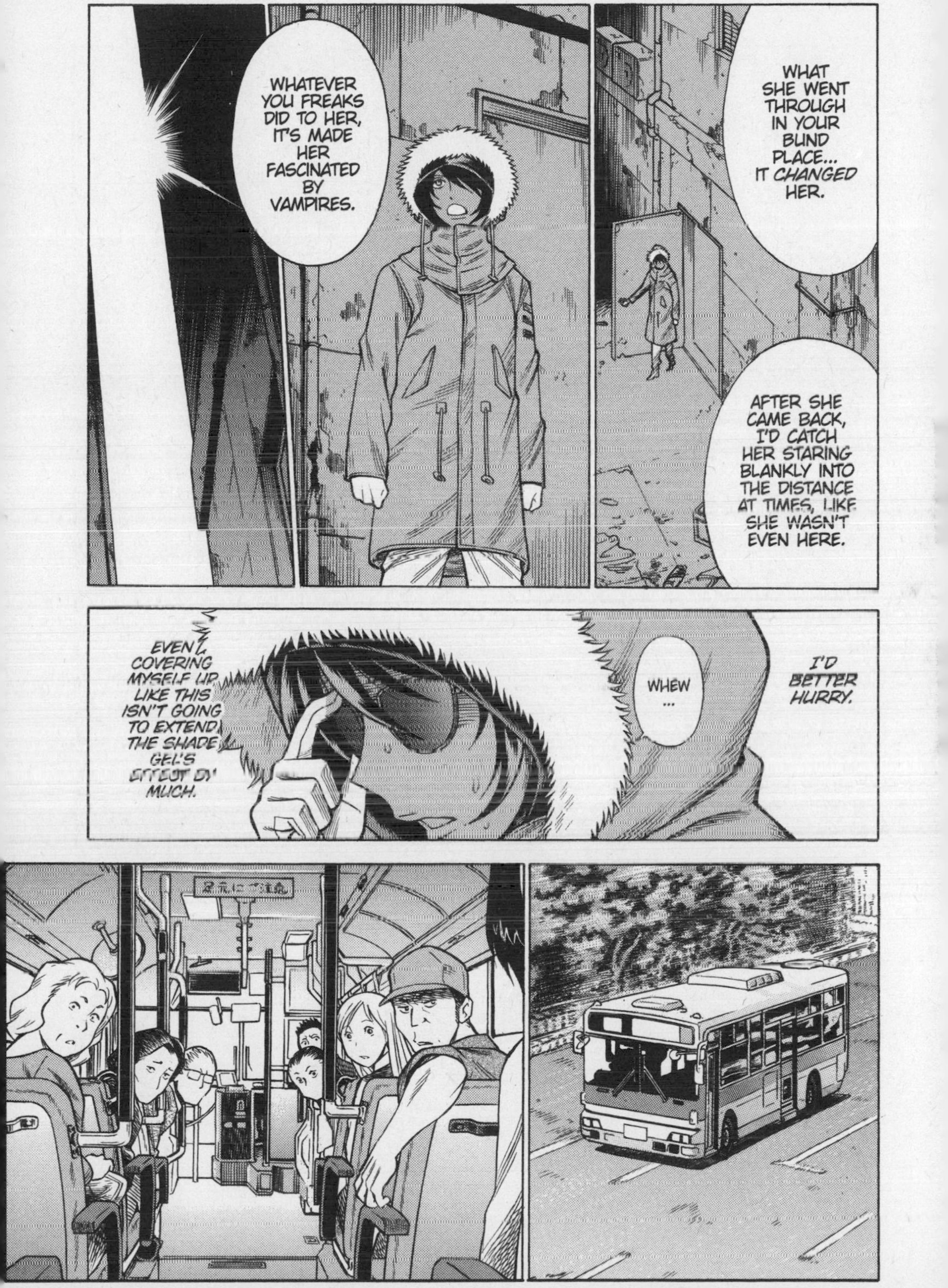
WHAT SHE WENT THROUGH IN YOUR BLIND PLACE... IT CHANGED HER.
AFTER SHE CAME BACK, I'D CATCH HER STARING BLANKLY INTO THE DISTANCE AT TIMES, LIKE SHE WASN'T EVEN HERE.
WHATEVER YOU FREAKS DID TO HER, IT'S MADE HER FASCINATED BY VAMPIRES.
I'D BETTER HURRY.
WHEW ...
EVEN COVERING MYSELF UP LIKE THIS ISN'T GOING TO EXTEND THE SHADE GEL'S EFFECT BY MUCH.

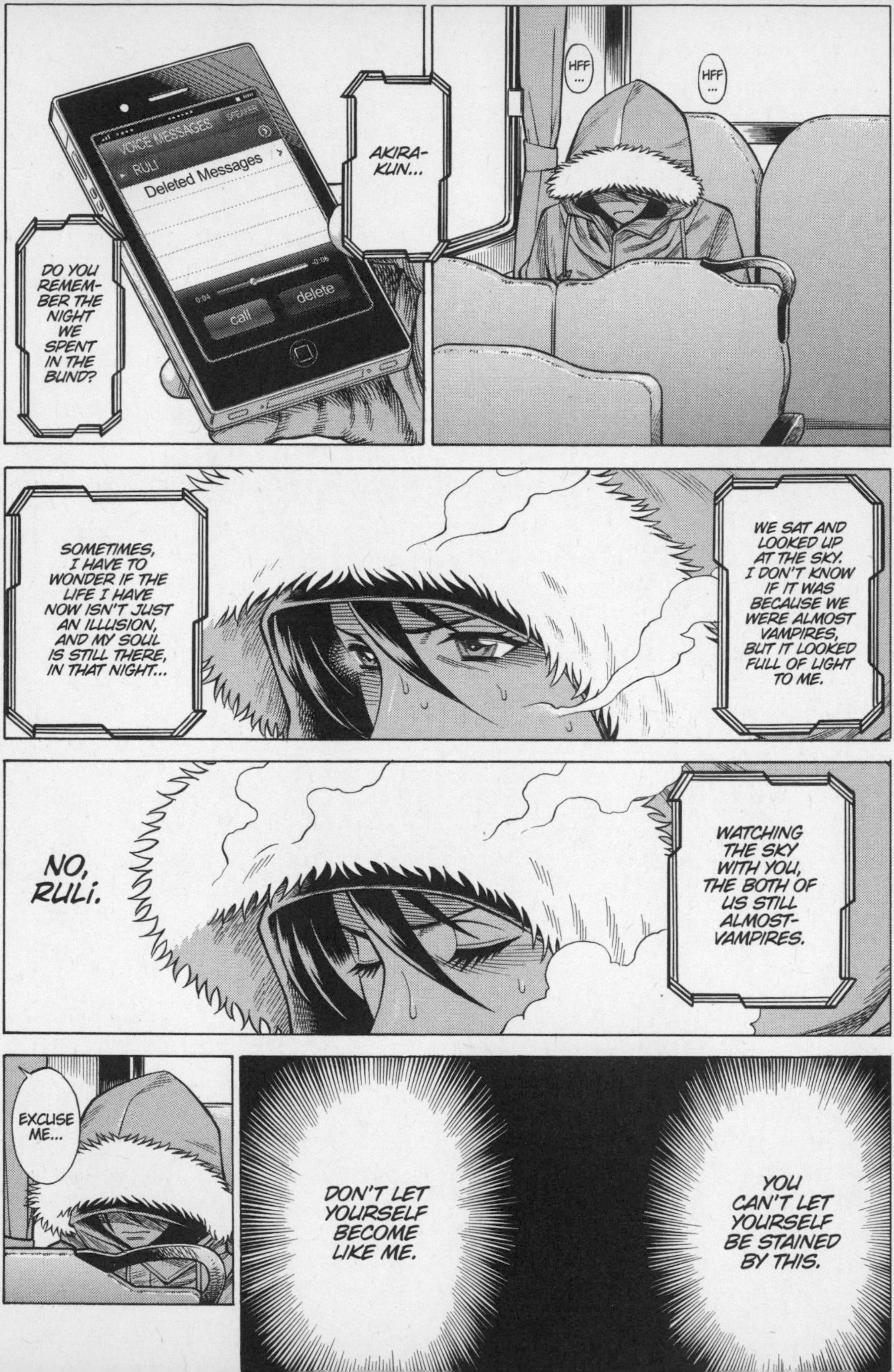
HFF...
HFF...
VOICE MESSAGES
SPEAKER
RULI
Deleted Messages
0:04
delete
call
AKIRA-KUN...
DO YOU REMEMBER THE NIGHT WE SPENT IN THE BUND?
WE SAT AND LOOKED UP AT THE SKY. I DON'T KNOW IF IT WAS BECAUSE WE WERE ALMOST VAMPIRES, BUT IT LOOKED FULL OF LIGHT TO ME.
SOMETIMES, I HAVE TO WONDER IF THE LIFE I HAVE NOW ISN'T JUST AN ILLUSION, AND MY SOUL IS STILL THERE, IN THAT NIGHT...
WATCHING THE SKY WITH YOU, THE BOTH OF US STILL ALMOST-VAMPIRES.
NO, RULi.
YOU CAN'T LET YOURSELF BE STAINED BY THIS.
DON'T LET YOURSELF BECOME LIKE ME.
EXCUSE ME...

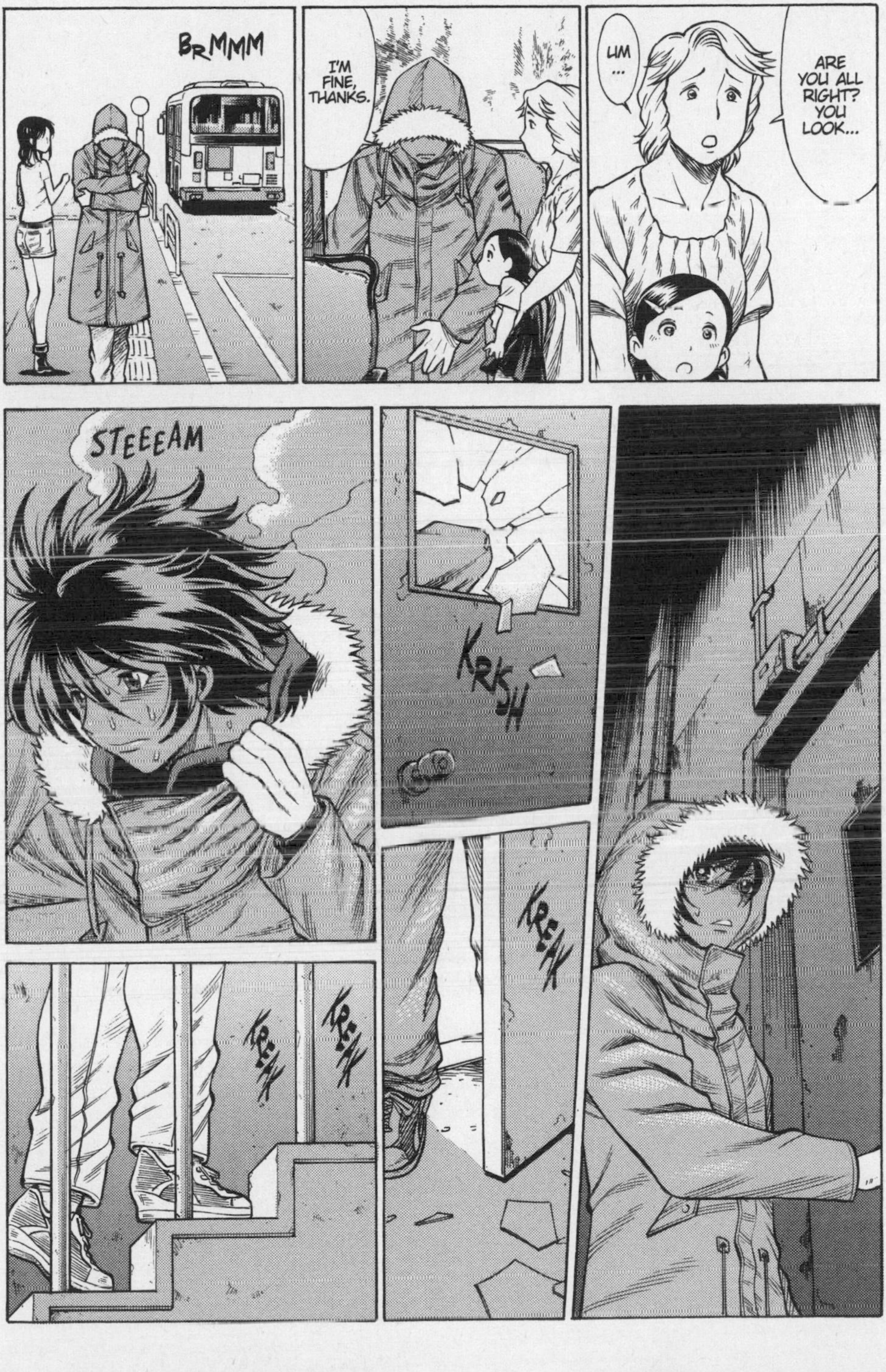
ARE YOU ALL RIGHT? YOU LOOK...
UM ...
I'M FINE, THANKS.
BRMMM
KRKSH
STEEEAM

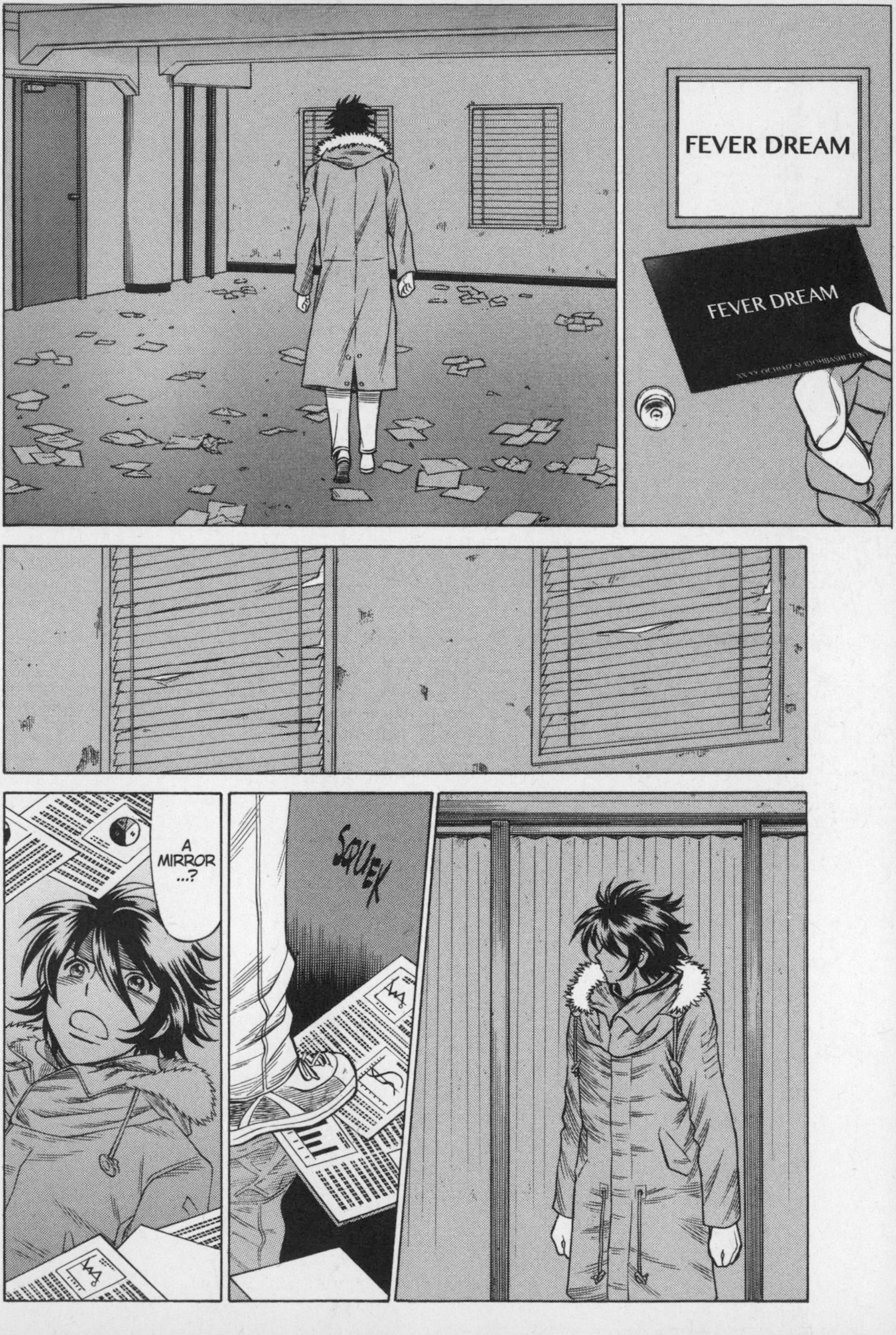
FEVER DREAM
FEVER DREAM
SQUEK
A MIRROR ...?

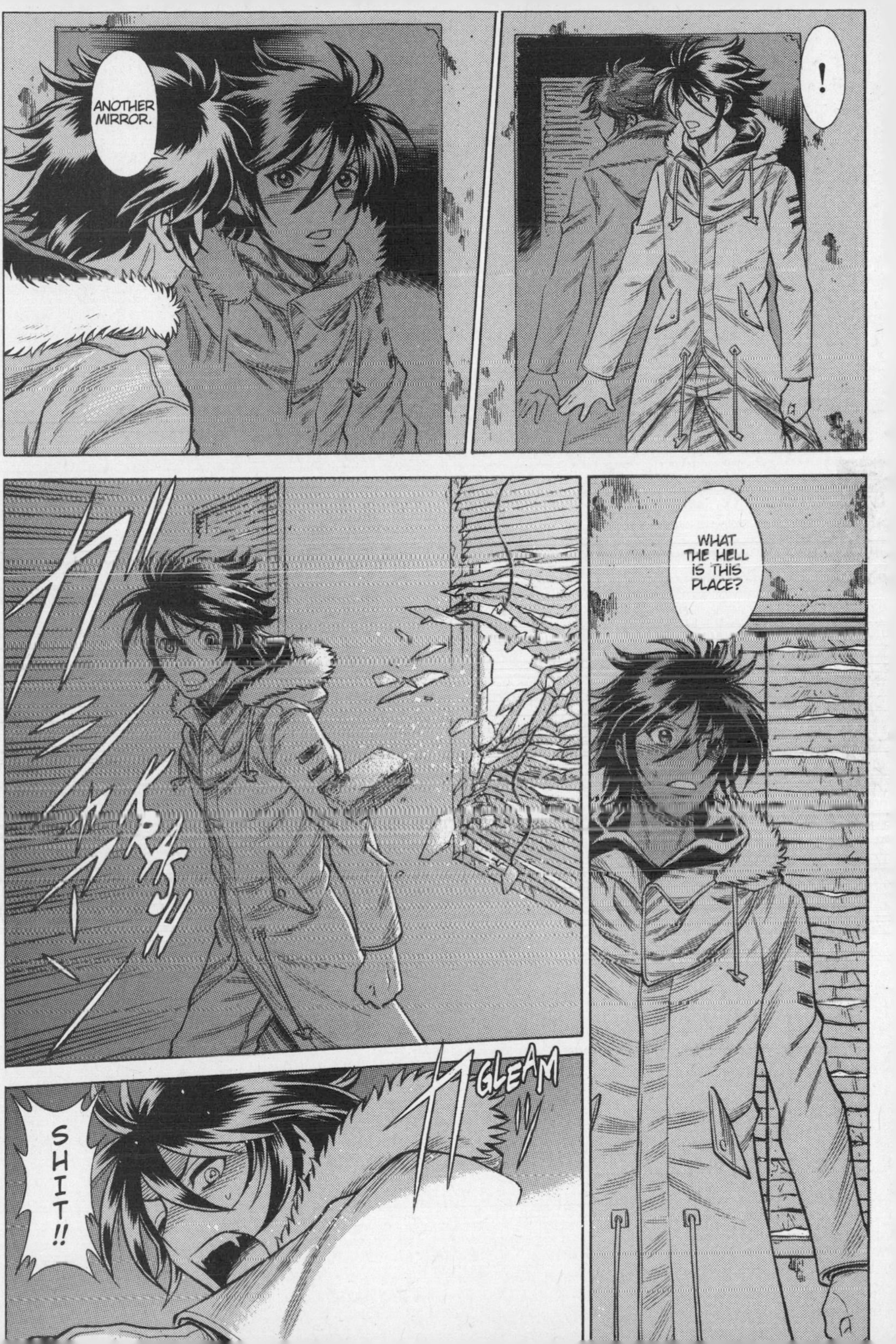
!
ANOTHER MIRROR.
WHAT THE HELL IS THIS PLACE?
KRASH
GLEAM!!
SHIT!!

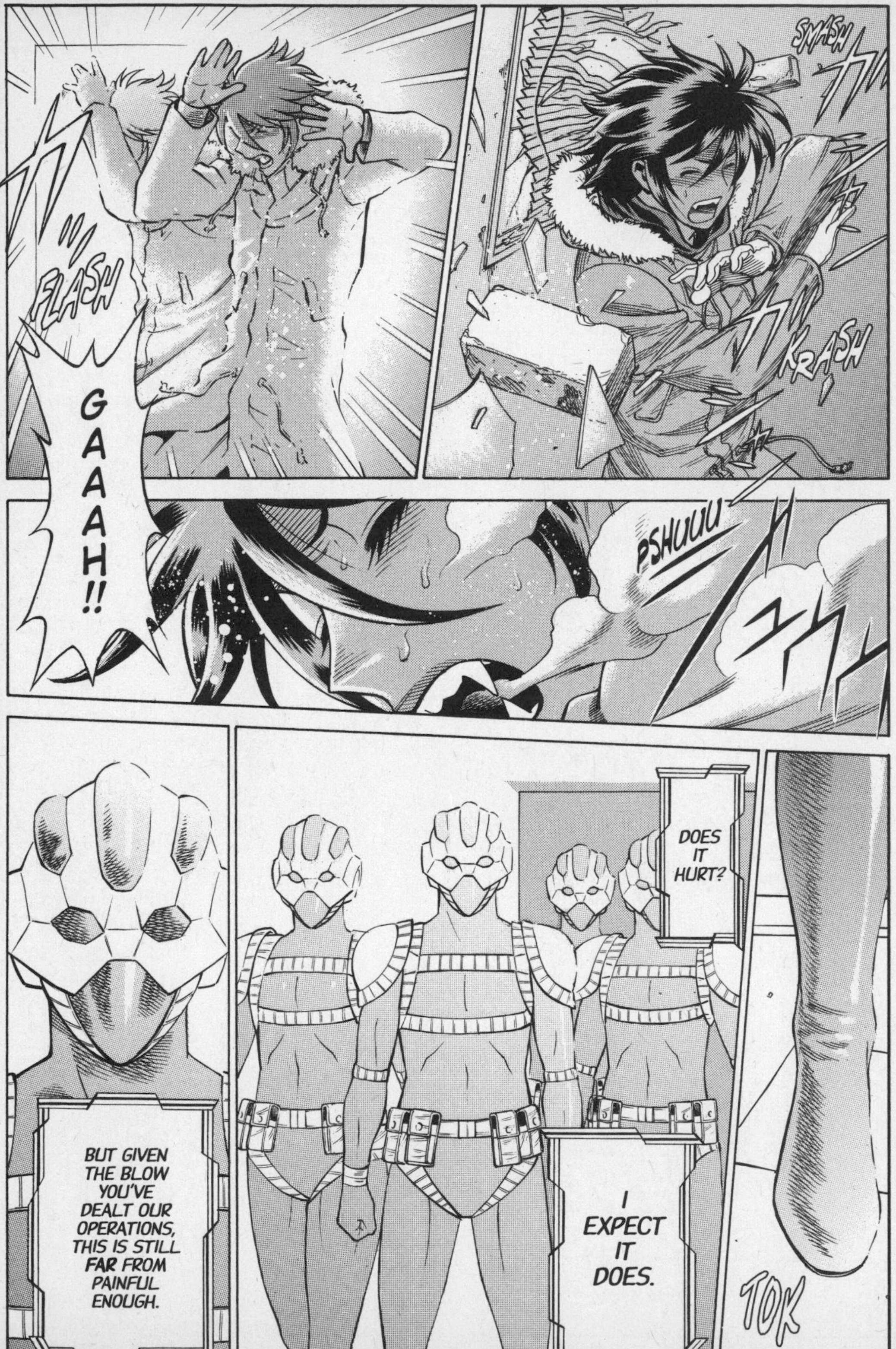
SMASH
KRASH
FLASH
GAAAAH!!
PSHUUU
TOK
DOES IT HURT?
I EXPECT IT DOES.
BUT GIVEN THE BLOW YOU'VE DEALT OUR OPERATIONS, THIS IS STILL FAR FROM PAINFUL ENOUGH.

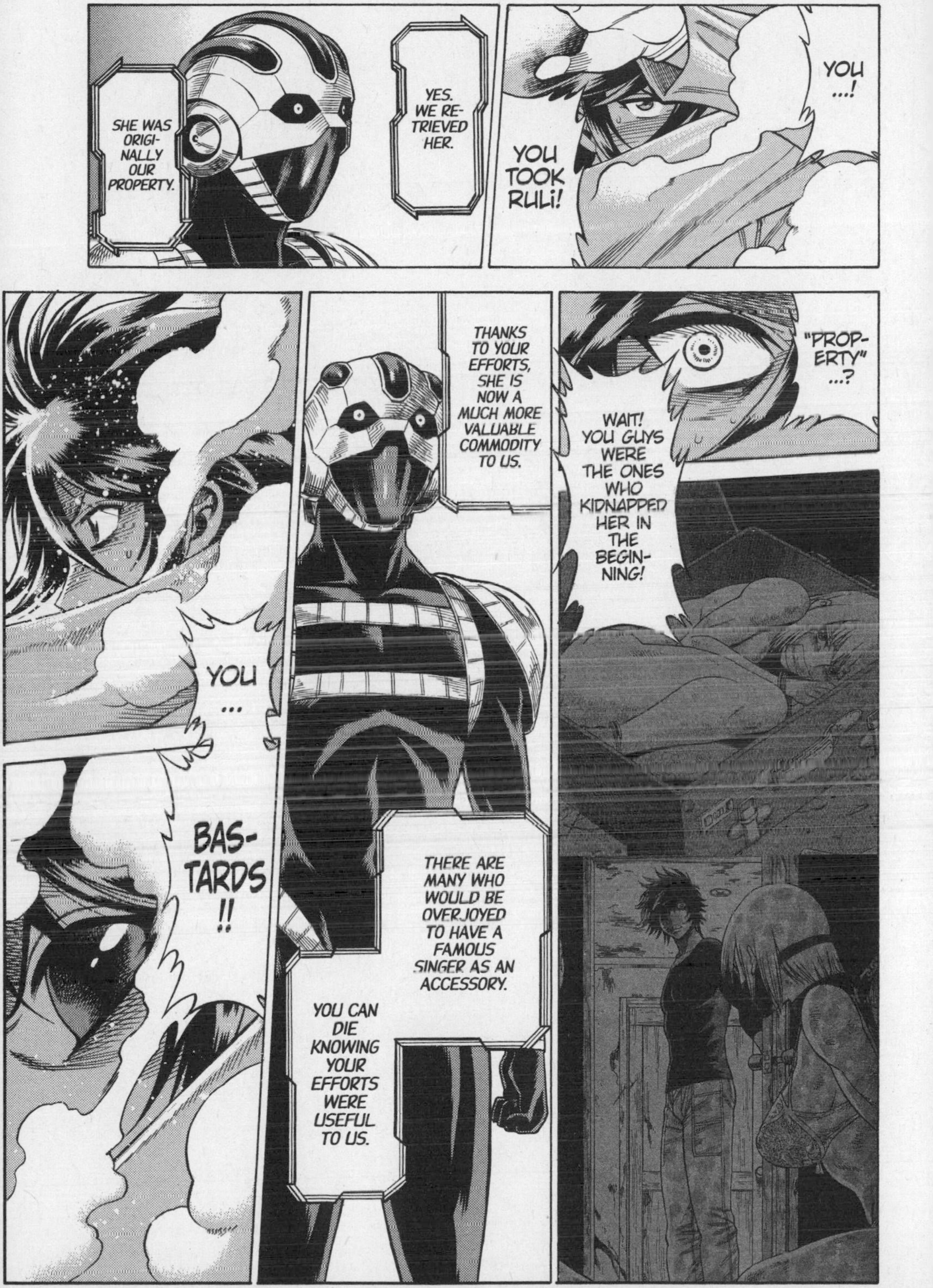

YOU ...!
YOU TOOK RULi!
YES. WE RE-TRIEVED HER.
SHE WAS ORIGI-NALLY OUR PROPERTY.
"PROP-ERTY" ...?
WAIT! YOU GUYS WERE THE ONES WHO KIDNAPPED HER IN THE BEGIN-NING!
THANKS TO YOUR EFFORTS, SHE IS NOW A MUCH MORE VALUABLE COMMODITY TO US.
THERE ARE MANY WHO WOULD BE OVERJOYED TO HAVE A FAMOUS SINGER AS AN ACCESSORY.
YOU CAN DIE KNOWING YOUR EFFORTS WERE USEFUL TO US.
YOU ...
BAS-TARDS !!

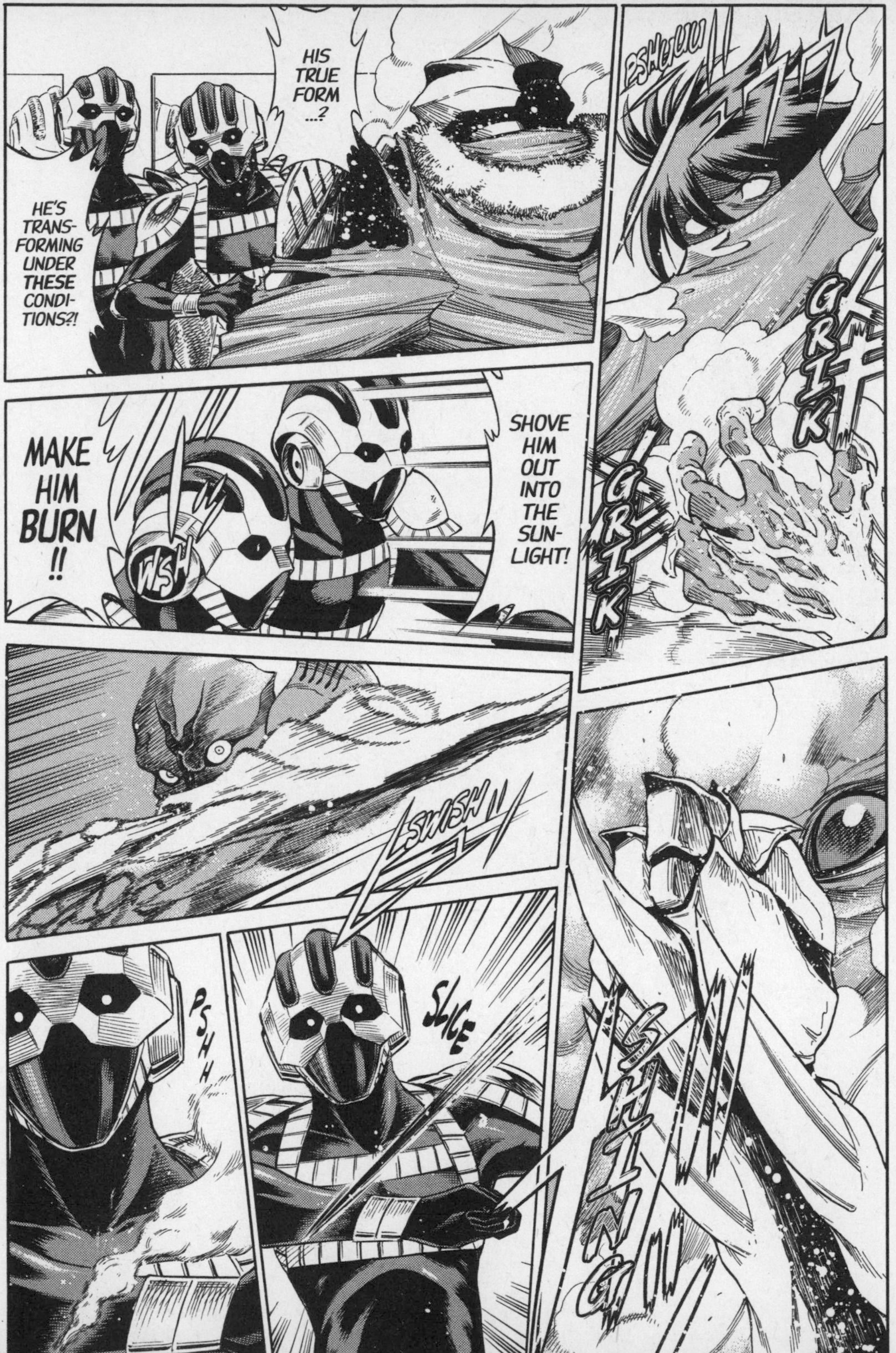
PSHUUU
GRIK
GRIK
HIS TRUE FORM ...?
HE'S TRANS-FORMING UNDER THESE CONDI-TIONS?!
SHOVE HIM OUT INTO THE SUN-LIGHT!
WSH
MAKE HIM BURN!!
SHING
SWISH
SLICE
PSHH...

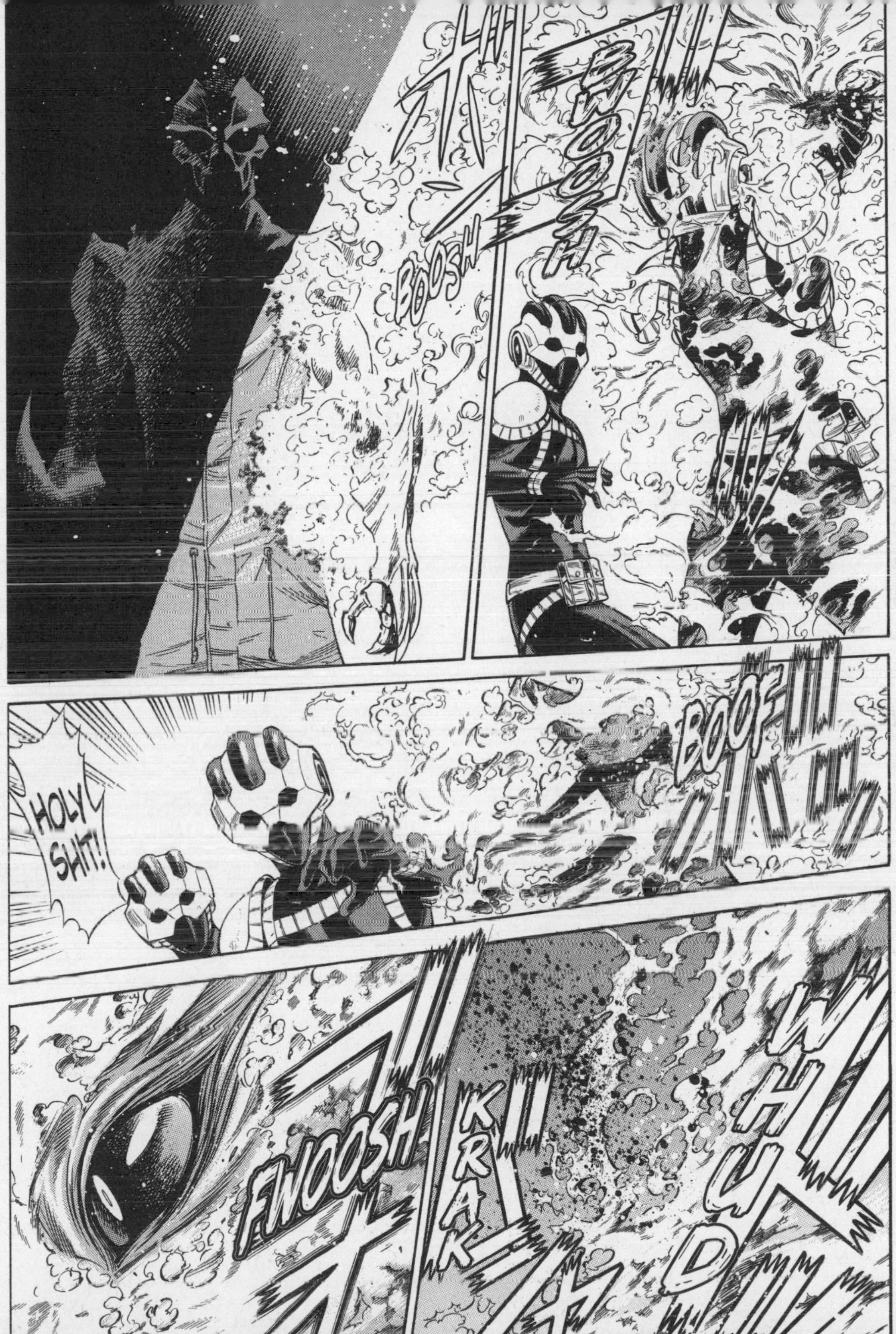
BWOOSH
BOOSH
BOOF!!!
HOLY SHIT!
WHUD!!
KRAK
FWOOSH

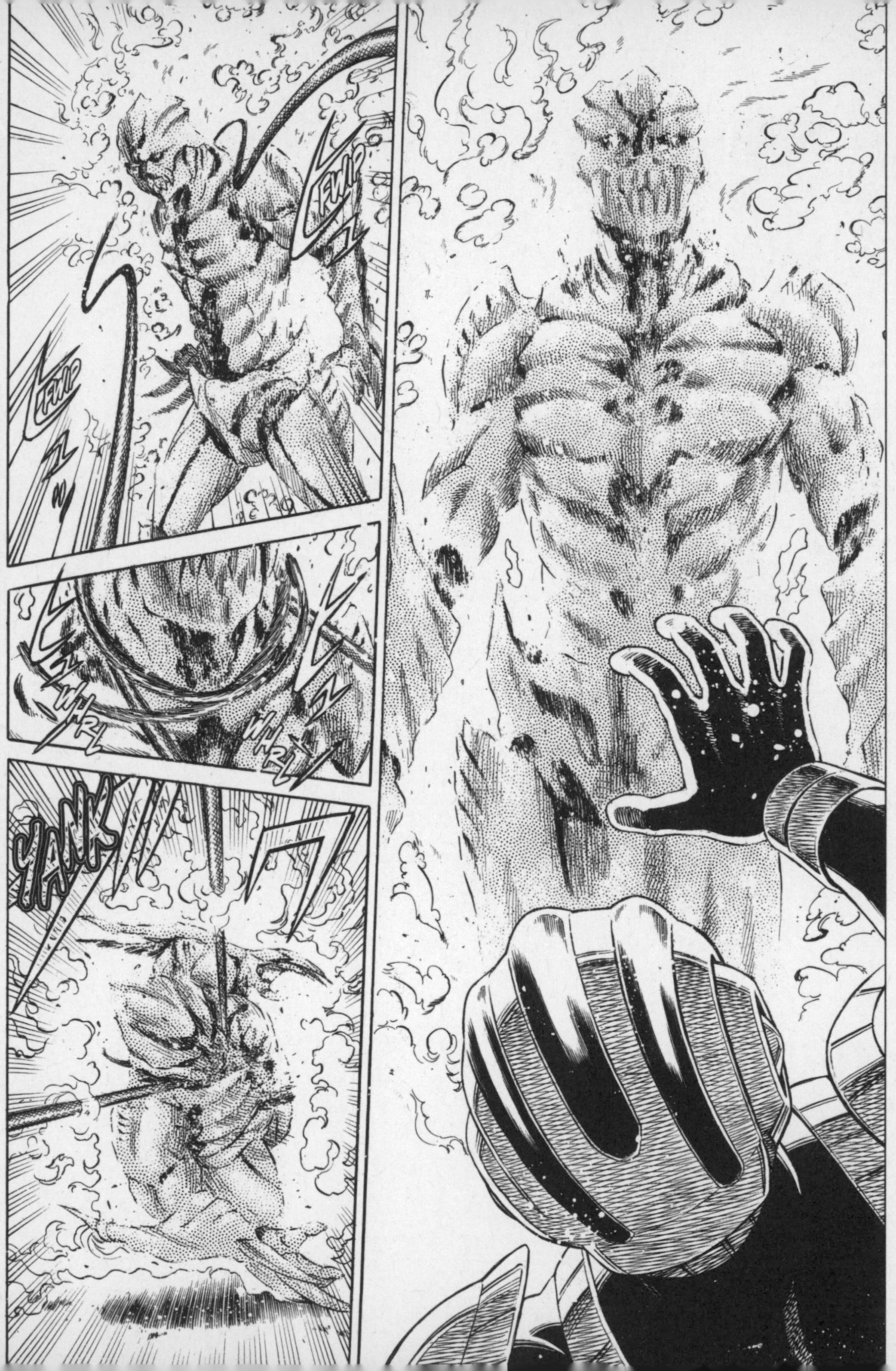
FWIP
FWIP
WHRL
WHRL
YANK

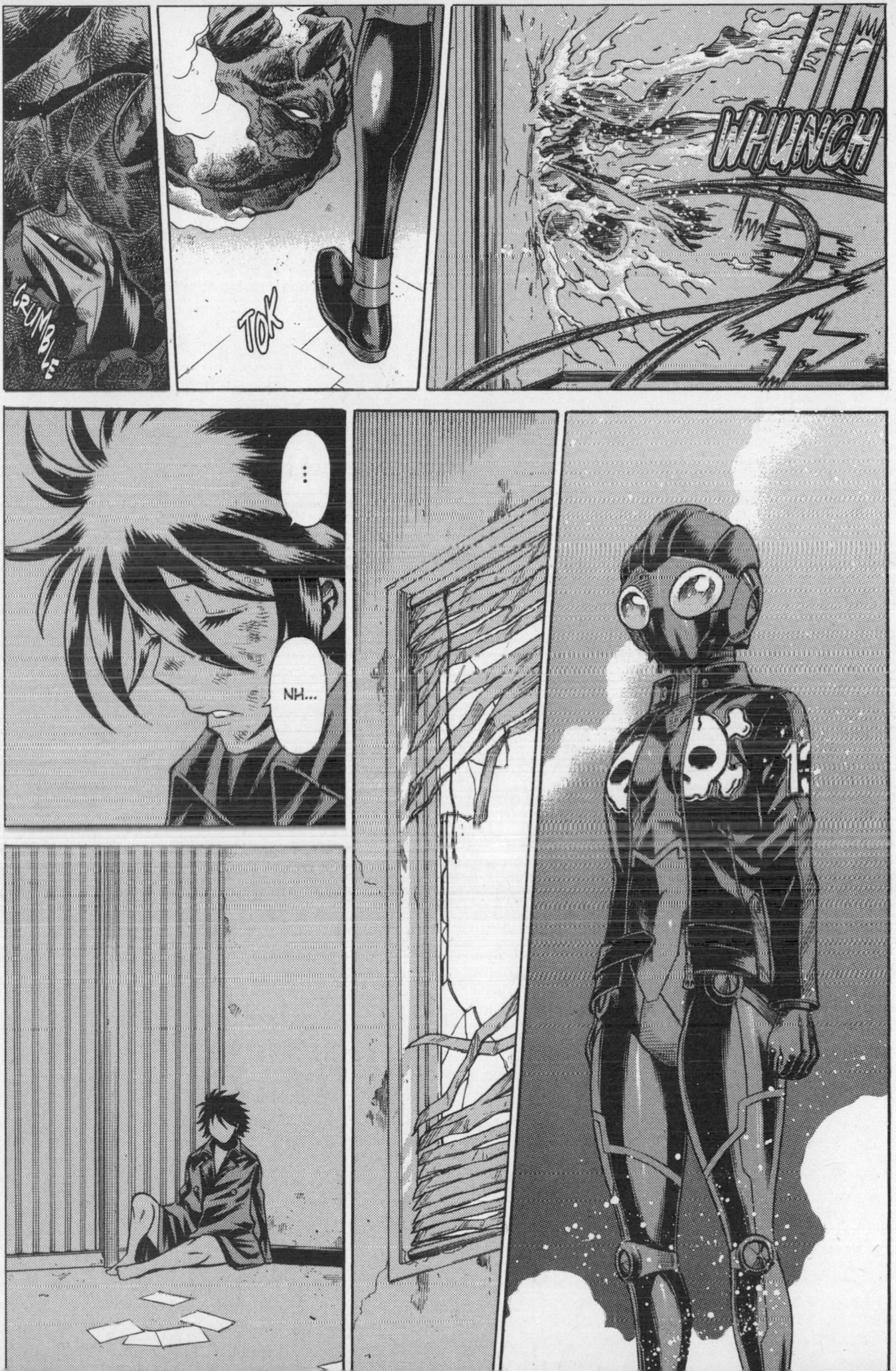
WHUNCH
TOK
CRUMBLE
...
NH...

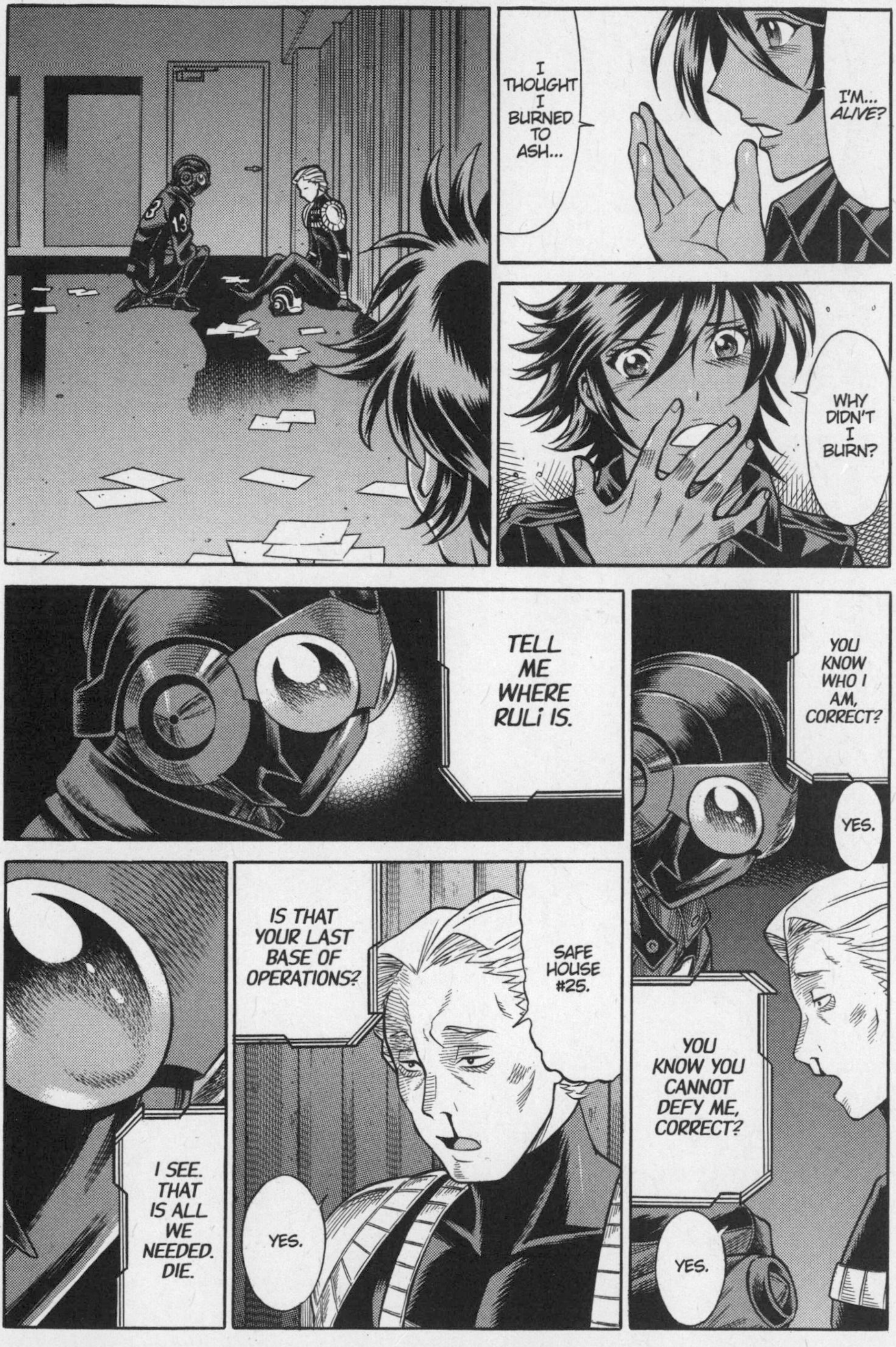
I'M... ALIVE?
I THOUGHT I BURNED TO ASH...
WHY DIDN'T I BURN?
YOU KNOW WHO I AM, CORRECT?
YES.
TELL ME WHERE RULi IS.
YOU KNOW YOU CANNOT DEFY ME, CORRECT?
YES.
SAFE HOUSE #25.
IS THAT YOUR LAST BASE OF OPERATIONS?
YES.
I SEE. THAT IS ALL WE NEEDED. DIE.

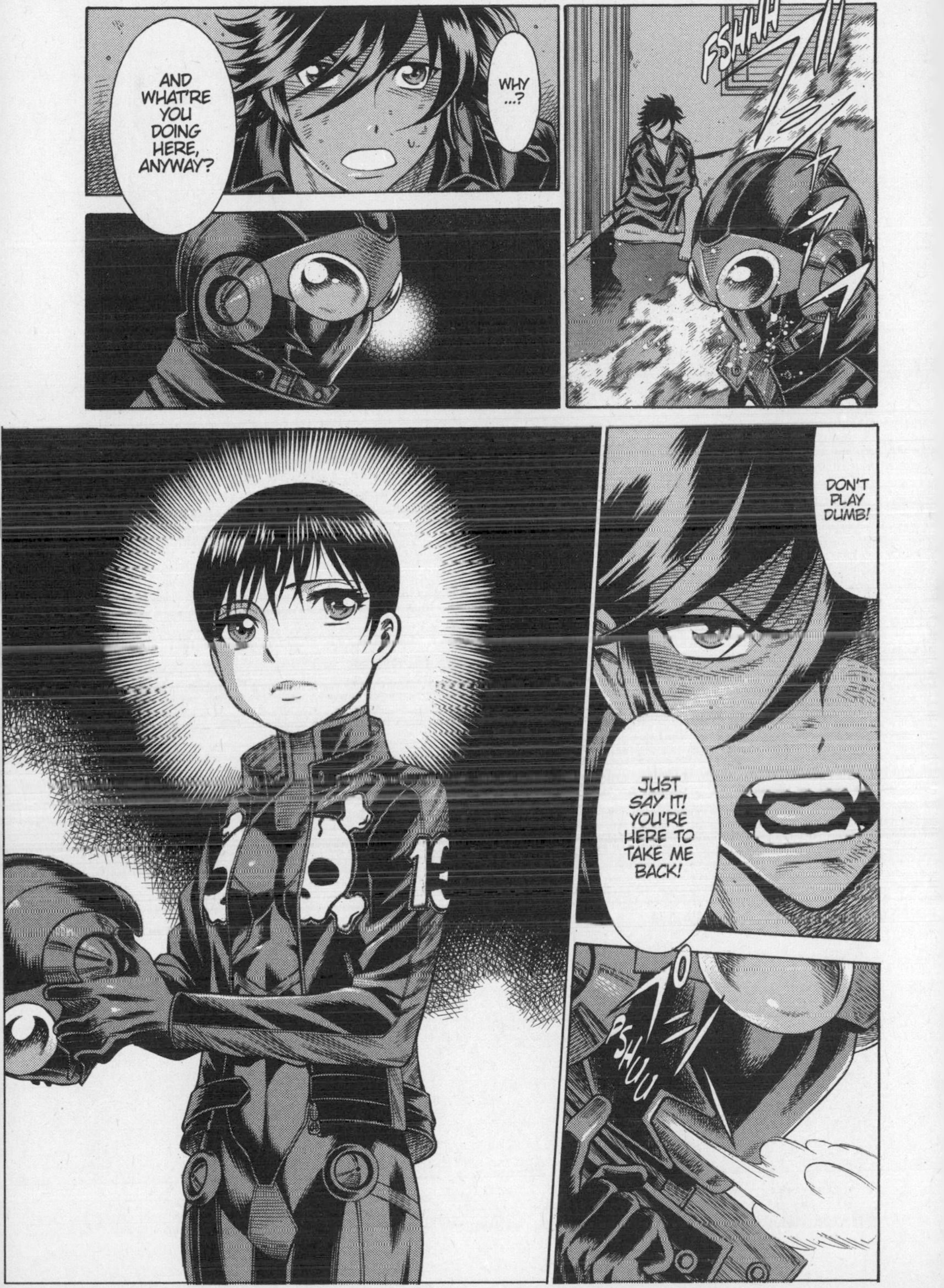
FSHHH
WHY ...?
AND WHAT'RE YOU DOING HERE, ANYWAY?
DON'T PLAY DUMB!
JUST SAY IT! YOU'RE HERE TO TAKE ME BACK!
PSHUUU

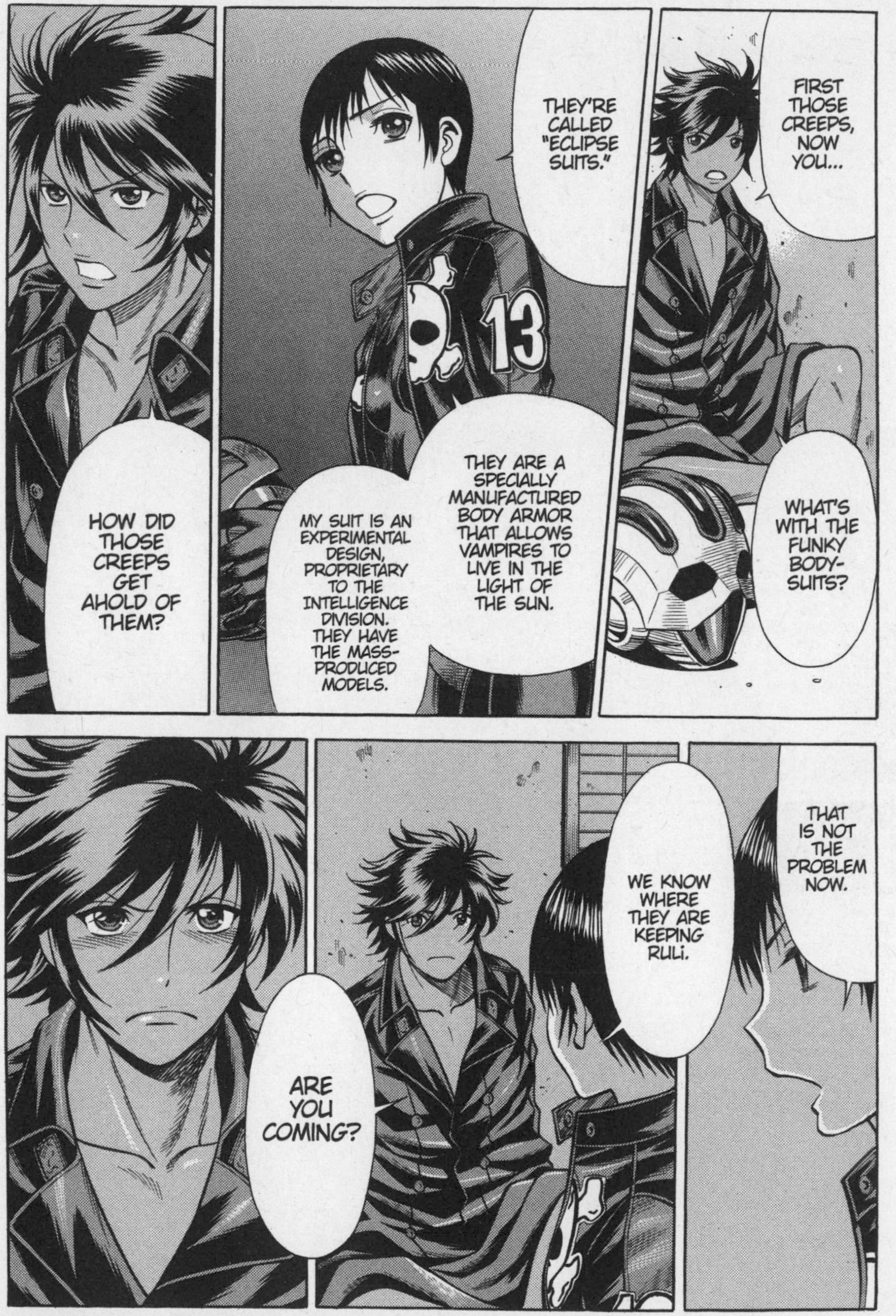
FIRST THOSE CREEPS, NOW YOU...
WHAT'S WITH THE FUNKY BODY-SUITS?
THEY'RE CALLED "ECLIPSE SUITS."
THEY ARE A SPECIALLY MANUFACTURED BODY ARMOR THAT ALLOWS VAMPIRES TO LIVE IN THE LIGHT OF THE SUN.
MY SUIT IS AN EXPERIMENTAL DESIGN, PROPRIETARY TO THE INTELLIGENCE DIVISION. THEY HAVE THE MASS-PRODUCED MODELS.
HOW DID THOSE CREEPS GET AHOLD OF THEM?
THAT IS NOT THE PROBLEM NOW.
WE KNOW WHERE THEY ARE KEEPING RULi.
ARE YOU COMING?

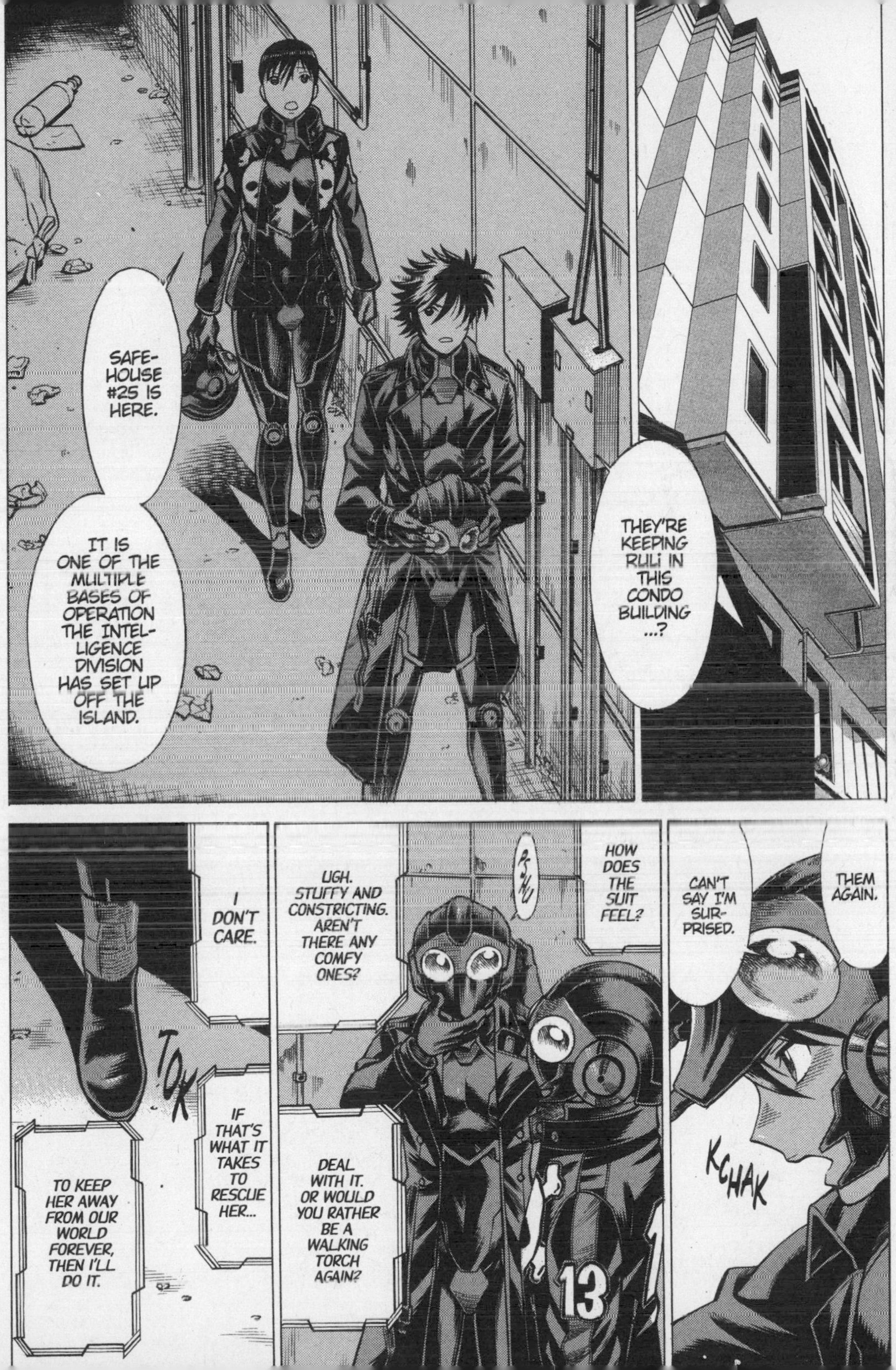

THEY'RE KEEPING RULi IN THIS CONDO BUILDING ...?
SAFE-HOUSE #25 IS HERE.
IT IS ONE OF THE MULTIPLE BASES OF OPERATION THE INTEL-LIGENCE DIVISION HAS SET UP OFF THE ISLAND.
THEM AGAIN.
CAN'T SAY I'M SUR-PRISED.
KCHAK
HOW DOES THE SUIT FEEL?
PSHU
UGH. STUFFY AND CONSTRICTING. AREN'T THERE ANY COMFY ONES?
DEAL WITH IT. OR WOULD YOU RATHER BE A WALKING TORCH AGAIN?
13
I DON'T CARE.
IF THAT'S WHAT IT TAKES TO RESCUE HER...
TOK
TO KEEP HER AWAY FROM OUR WORLD FOREVER, THEN I'LL DO IT.

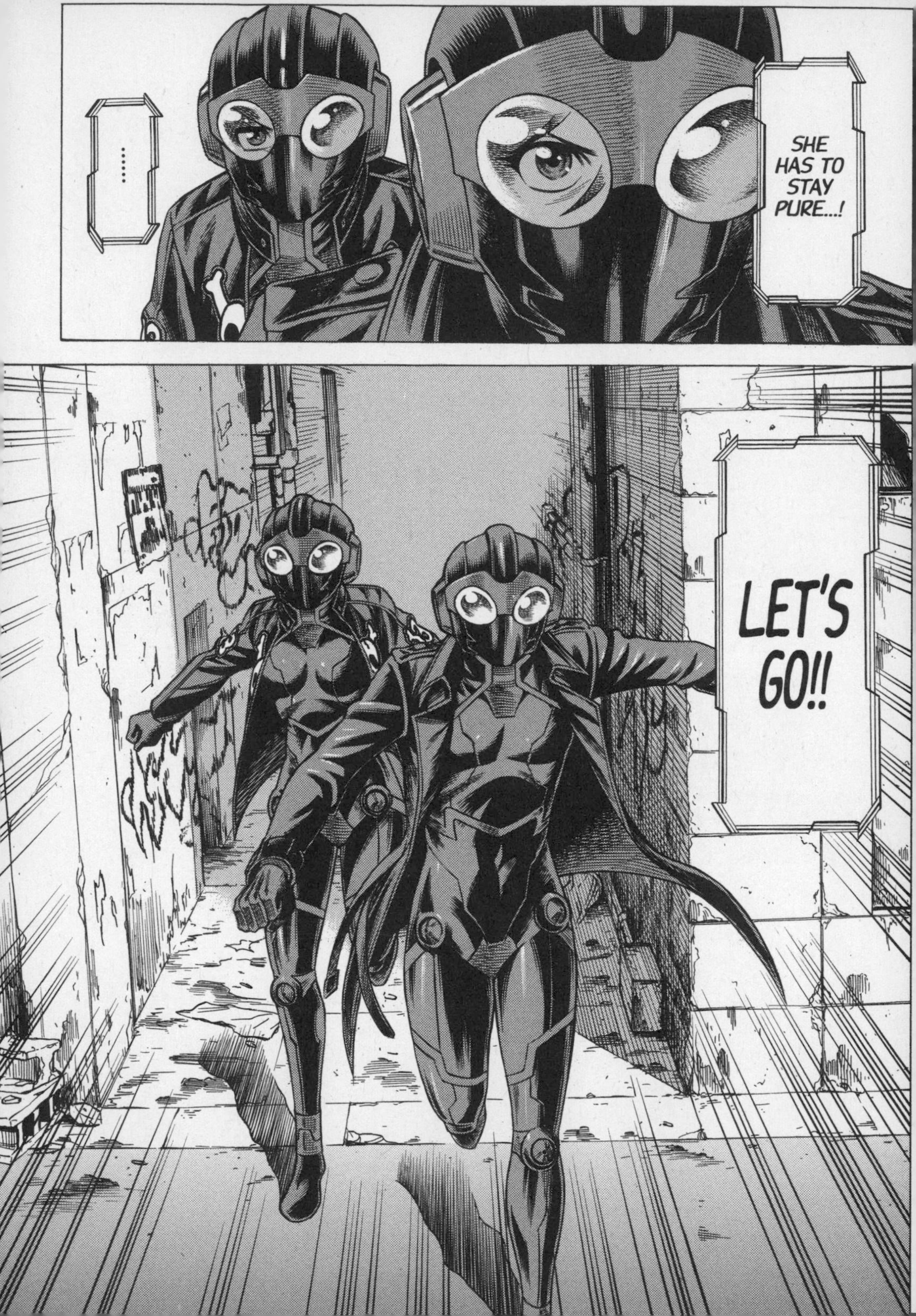
SHE HAS TO STAY PURE...!
......
LET'S GO!!

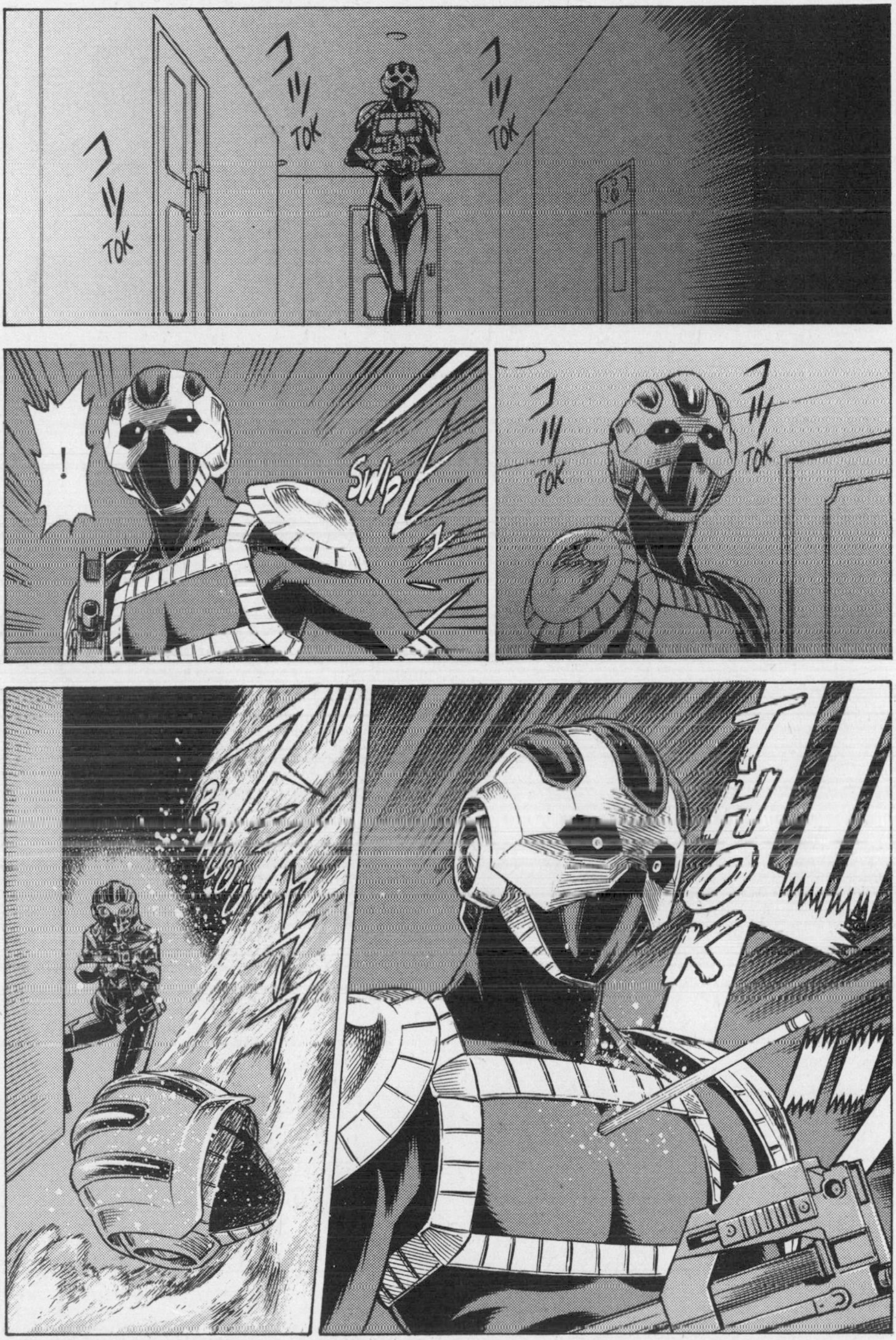
ゴッ TOK
ゴッ TOK
ゴッ TOK
ゴッ TOK
ゴッ TOK
!
SWIP
THOK
BSHUUU

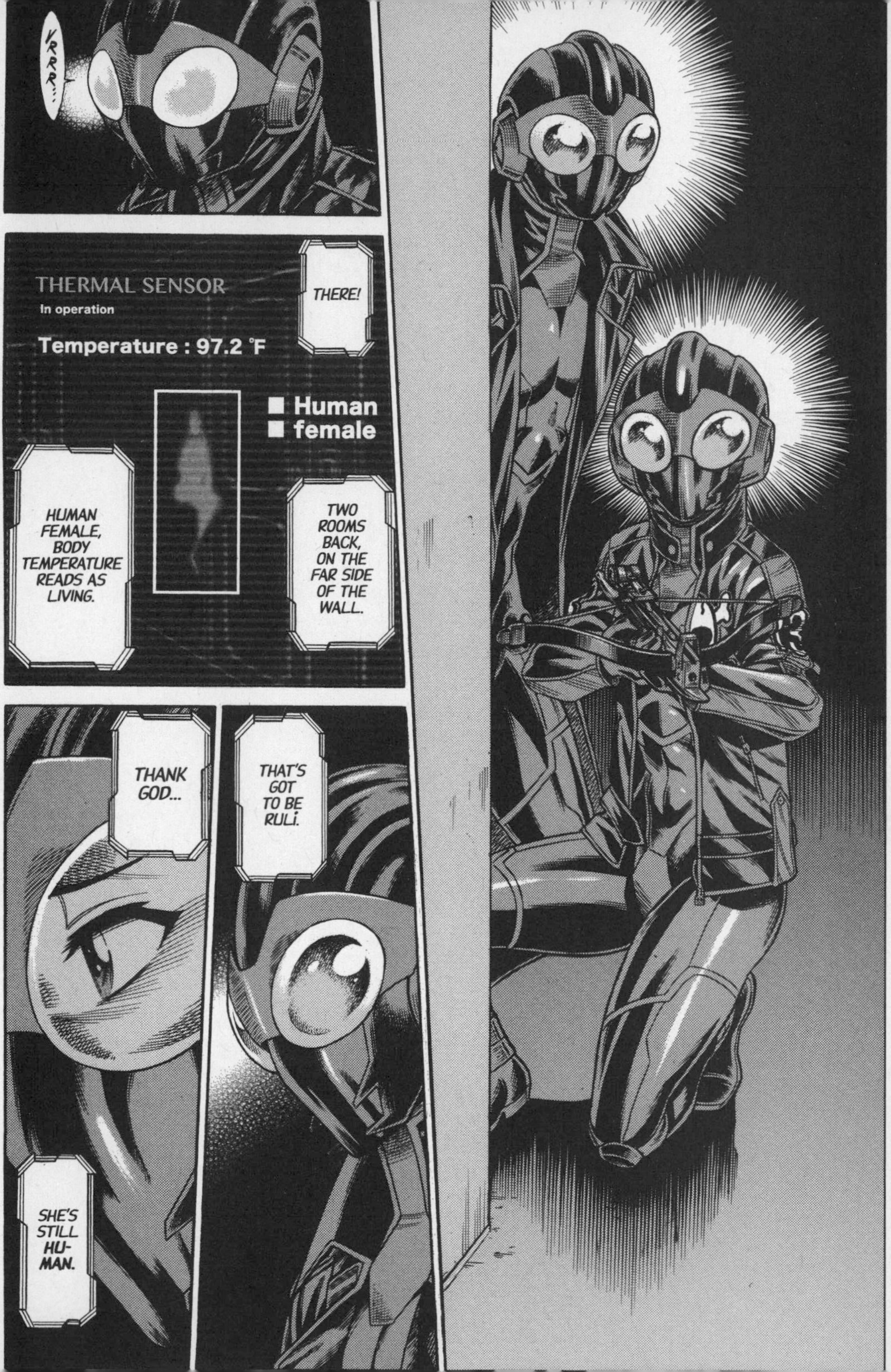
VRRR...
THERE!
THERMAL SENSOR
In operation
Temperature : 97.2 °F
■ Human
■ female
TWO ROOMS BACK, ON THE FAR SIDE OF THE WALL.
HUMAN FEMALE, BODY TEMPERATURE READS AS LIVING.
THAT'S GOT TO BE RULI.
THANK GOD...
SHE'S STILL HU-MAN.

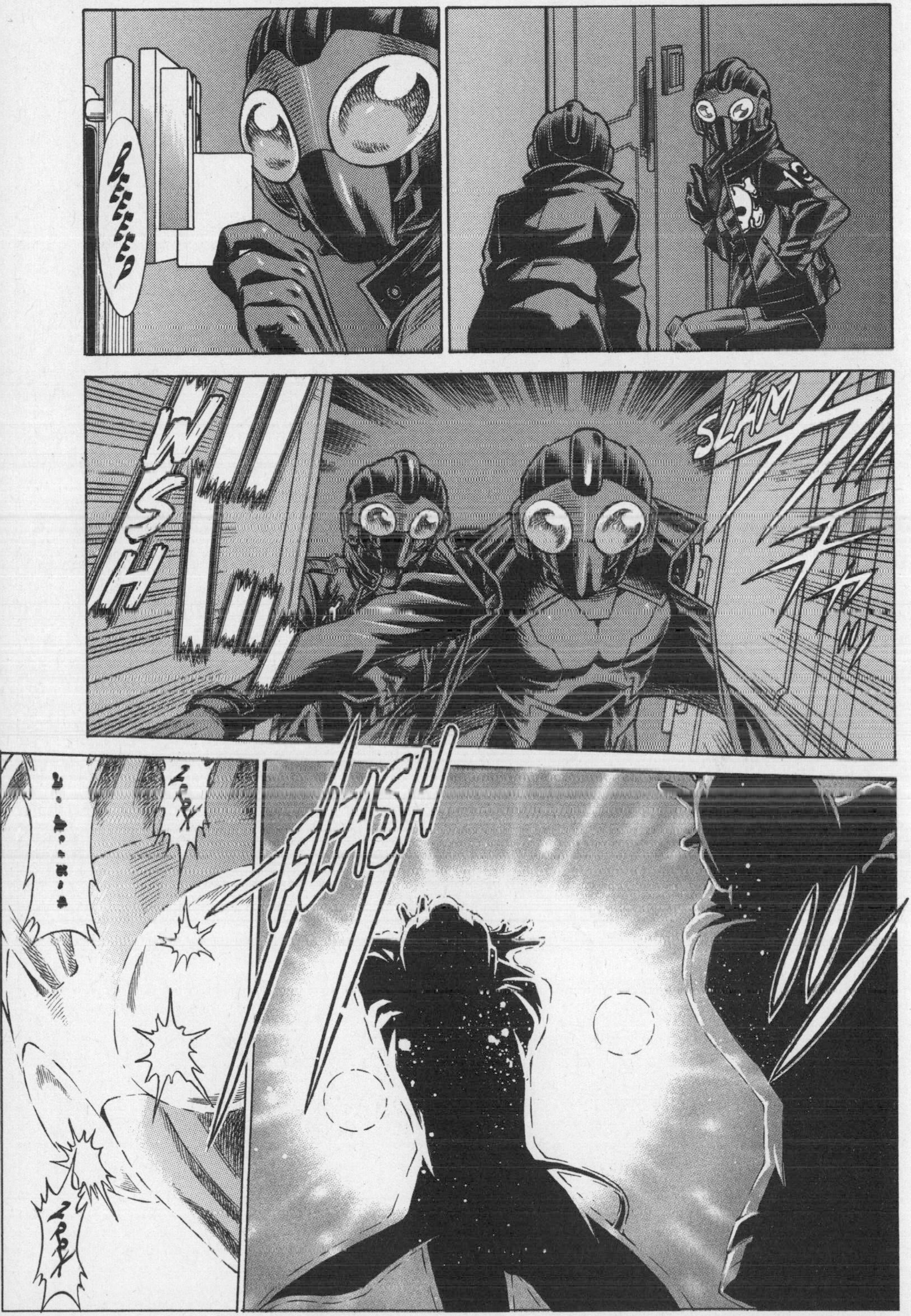
BEEEEEP
SLAM
WSSH
FLASH

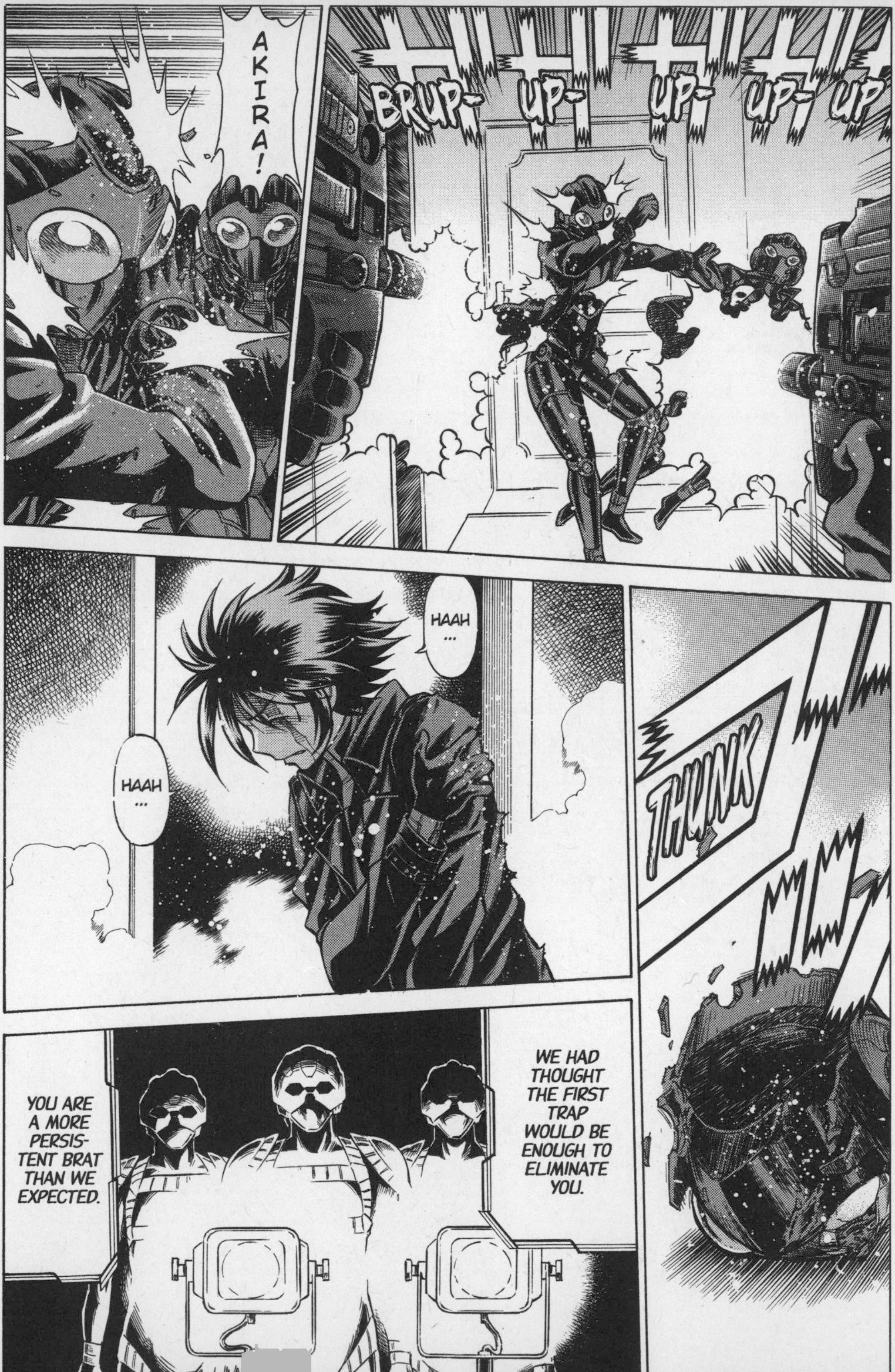
BRUP- UP- UP- UP- UP
AKIRA!
THUNK
HAAH ...
HAAH ...
WE HAD THOUGHT THE FIRST TRAP WOULD BE ENOUGH TO ELIMINATE YOU.
YOU ARE A MORE PERSIS- TENT BRAT THAN WE EXPECTED.

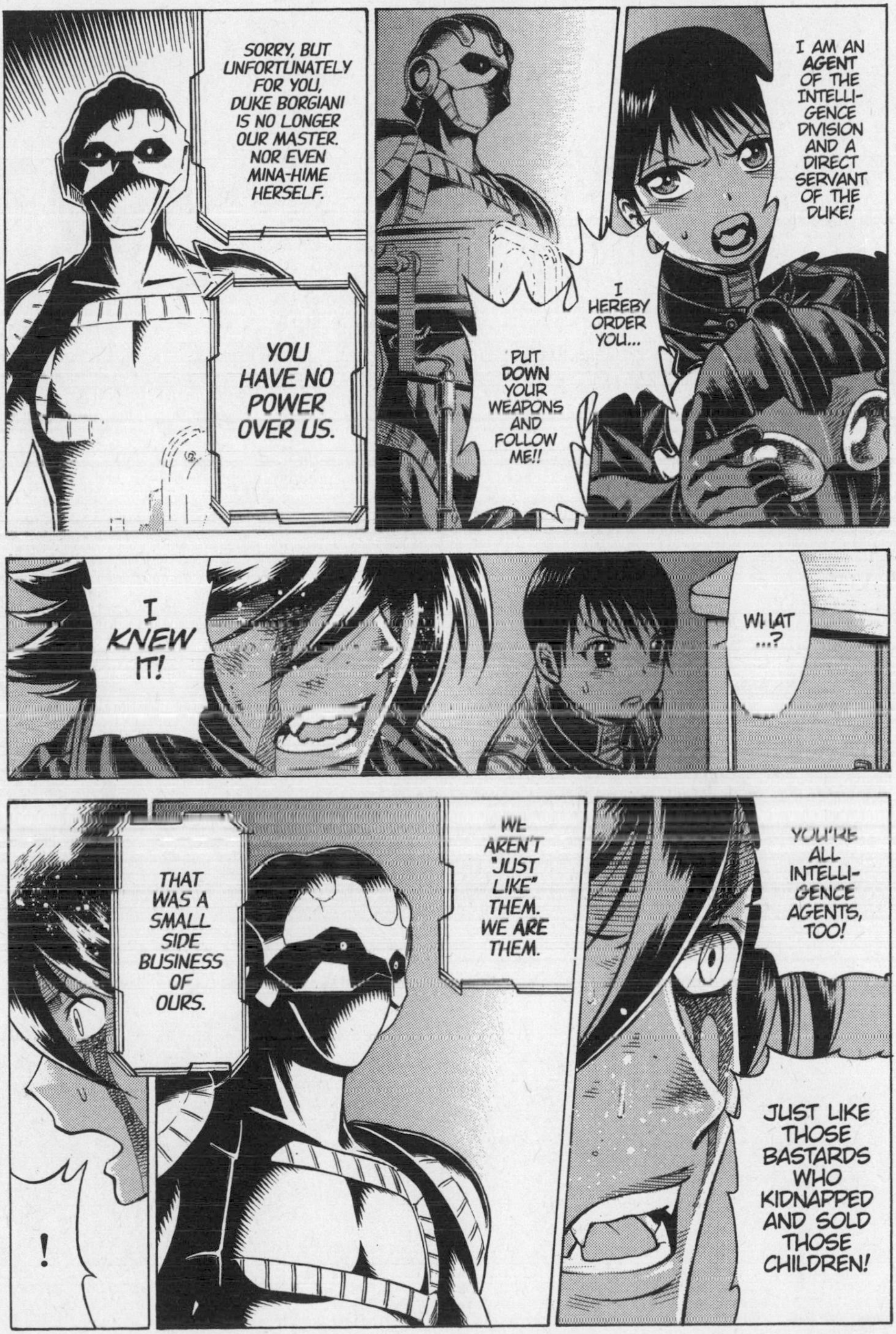
I AM AN AGENT OF THE INTELLIGENCE DIVISION AND A DIRECT SERVANT OF THE DUKE!
I HEREBY ORDER YOU...
PUT DOWN YOUR WEAPONS AND FOLLOW ME!!
SORRY, BUT UNFORTUNATELY FOR YOU, DUKE BORGIANI IS NO LONGER OUR MASTER. NOR EVEN MINA-HIME HERSELF.
YOU HAVE NO POWER OVER US.
WHAT ...?
I KNEW IT!
YOU'RE ALL INTELLIGENCE AGENTS, TOO!
JUST LIKE THOSE BASTARDS WHO KIDNAPPED AND SOLD THOSE CHILDREN!
WE AREN'T "JUST LIKE" THEM. WE ARE THEM.
THAT WAS A SMALL SIDE BUSINESS OF OURS.
!

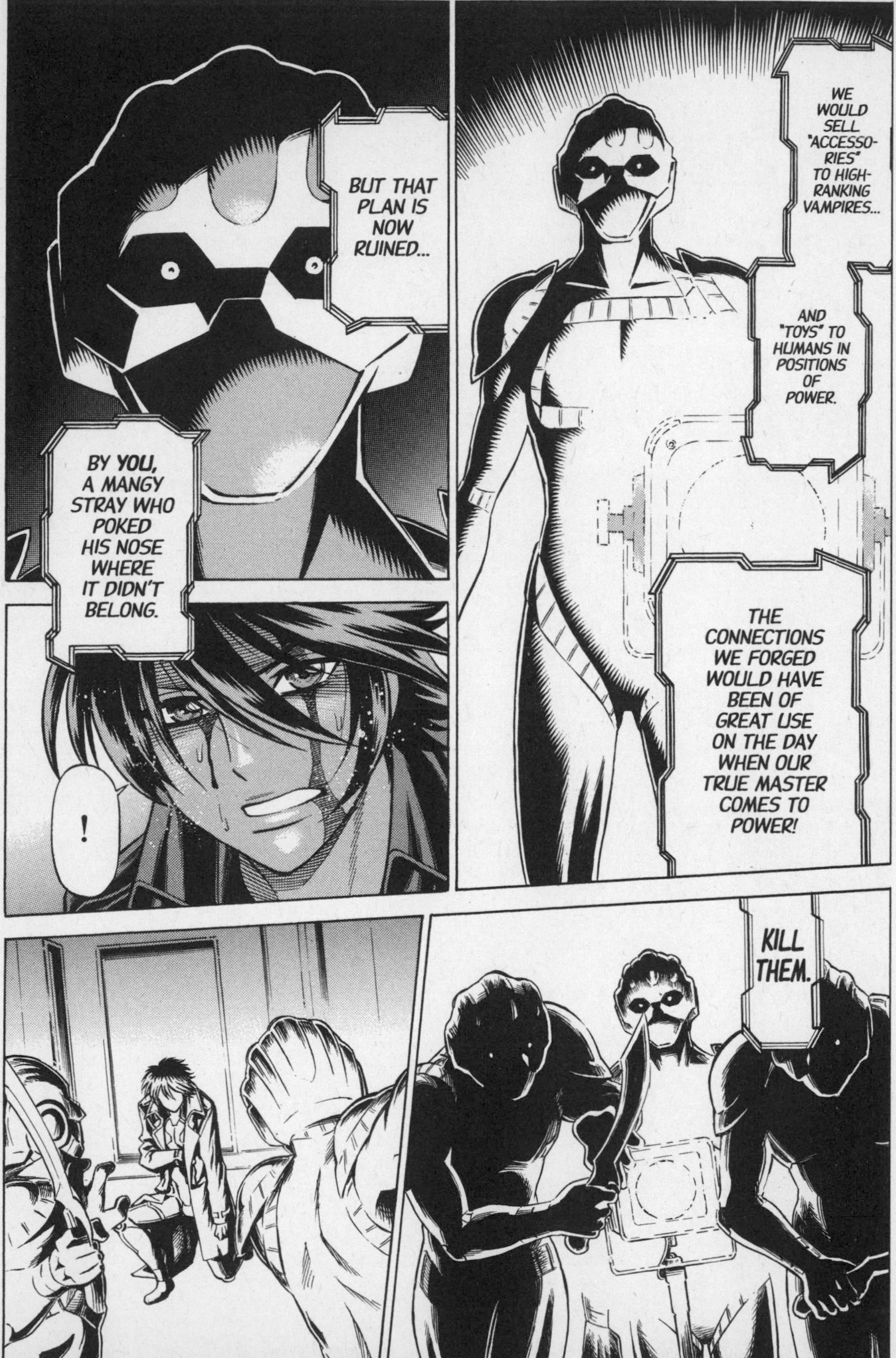
WE WOULD SELL "ACCESSORIES" TO HIGH-RANKING VAMPIRES...
AND "TOYS" TO HUMANS IN POSITIONS OF POWER.
THE CONNECTIONS WE FORGED WOULD HAVE BEEN OF GREAT USE ON THE DAY WHEN OUR TRUE MASTER COMES TO POWER!
BUT THAT PLAN IS NOW RUINED...
BY YOU, A MANGY STRAY WHO POKED HIS NOSE WHERE IT DIDN'T BELONG.
!
KILL THEM.

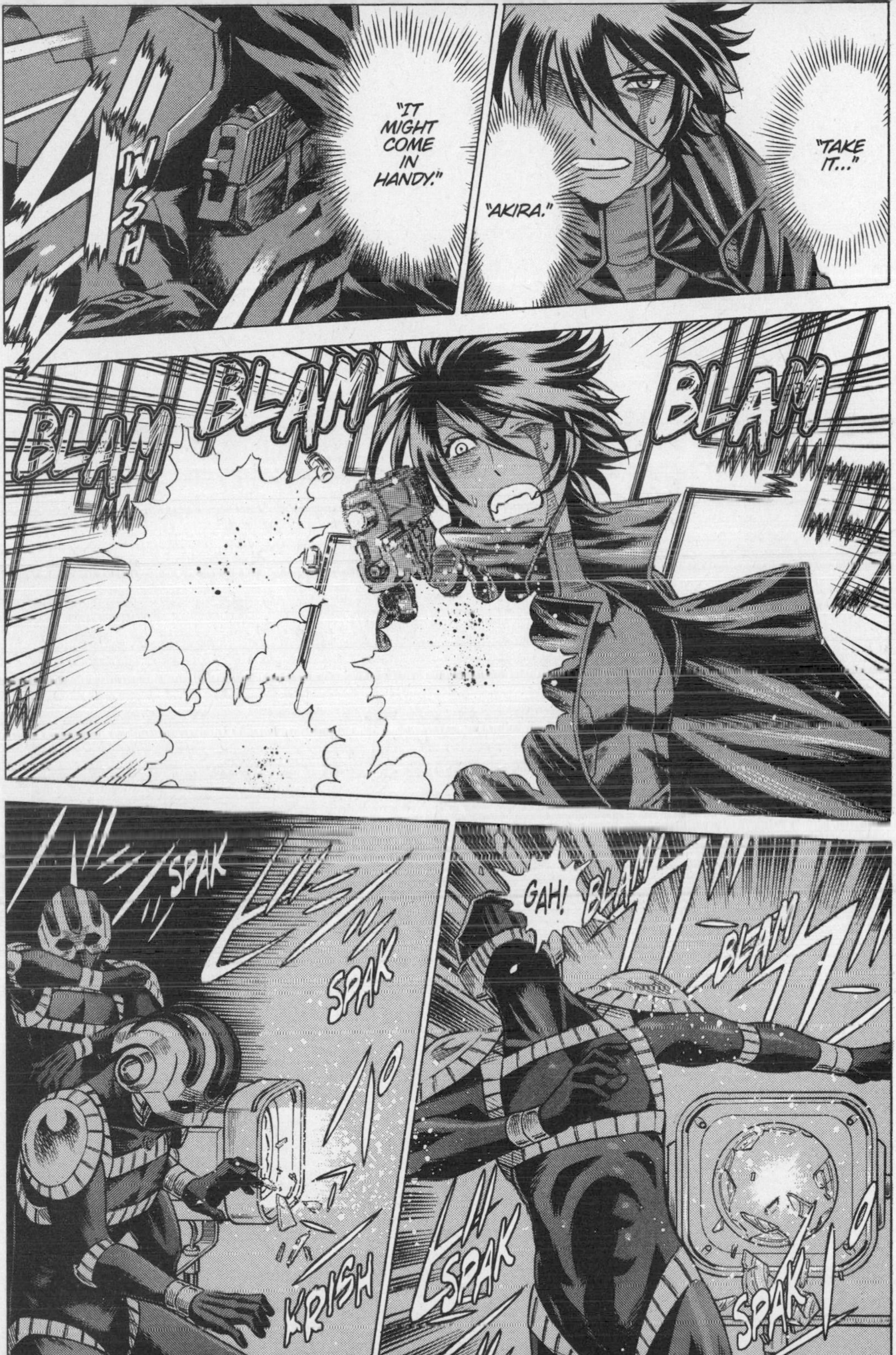
"TAKE IT..."
"AKIRA."
"IT MIGHT COME IN HANDY."
WSH
BLAM
BLAM
BLAM
GAH!
BLAM
BLAM
SPAK
SPAK
SPAK
SPAK
SPAK
KRISH

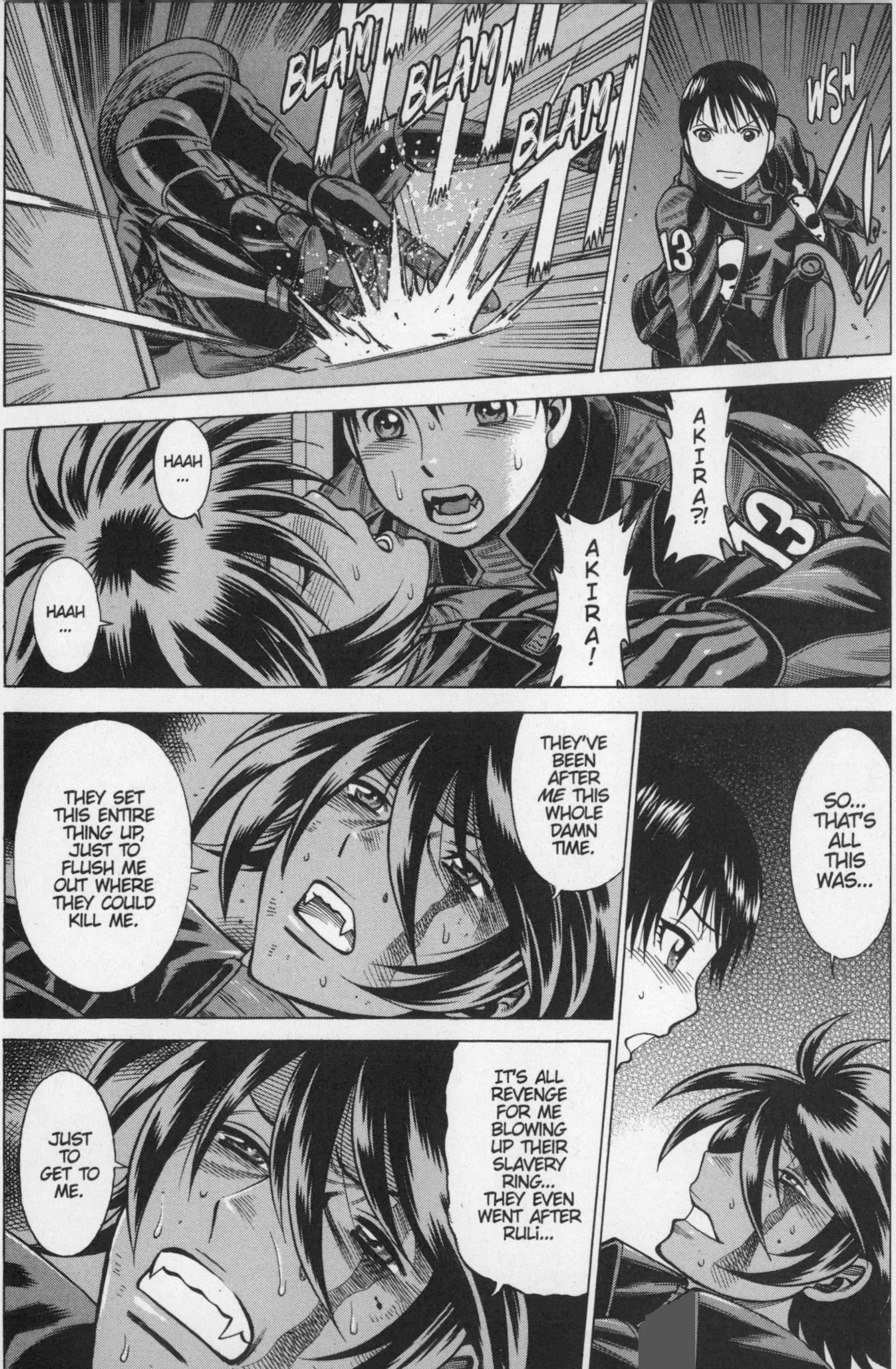
WSH
BLAM
BLAM
BLAM
AKIRA?!
AKIRA!
HAAH...
HAAH...
SO... THAT'S ALL THIS WAS...
THEY'VE BEEN AFTER *ME* THIS WHOLE DAMN TIME.
THEY SET THIS ENTIRE THING UP, JUST TO FLUSH ME OUT WHERE THEY COULD KILL ME.
IT'S ALL REVENGE FOR ME BLOWING UP THEIR SLAVERY RING... THEY EVEN WENT AFTER RULi...
JUST TO GET TO ME.

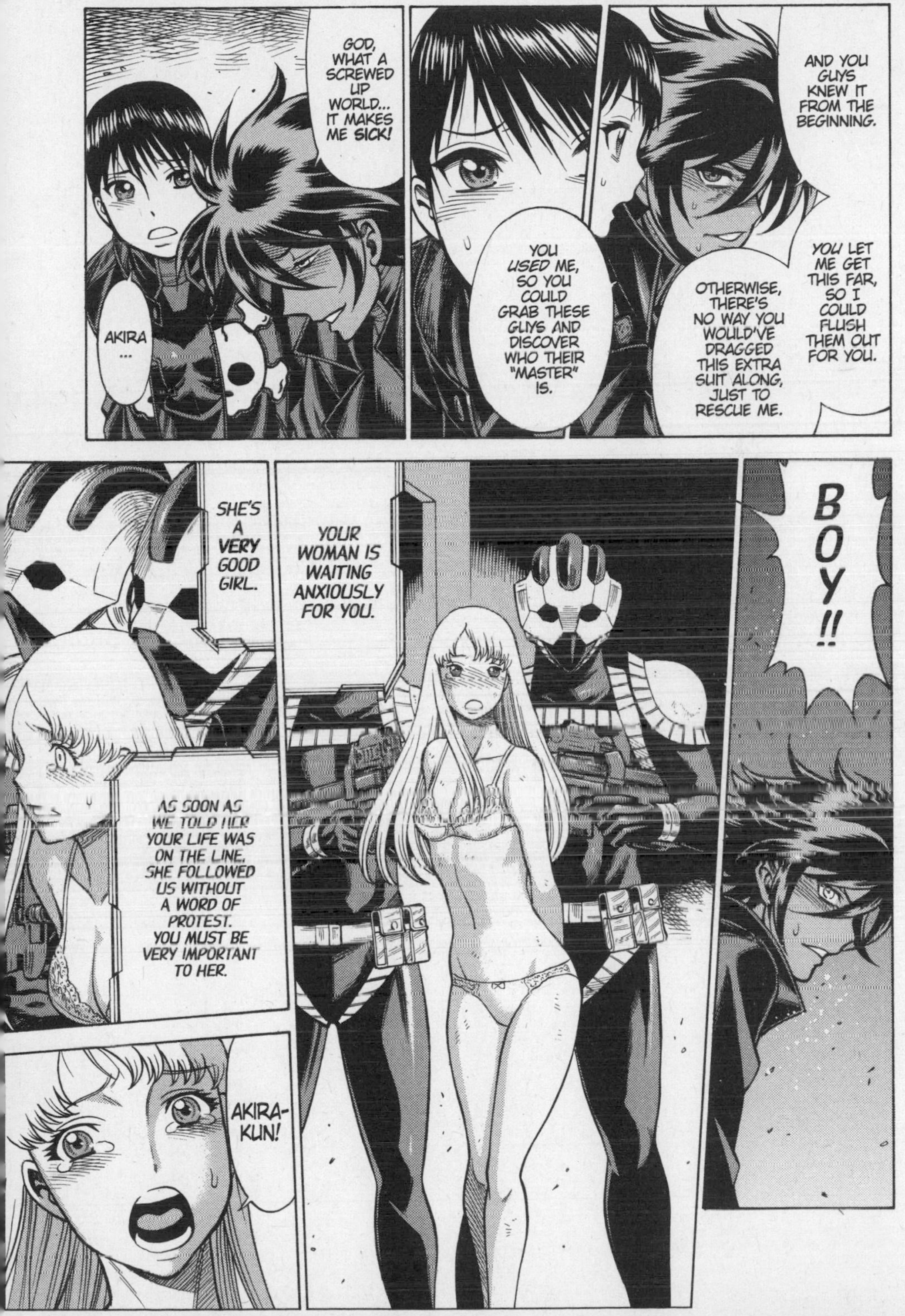
AND YOU GUYS KNEW IT FROM THE BEGINNING.
YOU LET ME GET THIS FAR, SO I COULD FLUSH THEM OUT FOR YOU.
YOU USED ME, SO YOU COULD GRAB THESE GUYS AND DISCOVER WHO THEIR "MASTER" IS.
OTHERWISE, THERE'S NO WAY YOU WOULD'VE DRAGGED THIS EXTRA SUIT ALONG, JUST TO RESCUE ME.
GOD, WHAT A SCREWED UP WORLD... IT MAKES ME SICK!
AKIRA ...
BOY!!
YOUR WOMAN IS WAITING ANXIOUSLY FOR YOU.
SHE'S A VERY GOOD GIRL.
AS SOON AS WE TOLD HER YOUR LIFE WAS ON THE LINE, SHE FOLLOWED US WITHOUT A WORD OF PROTEST. YOU MUST BE VERY IMPORTANT TO HER.
AKIRA-KUN!

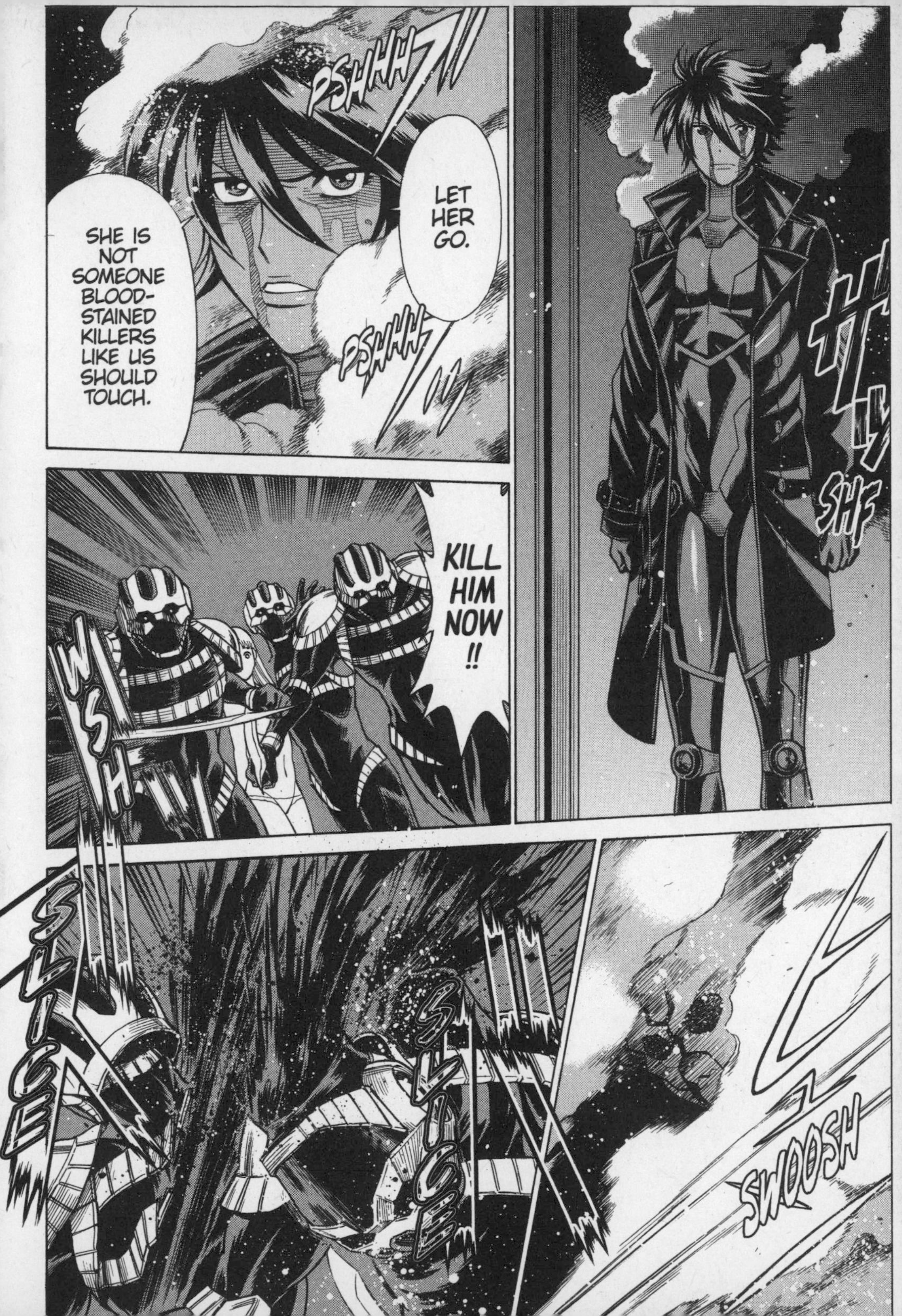
SHF
PSHHH
LET HER GO.
SHE IS NOT SOMEONE BLOOD-STAINED KILLERS LIKE US SHOULD TOUCH.
PSHHH
KILL HIM NOW!!
WSH
SWOOSH
SLICE
SLICE

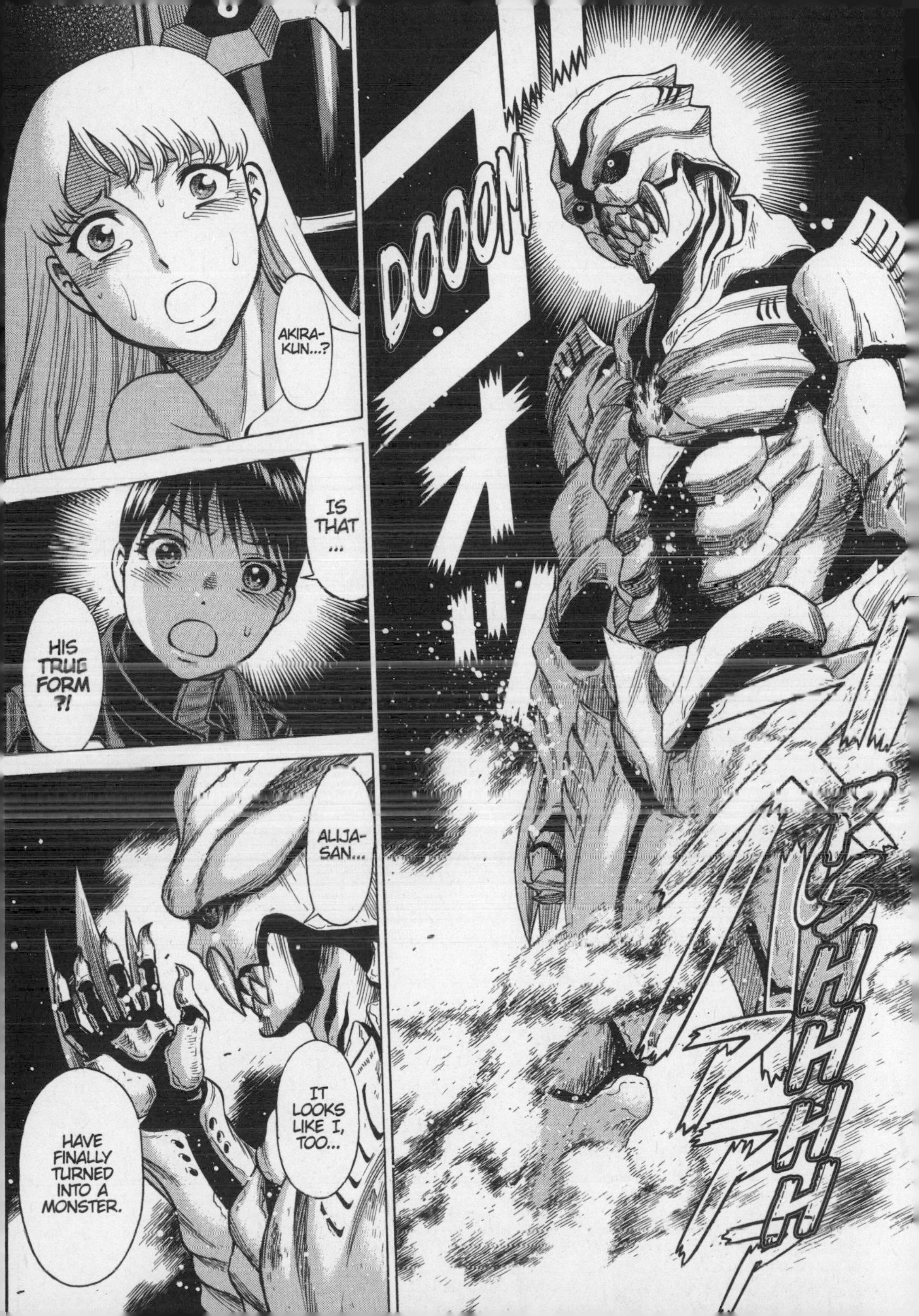
DOOOM
SHHHH
AKIRA-KUN...?
IS THAT ...
HIS TRUE FORM ?!
ALIJA-SAN...
IT LOOKS LIKE I, TOO...
HAVE FINALLY TURNED INTO A MONSTER.

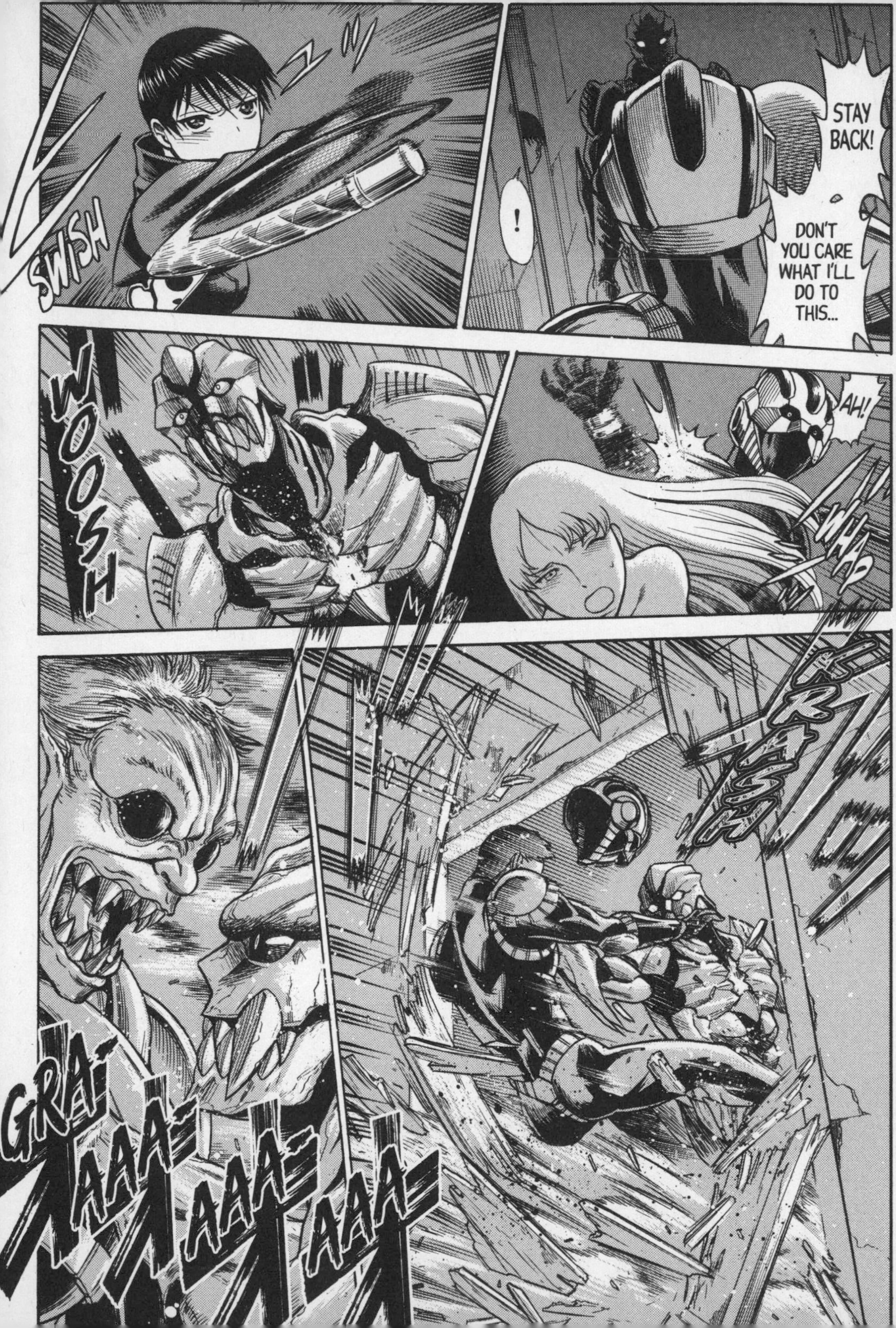
STAY BACK!
DON'T YOU CARE WHAT I'LL DO TO THIS...
!
SWISH
AH!
WHAP
WOOSH
KRASH
GRAAAAAAAAAA

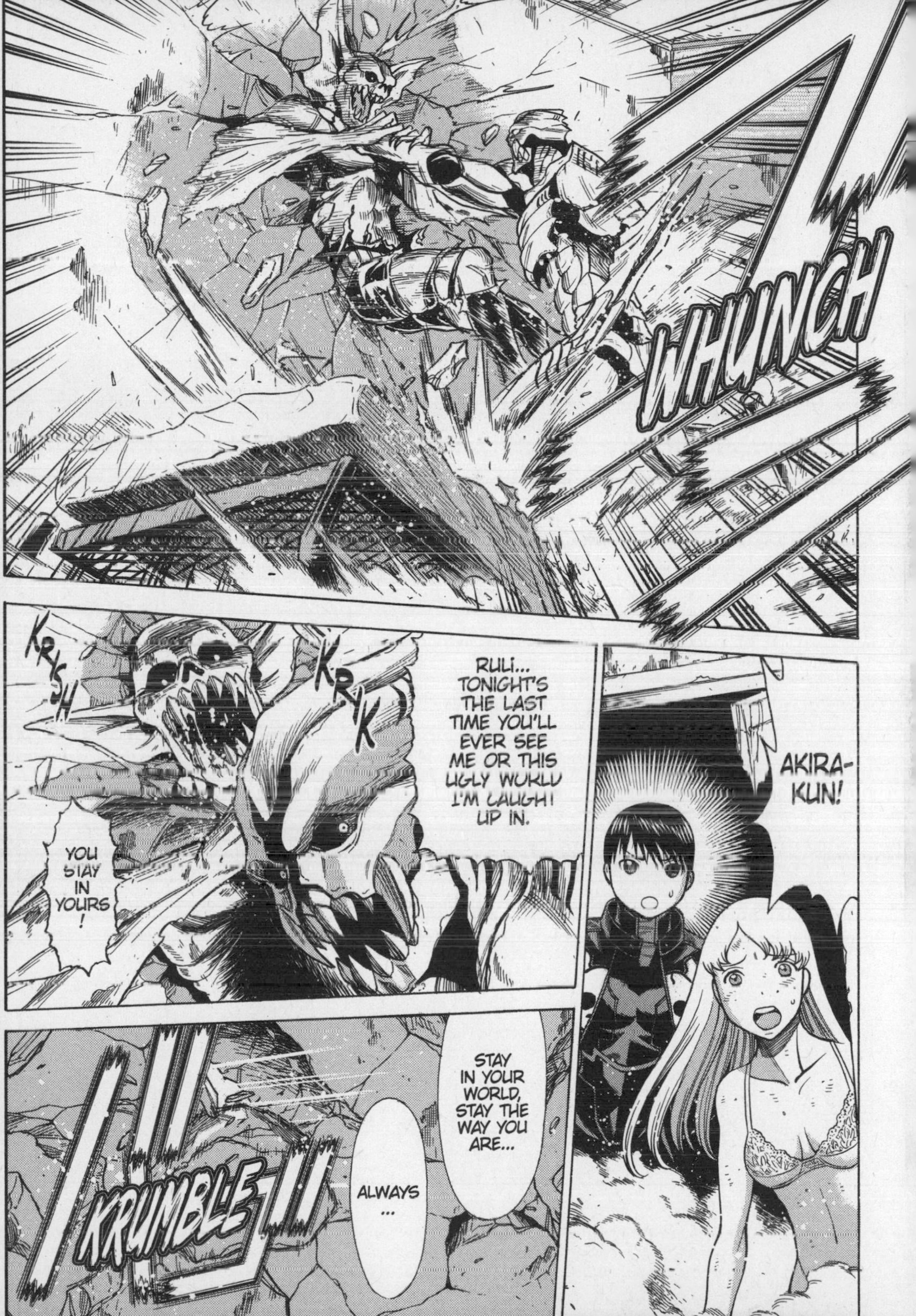
WHUNCH
AKIRA-KUN!
RULI... TONIGHT'S THE LAST TIME YOU'LL EVER SEE ME OR THIS UGLY WORLD I'M CAUGHT UP IN.
KRIK
KRISH
YOU STAY IN YOURS!
STAY IN YOUR WORLD, STAY THE WAY YOU ARE...
ALWAYS ...
KRUMBLE

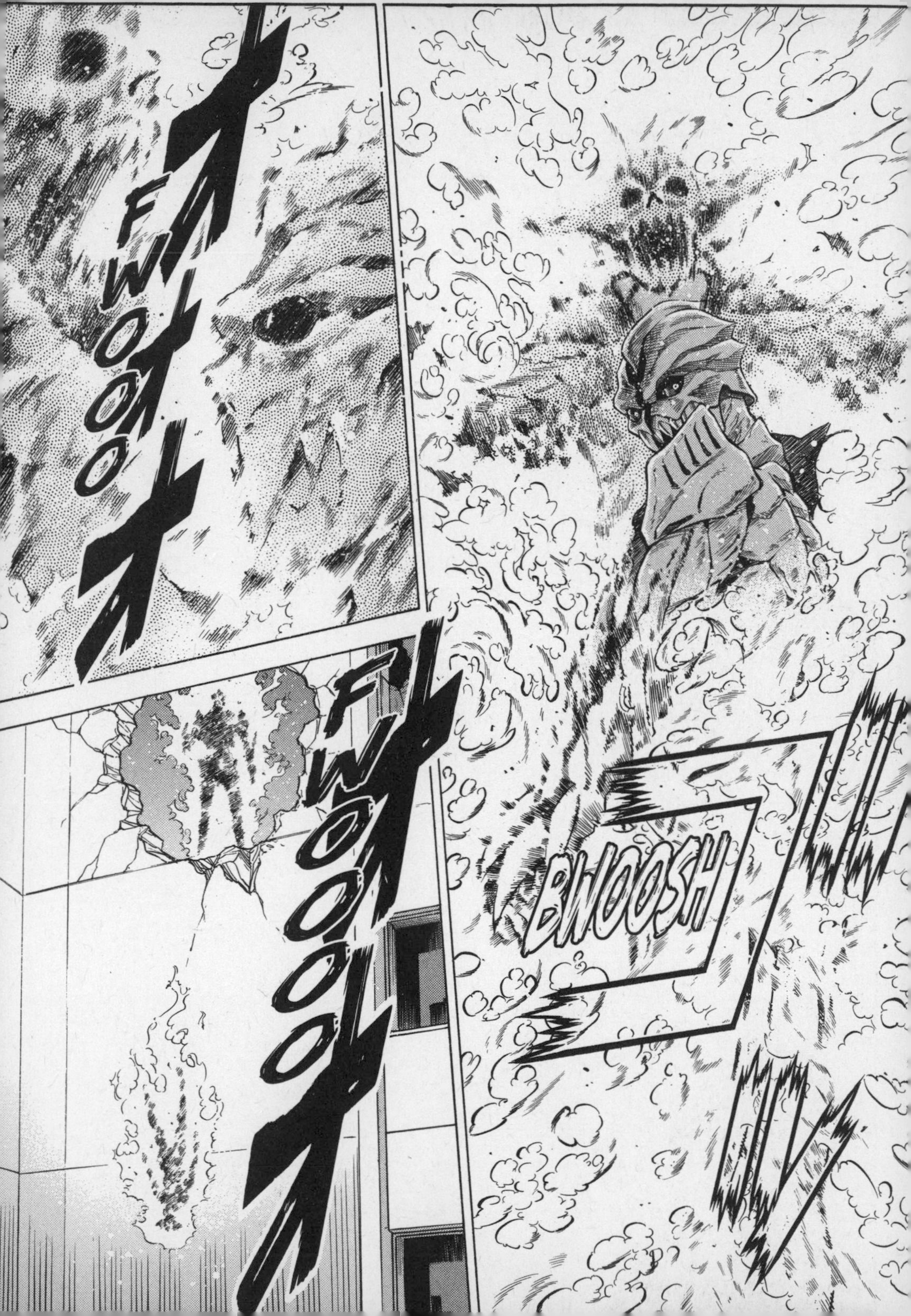
BWOOSH
FWOOO
FWOOOO

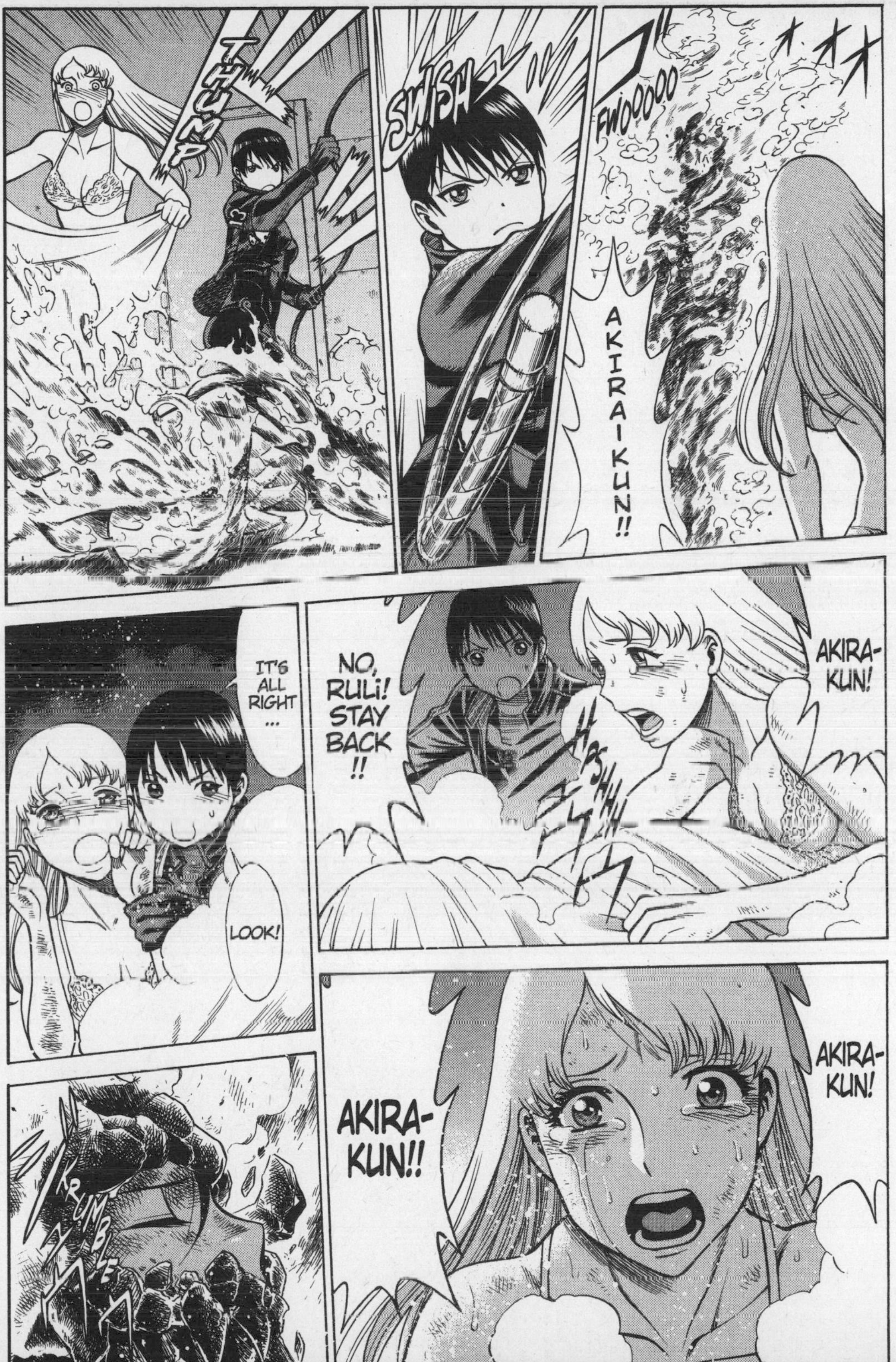
ゴ
オオオ
FWOOOOO
AKIRA-KUN!!
SWISH
THUMP
AKIRA-KUN!
NO, RULI! STAY BACK!!
HPSHHH
IT'S ALL RIGHT ...
LOOK!
AKIRA-KUN!
AKIRA-KUN!!
KRUMBLE

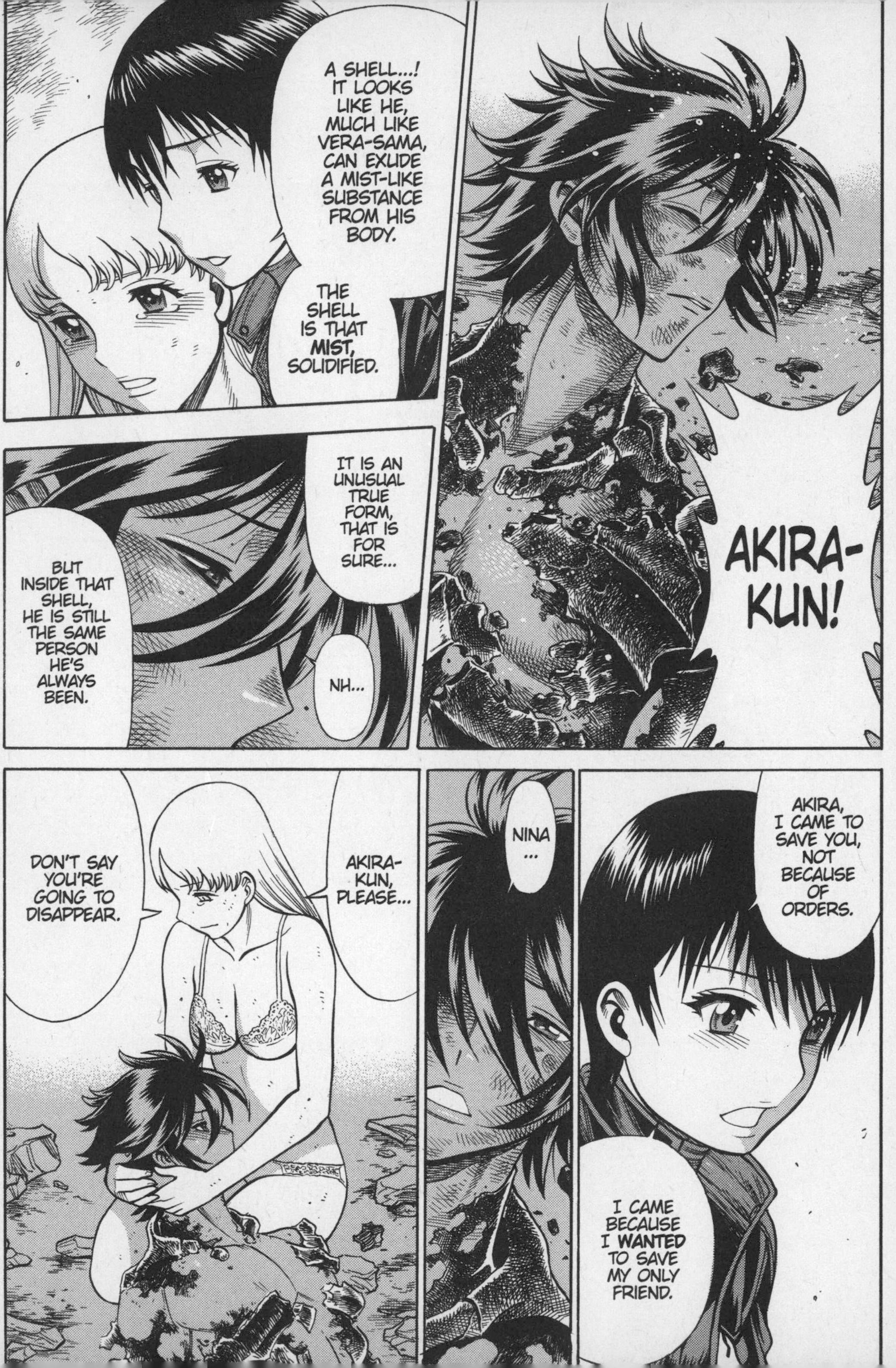
AKIRA-KUN!
A SHELL...! IT LOOKS LIKE HE, MUCH LIKE VERA-SAMA, CAN EXUDE A MIST-LIKE SUBSTANCE FROM HIS BODY.
THE SHELL IS THAT **MIST**, SOLIDIFIED.
IT IS AN UNUSUAL TRUE FORM, THAT IS FOR SURE...
BUT INSIDE THAT SHELL, HE IS STILL THE SAME PERSON HE'S ALWAYS BEEN.
NH...
AKIRA, I CAME TO SAVE YOU, NOT BECAUSE OF ORDERS.
I CAME BECAUSE I **WANTED** TO SAVE MY ONLY FRIEND.
NINA ...
AKIRA-KUN, PLEASE...
DON'T SAY YOU'RE GOING TO DISAPPEAR.

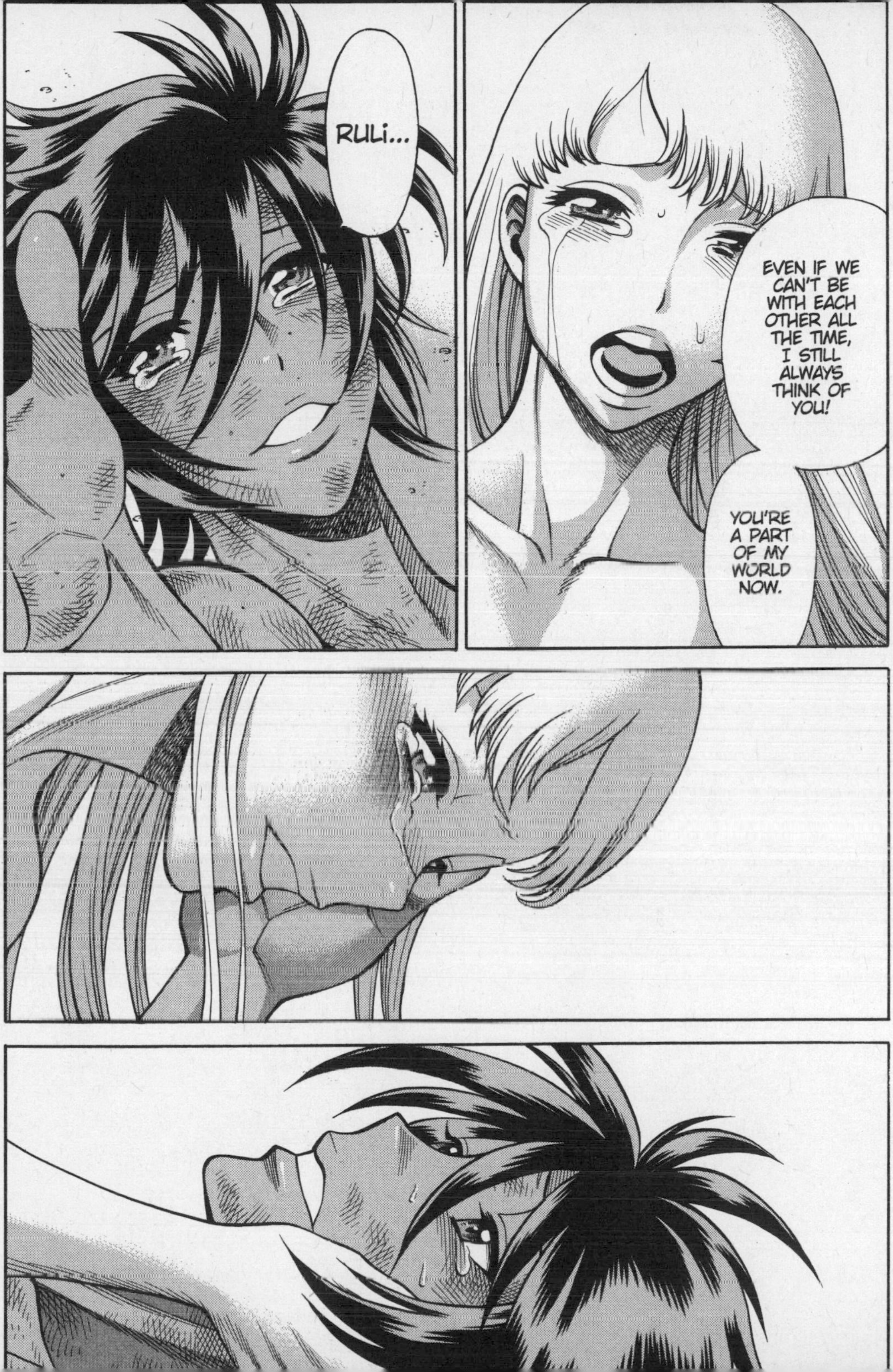
EVEN IF WE CAN'T BE WITH EACH OTHER ALL THE TIME, I STILL ALWAYS THINK OF YOU!
YOU'RE A PART OF MY WORLD NOW.
RULi...

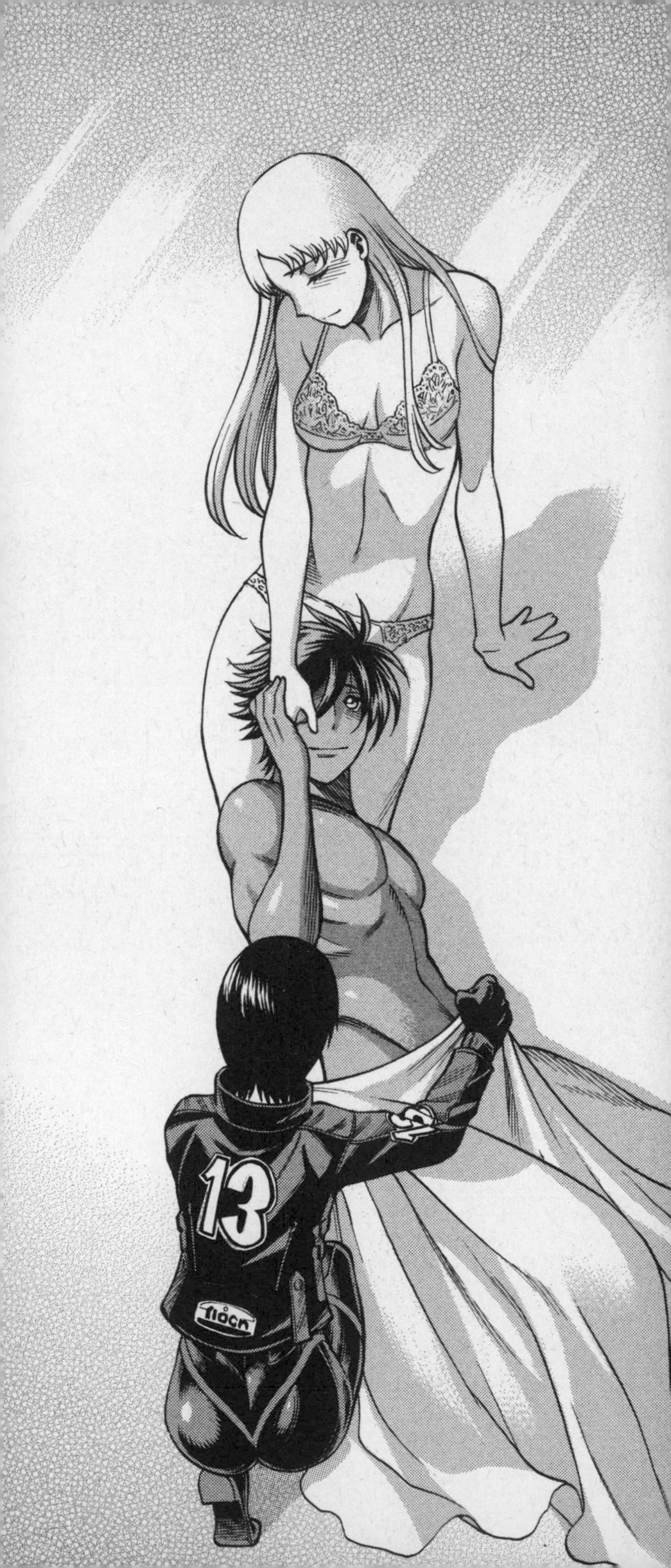
13

Epilogue

I SEE. HOW IS HE FARING?

Well...

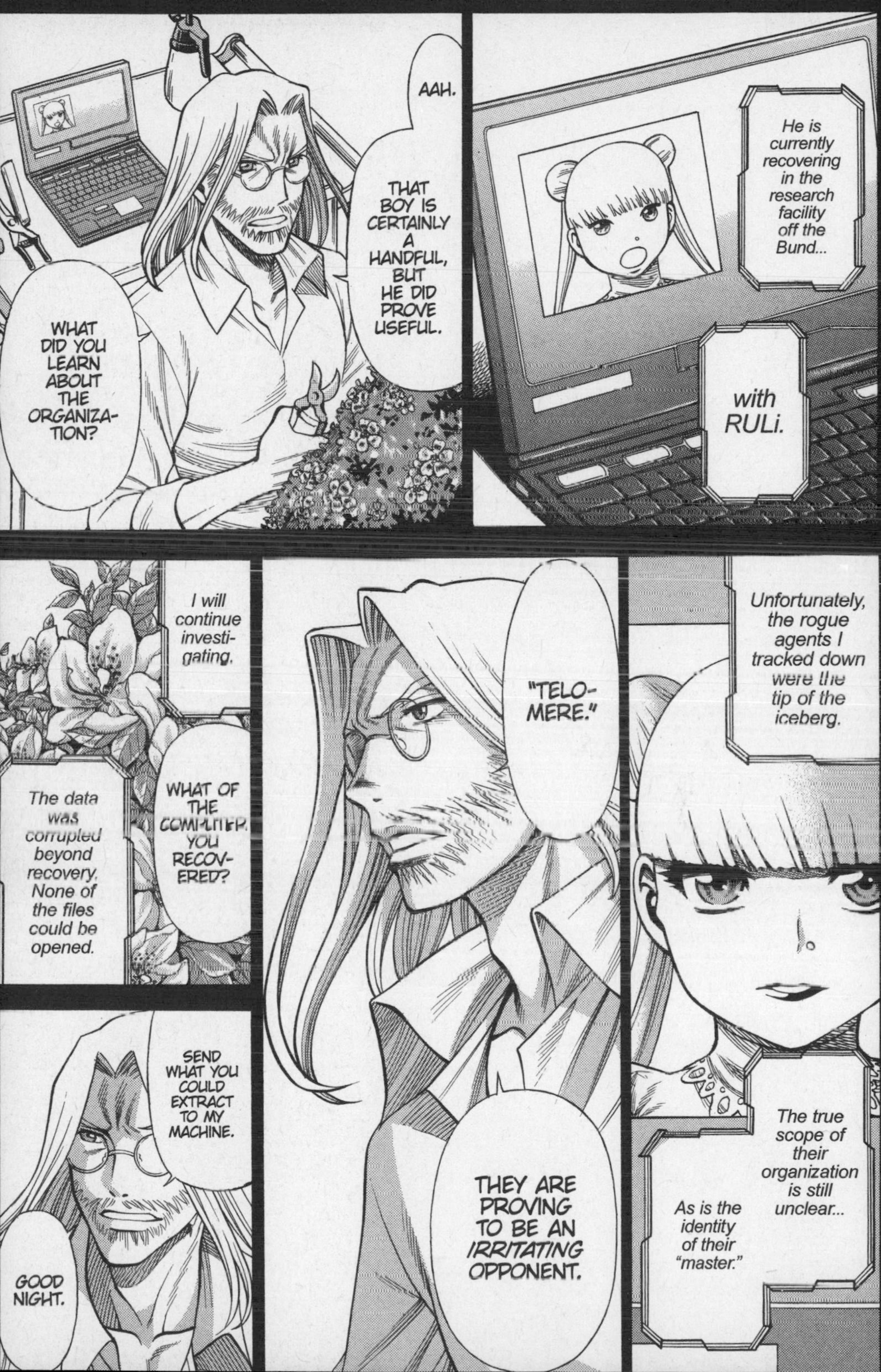
He is currently recovering in the research facility off the Bund...
with RULi.
AAH.
THAT BOY IS CERTAINLY A HANDFUL, BUT HE DID PROVE USEFUL.
WHAT DID YOU LEARN ABOUT THE ORGANIZATION?
Unfortunately, the rogue agents I tracked down were the tip of the iceberg.
The true scope of their organization is still unclear...
As is the identity of their "master."
"TELOMERE."
THEY ARE PROVING TO BE AN *IRRITATING* OPPONENT.
I will continue investigating.
WHAT OF THE COMPUTER YOU RECOVERED?
The data was corrupted beyond recovery. None of the files could be opened.
SEND WHAT YOU COULD EXTRACT TO MY MACHINE.
GOOD NIGHT.

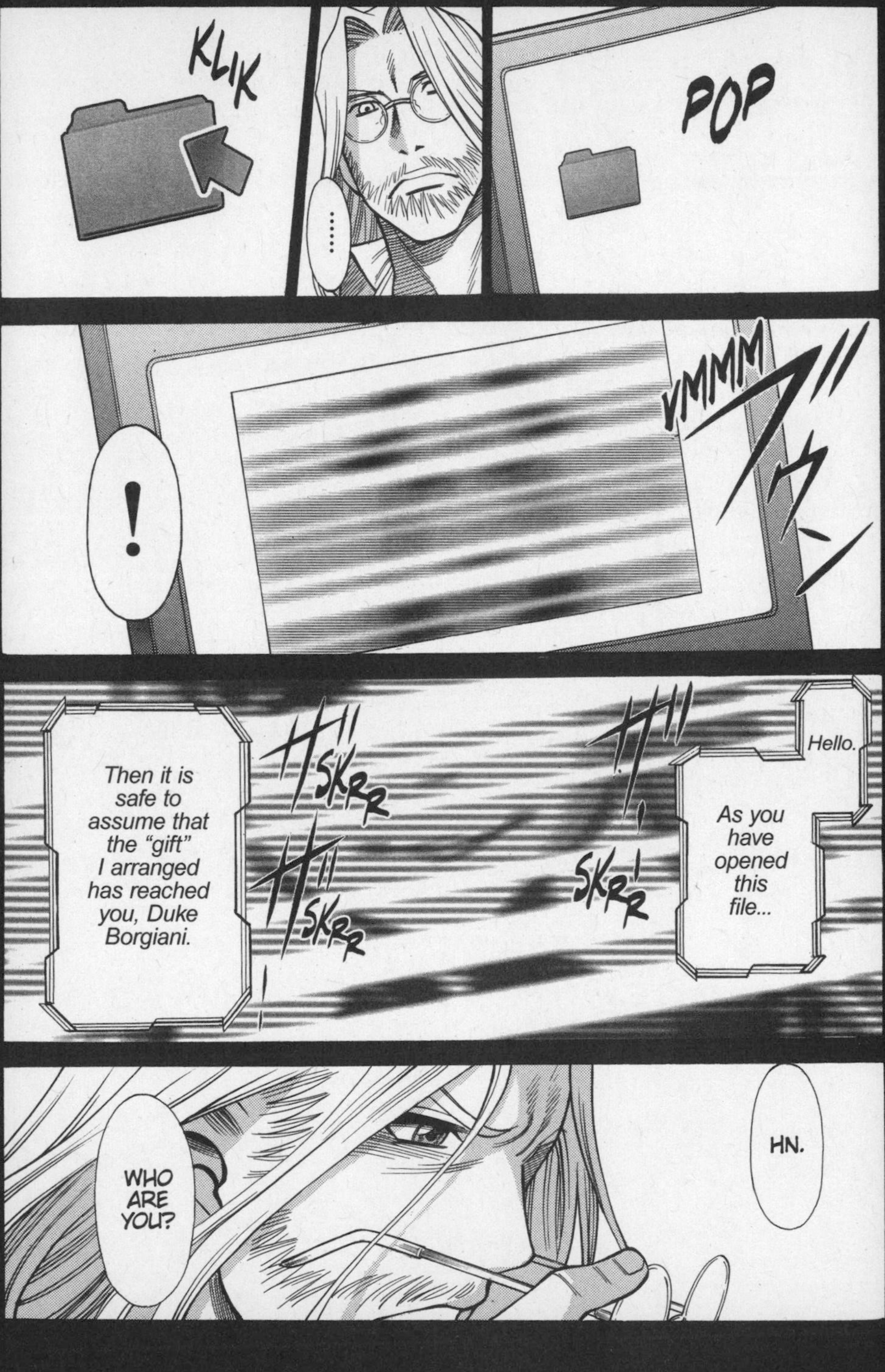
POP
......
KLIK
VMMM
!
Hello.
As you have opened this file...
SKRR
SKRR
SKRR
Then it is safe to assume that the "gift" I arranged has reached you, Duke Borgiani.
HN.
WHO ARE YOU?

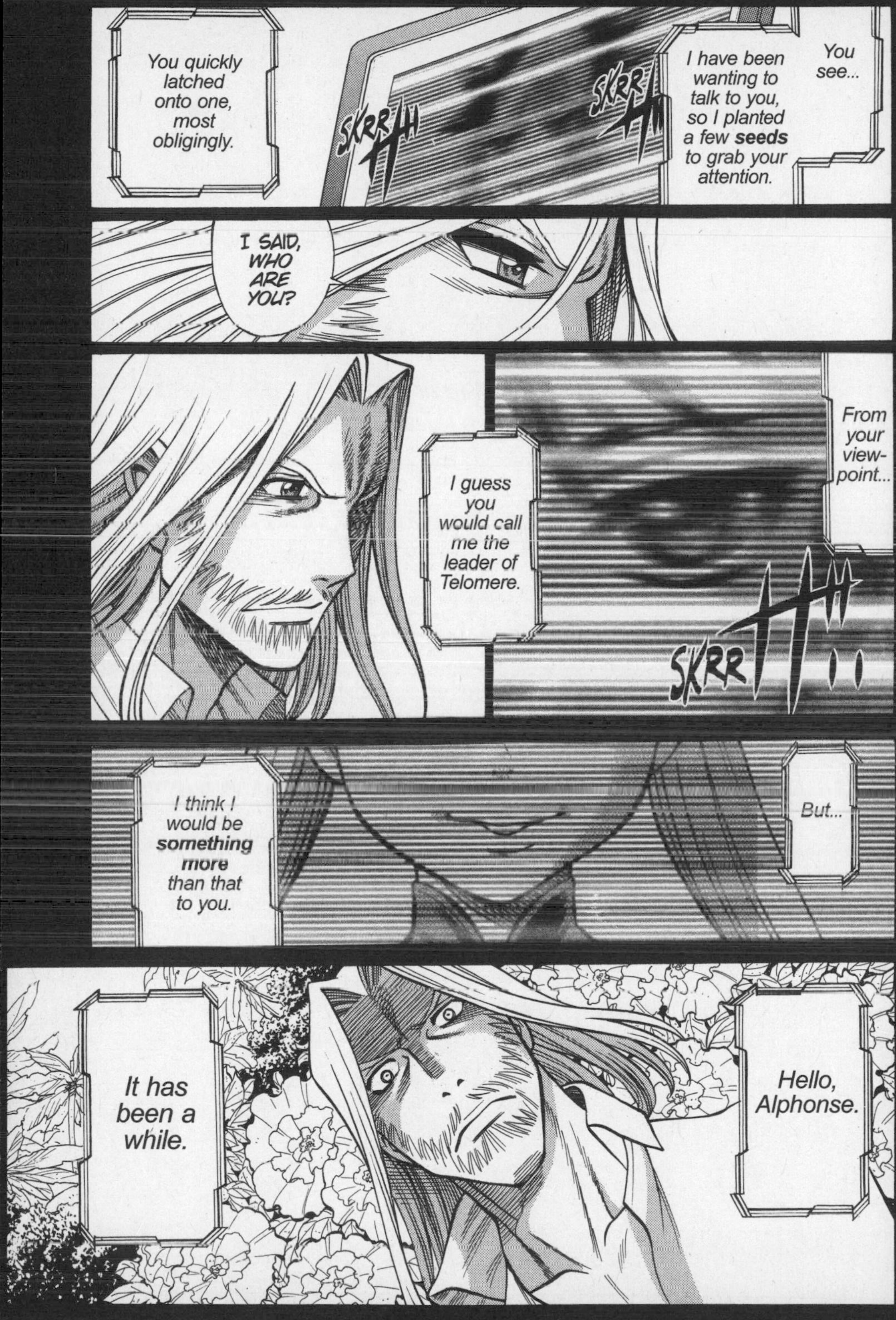
You see...
I have been wanting to talk to you, so I planted a few **seeds** to grab your attention.
SKRRHH
SKRRHH
You quickly latched onto one, most obligingly.
I SAID, WHO ARE YOU?
From your viewpoint...
SKRRHH!!
I guess you would call me the leader of Telomere.
But...
I think I would be **something more** than that to you.
Hello, Alphonse.
It has been a while.

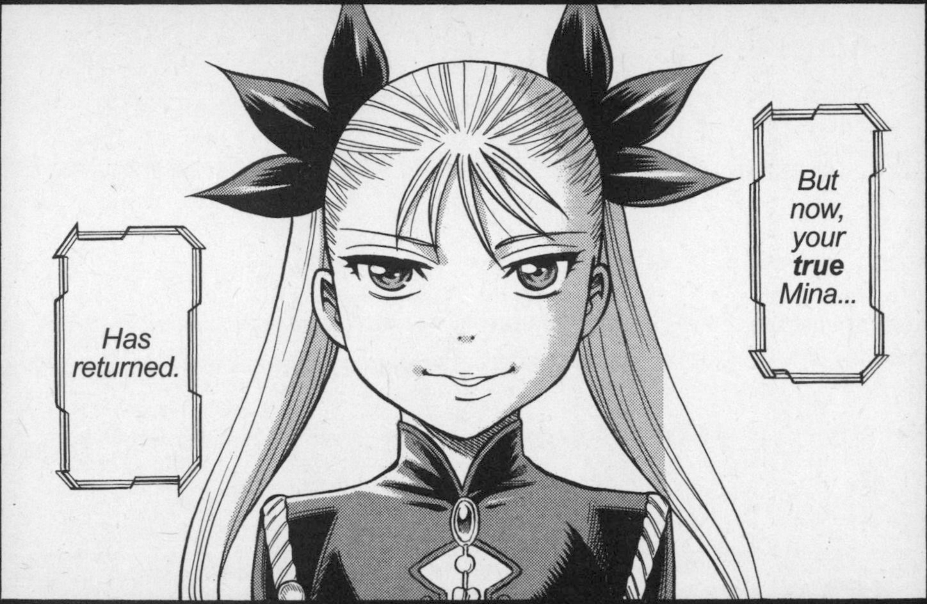
But now, your **true** Mina...
Has returned.

DIVE IN THE VAMPIRE BUND
SEASON II
END

Dive in the
Vampire Bund

DANCE IN THE VAMPIRE BUND: THE MEMORIES OF SLEDGEHAMMER

UNDER THE LIGHT OF THE FULL MOON... THE UNCERTAIN LOVE BETWEEN A WOMAN AND AN INHUMAN MAN DRIFTS IN SEARCH OF MEANING.

It has been three months since Mina Tepes reclaimed her Bund from the impostor, and both human and vampire societies are still trying to recover. In the midst of this effort, former Special Liaison to the Vampire Bund Reiko Gotoh is nearly kidnapped. Strangely, the attempt does not connect to the recent vampire-related upheaval, but to an incident nearly 10 years ago, when Gotoh and Hama Seiji first met...

So begins the story that will bridge not only the gap between *Dance in the Vampire Bund* Parts I & II, but also between the Bund's present and its past!

Dance in the Vampire Bund

READING ORDER

Dance in the Vampire Bund Vol. 1 ········· Chapter 1-6

Dance in the Vampire Bund Vol. 2 ········· Chapter 7-12

Dance in the Vampire Bund Vol. 3 ········· Chapter 13-19

Dance in the Vampire Bund Vol. 4 ········· Chapter 20-24

Dance in the Vampire Bund Vol. 5 ········· Chapter 25-31

Young Miss Holmes Casebook 1-2 ········· Sussex Vampire 1-5

Dance in the Vampire Bund Vol. 6 ········· Chapter 32-33

Dive in the Vampire Bund Vol. 1 ············ Chapter 1-10

Dive in the Vampire Bund Vol. 2 ············ Chapter 11-16

Dance in the Vampire Bund Vol. 6 ········· Chapter 34-37

Dance in the Vampire Bund Vol. 7 ········· Chapter 38-45

Dance in the Vampire Bund Vol. 8 ········· Chapter 44-49

Dance in the Vampire Bund Vol. 9 ········· Chapter 50-53

Dance in the Vampire Bund Vol. 10 ········· Chapter 54-59

Dance in the Vampire Bund Vol. 11 ········· Chapter 60-64

Dance in the Vampire Bund Vol. 12 ········· Chapter 65-70

Dance in the Vampire Bund Vol. 13 ········· Chapter 71-75

Dance in the Vampire Bund Vol. 14 ········· Chapter 76-82

The Memories of Sledgehammer Vol. 1 ···· Chapter 1-4

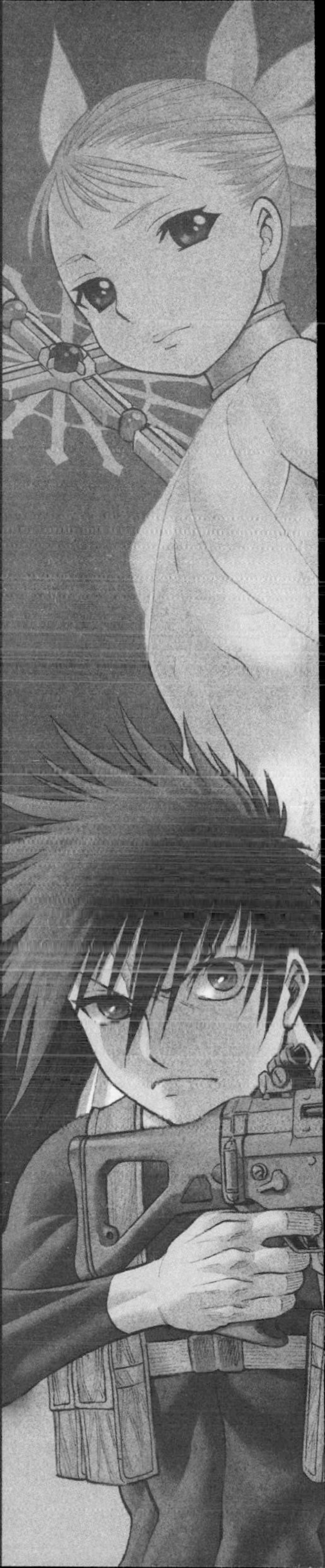

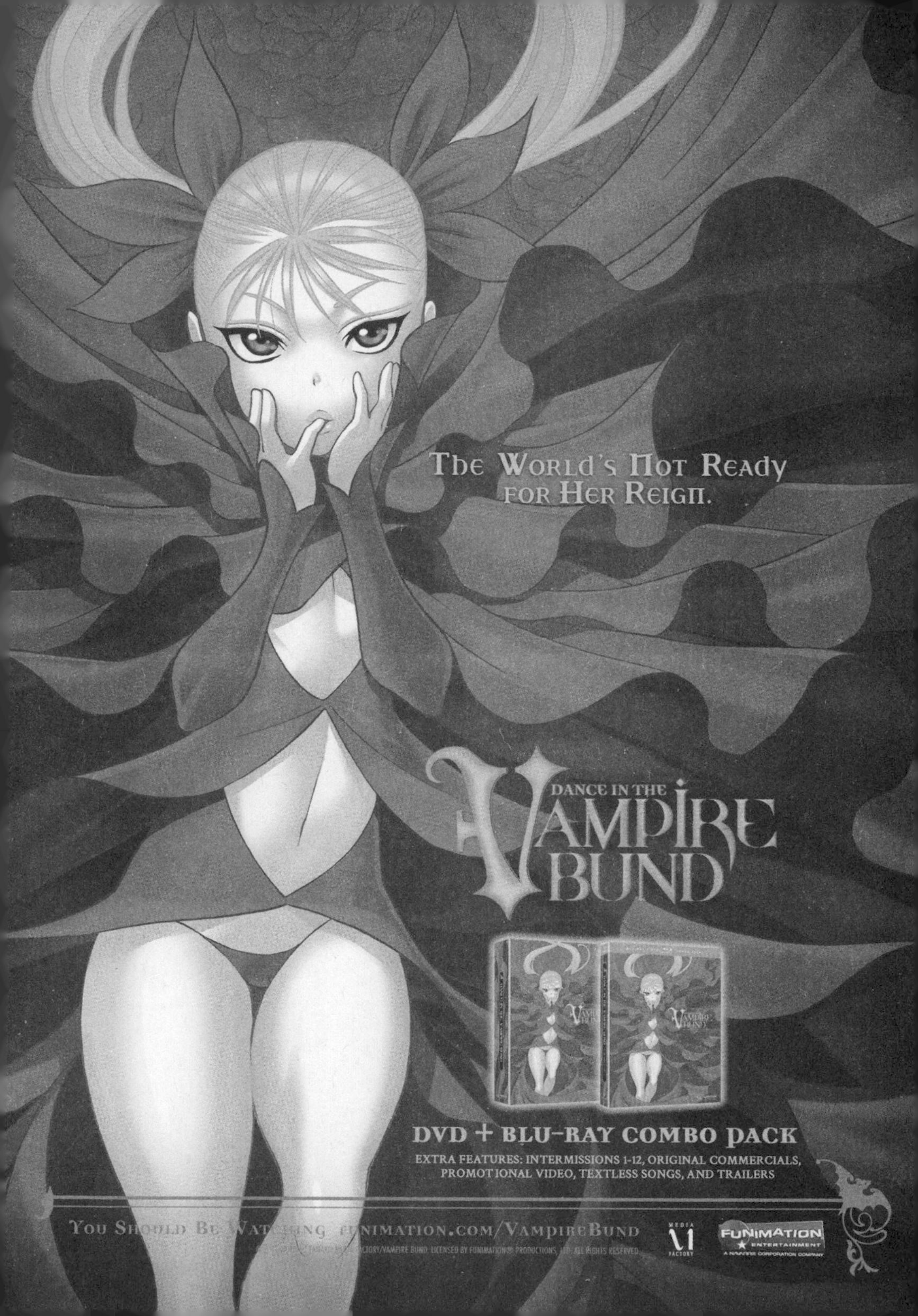

The World's Not Ready
for Her Reign.
DANCE IN THE
VAMPIRE BUND
DVD + BLU-RAY COMBO PACK
EXTRA FEATURES: INTERMISSIONS 1-12, ORIGINAL COMMERCIALS,
PROMOTIONAL VIDEO, TEXTLESS SONGS, AND TRAILERS
You Should Be Watching funimation.com/VampireBund
MEDIA FACTORY
FUNIMATION ENTERTAINMENT

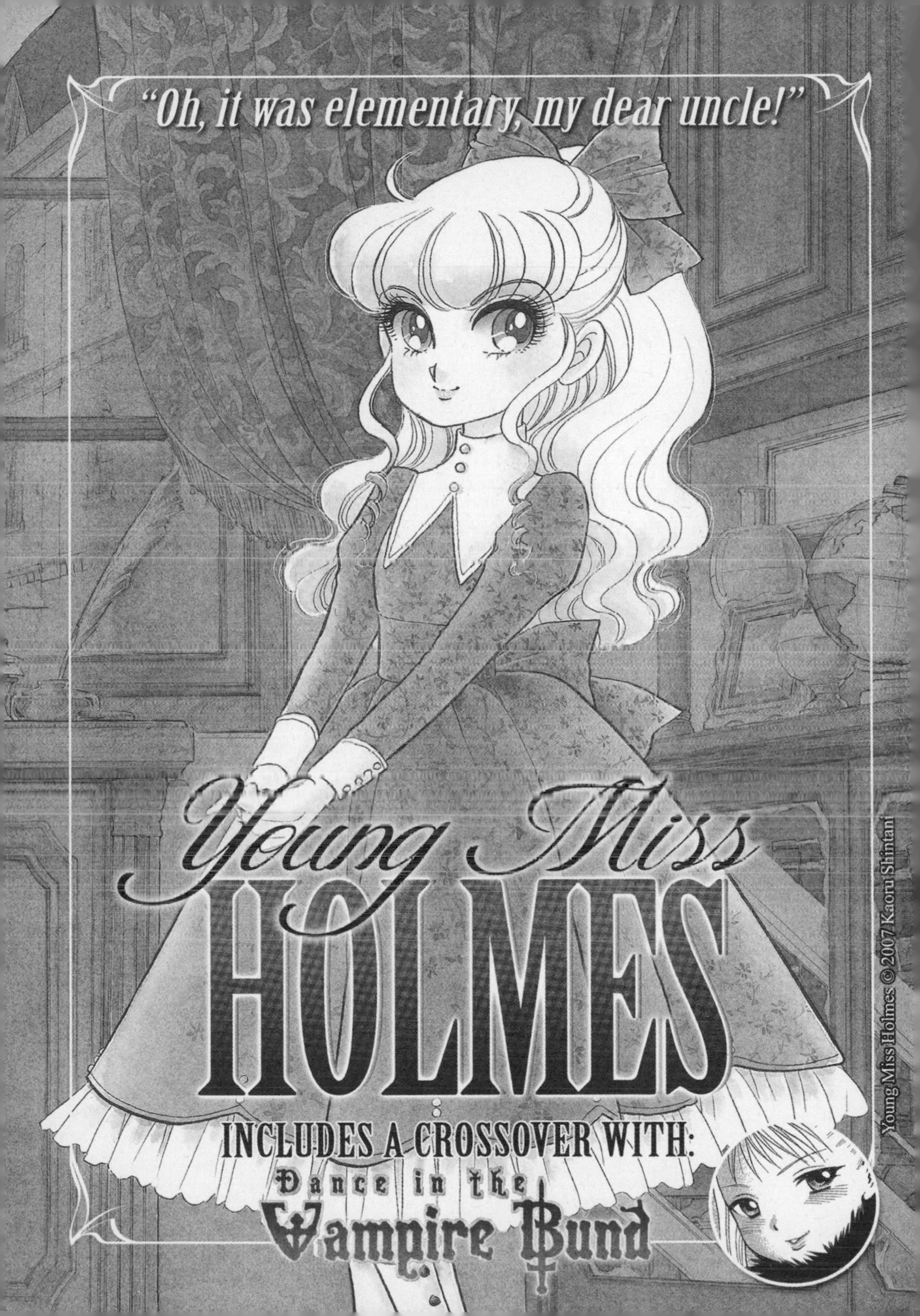
"Oh, it was elementary, my dear uncle!"
Young Miss
HOLMES
INCLUDES A CROSSOVER WITH:
Dance in the
Vampire Bund
Young Miss Holmes © 2007 Kaoru Shintani

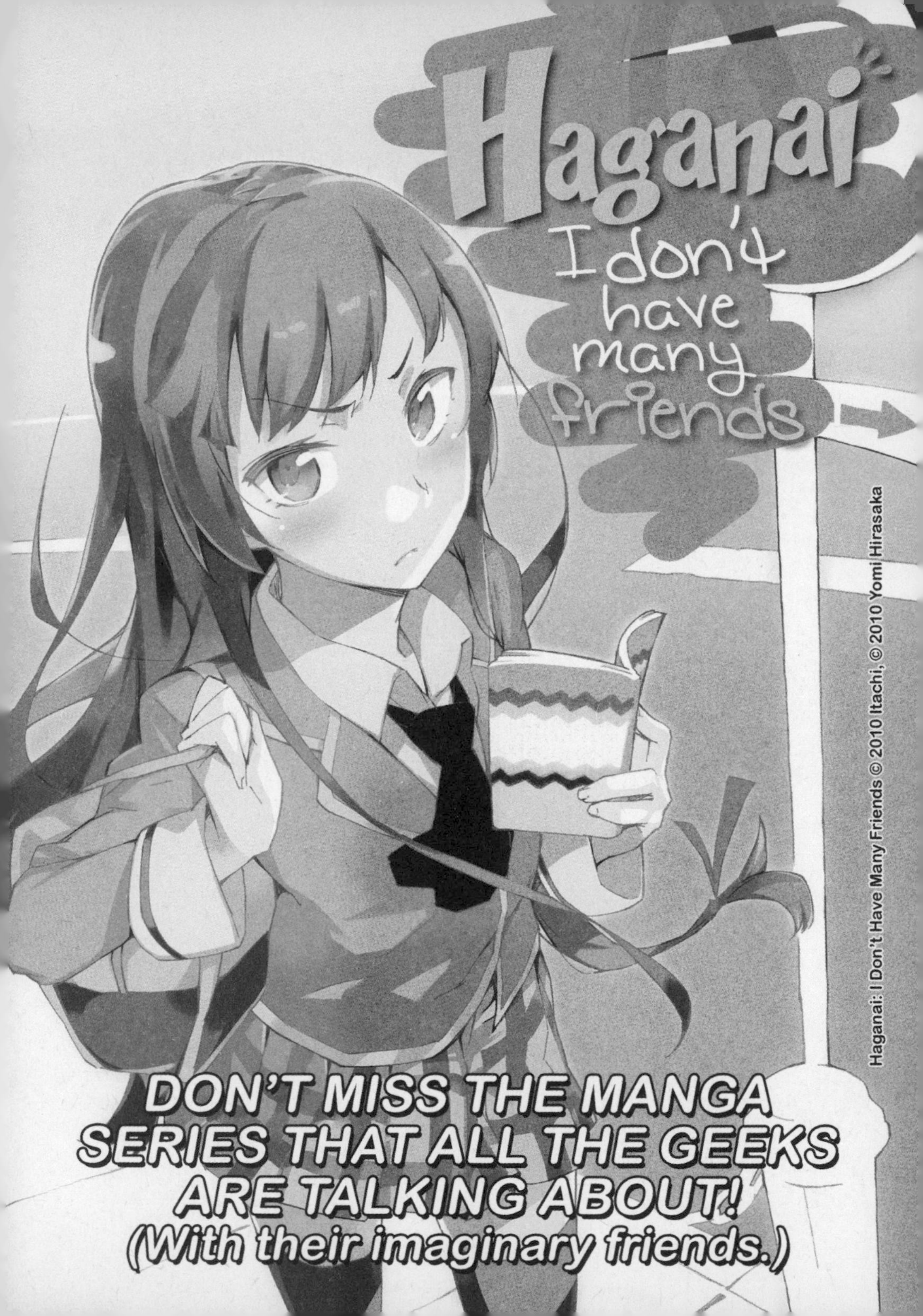
Haganai
I don't have many friends
DON'T MISS THE MANGA SERIES THAT ALL THE GEEKS ARE TALKING ABOUT!
(With their imaginary friends.)

MAYO CHIKI!

ARE YOU NORMAL? THIS MANGA IS DEFINITELY NOT!

P.S. CHECK OUT THE ANIME FROM SENTAI FILMWORKS!

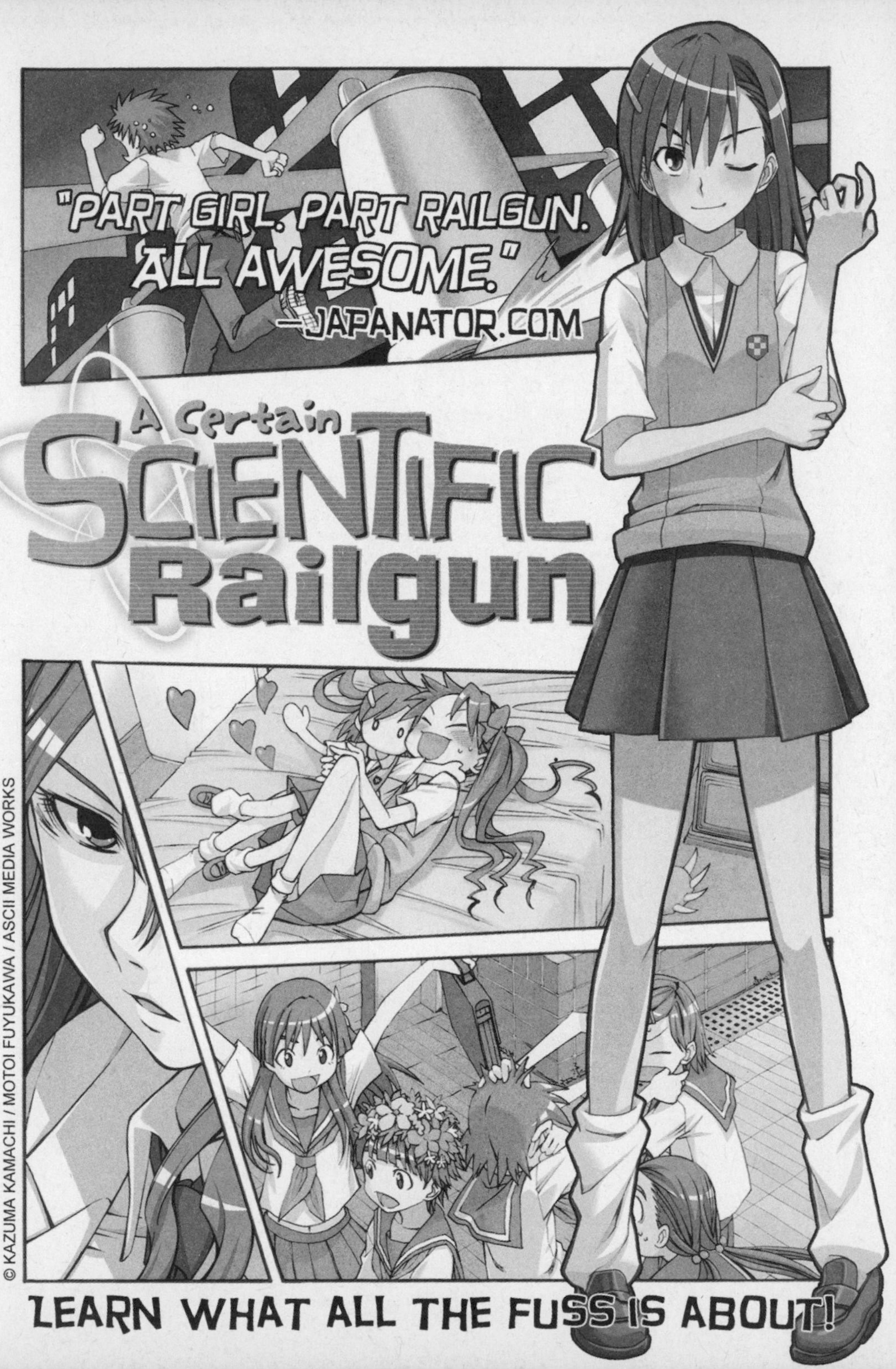

"PART GIRL. PART RAILGUN. ALL AWESOME."
—JAPANATOR.COM
A Certain SCIENTIFIC Railgun
LEARN WHAT ALL THE FUSS IS ABOUT!
© KAZUMA KAMACHI / MOTOI FUYUKAWA / ASCII MEDIA WORKS

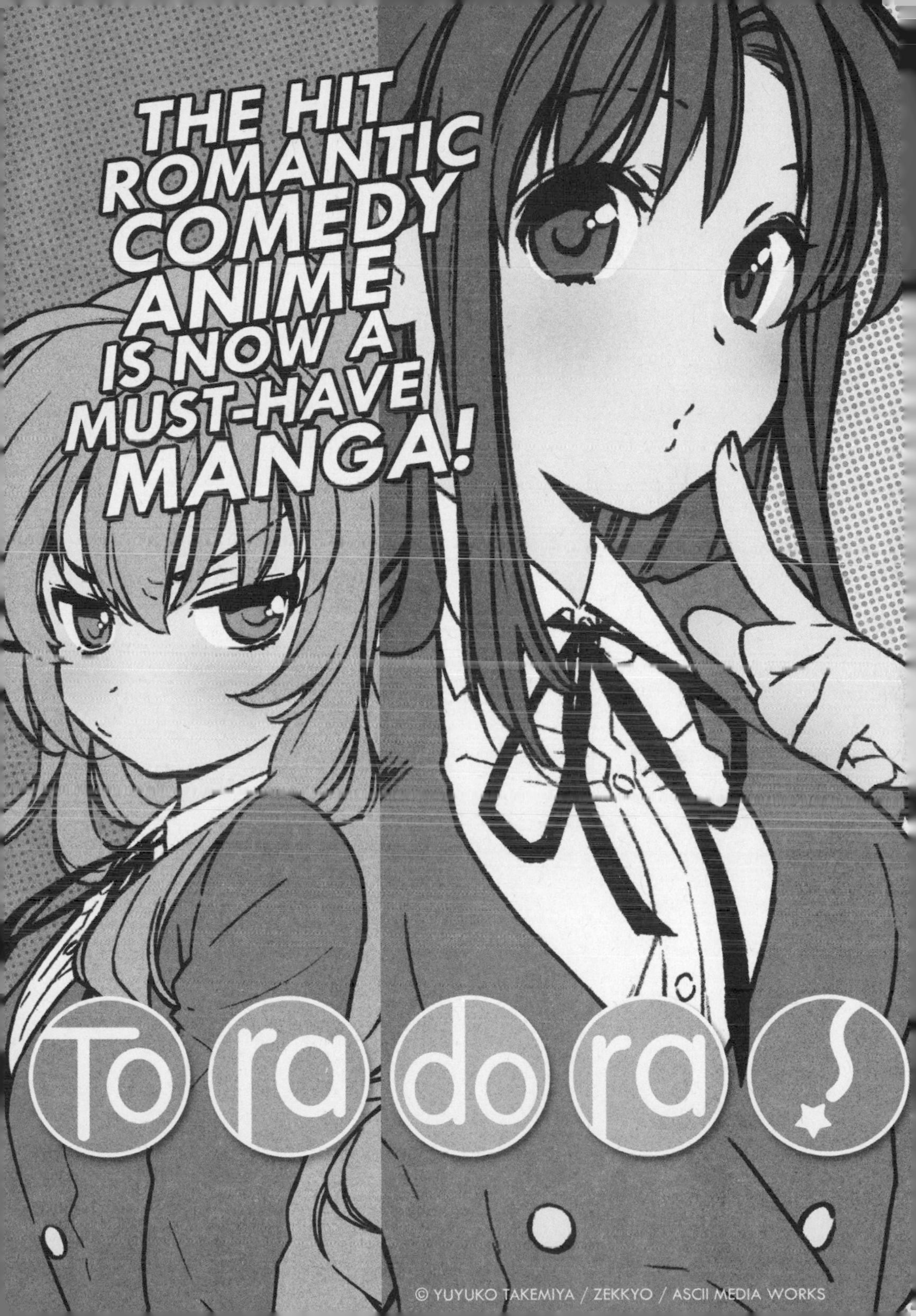
THE HIT ROMANTIC COMEDY ANIME IS NOW A MUST-HAVE MANGA!
Toradora!
© YUYUKO TAKEMIYA / ZEKKYO / ASCII MEDIA WORKS

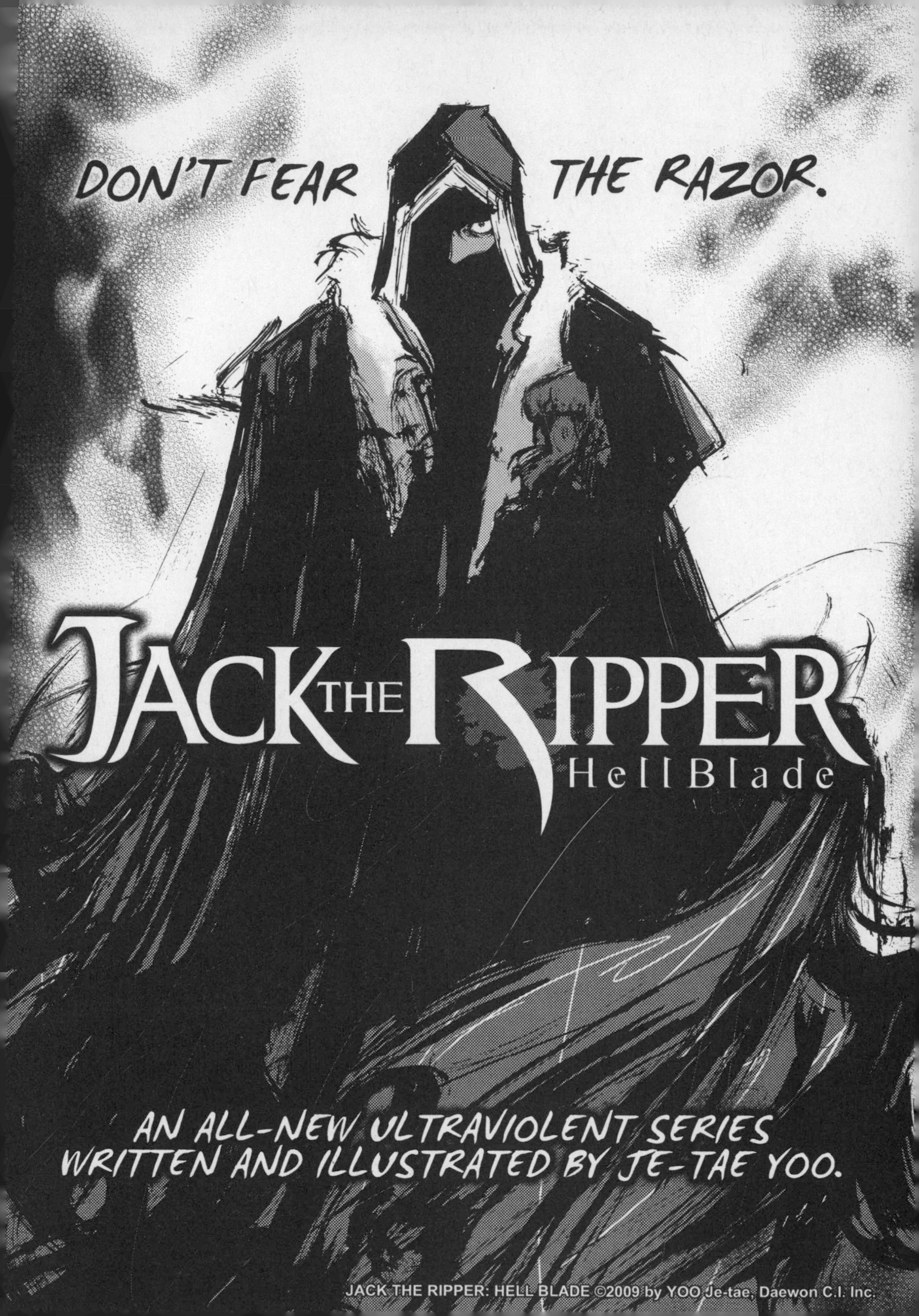
DON'T FEAR THE RAZOR.
JACK THE RIPPER
Hell Blade
AN ALL-NEW ULTRAVIOLENT SERIES
WRITTEN AND ILLUSTRATED BY JE-TAE YOO.

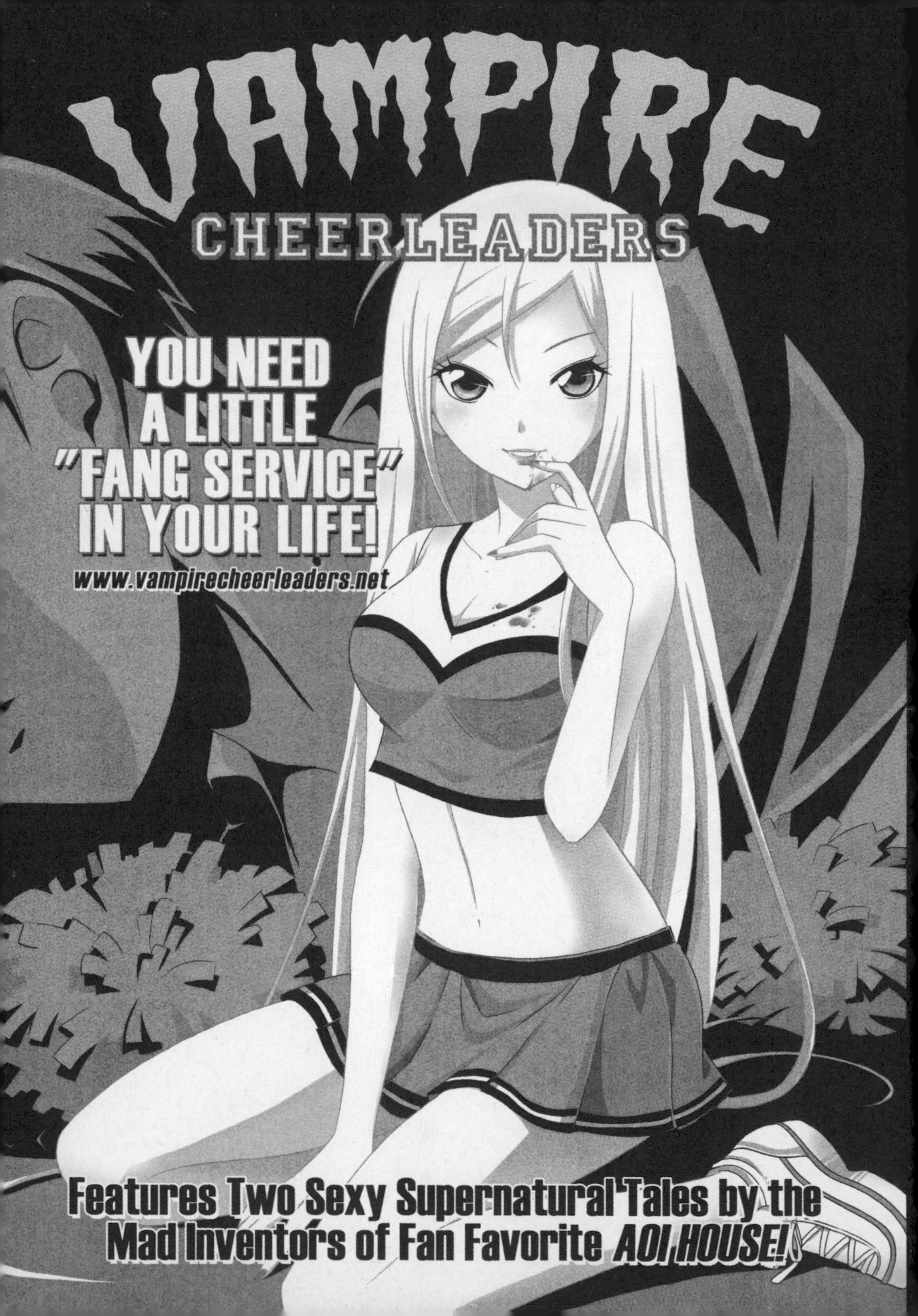
VAMPIRE
CHEERLEADERS
YOU NEED A LITTLE "FANG SERVICE" IN YOUR LIFE!
www.vampirecheerleaders.net
Features Two Sexy Supernatural Tales by the Mad Inventors of Fan Favorite AOI HOUSE!